Mathematical Modeling of Biological Systems

Mathematical Modeling of Biological Systems: Geometry, Symmetry and Conservation Laws

Editors

Federico Papa
Carmela Sinisgalli

MDPI • Basel • Beijing • Wuhan • Barcelona • Belgrade • Manchester • Tokyo • Cluj • Tianjin

Editors
Federico Papa
Institute for Systems Analysis and Computer Science "A. Ruberti"
National Research Council
Rome, Italy

Carmela Sinisgalli
Institute for Systems Analysis and Computer Science "A. Ruberti"
National Research Council
Rome, Italy

Editorial Office
MDPI
St. Alban-Anlage 66
4052 Basel, Switzerland

This is a reprint of articles from the Special Issue published online in the open access journal *Symmetry* (ISSN 2073-8994) (available at: https://www.mdpi.com/journal/symmetry/special_issues/Mathematical_Modeling_Biological_Systems_Geometry_Symmetry_Conservation_Laws).

For citation purposes, cite each article independently as indicated on the article page online and as indicated below:

LastName, A.A.; LastName, B.B.; LastName, C.C. Article Title. *Journal Name* **Year**, *Volume Number*, Page Range.

ISBN 978-3-0365-2764-2 (Hbk)
ISBN 978-3-0365-2765-9 (PDF)

© 2022 by the authors. Articles in this book are Open Access and distributed under the Creative Commons Attribution (CC BY) license, which allows users to download, copy and build upon published articles, as long as the author and publisher are properly credited, which ensures maximum dissemination and a wider impact of our publications.

The book as a whole is distributed by MDPI under the terms and conditions of the Creative Commons license CC BY-NC-ND.

Contents

Angiolo Farina, Antonio Fasano and Fabio Rosso
Mathematical Models for Some Aspects of Blood Microcirculation
Reprinted from: *Symmetry* **2021**, *13*, 1020, doi:10.3390/sym13061020 1

Hasan S. Panigoro, Agus Suryanto, Wuryansari Muharini Kusumawinahyu and Isnani Darti
Dynamics of an Eco-Epidemic Predator–Prey Model Involving Fractional Derivatives with Power-Law and Mittag–Leffler Kernel
Reprinted from: *Symmetry* **2021**, *13*, 785, doi:10.3390/sym13050785 39

Bruno F. F. Flora, Armando Ciancio and Alberto d'Onofrio
On Systems of Active Particles Perturbed by Symmetric Bounded Noises: A Multiscale Kinetic Approach
Reprinted from: *Symmetry* **2021**, *13*, 1604, doi:10.3390/sym13091604 69

Vincenzo Bonifaci
An Entropic Gradient Structure in the Network Dynamics of a Slime Mold
Reprinted from: *Symmetry* **2021**, *13*, 1385, doi:10.3390/sym1308138 93

Yolocuauhtli Salazar, Emmanuel Rodriguez, Paul A. Valle and Blanca E. Garcia
Primary Model for Biomass Growth Prediction in Batch Fermentation
Reprinted from: *Symmetry* **2021**, *13*, 1468, doi:10.3390/sym13081468 109

Paolo Di Giamberardino, Rita Caldarella and Daniela Iacoviello
A Control Based Mathematical Model for the Evaluation of Intervention Lines in COVID-19 Epidemic Spread: The Italian Case Study
Reprinted from: *Symmetry* **2021**, *13*, 890, doi:10.3390/sym13050890 125

Charles Roberto Telles, Henrique Lopes and Diogo Franco
SARS-COV-2: SIR Model Limitations and Predictive Constraints
Reprinted from: *Symmetry* **2021**, *13*, 676, doi:10.3390/sym13040676 147

Alessandro Borri, Francesco Carravetta and Pasquale Palumbo
The Double Phospho/Dephosphorylation Cycle as a Benchmark to Validate an Effective Taylor Series Method to Integrate Ordinary Differential Equations
Reprinted from: *Symmetry* **2021**, *13*, 1684, doi:10.3390/sym13091684 161

Diana Gamboa, Carlos E. Vázquez-López, Rosana Gutierrez and Paul J. Campos
Nonlinear Analysis of the C-Peptide Variable Related to Type 1-Diabetes Mellitus
Reprinted from: *Symmetry* **2021**, *13*, 1238, doi:10.3390/sym13071238 175

Petras Rupšys and Edmundas Petrauskas
Symmetric and Asymmetric Diffusions through Age-Varying Mixed-Species Stand Parameters
Reprinted from: *Symmetry* **2021**, *13*, , doi:10.3390/sym13081457 191

Article

Mathematical Models for Some Aspects of Blood Microcirculation

Angiolo Farina [1,*,†], Antonio Fasano [2,3,†], Fabio Rosso [1,†]

1. Dipartimento di Matematica e Informatica "U. Dini", Università degli Studi di Firenze, Viale Morgagni 67/a, 50134 Firenze, Italy; fabio.rosso@unifi.it
2. FIAB SpA, Vicchio, 50039 Firenze, Italy; a.fasano@fiab.it
3. Istituto di Analisi dei Sistemi ed Informatica "Antonio Ruberti"—Consiglio Nazionale delle Ricerche, Via dei Taurini 19, 00185 Roma, Italy
* Correspondence: angiolo.farina@unifi.it
† All authors contributed equally to this work.

Abstract: Blood rheology is a challenging subject owing to the fact that blood is a mixture of a fluid (plasma) and of cells, among which red blood cells make about 50% of the total volume. It is precisely this circumstance that originates the peculiar behavior of blood flow in small vessels (i.e., roughly speaking, vessel with a diameter less than half a millimeter). In this class we find arterioles, venules, and capillaries. The phenomena taking place in microcirculation are very important in supporting life. Everybody knows the importance of blood filtration in kidneys, but other phenomena, of not less importance, are known only to a small class of physicians. Overviewing such subjects reveals the fascinating complexity of microcirculation.

Keywords: blood microcirculation; ultrafiltration process; vasomotion; Fårhæus–Lindquist effect

Citation: Farina, A.; Fasano, A.; Rosso, F. Mathematical Models for Some Aspects of Blood Microcirculation. *Symmetry* **2021**, *13*, 1020. https://doi.org/10.3390/sym13061020

Academic Editors: Alice Miller and Alexander Shapovalov

Received: 5 May 2021
Accepted: 1 June 2021
Published: 6 June 2021

Publisher's Note: MDPI stays neutral with regard to jurisdictional claims in published maps and institutional affiliations.

Copyright: © 2021 by the authors. Licensee MDPI, Basel, Switzerland. This article is an open access article distributed under the terms and conditions of the Creative Commons Attribution (CC BY) license (https://creativecommons.org/licenses/by/4.0/).

1. Introduction

It is well known that blood is a mixture of plasma (a liquid slightly denser than water carrying a large number of molecular species performing a huge amount of tasks) and of a variety of cell populations: red blood cells (RBCS), white blood cells (WBCS), platelets. In particular, RBCs make 40–50% of total blood volume. Their density is practically the same as that of plasma. The RBCs volume fraction in blood is called the hematocrit. Cells of the other families, though extremely important, contribute only 1% to blood volume, so they do not play any significant role in blood rheology. Such a composite nature is a source of considerable difficulties in modeling blood rheology. Nevertheless, in sufficiently large vessels, blood can be safely considered a homogeneous fluid, for which several different rheological models have been proposed (see, e.g., the book [1] and the review papers [2,3]). The situation changes in small vessels (arterioles, venules, capillaries) where the fact that almost half of the volume is occupied by RBCs comes significantly into play. Geometrical symmetries play an important role, since all flows considered are axisymmetric, and this is largely exploited throughout the paper in connection with the smallness of the vessel's aspect ratio.

In the present paper, we review some recent results in modeling blood flow in such small vessels, considering three areas:

(i) Flow in capillaries, i.e., vessels whose size is even smaller than RBCs diameter, taking into account that capillaries allow some plasma to seep through the walls, owing to the presence of fenestration. An interesting aspect is that when blood enters a capillary the typical symmetry of the flow in larger vessels breaks down and the classical fluid dynamic approach has to be abandoned. The main application of this study is to model the ultra-filtration process taking place in the kidneys.

(ii) The peristaltic action occurring in arterioles and venules due to the periodic contraction of their walls (vasomotion). The presence of valves in venules turns vasomotion into a propulsive action, thus enhancing the flow under the modest venous hydraulic pressure gradient. The action of valves deeply modifies the classical symmetry of the normal flow with their alternating openings and closures.

(iii) The amazing phenomenon of the progressive reduction of blood apparent viscosity when the vessel diameter is reduced (roughly in the range 30 µm to 300 µm). This phenomenon, discovered about ninety years ago, known as the Fårhæus–Lindquist effect, has received a satisfactory explanation and a correct interpretation only very recently. The phenomenon originated from an entrance effect, creating a motion of the red blood cells toward the vessel axis. Preservation of symmetry is a crucial feature making the formulation of a model possible.

The focus of our exposition will be on modeling, but we will also try to elucidate the role of such phenomena in supporting life. We will also take this opportunity to present further elaborations of the various models.

2. Modeling the Flow through Fenestrated Capillaries

Capillaries are responsible for delivering to body cells the oxygen and the nutrients carried by blood. Transfer of such substances takes place by diffusion. Due to cells uptake, they can travel only a short distance, say 0.1 mm. Therefore, capillaries may feed only a region around them having that radius. That explains why as much as one billion capillaries are needed to fulfil their task in a body of average size. Capillaries connect the circulatory system carrying oxygenated blood to the one carrying oxygen deprived blood.

Capillaries are generally fenestrated, meaning that they allow some plasma cross their walls. Clearly, this is a further complication in the description of circulation at that level.

Blood flow in vessels whose size is comparable to the RBCs dimensions has very little to do with traditional fluid dynamics. Healthy RBCs have the shape of a disc with a diameter up to 8 µm and a thickness of 2–3 µm at the edge, slightly less in the middle. They are not rigid, but flexible and they exploit such a property to enter capillaries where they proceed in a single file. Occasionally they may stick to each other, forming the so-called ruleaux, but normally they form a travelling sequence [4], in which it is very reasonable to suppose (referring to an average situation) that cells are evenly spaced. This is the starting point of the flow model presented in [5]. This situation is depicted in Figure 1.

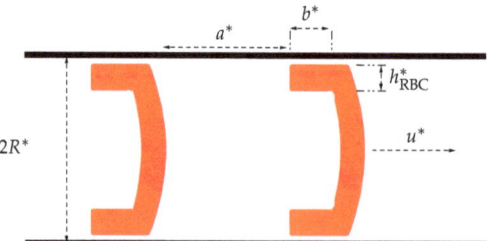

Figure 1. Sketch of the RBC/plasma element translating along the capillary (starred symbols refer to dimensional quantities, see the list of the main symbols below).

RBCs, represented in red (with a simplified geometry), take a shape letting them exploit the hydraulic pressure gradient. A portion of the RBCs surface slides on the capillary wall, separated by a thin plasma layer. The no-slip condition at the plasma/cell and the plasma/wall surface induces a strain rate in the layer. The same is true for the plasma element between two RBCs, since its translation is accompanied by the presence of a stressed layer at the wall. This is the origin of energy dissipation and drag. In our model we are going to neglect the influence of the capillary tortuosity.

Let us list the main symbols, warning that starred symbols refer to dimensional quantities (all of them positive):

ϕ, hematocrit.
ϕ_{in}, inlet hematocrit (typically 0.45).
x^*, longitudinal space coordinate.
t^*, time.
G^*, typical pressure gradient (calculated for a capillary in a renal glomerulus as the difference between the pressures in the afferent and efferent arterioles (5 mmHg $\approx$ 6.7 $\times$ 10^2 Pa) [6] divided by the glomerulus length (0.16 mm)). ($\sim$4.1 $\times$ 10^6 Pa/m).
u^*, translation speed.
u_0^*, characteristic translation speed ($\sim$1.7 mm/s).
R^*, vessel radius ($\sim$3 μm).
L^*, vessel length (0.16 mm).
$t_0^* = L^*/u_0^*$, characteristic transit time ($\sim$9.4 $\times$ 10^{-2} s).
R_{RBC}^*, RBC radius ($\sim$4 μm).
h_{RBC}^*, avg. RBC thickness ($\sim$1.8 μm)
V_{RBC}^*, RBC volume (typically $\sim$90 fl, where 1 fl = 1 μm^3).
ρ^*, blood density (1.06 $\times$ 10^3 Kg/m^3, same as RBCs density).
η_{pl}^*, plasma viscosity ($\sim$3.5 $\times$ 10^{-3} Pa s).
a^*, distance between two consecutive cells in the sequence.
b^*, length of the RBC portion sliding over the vessel wall.
ε_{RBC}^*, thickness of the plasma layer between the wall and the RBC.
ε_{pl}^*, thickness of the plasma layer between the wall and the plasma element.
$$\varepsilon = \frac{\varepsilon_{RBC}^*}{\varepsilon_{pl}^*}.$$
V_{el}^*, volume of a translating element.
L_{el}^*, element length.
Δp_{el}^*, pressure difference across the element length.
p^*, blood pressure.
p_e^*, pressure of external fluid.
F_{drag}^*, drag force originated by the friction in the strained layers.
$t_0^* = L^*/u_0^*$, characteristic transit time ($\sim$9.4 $\times$ 10^{-2} s).
c^*, protein concentration in blood.
c_{in}^*, inlet protein concentration in blood ($\sim$7 gr/dl).
K^*, permeability of the capillary wall.

In the sequel any length divided by R^* will be denoted by the corresponding symbol without the "*" (e.g., $a = a^*/R^*$, etc.). Note that both ε_{pl} and ε_{RBC} are $\ll 1$.

From the geometry represented in Figure 1 we deduce

$$V_{el}^* = \pi R^{*2} a^* + V_{RBC}^* + \pi b^* \left(R^{*2} - h_{RBC}^{*2} \right) \qquad (1)$$

$$V_{RBC}^* = \pi h_{RBC}^* R_{RBC}^{*2} = V_1^* + V_2^*, \qquad (2)$$

where

$$V_1^* = \pi b^* \left[R^{*2} - (R^* - h_{RBC}^*)^2 \right], \qquad (3)$$

is the volume of the RBC portion in contact with the wall. Concerning V_2^*, we take a slightly better approximation than the one assumed in [5], as illustrated in Figure 2.

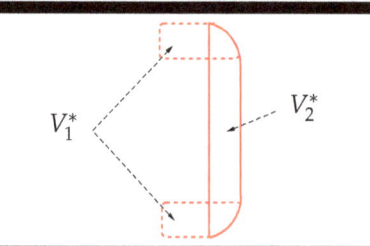

Figure 2. Splitting the RBC volume into V_1^* and V_2^*.

The total volume V_2^* can be calculated as $\pi \int_0^{h_{RBC}^*} f^2(x^*)\,dx^*$, where $f(x^*) = R^* - h_{RBC}^* + \sqrt{h_{RBC}^{*2} - x^{*2}}$, hence (in [5] V_2^* is simply estimated as $\pi h_{RBC}^* R^{*2}$).

$$V_2^* = \pi h_{RBC}^* R^{*2}\, \Xi, \quad \text{with} \quad \Xi = 1 - \left(2 - \frac{\pi}{2}\right) h_{RBC} + \left(\frac{5}{3} - \frac{\pi}{2}\right) h_{RBC}^2. \tag{4}$$

Considering $h \approx 1.8$ µm, we obtain $\Xi \approx 0.78$ if $R^* = 3$ µm. Actually R^* is not allowed to approach h^*, otherwise the flow becomes impossible (see [4] for a discussion).

Equations (2)–(4) provide an expression for b^*, which we write directly in dimensionless form

$$b = \frac{R_{RBC}^2 - \Xi}{2 - h_{RBC}}. \tag{5}$$

For instance, when $R^* = 3$ µm, we get (in [5] $b = \frac{R_{RBC}^2 - 1}{2 - h_{RBC}}$, thus giving $b^* = 1.6$ µm, if $R^* = 3$ µm). $b^* = 2.1$ µm. The approximation is valid as long as $b^* > h^*$, since on one side we have written $V^* = \pi h^* R_{RBC}^{*2}$, (RBC of cylindrical shape) but when $b^* = 0$ the domain left V_2^* is slightly smaller. Actually, since the RBC boundary is round there is some interval of values of R, before it reaches R_{RBC}^*, in which $b^* \approx 0$, and we should simply replace V_2^* with V^*.

The length a^* is a function of the hematocrit ϕ and is found by imposing the condition

$$\phi = \frac{V_{RBC}^*}{V_{el}^*}. \tag{6}$$

Hence, from (1),

$$a(\phi) = H\frac{1-\phi}{\phi} - b\left(1 - h_{RBC}^2\right), \tag{7}$$

where b is given by (5) and

$$H = \frac{V_{RBC}^*}{\pi R^{*3}} \underset{(2)}{=} h_{RBC} R_{RBC}^2, \tag{8}$$

is a dimensionless constant (if, e.g., $R^* = 3$ µm, then $H \approx 1$). Note that b does not depend on ϕ. Moreover, the total length of a single element is

$$L_{el}^* = a^* + b^* + h_{RBC}^*. \tag{9}$$

Now recalling (7), we introduce the $\mathcal{O}(1)$ dimensionless quantity

$$\lambda(\phi) = \frac{R^*}{L_{el}^*} = \left[H\frac{1-\phi}{\phi} + h_{RBC}(1 + bh_{RBC})\right]^{-1}. \tag{10}$$

Figure 3 shows the behaviour of λ and L_{el}^* versus ϕ.

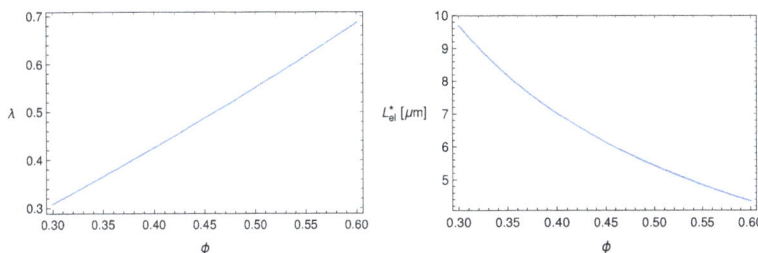

Figure 3. Plots of $\lambda(\phi)$ (**left panel**) and of $L_{el}^*(\phi)$ (**right panel**) for $R^* = 3$ µm, $h_{RBC}^* = 1.8$ µm, $R_{RBC}^* = 4$ µm, b given by (5), Ξ by (4), and H by (8). We remark that about twenty elements are simultaneously present in the capillary.

If plasma filtrates through the vessel wall, the distance a^* and the volume element V_{el}^* will decrease in time. Thus, the element motion equation takes the following form

$$\rho^* \frac{d}{dt^*}(u^* V_{el}^*) = \pi R^{*2} \Delta p_{el}^* - F_{drag}^* . \tag{11}$$

The expression for F_{drag}^* can be obtained as follows: compute the power dissipation in each stressed plasma layer for some translational velocity u^*, imposing the no-slip condition at both layer boundaries, then write that the overall power dissipation equals the product $F_{drag}^* u^*$. Omitting standard calculations (for more details we refer the readers to [5]), the result is

$$F_{drag}^* = 2\pi \eta_{pl}^* u^* R^* \left[\frac{a(\phi)}{\left|\ln(1-\varepsilon_{pl})\right|} + \frac{b}{\left|\ln(1-\varepsilon_{RBC})\right|} \right] \approx 2\pi \eta_{pl}^* u^* R^* \left[\frac{a(\phi)}{\varepsilon_{pl}} + \frac{b}{\varepsilon_{RBC}} \right]. \tag{12}$$

Hence, recalling (6), we rewrite (11) as

$$\rho^* V_{RBC}^* \frac{d}{dt^*}\left(\frac{u^*}{\phi}\right) = \pi R^{*2} L_{el}^* \left|\frac{\partial p^*}{\partial x^*}\right| - F_{drag}^* , \tag{13}$$

where we set $\Delta p_{el}^* = L_{el}^* \left|\frac{\partial p^*}{\partial x^*}\right|$, to put the equation in a form applicable to a continuum. This is justified by the fact that the number of elements in the capillary is sufficiently large (≈ 40).

Let us now recall that $\frac{d}{dt^*} = \frac{\partial}{\partial t^*} + u^* \frac{\partial}{\partial x^*}$ and (10). So, (13) takes the form

$$\rho^* V_{RBC}^* \lambda(\phi) \left(\frac{\partial}{\partial t^*} + u^* \frac{\partial}{\partial x^*}\right)\left(\frac{u^*}{\phi}\right) = \pi R^{*3} \left|\frac{\partial p^*}{\partial x^*}\right| - \lambda(\phi) F_{drag}^* . \tag{14}$$

At this point it is convenient to recall the ratio $\varepsilon = \varepsilon_{RBC}^*/\varepsilon_{pl}^*$ that we are going to use as a fitting parameter (the only one in the model). With the help of it and recalling (12), we rewrite the expression of F_{drag}^*

$$F_{drag}^* = \frac{2\pi \eta_{pl}^* u^* R^*}{\varepsilon_{RBC}} [\varepsilon a(\phi) + b], \tag{15}$$

which, being proportional to u^*, has the character of a viscous force.

Concerning ε_{RBC}, we estimate it by considering a steady flow in typical conditions, imposing that the l.h.s. of (14) vanishes and taking the guess $\varepsilon = 0.5$, to be verified a posteriori. This has been done in [5] obtaining

$$\varepsilon_{RBC} \approx 6 \times 10^{-2} .$$

Let us now derive the dimensionless form of (14) recalling the characteristic transit time $t_0^* = L^*/u_0^* \approx 9.4 \times 10^{-2}$ s, and introducing the dimensionless variables $u = u^*/u_0^*$, $x = x^*/L^*$, $t = t^*/t_0^*$, and

$$p = \frac{p^* - p_e^*}{L^* G^*}. \tag{16}$$

Dividing (14) by $\pi R^{*3} G^*$, we obtain

$$\lambda(\phi)\Gamma\left(\frac{\partial}{\partial t} + u\frac{\partial}{\partial x}\right)\left(\frac{u}{\phi}\right) = -\frac{\partial p}{\partial x} - \lambda(\phi)\Lambda u[\varepsilon a(\phi) + b], \tag{17}$$

where $a(\phi)$ and $\lambda(\phi)$ are given by (7) and (10), respectively, and

$$\Gamma = \frac{\rho^* V_{RBC}^* u_0^*}{\pi R^{*3} G^* t_0^*}, \qquad \Lambda = \frac{2\eta_{pl}^* u_0^*}{R^{*2} G^* \varepsilon_{RBC}}.$$

We recall that λ is $\mathcal{O}(1)$ and (if, e.g., $R^* = 3$ μm) we find $\Gamma \approx 10^{-6}$. Thus, inertia has no role in (17). With the same value of R^* we get $\Lambda \approx 5.4$, which confirms that the performed rescaling is suitable. Eventually, (17) reduces to

$$\frac{1}{\Lambda}\frac{\partial p}{\partial x} = -\lambda(\phi)u[\varepsilon a(\phi) + b]. \tag{18}$$

Now we shift our attention to the dynamics of plasma filtration through the capillary wall, in other words to the evolution of ϕ. On one side we have that no RBCs are loss during the flow, thus their concentration ϕ obeys the continuity equation

$$\frac{\partial \phi}{\partial t^*} + \frac{\partial(u^* \phi)}{\partial x^*} = 0. \tag{19}$$

The plasma loss rate through the capillary wall is driven by the difference $p^* - p_e^*$, p_e^* being the external fluid pressure, and is opposed by the so called oncotic pressure resulting from the presence of proteins in plasma (mainly albumin), responsible for osmosis. Since the plasma volume fraction is $1 - \phi$, the plasma balance can be written as follows (Starling's law)

$$\frac{\partial(1-\phi)}{\partial t^*} + \frac{\partial(u^*(1-\phi))}{\partial x^*} = -K^*[p^* - p_e^* - \Pi^*(c^*)], \tag{20}$$

where K^* in the permeability of the capillary wall and $\Pi^*(c^*)$ is the oncotic pressure, a function of the total proteins concentration in blood c^*, usually given in g/dL,

$$\Pi^*(c^*) = \sum_{j=1}^{3} A_j^* c^{*j}, \tag{21}$$

given by the Landis–Pappenhaimer formula (see [7], vol. 2, Chapt. 29). The three coefficients A_j^*, $j = 1, 2, 3$, have the values reported in Table 1.

Table 1. Values of the three coefficients A_j^*, $j = 1, 2, 3$ in (21).

A_1^* [Pa/(g/dL)]	A_2^* [Pa/(g/dL)^2]	A_3^* [Pa/(g/dL)^3]
280	21.3	1.2

As plasma flows out, proteins keep concentrating, since the product $a^* c^*$ remains constant

$$a^* c^* = a_{in}^* c_{in}^*, \tag{22}$$

where the quantities on the r.h.s. are the ones in circulating blood, hence the values at the capillary inlet. Note that a_{in}^* is deducible from (7) putting $\phi = \phi_{in}$. Hence, considering c_{in}^* as reference protein concentration, and introducing $c = c^*/c_{in}^*$, (22) rewrites as (in [5], where the term b is neglected, $c(\phi) = (1-\phi_o)\phi[(1-\phi)\phi_o]^{-1}$)

$$c(\phi) = \frac{a_{in}^*}{a} = \frac{H\dfrac{1-\phi_{in}}{\phi_{in}} - b(1-h_{RBC}^2)}{H\dfrac{1-\phi}{\phi} - b(1-h_{RBC}^2)}. \tag{23}$$

Combining (19) and (20) yields

$$\frac{\partial u^*}{\partial x^*} = -K^*[p^* - p_e^* - \Pi^*(c^*)]. \tag{24}$$

Equation (19) is readily written in dimensionless form

$$\frac{\partial \phi}{\partial t} + \frac{\partial (u\phi)}{\partial x} = 0. \tag{25}$$

In order to reduce (24) to a dimensionless form too, we define the dimensionless constants

$$K = K^* G^* L^* t_0^*, \quad A_j = \frac{A_j^* c_{in}^{*j}}{G^* L^*}, \quad j = 1, 2, 3. \tag{26}$$

Recalling (16) and (21), Equation (24) can be rewritten as

$$-\frac{1}{K}\frac{\partial u}{\partial x} = p - \sum_{j=1}^{3} A_j (c(\phi))^j, \tag{27}$$

with $c(\phi)$ given by (23). Thus, the model consists of solving the differential system (18), (25) and (27), for the determination of the unknowns ϕ, u and p.

The main physiological application refers to the steady flows. Eliminating time dependence is a great simplification. First, Equation (25) implies

$$u\phi = u_{in}\phi_{in}, \tag{28}$$

where $u_{in} = u^*/u_0^*$, is the dimensionless blood velocity at the capillary inlet. Assuming $u_{in} = 1$, then u can be seen as a function of ϕ

$$u(x) = \frac{\phi_{in}}{\phi(x)}, \tag{29}$$

and so (27) rewrites as (here, and in the sequel, we have set $(\bullet)' = d(\bullet)/dx$).

$$\frac{1}{\phi_{in} K}\phi' = \phi^2 \left[p - \sum_{j=1}^{3} A_j (c(\phi))^j \right].$$

Next, plugging (18) in (29) we obtain

$$\frac{1}{\Lambda \phi_{in}} p' = -\frac{\lambda(\phi)}{\phi}[\varepsilon a(\phi) + b].$$

Hence, $\phi(x)$ and $p(x)$ are obtained solving this Cauchy for $x \in (0,1)$

$$\begin{cases} \phi' = \phi_{in} K \phi^2 \left[p - \sum_{j=1}^{3} A_j (c(\phi))^j \right], \\ p' = -\Lambda \phi_{in} \dfrac{\lambda(\phi)}{\phi} [\varepsilon a(\phi) + b], \\ \phi(0) = \phi_{in}, \quad p(0) = p_{in}, \end{cases} \quad (30)$$

where $c(\phi)$, $\lambda(\phi)$ and $a(\phi)$ are given by (7), (10) and (23), respectively, and where, recalling (16),

$$p_{in} = \frac{p_{in}^* - p_e^*}{L^* G^*}, \quad (31)$$

$p_{in}^* - p_e^*$, being the characteristic transmembrane pressure. In particular, following [8,9], we introduce the *osmotic number*

$$\text{Os} = \frac{A_1^* c_{in}^*}{p_{in}^* - p_e^*}, \quad (32)$$

and, recalling (26), we rewrite (31) as

$$p_{in} = \frac{A_1}{\text{Os}}. \quad (33)$$

Figure 4 shows $\phi(x)$, when $\text{Os} = 0.1$, and $\phi_{in} = 0.45$. In Figure 5 we report the corresponding $u(x)$, given by (29).

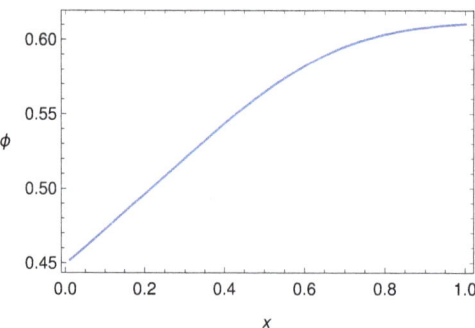

Figure 4. Behaviour of $\phi(x)$ for $\varepsilon = 0.5$ and $K = 0.15$, when $\text{Os} = 0.1$.

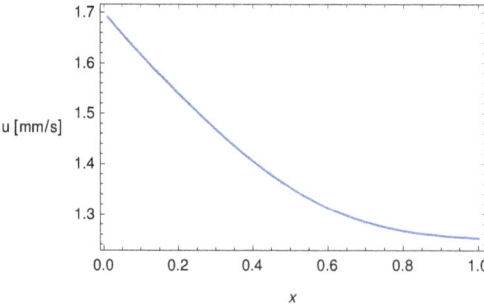

Figure 5. Behaviour of $u(x)$ given by (29) for $\varepsilon = 0.5$ and $K = 0.15$, $\text{Os} = 0.1$.

In [5], the steady-flow model (30) has been applied to the capillaries in the renal glomerulus obtaining the physiological value of the renal filtration rate. For more references and details, also on historical aspects, see [1].

Modeling the Flow through Fenestrated Capillaries: Conclusions

We have reviewed a model for blood flow in fenestrated capillaries based on an approach outside the standard fluid dynamical context. Indeed, the model considers the motion of plasma-RBC elements imposing the balance between the driving force produced by the hydraulic pressure gradient and the drag caused by friction at the vessel wall. The latter takes place in the thin plasma layer confined by the RBC portion facing the capillary wall (see Figure 1) and in a layer of the plasma segment between two consecutive RBCs in the flowing sequence. Plasma loss through fenestrations, altering the system configuration, is particularly intense in the highly fenestrated capillaries making the renal glomeruli, and is driven by the pressure across the vessel wall, which includes the effect of osmosis. Osmosis plays a fundamental role, since proteins (mainly albumin) in blood are not allowed to leave the capillary, whose wall behaves as a semi-permeable membrane. The progressive plasma loss increases the albumin concentration thus enhancing osmosis. The model has been applied in [5] to compute the glomerural filtration rate (i.e., the amount of the plasma filtrated by kidneys in one minute). The physiological value has been successfully retrieved.

3. Modeling Vasomotion

Rhythmic contractions of blood vessels equipped with smooth muscle are normally independent on heart pulsation or respiratory rhythm. This phenomenon, called vasomotion, is easily observed in the veins in the bat's wing and was first noticed by T.W. Jones [10] in 1852. The biological mechanisms driving the onset of persisting oscillations have been studied in a number of papers, [11–20]. Vasomotion ordinary values for frequency and amplitude are 10 cpm and 25% of mean diameter, though values of 25 cpm and 100% are possible [21].

Literature on vasomotion physiology is rather numerous since one of the main concern is about its benefit to microcirculation. Indeed, vasomotion is particularly active at the level of microcirculation where vessels resistance becomes large. Jones, in their paper [10], conjectured that vasomotion reduces the vessel resistance thus favoring blood flow. However, vasomotion appears reduced during pregnancy [22]. On the other hand, unexpectedly, it is upregulated in hypertensive states like preeclampsia (pregnancy induced severe hypertension), while a decrease in vessels resistance is believed to be advantageous in pregnant mammals. Clearly, this does not help to clarify the role of this phenomenon.

The paper [23] takes a shortcut to show that vasomotion enhances flow in arteries, but their argument was pointed out to be incorrect in [24]. Experiments with bat wings (see [25]) suggest that venules vasomotion acts as a reciprocating pump, increasing blood flow rate, due to to valves preventing backflow. Indeed the phenomenon presents very different features in arterioles and in venules. The interaction flow-vasomotion is much more complicated in venules, because of the action of valves. The experiments illustrated in [25] show that pressure exhibits large peaks during the vessel contraction, which is compatible with the presence of an inlet and an outlet valve.

The whole matter of blood dynamics in the presence of vasomotion has been recently reconsidered in [24,26,27] (see [1] for a review). In [24] the authors make a clear distinction between the flow in the venules and in arterioles, while in [26,27] the effect of the presence of valves was investigated on the basis of a mathematical model with the aim of clarifying their real influence on blood flow. Comparing the model results with the experimental data by Dongaonkar et al. [25], it was concluded that in valves equipped venules, oscillations are converted in blood propulsion. On the contrary, in the valveless vessels (i.e., arterioles), vasomotion has little effect, and actually increases the hydraulic resistance thus reducing the flow rate, contrary to what was stated in [23].

In the paper [28] the case of vessels with distributed valves was considered, resulting in a model with a free boundary (the moving location of the engaged valve). The existence of distributed microvalves in venules has been reported in [29], where a condition of pressure continuity forces that value to remain between the imposed inlet and outlet values.

In this paper, we review the mathematical models for incompressible Newtonian flows in oscillating arterioles and venules. In our derivation we exploit the smallness of the ratio (we recall that the symbol " * " denotes dimensional quantities).

$$\varepsilon = \frac{R_o^*}{L^*} \ll 1. \tag{34}$$

where R_o^* is the maximum vessel radius and L^* is the vessel length.

Concerning arterioles, which are characterized by the absence of valves, in Section 3.1 we investigate the influence of vasomotion on the flow. Concerning venules, Section 3.2, the model requires to impose very peculiar boundary conditions (unilateral, or Signorini, boundary conditions), that take the valves action into account. We thus formulate a mathematical model for a peristaltic wave travelling along the vessel. In particular, denoting by λ^* the wavelength of the peristaltic oscillation, we investigate the flow analyzing two cases:

- $\lambda^* \gg L^*$, referred to as synchronous oscillation.
- $\lambda^* \approx L^*$, referred to as non synchronous oscillation.

The former consists of a uniform oscillation of the vessel walls, while in the second case a wave profile travels along the vessel.

The first case (synchronous oscillation) can, indeed, be recovered from the second one in the limit of "long" wavelengths, which guarantees the physical consistency of the model. In Section 3.8 we show numerical solutions that match the experimentally detected pressure behavior displayed in [25]. Since we are interested in the average flow, in the following we will systematically ignore pressure pulses by heartbeats, just considering the average hydraulic pressure gradient present in the studied vessels.

3.1. Vasomotion in Arterioles

We start considering vasomotion in arterioles, where usually ε ranges around 10^{-2}, and model these vessels as cylindrical tubes. We denote by x^*, and r^* the longitudinal and radial coordinates and assume azimuthal symmetry so that the angular coordinate never appears and the velocity field is

$$v^* = v_1^* e_x + v_2^* e_r.$$

We note that the muscle fibers surrounding the vessel can only contract and not dilate, so that the vessel radius is maximal in the rest configuration. Consequently the oscillation of the vessel wall causes a lumen narrowing. Hence we model the vessel oscillations as

$$R(t^*) = R_o^*[1 - \delta(1 - \cos(\omega^* t^*))],$$

where R_o^* is the radius of the rest (undeformed) state, $\delta \in (0, 1/2)$, and ω^* is the oscillations pulsation. Denoting by $\langle \cdot \rangle$ the time average over the period T^*, we find $\langle R^* \rangle = R_o^*(1 - \delta)$. The periodic oscillations thus cause an average a reduction of the vessel lumen by δR_o^*.

Dealing with arterioles, where the flow is dominated by hydraulic pressure imposed by the heart, a natural scale for the longitudinal flow is

$$v_{1,\text{ref}}^* = \frac{R_o^{*\,2}}{\mu^*} \frac{\Delta p_c^*}{L^*}, \tag{35}$$

where Δp_c^*, denotes the typical pressure drop and μ^* is the blood viscosity (typically $\mu^* \approx 3$ mPa s). If we take as approximate values $\Delta p^* \approx 18$ mmHg $= 2.4 \times 10^3$ Pa, and

$L^* \approx 3$ mm, $R_o^* \approx 20$ μm, it turns out that the formula above captures the correct magnitude order $v_{1,\text{ref}}^* \approx 10$ cm/s. In particular, exploiting (35) we can estimate the transit time as

$$t_{\text{tr}}^* = L^*/v_{1,\text{ref}}^* = \varepsilon^{-2}\left(\frac{\mu^*}{\Delta p_c^*}\right),$$

getting $t_{\text{tr}}^* \approx 2.5 \times 10^{-2}$s. Hence, if the period of the walls oscillations is $T^* = 6$s (which roughly corresponds to ≈ 10 cpm, i.e., $\omega^* \approx 1\,\text{s}^{-1}$), we have

$$\frac{T^*}{t_{\text{tr}}^*} \approx \varepsilon^{-1}.$$

Concerning the characteristic radial velocity, we set

$$v_{2,\text{ref}}^* = \delta R_o^* \omega^* = 2\pi\delta\frac{R_o^*}{T^*}, \tag{36}$$

Taking $\delta = 0.25$, and a frequency of ≈ 10 cpm, we have $v_{2,\text{ref}}^* \approx 5 \times 10^{-4}$ cm/s, so that

$$\frac{v_{1,\text{ref}}^*}{v_{2,\text{ref}}^*} = \frac{L^*\,T^*}{R^*\,t_{\text{tr}}^*} \approx \varepsilon^{-2}. \tag{37}$$

Defining

$$x = \frac{x^*}{L^*}, \quad r = \frac{r^*}{R_o^*}, \quad t = \frac{t^*}{T^*}, \tag{38}$$

$$v_1 = \frac{v_1^*}{v_{1,\text{ref}}^*}, \quad v_2 = \frac{v_2^*}{v_{2,\text{ref}}^*}, \quad p = \frac{p^*}{\Delta p_c^*}$$

and recalling (35) and (36), the dimensionless version of the Navier–Stokes and continuity equations is

$$\begin{cases}
\dfrac{\partial v_1}{\partial x} + \varepsilon^3\dfrac{1}{r}\dfrac{\partial(rv_2)}{\partial r} = 0, & (39) \\[6pt]
\dfrac{\rho^* R_o^{*2}}{T^*\mu^*}\left[\dfrac{\partial v_1}{\partial t} + 2\pi\delta\left(\varepsilon^{-1}v_1\dfrac{\partial v_1}{\partial x} + v_2\dfrac{\partial v_1}{\partial r}\right)\right] \\[4pt]
\quad = -\dfrac{\partial p}{\partial x} + \dfrac{1}{r}\dfrac{\partial}{\partial r}\left(r\dfrac{\partial v_1}{\partial r}\right) + \varepsilon^2\dfrac{\partial^2 v_1}{\partial x^2}, & (40) \\[6pt]
\dfrac{\rho^* R_o^{*2}}{T^*\mu^*}\varepsilon^{-3}\left[\dfrac{\partial v_2}{\partial t} + \varepsilon^{-1}\left(v_1\dfrac{\partial v_2}{\partial x} + v_2\dfrac{\partial v_2}{\partial r}\right)\right] \\[4pt]
\quad = -\varepsilon^{-5}\dfrac{\partial p}{\partial r} + \varepsilon^{-2}\dfrac{1}{r}\dfrac{\partial}{\partial r}\left(r\dfrac{\partial v_2}{\partial r}\right) + \dfrac{\partial^2 v_2}{\partial x^2}, & (41)
\end{cases}$$

where

$$\frac{\rho^* R_o^{*2}}{T^*\mu^*} \approx \varepsilon^3.$$

We remark that the Reynolds number of the flow is rather small (less than 10), so that chaotic turbulence never occurs. At the leading order (40) reduces, as expected, to the classical Hagen–Poiseuille equation

$$-\frac{\partial p}{\partial x} + \frac{1}{r}\frac{\partial}{\partial r}\left(r\frac{\partial v_1}{\partial r}\right) = 0.$$

Equation (41) implies that p is independent of r. while the continuity Equation (39) shows that v_1 is independent of x, so that p is linear in x. This fact fully justifies the shortcut adopted in [23] where the quasi steady Poiseuille discharge through the vessel is averaged over a period.

Denoting by Q^* the discharge

$$Q^* = 2\pi \int_0^{R^*} v_1^* r^* \, d r^*,$$

we find, after a little algebra, that the average discharge is

$$\langle Q^* \rangle = \frac{1}{T^*} \int_0^{T^*} Q^* \, d t^* = Q_0^*(1 + f(\delta)), \tag{42}$$

where

$$Q_0^* = \frac{\pi R_o^{*\,4}}{8\mu^*} \frac{\Delta p^*}{L^*},$$

is the discharge corresponding to the radius at the rest state (in [23] the authors obtained a similar formula, but they compared the average flow rate with the one corresponding to the average vessel radius, which is not the rest state radius. Hence they erroneously concluded that vasomotion is advantageous for any amplitude), i.e., the undeformed configuration, and

$$f(\delta) = \frac{35}{8}\delta^4 - 10\delta^3 + 9\delta^2 - 4\delta. \tag{43}$$

In particular, since $-1 < f(\delta) < 0$ for $\delta \in (0,1)$, and $f(\delta) = 0$ when $\delta = 0$, we remark that $\langle Q^* \rangle$ is maximum for when $\delta = 0$. For any $\delta \in (0,1]$ we have $\langle Q^* \rangle < Q_0^*$, so that vascular contractions due to vasomotor activity are disadvantageous for flow, at least in this simple framework. Indeed, the arteriole smooth muscle cells contract from a rest state corresponding to the maximum vessel size R_o^*, and the lumen reduction can only hinder the flow. Thus, the question of the possible benefit of vasomotion in arterioles is left open and should be investigated in a scenario different from the one of a simple Newtonian flow in a vessel with synchronous oscillations.

The above analysis is correct within the $\mathcal{O}(\varepsilon)$ order. Higher order approximations provide corrections not exceeding 1% and are neglected.

3.2. Vasomotion in Venules

Because of the presence of valves which prevent backflow, vasomotion in venules produces a completely different effect. Indeed the pumping action generated by vasomotion on the flow is definitely comparable to the one due to the available pressure gradient.

Valves in the major veins had been observed since the early times of anatomy (see [1] at p. 60). On the contrary, the presence of valves in small veins has been underestimated or even ignored. An historical review on this subject is due to Caggiati et al. [29]. In particular, microscopic valves has been observed in venules as small as 25 μm diameter, where they may be arranged in series (see [30,31]).

3.3. The Mathematical Model

We illustrate a model for venules equipped with just two valves placed at the inlet and outlet, corresponding to $x^* = 0$ and $x^* = L^*$. We attack the problem from a more general point of view, supposing that the vessel radius R^* evolves as a travelling wave with wavelength λ^*, i.e.,

$$R^*(x^*, t^*) = R_o^* R(x^*, t^*) \qquad R(x^*, t^*) = 1 + \delta\Phi\left(\frac{x^*}{\lambda^*} - \frac{t^*}{T^*}\right), \tag{44}$$

where:

A.1 $\Phi(\eta)$ is a periodic function (with period 1) such that $\max \Phi = 0$, $\min \Phi = -1$. Moreover we suppose that Φ is decreasing in a fraction of the period (contraction phase) and increasing in the remaining fraction (expansion phase). Therefore, as in Section 3.1, the vessel radius in the natural undeformed state is R_o^* (maximum cylinder lumen).

A.2 $0 < \delta < 1$, is a dimensionless parameter, so that $R_o^* \delta$, gives the oscillation amplitude (producing a lumen reduction with respect to the rest state).

A.3 λ^* is the wavelength and T^* is the wave period, which are linked to the wave velocity c^* by

$$c^* = \frac{\lambda^*}{T^*}. \tag{45}$$

We denote by u^* the radial surface velocity. From (44)

$$u^* = \frac{\partial R^*}{\partial t^*} e_r = -\dot{R}_{ref}^* \Phi'\left(\frac{x^*}{\lambda^*} - \frac{t^*}{T^*}\right) e_r, \tag{46}$$

where $\Phi'(\eta) = d\Phi/d\eta$ and where

$$\dot{R}_{ref}^* = \frac{R_o^* \delta}{T^*}, \tag{47}$$

represents the average contraction velocity, so that we replace (36) with $v_{2,ref}^* = \dot{R}_{ref}^*$. In vasomotion $\dot{R}_{ref}^*$ is available from experiments. Recalling the scaling (38), we introduce $\lambda = \lambda^*/L^*$. We will focus on the following cases:

1. λ^* much larger than L^* (more precisely $\lambda^{-1} \leq \varepsilon$), meaning that at the leading order the vessel undergoes spatially synchronous oscillations.
2. λ^* comparable with L^*, i.e., $\lambda = \mathcal{O}(1)$.

We do not consider the case $\lambda^* \ll L^*$, since in [32] we proved that in this case the peristalsis has basically no effect on the flow.

Considering (38) and setting $\lambda = \lambda^*/L^*$, Equation (44) becomes

$$R(x,t) = 1 + \delta \Phi\left(\frac{x}{\lambda} - t\right), \tag{48}$$

so that

$$\lambda \frac{\partial R}{\partial x} + \frac{\partial R}{\partial t} = 0.$$

Differently from the case of arterioles, the pressure gradient in venules is low (few mmHg/mm) and we may assume that the flow is dominated by peristalsis. Therefore we choose the longitudinal reference velocity v_{ref}^* as follows

$$v_{ref}^* = \frac{1}{\varepsilon} \dot{R}_{ref}^* = \frac{1}{\varepsilon} \frac{R_o^* \delta}{T^*}, \tag{49}$$

and set

$$v_1 = \frac{v_1^*}{v_{ref}^*}, \quad v_2 = \frac{v_2^*}{\dot{R}_{ref}^*} = \frac{v_2^*}{\varepsilon v_{ref}^*},$$

so that $v = v_1 e_x + \varepsilon v_2 e_r$. The reference pressure gradient is defined as

$$\frac{\Delta p_{ref}^*}{L^*} = \frac{\mu^*}{R_o^{*2}} v_{ref}^*.$$

The quantity Δp_{ref}^* represents the order of magnitude of the "effective pressure drop" caused by the oscillations of the vessel (inspired to Poiseuille's formula). The known imposed pressure difference is $\Delta p^* = p^*(0, t^*) - p^*(L^*, t^*)$, and we consider

$$\Delta p = \frac{\Delta p^*}{\Delta p^*_{\text{ref}}} = \mathcal{O}(1). \tag{49}$$

When $\Delta p \gg 1$, the flow is essentially dominated by the externally imposed pressure gradient and the effects due to the wall oscillations are hardly observable (which is exactly the case occurring in arterioles). We also introduce the dimensionless pressure

$$p = \frac{p^*(x^*, t^*) - p^*(L^*, t^*)}{\Delta p^*_{\text{ref}}}, \tag{50}$$

so that

$$p|_{\text{inlet}} = \Delta p, \qquad p|_{\text{outlet}} = 0. \tag{51}$$

We finally rescale the radial velocity of the vessel walls u^* by $\dot{R}^*_{\text{ref}}$, namely, by using (48),

$$u^* = \dot{R}^*_{\text{ref}} \, u \, \mathbf{e}_r, \quad \text{with} \quad u = -\Phi'\left(\frac{x}{\lambda} - t\right) = \frac{\lambda}{\delta} \frac{\partial R}{\partial x} = \frac{1}{\delta} \frac{\partial R}{\partial t}. \tag{52}$$

3.4. Flow Equations

On the tube surface we set $v^*|_{r^* = R^*} = u^*$ so that, from (46) and (52),

$$v_1|_{r=R} = 0, \tag{53}$$

$$v_2|_{r=R} = u = -\Phi'\left(\frac{x}{\lambda} - t\right) = \frac{\partial \Phi}{\partial t} = -\frac{1}{\lambda} \frac{\partial \Phi}{\partial x}. \tag{54}$$

The line $r = 0$ is a symmetry axis so that

$$v_2|_{r=0} = 0, \quad \text{and} \quad \left.\frac{\partial v_1}{\partial r}\right|_{r=0} = 0. \tag{55}$$

The fluid mechanical incompressibility yields

$$\frac{\partial v_1}{\partial x} + \frac{1}{r}\frac{\partial (r v_2)}{\partial r} = 0, \tag{56}$$

and the motion equation reduces to Stokes equation

$$-\nabla^* p^* + \mu^* \Delta^* v^* = 0, \tag{57}$$

since the Reynolds number characterizing the flow is small (referring, for instance, to the data of [25] we have $\text{Re} \approx 10^{-2}$). So (57) yields

$$-\frac{\partial p}{\partial x} + \varepsilon^2 \frac{\partial^2 v_1}{\partial x^2} + \frac{1}{r}\frac{\partial}{\partial r}\left(r \frac{\partial v_1}{\partial r}\right) = 0, \tag{58}$$

$$-\frac{1}{\varepsilon^2}\frac{\partial p}{\partial r} + \varepsilon^2 \frac{\partial^2 v_2}{\partial x^2} + \frac{1}{r}\frac{\partial}{\partial r}\left(r \frac{\partial v_2}{\partial r}\right) - \frac{v_2}{r^2} = 0, \tag{59}$$

which, at the leading order imply $p = p(x, t)$, and

$$-\frac{\partial p}{\partial x} + \frac{1}{r}\frac{\partial}{\partial r}\left(r \frac{\partial v_1}{\partial r}\right) = 0. \tag{60}$$

Recalling boundary conditions (53) and (55), we find

$$v_1(x, r, t) = -\frac{1}{4}\frac{\partial p}{\partial x}\left(R^2 - r^2\right), \tag{61}$$

with $R(x,t)$ given by (48). We now insert (56) in (61), getting

$$4\frac{\partial}{\partial r}(r v_2) = \frac{\partial^2 p}{\partial x^2} r(R^2 - r^2) + 2r\frac{\partial p}{\partial x} R \frac{\partial R}{\partial x}.$$

Integrating between 0 and R and exploiting (54) we obtain

$$\frac{\partial}{\partial x}\left(\frac{R^4}{4}\frac{\partial p}{\partial x}\right) = 4Ru, \tag{62}$$

with u given by (52). The average longitudinal velocity is

$$\langle v_1 \rangle = \frac{2}{R^2}\int_0^R \left(-\frac{1}{4}\frac{\partial p}{\partial x}\right)(R^2 - r^2) r\, dr = -\frac{1}{8}\frac{\partial p}{\partial x} R^2.$$

The local dimensionless discharge at time t (within an $\mathcal{O}(\varepsilon)$ approximation) is

$$Q(x,t) = \pi R^2 \langle v_1 \rangle = -\pi \frac{R^4}{8}\frac{\partial p}{\partial x}, \tag{63}$$

corresponding to the physical quantity

$$Q^*(x^*,t^*) = \left(\frac{L^*\delta}{T^*} R_0^{*2}\right) \pi R^2 \langle v_1 \rangle. \tag{64}$$

3.5. Boundary Conditions at the Vessel Ends

The valves are placed at the vessels ends, and act to prevent backflow. Valves are considered as massless devices with a simple dynamics: when pressure exceeds the inlet one, the inlet valve closes; when pressure falls below the outlet one, the outlet valve closes. Let us express the corresponding boundary conditions. At $x = 0$, inlet valve, two conditions have to be fulfilled

$$Q(0,t) \geq 0, \Leftrightarrow \left.\frac{\partial p}{\partial x}\right|_{x=0} \leq 0, \tag{65}$$

$$p(0,t) \geq \Delta p. \tag{66}$$

The first condition simply states that backflow cannot occur (pressure is allowed to grow beyond Δp when the valve is closed), while the second one guarantees that $p(0,t)$ can never drop below the imposed pressure. Evidently, at least one of such conditions must be verified as an equality. As a consequence, the inlet boundary conditions summarize as follows

$$\begin{cases} \left.\frac{\partial p}{\partial x}\right|_{x=0} (p(0,t) - \Delta p) = 0 \\ \left.\frac{\partial p}{\partial x}\right|_{x=0} \leq 0, \\ p(0,t) \geq \Delta p. \end{cases} \tag{67}$$

This is a typical unilateral boundary condition (also known as Signorini type condition) which is frequently encountered in continuum mechanics (see, for instance, [33]). Similarly, the boundary conditions at $x = 1$ are

$$\begin{cases} \dfrac{\partial p}{\partial x}\bigg|_{x=1} p(1,t) = 0, \\ \dfrac{\partial p}{\partial x}\bigg|_{x=1} \leq 0, \\ p(1,t) \leq 0. \end{cases} \tag{68}$$

These conditions (graphically represented by the step functions, i.e., solid lines, in Figure 6) allow, as we shall see, to find an explicit formula for pressure and discharge. In this way the valves are modeled as massless devices which open/close instantaneously as the pressure in the vessel becomes larger/smaller than the one outside. Such an approach, though providing a significant agreement with the experiments reported in [25], have been improved in [27] where the valves inertia, which induces a delay in their action, has been considered.

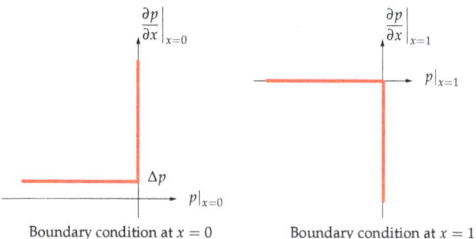

Figure 6. Signorini type boundary conditions at $x = 0$ and $x = 1$ (pressure gradient vs. pressure).

3.6. Synchronous Oscillation: $\lambda^{-1} \leq \varepsilon$

This case essentially corresponds to a spatially uniform contraction/expansion of the vessel, i.e., $R = R(t)$. In particular, using the same notation of Formula (44), we take

$$R = R(t) = 1 + \delta \Phi(t), \tag{69}$$

with Φ periodic function of period 1, and, recalling A.1 of Section 3.3, $\Phi \leq 0$. Next, because of (52)

$$u = \dfrac{1}{\delta} \dot{R}(t) = \dot{\Phi}(t). \tag{70}$$

Formula (62) can be rewritten as

$$\dfrac{\partial^2 p}{\partial x^2} = \dfrac{16}{\delta} \dfrac{\ddot{R}}{R^3},$$

yielding

$$\begin{cases} p(x,t) = \dfrac{8}{\delta} \dfrac{\ddot{R}(t)}{R^3(t)} x^2 + A(t)x + B(t), \\ \dfrac{\partial p(x,t)}{\partial x} = \dfrac{16}{\delta} \dfrac{\ddot{R}(t)}{R^3(t)} x + A(t). \end{cases} \tag{71}$$

Functions $A(t)$, and $B(t)$ are unknown and have to be determined. Condition (67) rewrites as

$$\begin{cases} A(t)(B(t) - \Delta p) = 0, \\ A(t) \leq 0, \\ B(t) - \Delta p \geq 0, \end{cases} \quad (72)$$

while (68) takes the form

$$\begin{cases} \left(\dfrac{8}{\delta}\dfrac{\dot{R}(t)}{R^3(t)} + A(t) + B(t)\right)\left(\dfrac{16}{\delta}\dfrac{\dot{R}(t)}{R^3(t)} + A(t)\right) = 0, \\ \dfrac{16}{\delta}\dfrac{\dot{R}(t)}{R^3(t)} + A(t) \leq 0, \\ \dfrac{8}{\delta}\dfrac{\dot{R}(t)}{R^3(t)} + A(t) + B(t) \leq 0. \end{cases} \quad (73)$$

We now assume the entrance valve engaged, that is $A = 0$, and consider the compression phase $\dot{R} < 0$. From the first of (73)

$$B(t) = -\dfrac{8}{\delta}\dfrac{\dot{R}}{R^3},$$

which, exploiting (71), gives $p(1,t) = 0$. Of course the third condition of (72) has to be fulfilled so that

$$\dfrac{8}{\delta}\dfrac{|\dot{R}|}{R^3} \geq \Delta p. \quad (74)$$

On the other hand if

$$\dfrac{8}{\delta}\dfrac{|\dot{R}|}{R^3} < \Delta p, \quad (75)$$

the entrance valve is open and the solution is

$$B(t) = \Delta p \quad \text{and} \quad A(t) = -\left(\dfrac{8}{\delta}\dfrac{\dot{R}(t)}{R^3(t)} + \Delta p\right).$$

Hence, during the compression phase, i.e., $\dot{R} < 0$, we have

$$p(x,t) = \begin{cases} \dfrac{8}{\delta}\dfrac{\dot{R}}{R^3}(x^2 - 1), & \text{if } \dfrac{8}{\delta}\dfrac{|\dot{R}|}{R^3} \geq \Delta p, \\ \dfrac{8}{\delta}\dfrac{\dot{R}}{R^3}(x^2 - x) - \Delta p(x - 1), & \text{if } \dfrac{8}{\delta}\dfrac{|\dot{R}|}{R^3} < \Delta p. \end{cases} \quad (76)$$

In the expansion phase $\dot{R} > 0$, we first consider

$$A = -\dfrac{16}{\delta}\dfrac{\dot{R}}{R^3},$$

i.e., the exit valve is closed. The conclusion is that $B(t) = \Delta p$ (the inlet dimensionless pressure). Then, recalling the third condition in (73), we notice that the compatibility condition (74) must once again be fulfilled. On the contrary, when condition (75) is fulfilled the exit valve is open and the condition $p(1,t) = 0$ yields

$$A(t) = -\left(\frac{8}{\delta}\frac{\dot{R}(t)}{R^3(t)} + \Delta p\right) \quad \text{and} \quad B(t) = \Delta p.$$

Summarizing, during the expansion phase, i.e., $\dot{R} > 0$, the pressure is

$$p(x,t) = \begin{cases} \Delta p + \dfrac{8}{\delta}\dfrac{\dot{R}}{R^3}(x^2 - 2x), & \text{if } \dfrac{8}{\delta}\dfrac{\dot{R}}{R^3} \geq \Delta p, \\[2mm] \dfrac{8}{\delta}\dfrac{\dot{R}}{R^3}(x^2 - x) - \Delta p(x - 1), & \text{if } \dfrac{8}{\delta}\dfrac{\dot{R}}{R^3} < \Delta p, \end{cases} \qquad (77)$$

We remark that when $\dot{R} = 0$ Equations (76) and (77) provide the classical linear profile

$$p(x,t) = \Delta p\,(1 - x).$$

We also observe that the flux has no interruption. Indeed, when a valve at one end is closed the one at the opposite end is open. Formula (63) allows to estimate the dimensionless discharge, which depends on the abscissa x along the vessel. In particular, when $\Delta p = 0$, we have (the case $\Delta p \neq 0$, has been extensively analyzed in [26]).

$$Q(x,t) = 2\pi\frac{R}{\delta}\begin{cases} |\dot{R}|x, & \text{when } \dot{R} < 0, \\[2mm] \dot{R}(1 - x), & \text{when } \dot{R} > 0. \end{cases} \qquad (78)$$

Therefore, during compression phase, i.e., when $\dot{R} < 0$, the inlet discharge vanishes, while in the expansion phase we have $Q(1,t) = 0$, and the inlet flow rate becomes maximum. It is trivial to verify that the total inlet discharge equals the total output discharge. Moreover, the average flow in a period is not zero (as it would occur in absence of valves). Indeed, if a single oscillation over the period is considered, namely

$$\dot{R} < 0, \quad \text{for} \quad 0 \leq t < \alpha,$$

$$\dot{R} = 0, \quad \text{for} \quad t = \alpha,$$

$$\dot{R} > 0, \quad \text{for} \quad \alpha < t < 1,$$

the total volume (dimensionless) coming out of the vessel in a period (and which therefore enters the tube during the subsequent expansion phase) is

$$V_{out} = \int_0^1 Q(1,t)\,dt = -\frac{\pi}{\delta}\int_0^\alpha \frac{dR^2}{dt}\,dt = \frac{\pi}{\delta}\left[R^2(0) - R^2(\alpha)\right] = \pi(2 - \delta),$$

since, $R(0) = 1$ and $R(\alpha) = \min R(t) = 1 - \delta$. Hence, recalling (64), we have

$$V^*_{out} = \pi R_o^{*2}\left(2\delta - \delta^2\right)L^* = \pi L^*\left(R_o^{*2} - \min R^{*\,2}\right),$$

that is the volume by which the cylinder is reduced during an oscillation.

The typical behavior of the outflux and influx, i.e., $Q(1,t)$ and $Q(0,t)$, is displayed in Figure 7. The top panel shows the radius oscillation during a period (in this case $\delta = 0.3$), while in the bottom panel $Q(1,t)$ and $Q(0,t)$, given by (78). We remark that, during the compression phase, $Q(0,t)$ vanishes and $Q(1,t) \neq 0$ since the outlet valve is open. During the expansion phase, $\dot{R} > 0$, exactly the opposite occurs since the inlet valve is open.

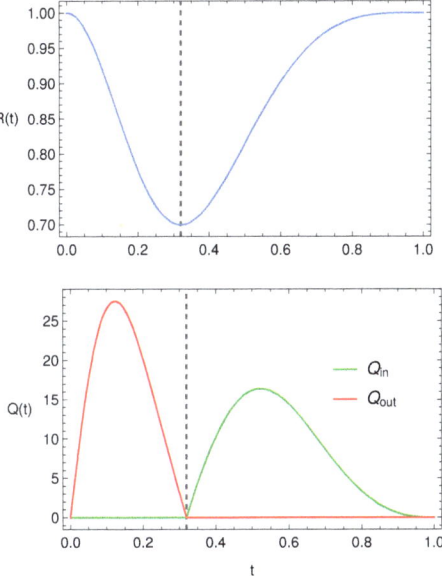

Figure 7. Typical behaviour of $R(t)$, $Q(0,t)$ and $Q(1,t)$.

3.7. Non-Synchronous Oscillation: $\lambda = \mathcal{O}(1)$

The case in which $\lambda = \mathcal{O}(1)$, i.e., non-synchronous oscillations, has been analyzed in detail in [26]. Here we recall briefly the main steps, considering, for the sake of simplicity, $\Delta p = 0$. Recalling (52) and (62), we write

$$\frac{\partial}{\partial x}\left(\frac{R^4}{8}\frac{\partial p}{\partial x}\right) = -\frac{\lambda}{\delta}\frac{\partial R^2}{\partial x}, \qquad (79)$$

which gives

$$p(x,t) = \mathcal{B}(t) - \frac{8\lambda}{\delta}\int_0^x \frac{dx'}{R^2} + \mathcal{A}(t)\int_0^x \frac{dx'}{R^4},$$

where $\mathcal{A}(t)$ and $\mathcal{B}(t)$ are unknown at this stage.

We introduce

$$R_{\text{in}}(t) = R(0,t), \quad R_{\text{out}}(t) = R(1,t), \quad S_{\text{in}}(t) = \pi R_{\text{in}}^2(t), \quad S_{\text{out}}(t) = \pi R_{\text{out}}^2(t),$$

and define

$$\mathcal{I}_2(t) = \int_0^1 \frac{dx}{R^2(x,t)}, \qquad \mathcal{I}_4(t) = \int_0^1 \frac{dx}{R^4(x,t)}.$$

Proceeding as in Section 3.6, we consider two cases:

(a) $\quad S_{\text{in}}(t) < S_{\text{out}}(t) \quad \Leftrightarrow \quad R_{\text{in}}(t) < R_{\text{out}}(t),$

(b) $\quad S_{\text{in}}(t) \geq S_{\text{out}}(t) \quad \Leftrightarrow \quad R_{\text{in}}(t) \geq R_{\text{out}}(t).$

Case (a). The boundary conditions (67) and (68) yield

$$\mathcal{A}(t) = \frac{8\lambda}{\delta}R_{\text{in}}^2(t),$$

and
$$B(t) = \frac{8\lambda}{\delta}\left[\mathcal{I}_2(t) - R_{in}^2(t)\mathcal{I}_4(t)\right],$$

provided
$$\left[\mathcal{I}_2(t) - R_{in}^2(t)\mathcal{I}_4(t)\right] \geq 0 \qquad (80)$$

If (80) is violated, i.e.,
$$\left[\mathcal{I}_2(t) - R_{in}^2(t)\mathcal{I}_4(t)\right] < 0, \qquad (81)$$

we take
$$B(t) = 0, \text{ and } \mathcal{A}(t) = \frac{8\lambda}{\delta}\frac{\mathcal{I}_2(t)}{\mathcal{I}_4(t)}, \qquad (82)$$

Since conditions the third of both (67) and (68) are fulfilled, we need to prove only the second of (67) from which the second of (68) automatically follows because $R_{in}^2 < R_{out}^2$. Rewriting the second of (67) as
$$\mathcal{A} \leq \frac{8\lambda}{\delta} R_{in}^2$$

and using (82), we immediately obtain (81).

Case (b). We now have
$$B = 0,$$
and
$$\mathcal{A}(t) = \frac{8\lambda}{\delta}R_{out}^2(t), \text{ if } \left[\mathcal{I}_2(t) - R_{out}^2(t)\mathcal{I}_4(t)\right] \geq 0,$$

or $\mathcal{A}$ given by (82) in case $\left[\mathcal{I}_2(t) - R_{out}^2(t)\mathcal{I}_4(t)\right] < 0$. Hence, recalling (63) and introducing
$$\mathfrak{T}_{in}(t) = \mathcal{I}_2(t) - R_{in}^2(t)\mathcal{I}_4(t), \qquad \mathfrak{T}_{out}(t) = \mathcal{I}_2(t) - R_{out}^2(t)\mathcal{I}_4(t),$$

we have

if $S_{in}(t) < S_{out}(t)$, $Q(x,t) = -\pi\frac{\lambda}{\delta}\begin{cases} R_{in}^2(t) - R^2(x,t), & \text{if } \mathfrak{T}_{in}(t) \geq 0, \\ \dfrac{\mathcal{I}_2(t)}{\mathcal{I}_4(t)} - R^2(x,t), & \text{if } \mathfrak{T}_{in}(t) < 0, \end{cases}$

if $S_{in}(t) \geq S_{out}(t)$, $Q(x,t) = -\pi\frac{\lambda}{\delta}\begin{cases} R_{out}^2(t) - R^2(x,t), & \text{if } \mathfrak{T}_{out}(t) \geq 0, \\ \dfrac{\mathcal{I}_2(t)}{\mathcal{I}_4(t)} - R^2(x,t), & \text{if } \mathfrak{T}_{out}(t) < 0. \end{cases}$

In order to highlight the difference between the two cases, we consider $\Phi(\eta) = -[1 - \cos^2(\pi\eta)]$, which fulfils A.1, so that
$$R(x,t) = 1 - \delta\left[1 - \cos^2\left(\pi\left(\frac{x}{\lambda} - t\right)\right)\right]. \qquad (83)$$

Figure 8 displays the in influx, $Q_{in} = Q(0,t)$ and the outflux $Q_{out} = Q(0,t)$, when $R(x,t)$ is given by (83) with $\delta = 0.3$, and $\lambda = 3/4$. In Figure 9 we still report Q_{in} and Q_{out} but in case of synchronous oscillations, i.e., when $R(t) = 1 - \delta[1 - \cos^2(\pi t)]$, with the same δ. The differences between the profiles reported in Figures 8 and 9 are evident even if the flow rates peaks are the same. In case of synchronous oscillations, Figure 9, the two valves are never open at the same time and the inlet and outlet flow rates are symmetrical (because of to the peculiar behavior of $R(t)$). In case of non-synchronous oscillations, i.e., Figure 8, there exists a time interval in which both valves are open. This is evidently attributable to the fact that the vessel contraction occurs as a traveling wave.

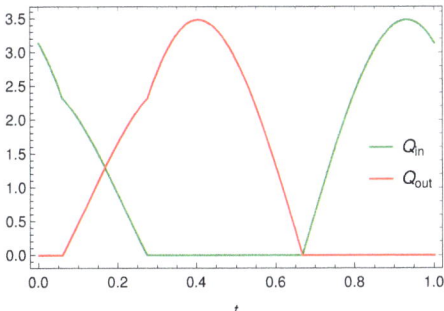

Figure 8. Inlet and outlet discharge when $R(x,t)$ is given by (83), with $\delta = 0.3$ and $\lambda = 3/4$.

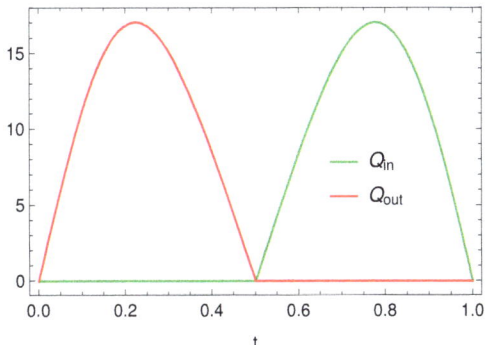

Figure 9. Inlet and outlet discharge when $R(t) = 1 - \delta[1 - \cos^2(\pi t)]$ with $\delta = 0.3$.

3.8. Model Validation

The comparison between the model and the experimental data by Dongaonkar et al. [25] has been discussed in details in [26,27].

We consider the experimental data reported in Figure 3 of [25], which represents the diameter oscillations of a bat wing venule. In particular, we select (recall that δ denotes the oscillation amplitude)

$$R(t) = at^3(1-t^3)^3 + (1-\delta). \tag{84}$$

where we set $R_o^* \approx 70$ μm, $T^* \approx 6$ s, $\delta = 0.25$, and $a \approx 2.37$.

The comparison between the experimental data of [25] (Figure 5, luminal pressure) and the pressure profile predicted by the model is shown in Figure 10. Considering the simplicity of the model (only two valves, inertia neglected, Newtonian context), the agreement appears rather satisfactory.

In the left panel of Figure 11 we show $P(x,t)$ when $R(t)$ is given by (84), and $\Delta p = 1$. The right panel shows $P(x,t)$ when $R(t)$ is given by (84), and $\Delta p = 50$. We remark that in the latter case the effect on the pressure caused by the vessel contraction is comparable with the driving pressure difference.

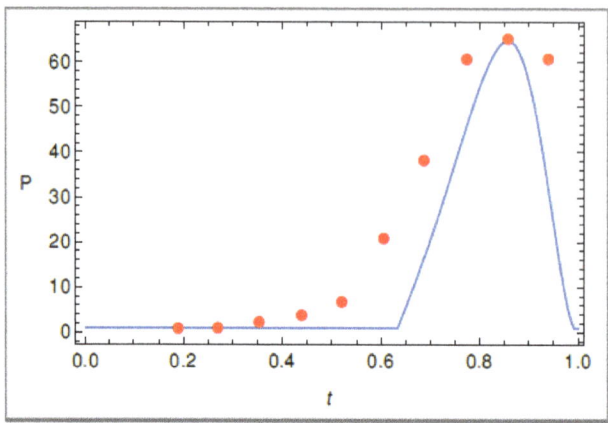

Figure 10. Pressure pulse at $x = 0$ when $R(t)$ is given by (84) and the experimental data extracted from Figure 5 of [25].

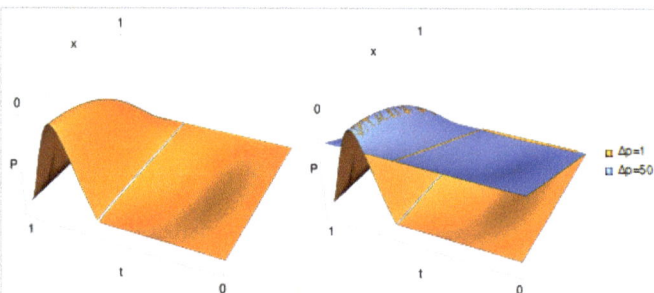

Figure 11. The pressure $P(x,t)$ given by (76) and (77), and $R(t)$ given by (84). In the left panel $\Delta p = 1$; in right one, the two surfaces correspond to $\Delta p = 1$ and $\Delta p = 50$, respectively.

3.9. Modeling Vasomotion: Conclusions

Periodic contraction-expansion of blood vessels have been recorded since 1852. Such phenomenon, usually referred to as vasomotion, concerns small (but not too small) vessels (arterioles and venules). The basic laws of fluid dynamics and the smallness of the radius/length ratio have been exploited to formulate a mathematical model which appears to be rather accurate.

First we have focused on arterioles, where the blood flow is essentially driven by hydraulic pressure gradient imposed by heart, concluding that the vessel resistance is increased by vasomotion. This is due to the lumen reduction caused by the vessel contraction (generated by the smooth muscle cells surrounding the arterioles) which actually hinders the flow. Actually such a result agrees with [22]: the resistance in a vessel with vasomotion is larger than the one of a static vessel with relaxed radius.

We then analyzed vasomotion in venules provided with just two compliant valves (one at the inlet and one at the outlet). We considered first the case of synchronous vessel oscillation. This can be seen as the limit of the peristaltic motion when the wavelength is much larger than the vessel length. The model has been tested versus the experimental measures by Dongaonkar et al. [25] performed on bat wing venules, which are characterized by periodic pressure pulses. Regardless of the simplicity of the model, the agreement obtained is remarkable. In particular, the model discussed in [27] which accounts effectively for valve inertia, reproduces the recorded pressure pulse almost perfectly. This suggests that the scheme with two valves provides a quite reasonable description of the phenomenon.

On the contrary, the many valves model discussed in [28] produces a different qualitative behavior which is not compatible with the experimental measures of [25].

We have confined our analysis to the propulsive effect. In larger veins, valves exert a modulation effect that enhances the centripetal blood flow [34]. We finally emphasize that the two-valve model may be applicable to lymphagiones, the valves equipped elements making a lymphatic vessel.

4. The Fåhræus–Lindqvist Effect

The Fåhræus–Lindqvist (FL) effect is a phenomenon that occurs in blood vessels with diameter in the range $\approx$ 30–300 µm and is named after the two Swedish scientists Robin Fåhræus and Johann Torsten Lindqvist [35]. It consists in a progressive reduction of the apparent blood viscosity as the blood vessel radius decreases. The FL effect is clearly related to the rheological properties of blood. Indeed, despite the blood composite nature, in tubes like veins and arteries above the size specified above and at relatively high shear rate ($\geq$100 s^{-1}), this fluid shows the characteristic Newtonian behaviour of an incompressible liquid. At a smaller scale this is no longer true since inhomogeneity effects become highly significant and must be considered. Notwithstanding the great importance of this topic in physiology, until the fifties papers on blood rheology were scarce and not properly connected in textbooks or manuals dealing with blood or the blood circulation. Quoting Copley [36]

> reviews on the viscosity of blood deal largely with data on apparent viscosities. The relative paucity of rheological treatments of blood is contrasted by the large number of observations of rheological phenomena of this humor.

Despite all the efforts and hundreds of studies devoted to the FL effect in the last ninety years, an explanation based on the principles of fluid dynamics has been achieved only very recently [37].

The physiologist and physicist Jean Poiseuille [38], in 1836, was the first to investigate the flow of human blood in narrow tubes. Experiments lead them to formulate their famous law that relates the fluid dynamic viscosity (as previously stated, starred quantities are dimensional) η^* to the in-out pressure difference ΔP^* in the tube, the volumetric flux Q^*, and the tube length L^* and radius R^*, namely

$$\eta^* = \frac{\pi R^{*4}}{8 L^* Q^*} \Delta P^* \tag{85}$$

Poiseuille experiments found their theoretical justification some years later, thanks to Navier and Stokes. Indeed, (85) can be proved to be a direct consequence of the Navier–Stokes equations of fluid mechanics. If blood is considered a *homogeneous* Newtonian fluid, then the stress and shear rate are directly proportional through a *constant* viscosity η^*, which depends on temperature. In case of flow in a tube, Navier–Stokes equations can be solved explicitly for the velocity which shows a parabolic profile along a tube cross-section. Thus, being

$$Q^* = 2\pi \int_0^{R^*} r^* v^*(r^*) \, d r^*, \tag{86}$$

the flow rate can be calculated by integrating $v^*(r^*)$, and (85) is theoretically justified.

What has all this to do with the FL effect? If blood were really Newtonian, its viscosity should not depend, in particular, on the tube radius. On the contrary Figure 12 shows that this is not true.

Moreover, viscosity is measured at a given shear rate, an so, in principle, it could also depend on the latter. For a Newtonian fluid this ratio is a material constant which shows dependence only on temperature. Otherwise, viscosity is referred to with the name of "apparent" viscosity and denoted by η^*_{app}. Figure 12 shows that blood turns from a

Newtonian to a non-Newtonian behaviour as soon as the vessel diameter reduces below a threshold value.

The FL effect has an important physiological implication: *the heart can drive a given volume of blood through the arterioles at a much lower pressure than would be the case if the blood were a Newtonian fluid*.

The non-Newtonian behaviour of blood in small tubes has received several *qualitative* explanations, the most important one being related to the fact that blood is not a simple a liquid, but rather a non-homogeneous suspension of various particles. Among all these particles, RBCs contribute by far the highest percentage. In the next section we outline the Haynes' conjecture, which was the first tentative to interpret the FL effect as a consequence of a "smart" response of the RBCs to the narrowing of the vessel diameter.

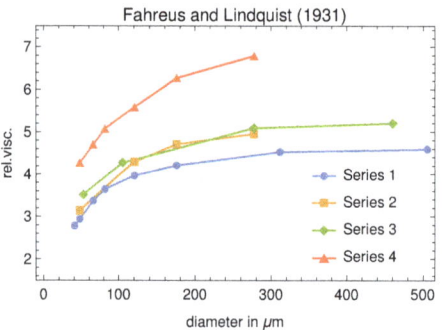

Figure 12. Original data of the Fåhræus–Lindqvist experiment. The measured viscosity is relative to that of plasma. It should be emphasized that one of the blood samples (series 4) shows higher relative viscosity values than that the others, since was partially depleted of plasma by centrifugation.

4.1. The Haynes' Conjecture and Its Physiological Implications

According to Haynes [39], in vessels with diameter smaller than 300 µm, RBCs tend to migrate towards the central part of the vessel, while a less viscous layer of plasma, named "marginal zone" or "cell-free layer" (CFL), forms close to the walls. The viscosity in the marginal zone is basically the one of the suspending liquid (plasma), denoted by η_p^*. The viscosity of the RBCs suspension in the central core of the tube is assumed to be uniform and is denoted by η_c^*. Haynes' leading idea is that the presence of the marginal zone reduces the apparent viscosity in tubes of small diameter. This reminds Jeffery [40] who heuristically hypothesized that

the particles will tend to adopt that motion which, of all motions possible under the approximate equations, corresponds to the least dissipation of energy.

Indeed, since the viscosity of the marginal layer is from 4 to 5 times less than that of the core, the wall stress is drastically reduced. In the Haynes' view, the physiological motivation of the migration of the RBCs toward the center of the tube is to reduce the pumping effort of the heart. Recently, Ascolese et al. [41] showed that this heuristic explanation is misleading.

Following their approach, we first recall that blood is treated as an inhomogeneous incompressible linear viscous fluid, whose viscosity depends on the hematocrit ϕ. If **u** is the velocity, the model equations are

$$\begin{cases} \dfrac{\partial^* \phi}{\partial t^*} + \boldsymbol{u}^* \cdot \nabla^* \phi = 0, \\ \nabla^* \cdot \boldsymbol{u}^* = 0, \\ \varrho \left(\dfrac{\partial^* \boldsymbol{u}^*}{\partial t^*} + (\nabla^* \boldsymbol{u}^*) \boldsymbol{u}^* \right) = -\nabla^* p^* + \nabla^* \cdot \mathbb{T}^*, \end{cases} \quad (87)$$

where the differential operators are referred to dimensional variables, ϱ^* is the blood density, p^* the pressure, and $\mathbb{T}^* = 2\eta^*(\phi)\mathbb{D}^*$, with $\eta^*(\phi)$ the hematocrit-dependent blood viscosity, and $\mathbb{D}^* = (1/2)\left(\nabla^* u^* + \nabla^* u^{*T}\right)$. Concerning $\eta^*(\phi)$, the current literature offers a variety of empirical laws (see, for example, [42–47]).

Although blood generally shows shear thinning and stress relaxation proprieties [1,48] these non-Newtonian effects can be neglected for the flow regimes and vessel sizes considered in [41].

Let us now specialize model (87) to the steady flow in a cylindrical tube whose diameter is $D^* = 2R^*$ and whose length is L^*. If we denote by r^* the radial coordinate, and suppose that the flow attains a steady laminar state

$$u^* = u^*(r^*) e_x, \quad \phi = \phi(r^*), \tag{88}$$

where e_x is the unit vector parallel to the cylinder axis, the first two equations in (87) are identically satisfied, and the third reduces to

$$0 = -\frac{\partial^* p^*}{\partial x^*} + \frac{1}{r^*} \frac{\partial}{\partial r^*}\left(r^* \eta^*(\phi) \frac{\partial u^*}{\partial r^*}\right). \tag{89}$$

Equation (89) can solved for $(u^*(r^*), \phi(r^*))$ under standard (no-slip) boundary conditions:

$$u^*(r^*) = \frac{\Delta P^*}{2L^*} \int_{r^*}^{R^*} \frac{\zeta^*}{\eta^*(\phi(\zeta^*))} d\zeta^*, \tag{90}$$

and

$$\phi_B \int_0^{R^*} \frac{r^{*3}}{\eta^*(\phi(r^*))} dr^* = \int_0^{R^*} \frac{2r^*}{\eta^*(\phi(r^*))} \left(\int_0^{r^*} \phi(\zeta^*)\zeta^* d\zeta^*\right) dr^*, \tag{91}$$

where ϕ_B is the inlet hematocrit (usually between 0.35 and 0.5) and $\Delta P^* = P^*(0) - P^*(L^*)$ the in-out pressure difference.

According to Haynes' conjecture, in vessels with diameter D^* less than 0.3 mm, the RBCs migrate towards the center so that the flow region consists of an outer layer in which $\phi = 0$ (also referred to as cell-free layer, CFL) and the complementary axisymmetric region to which all RBCs are segregated, where the hematocrit ϕ_c is constant and uniform. The two regions are separated by an interface with constant but unknown radius s. Therefore, $\phi(r^*)$ is a stepwise function

$$\phi(r^*) = \begin{cases} \phi_c, & 0 \le r^* \le s^*, \\ 0, & s^* < r^* \le R^*, \end{cases} \tag{92}$$

and the flow has the so-called core-annulus structure (CAS). Since Equation (91) has to be fulfilled, s is not arbitrary. Although other choices of $\phi(r^*)$ are possible (see, for example, Phillips et al. [49]), the advantage of (92) is that it allows to solve the flow problem explicitly.

The continuity of velocity and shear stress at the unknown interface s leads, after standard calculations, to obtain the velocity profile in the tube and to evaluate, consequently, the discharge: indeed

$$u^*(r^*) = \begin{cases} \dfrac{\Delta P^*}{4L^*}\left(\dfrac{s^{*2} - r^{*2}}{\eta^*(\phi_c)} + \dfrac{R^{*2} - s^{*2}}{\eta_p^*}\right), & 0 \le r^* \le s^* \\[2ex] \dfrac{\Delta P^*}{4L^*} \dfrac{R^{*2} - r^{*2}}{\eta_p^*}, & s^* \le r^* \le R^*, \end{cases} \tag{93}$$

and

$$Q_c^* = 2\pi \int_0^{s^*} r^* u^*(r^*)\, dr^* = \frac{\pi \Delta P^*}{8L^*}\left(\frac{s^{*4}}{\eta^*(\phi_c)} + \frac{2(R^{*2}-s^{*2})}{\eta_p^*}\right) \quad \text{(core)}, \quad (94)$$

$$Q_a^* = 2\pi \int_{s^*}^{R^*} r^* u^*(r^*)\, dr^* = \frac{\pi \Delta P^*}{8L^* \eta_p^*}\left(R^{*2}-s^{*2}\right)^2 \quad \text{(outer layer)}, \quad (95)$$

so that the total discharge is

$$Q^* = \frac{\pi \Delta P^*}{8L^*}\left(\frac{s^{*4}}{\eta^*(\phi_c)} + \frac{R^{*4}-s^{*4}}{\eta_p^*}\right). \quad (96)$$

Recalling (85), we get

$$\eta_{\text{app}}^* = \frac{\eta_p^*}{1+\sigma^4\left(\frac{\eta_p^*}{\eta^*(\phi_c)}-1\right)}, \quad (97)$$

where $\sigma = s^*/R^* \in (0,1]$. The derivation of sigma will be discussed in Section 4.2. The total power dissipation by the viscous friction along the tube is

$$\mathcal{P}^* = 2\pi \int_0^{L^*} \eta^*(\phi(r^*))\left(\frac{d^*}{dr^*} u^*(r^*)\right)^2 r^*\, dr^*\, dx^*, \quad (98)$$

while the total flow discharge for a given pressure drop ΔP is

$$\mathcal{Q}^* = \pi \frac{\Delta P^*}{L^*} \int_0^{R^*} r^* \int_{r^*}^{R^*} \frac{\zeta^*}{\eta^*(\phi(\zeta^*))}\, d\zeta^*\, dr^*. \quad (99)$$

Thus, by using (93), it follows

$$\mathcal{P}^* = \Delta P^*\, \mathcal{Q}^*. \quad (100)$$

The key point is that $\mathcal{P}^*$ can be expressed in the form $\mathcal{P}_B^* \Psi(\sigma)$, where

$$\mathcal{P}_B^* = \frac{\pi}{8}\frac{(\Delta P^*)^2}{L^*}\frac{R^{*4}}{\eta_B^*},$$

η_B^* is the blood viscosity before entering the vessel, and Ψ is a dimensionless strictly decreasing function of σ whose explicit form depends on the way one chooses to evaluate η_B^* as a function of the hematocrit. Ascolese et al. [41] evaluated Ψ for six different choices of $\eta_B^*(\phi)$ and for four different values of ϕ (see Figure 6 in the cited paper). In all cases considered, $\Psi' < 0$ for $\sigma \in (0,1)$ and $\Psi \to 1$ as $\sigma \to 1$. Thus, (100) implies that $\mathcal{P}$ increases as σ decreases, meaning greater dissipation when a CFL is present. At the same time $\mathcal{Q}$ increases above its value before entering the vessel, which in physiological terms means an increase of the perfusion effect towards the peripheral tissues. This conclusion elucidates, more than others, the crucial role of the FL effect in physiology.

Formula (97) follows almost directly from the Haynes' conjecture and from the calculus of the total (core and plasma layer) discharge. Far from giving a justification of the CFL, its utility is confined to provide an estimate of σ (difficult to measure) as a function of the other, experimentally measurable, parameters, provided a reliable $\eta^*(\phi)$ is given. However, two questions remain still unanswered: is a boundary layer already present also in "large" vessels? In the affirmative case, why the layer thickness increases when blood flows from a given vessel to a smaller one? The first question is usually explained in terms of the so-called *size exclusion effect* (see, for example [50–52]): RBCs cannot get close to the vessel wall for less than half of their minimal thickness ($\approx$ 2–3 µm). Thus, the CFL thickness cannot be lower than $\approx$ 1–1.5 µm. The second question has been fully answered by Guadagni and Farina in [53] by applying the Prandtl boundary layer theory (see, for example, [54]). They show that the marginal layer, after an "entrance effect", quickly reaches a steady value. The main contribution of that paper is to provide an exact relation which links the asymptotic thickness of the CFL to its initial (minimum) value dictated by the size exclusion effect. This is the key step towards a rigorous justification of the FL effect. In particular, in [37] we compared the marginal layer thickness, as predicted by the mathematical model, and some measured values taken from "in vivo" experiments by Maeda et al. [55] and by Kim et al. [56]. In all cases we obtained results that, considering the uncertainty due to the experimental errors, are quite satisfactory.

4.2. The CAF Evolution Explained as an Entrance Effect

In [53] the Authors, working in planar geometry, study the entrance effect. They show that the velocity has a transverse component which shifts streamlines towards the channel center and it is bound to vanish just beyond the entrance region. So the flow reaches very soon a stratified structure where the particle volume fraction close to the wall significantly lower than the one in the core. The proof is quite technical and cannot be reported here.

Here we partially extend the argument of [53] to cylindrical geometry. Furthermore, in this case, as expected, it turns out that flow soon reaches a CAF structure as the one hypothesised by Haynes [39].

Let us denote by a^* the minimum size of the outer layer, i.e., $a^* = R^* - s_0^*$, with $s_0^* = s^*|_{x=0}$. It is reasonable to guess that a^* is going to depend on the geometrical properties of the RBCs in the considered sample, thus a quantity whose value cannot be given a priori with great accuracy, though its range is limited around the RBC average thickness. We now rewrite system (87) in dimensionless form by introducing the following new variables

$$x = \frac{x^*}{\mathcal{L}^*}, \quad r = \frac{r^*}{R^*}, \quad u = \frac{u^*}{U^*}, \quad v = \frac{v^*}{V^*}, \quad p = \frac{p^*}{\rho^* U^{*2}}, \quad \eta(\phi) = \eta_p^* \eta^*(\phi)$$

where $\mathcal{L}^* (< L^*)$ is the longitudinal length scale, ρ^* is the constant and uniform suspension density, U^* the characteristic inlet velocity, η_p^* the plasma viscosity (taken as the reference one), and $V^*/U^* = R^*/\mathcal{L}^*$. Then, if $\text{Re} = \rho^* U^* R^*/\eta_{\text{ref}}^*$ is the Reynolds number, we define $R^*/\mathcal{L}^* = 1/\sqrt{\text{Re}} (< 1)$, meaning that the choice of Re defines the aspect ratio of the entrance region. We also denote by η_C and η_A the (dimensionless) core and marginal layer viscosities, respectively. Clearly, if the marginal layer is just pure plasma, then $\eta_A = 1$, but in Section 4.3 we will allow η_A to deviate slightly away from unity.

Because of symmetry, $\partial u/\partial r|_{r=0} = 0$, while $v|_{r=0} = 0$, and all unknowns are independent of the angular coordinate. Next, we assume that $\varepsilon = 1/\sqrt{\text{Re}}$ can be used as a small parameter. Then, neglecting all terms $O(\varepsilon^n)$, $n \geq 2$, system (87) in dimensionless form rewrites (in both layers)

$$\begin{cases} u\dfrac{\partial \phi}{\partial x} + v\dfrac{\partial \phi}{\partial r} = 0, \\[6pt] \dfrac{\partial (ru)}{\partial x} + \dfrac{\partial (rv)}{\partial r} = 0, \\[6pt] u\dfrac{\partial u}{\partial x} + v\dfrac{\partial u}{\partial r} = -\dfrac{\partial p}{\partial x} + \dfrac{\varepsilon}{r}\dfrac{\partial}{\partial r}\left(r\eta(\phi)\dfrac{\partial u}{\partial r}\right), \\[6pt] \dfrac{\partial p}{\partial r} = 0, \quad (\Rightarrow p = p(x)). \end{cases} \qquad (101)$$

where, of course, η is the viscosity of the layer considered. The following inlet conditions are assumed:

$$u(0,r) = 1, \quad v(0,r) = 0, \quad \phi_{in} = \begin{cases} \Phi_C, & 0 \leq r \leq 1-\delta, \\ \Phi_A, & 1-\delta < r \leq 1 \end{cases}, \quad (102)$$

with Φ_C, Φ_A constant and $\delta = a/R$, where a is the inlet thickness of the marginal layer (according to the size exclusion effect). The interface between the core and the marginal layer is denoted by Σ and given by

$$r = \sigma(x), \quad \text{with} \quad \sigma(0) \equiv \sigma_o = 1-\delta.$$

Since Σ is a (steady) material surface, we have

$$-u(x,\sigma(x))\sigma'(x) + v(x,\sigma(x)) = 0,$$

and, consequently,

$$\phi(x,r) = \begin{cases} \Phi_C, & 0 \leq r \leq \sigma(x), \\ \Phi_A, & \sigma(x) < r \leq 1 \end{cases}, \quad \eta(x,r) = \begin{cases} \eta(\Phi_C) \equiv \eta_C, & 0 \leq r \leq \sigma(x), \\ \eta(\Phi_A) \equiv \eta_A, & \sigma(x) < r \leq 1. \end{cases}$$

The whole problem consists in solving the following coupled systems of Prandtl equations

$$\begin{cases} \dfrac{\partial(ru)}{\partial x} + \dfrac{\partial(rv)}{\partial r} = 0, & x \geq 0, \ 0 \leq r < \sigma(x), \\ u\dfrac{\partial u}{\partial x} + v\dfrac{\partial u}{\partial r} = -\dfrac{\partial p}{\partial x} + \dfrac{\varepsilon \eta_C}{r}\dfrac{\partial}{\partial r}\left(r\dfrac{\partial u}{\partial r}\right), & x \geq 0, \ 0 \leq r < \sigma(x), \\ p = p(x), & x \geq 0, \\ \dfrac{\partial u}{\partial r} = 0, \quad v = 0, & x \geq 0 \ \ r = 0, \\ u = 1, \quad v = 0, & x = 0, \ 0 \leq r \leq 1-\delta, \end{cases} \quad (103)$$

$$\begin{cases} \dfrac{\partial(ru)}{\partial x} + \dfrac{\partial(rv)}{\partial r} = 0, & x \geq 0, \ \sigma(x) < r \leq 1, \\ u\dfrac{\partial u}{\partial x} + v\dfrac{\partial u}{\partial r} = -\dfrac{\partial p}{\partial x} + \dfrac{\varepsilon \eta_A}{r}\dfrac{\partial}{\partial r}\left(r\dfrac{\partial u}{\partial r}\right), & x \geq 0, \ \sigma(x) < r \leq 1, \\ p = p(x), & x \geq 0, \\ u = 0, \quad v = 0, & x \geq 0 \ \ r = 1, \\ u = 1, \quad v = 0, & x = 0, \ 1-\delta < r \leq 1, \end{cases} \quad (104)$$

to which the following free boundary conditions need to be added

$$\begin{cases} -u(x,\sigma(x))\sigma'(x) + v(x,\sigma(x)) = 0, \\ [\![u]\!] = [\![vs.]\!] = [\![p]\!] = 0, \\ \eta_C \dfrac{\partial u}{\partial r}\bigg|_{r=\sigma^-} = \eta_A \dfrac{\partial u}{\partial r}\bigg|_{r=\sigma^+}, \end{cases} \quad (105)$$

where $[\![\bullet]\!]$ denotes the jump through Σ. System (103)–(105) allows an asymptotic solution of Poiseuille type for $x \to \infty$, namely $v_\infty(r) = 0$ and

$$u_\infty(r) = \dfrac{2}{(1-\sigma_\infty^4)\dfrac{1}{\eta_A} + \dfrac{\sigma_\infty^4}{\eta_C}} \times \begin{cases} \dfrac{\sigma_\infty^2 - r^2}{\eta_C} + \dfrac{1-\sigma_\infty^2}{\eta_A}, & 0 \le r \le \sigma_\infty \\ \dfrac{1-r^2}{\eta_A}, & \sigma_\infty \le r \le 1, \end{cases} \qquad (106)$$

where $\sigma_\infty = \lim\limits_{x \to \infty} \sigma(x)$. Since Σ is a material curve

$$\int_0^{\sigma_0} u(0,r)\, r\, \mathrm{d}r = \int_0^{\sigma_\infty} u_\infty(r)\, r\, \mathrm{d}r.$$

Thus, the initial core radius and its asymptotic value are related through

$$\sigma_0^2 = \dfrac{1}{\sigma_\infty^4 \left(\dfrac{1}{\eta_C} - \dfrac{1}{\eta_A}\right) + \dfrac{1}{\eta_A}} \left[\sigma_\infty^4 \left(\dfrac{1}{\eta_C} - \dfrac{2}{\eta_A}\right) + \dfrac{2\sigma_\infty^2}{\eta_A}\right]. \qquad (107)$$

We notice that (107) is a fourth order algebraic equation in the unknown σ_∞, with only one physically significant solution i.e., $\sigma_\infty \in (0,1)$,

$$\sigma_\infty = \dfrac{\sigma_0}{\sqrt{1 + \sqrt{(1-\sigma_0^2)\left[1 - \sigma_0^2\left(1 - \dfrac{\eta_A}{\eta_C}\right)\right]}}}. \qquad (108)$$

We notice that (108) is independent of Re. The behaviour of σ_∞ as a function of σ_0 is shown in Figure 13. If we can solve system (103)–(105) in the whole region $x \ge 0$ and $t \ge 0$ and prove that $\sigma(x)$ decays rapidly to σ_∞, then (108) can be used to verify the FL effect versus the experimental data.

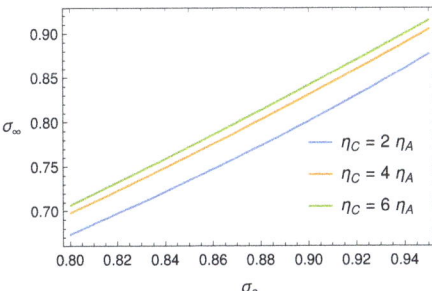

Figure 13. Function (108) for some values of the ratio η_C/η_A.

4.3. The Fåhræus–Lindqvist Effect Justified through Fluid Mechanics

In [53] Guadagni and Farina use the Langhaar's approach [57] to solve the boundary layer equation in plane geometry. In the tube geometry a similar argument can be developed (see, for example, Sparrow et al. [58], Avula [59], Gupta [60] and Campbell and Slattery [61]).

We confine ourselves to summarize the guidelines of the procedure and report the evolution of $\sigma(x)$ for various choices of the relevant parameters.

It is well-known that it is not possible to solve Prandtl's equations explicitly, so that special approximating techniques are needed. Here, the method consists in linearizing the inertia terms in the second of (103) and (104), in order to transform the momentum equation in the form

$$\frac{\varepsilon \eta_A}{r} \frac{\partial}{\partial r}\left(r \frac{\partial u}{\partial r}\right) = \varepsilon \beta^2 u - \kappa_{\text{outer}}(x). \tag{109}$$

where $\beta(x)$ and $\kappa_{\text{outer}}(x)$ are auxiliary functions still to be specified. Imposing the boundary condition $u(1, x) = 0$, the solution to (109) can be expressed as

$$u_{\text{outer}}(r, x) = C(x)\left[I_0\left(\frac{r\beta}{\sqrt{\eta_A}}\right) - I_0\left(\frac{\beta}{\sqrt{\eta_A}}\right)\frac{Y_0\left(-\frac{ir\beta}{\sqrt{\eta_A}}\right)}{Y_0\left(-\frac{i\beta}{\sqrt{\eta_A}}\right)}\right]$$

$$- \frac{\kappa_{\text{outer}}}{\varepsilon \beta^2}\left[1 - \frac{Y_0\left(-\frac{ir\beta}{\sqrt{\eta_A}}\right)}{Y_0\left(-\frac{i\beta}{\sqrt{\eta_A}}\right)}\right], \tag{110}$$

where $I_o(r)$ and $Y_o(r)$ are Bessel functions of the first modified and second type, respectively, and $C(x)$ has to be determined. The same argument applies to the inner layer and, by imposing the boundary condition $u'(0, x) = 0$, one obtains

$$u_{\text{in}}(r, x) = D(x) J_0\left(\frac{ir\beta}{\sqrt{\eta_C}}\right) - \frac{\kappa_{\text{inner}}}{\varepsilon \beta^2}, \tag{111}$$

where $D(x)$, as well as $\kappa_{\text{inner}}(x)$, have to be determined. If we insert (111) and (110) into the second of (105) and the third of (105), we get an algebraic system that allows to express κ_{inner} and κ_{outer} in terms of C and D. Substituting again into (111) and (110), entails

$$u(r,x) = \begin{cases} C\mathfrak{F}_{1,\text{out}}(r,\beta) + D\mathfrak{F}_{2,\text{out}}(r,\beta), & \sigma < r \leq 1, \\ C\mathfrak{F}_{1,\text{in}}(r,\beta) + D\mathfrak{F}_{2,\text{in}}(r,\beta), & 0 \leq r \leq \sigma, \end{cases} \tag{112}$$

where

$$\mathfrak{F}_{1,\text{out}}(\sigma, \beta) = \frac{Y_1\left(-\frac{i\sigma\beta}{\sqrt{\eta_A}}\right)\left(I_0\left(\frac{\sigma\beta}{\sqrt{\eta_A}}\right) - I_0\left(\frac{\beta}{\sqrt{\eta_A}}\right)\right)}{Y_1\left(-\frac{i\sigma\beta}{\sqrt{\eta_A}}\right)}$$

$$- i\frac{\left(Y_0\left(-\frac{i\beta}{\sqrt{\eta_A}}\right) - Y_0\left(-\frac{i\sigma\beta}{\sqrt{\eta_A}}\right)\right)I_1\left(\frac{\sigma\beta}{\sqrt{\eta_A}}\right)}{Y_1\left(-\frac{i\sigma\beta}{\sqrt{\eta_A}}\right)} \tag{113}$$

$$\mathfrak{F}_{2,\text{out}}(r, \beta) = \frac{\sqrt{\eta_C}\left(Y_0\left(-\frac{i\beta}{\sqrt{\eta_A}}\right) - Y_0\left(-\frac{i\sigma\beta}{\sqrt{\eta_A}}\right)\right)J_1\left(\frac{i\sigma\beta}{\sqrt{\eta_C}}\right)}{\sqrt{\eta_A} Y_1\left(-\frac{i\sigma\beta}{\sqrt{\eta_A}}\right)} \tag{114}$$

$$\mathfrak{F}_{1,\text{in}}(r,\beta) = I_0\left(\frac{\beta\sigma}{\sqrt{\eta_A}}\right) - I_0\left(\frac{\beta}{\sqrt{\eta_A}}\right)$$

$$- \frac{i\beta\sigma\left(Y_0\left(-\frac{i\beta}{\sqrt{\eta_A}}\right) - Y_0\left(-\frac{i\beta\sigma}{\sqrt{\eta_A}}\right)\right) F\left(2; \frac{\sigma^2\beta^2}{4\eta_A}\right)}{2\sqrt{\eta_A}Y_1\left(-\frac{i\sigma\beta}{\sqrt{\eta_A}}\right)} \quad (115)$$

$$\mathfrak{F}_{2,\text{in}}(r,\beta) = I_0\left(\frac{\sigma\beta}{\sqrt{\eta_C}}\right) - I_0\left(\frac{\beta\sigma}{\sqrt{\eta_C}}\right)$$

$$+ \frac{i\beta\sigma\left(Y_0\left(-\frac{i\beta}{\sqrt{\eta_A}}\right) - Y_0\left(-\frac{i\beta\sigma}{\sqrt{\eta_A}}\right)\right) F\left(2; \frac{\sigma^2\beta^2}{4\eta_C}\right)}{2\sqrt{\eta_A}Y_1\left(-\frac{i\sigma\beta}{\sqrt{\eta_A}}\right)}, \quad (116)$$

and

$$F(b;z) = \sum_{k=0}^{\infty} \frac{z^k}{\Gamma(b+k)k!}$$

is the regularized hyper-geometric function (from now on, we do not report the explicit expressions of the involved functions (which are, indeed, exceedingly long to be shown) and focus on the procedure).

To make the solution physically consistent we need to impose both the momentum balance and mass conservation (which, otherwise, may not be satisfied by the approximate solution), i.e.,

$$2\frac{d}{dx}\int_0^1 ru^2\,dr = -p' + 2\varepsilon\,\eta_A \left.\frac{\partial u}{\partial r}\right|_{r=1}, \quad \frac{d}{dx}\int_0^1 ru(r,x)\,dr = 0 \quad (117)$$

Now, by inserting (112) into the second of (117), we determine $C(\beta,\sigma)$ and $D(\beta,\sigma)$. For $u(x,r)$ to be consistent with the asymptotic solution (106), $\beta(x)$ must vanish as $x \to \infty$. This can be achieved by expanding (112) for $x \to \infty$ (that is for $\beta \to 0$) and verifying that at the zeroth order in β, $u(x,r)$ identifies with $u_\infty(r)$ given by (106). At this point, the final step is to obtain two equations for β and σ. The former follows by applying the second of (117) once again, in which p' is computed through the second of (103), evaluated at $r=0$. The latter follows by the kinematic condition (105). Finally we have to solve a system of two ODEs of type

$$\begin{cases} \beta' = \mathfrak{B}(\beta,\sigma), \\ \sigma' = \mathfrak{S}(\beta,\sigma), \end{cases} \quad (118)$$

to be coupled with "suitable" initial conditions (in the sense specified in [53]), one of them being $\sigma(0) = \sigma_0$. Figures 14–16 show, each for a given Re, the solution $\sigma(x)$ for $\sigma(0) = 0.9, 0.8$ and for five values of the ratio $\mu = \eta_C/\eta_A$.

The longitudinal interval Δx needed for $\sigma(x)$ to decrease from σ_0 to its asymptotic value σ_∞ is usually referred to as the "entrance length". The most evident effect outlined by Figures 14–16 is that, for fixed μ, the entrance length increases by increasing Re, while for any given Re, it decreases significantly by increasing μ. It must also be emphasized that simulations confirm that the asymptotic value σ_∞ depends only on μ, not on Re, as it must be, according to (108). In the next section, we compare the model with the experiments: in all cases we considered, the entrance length is rather small.

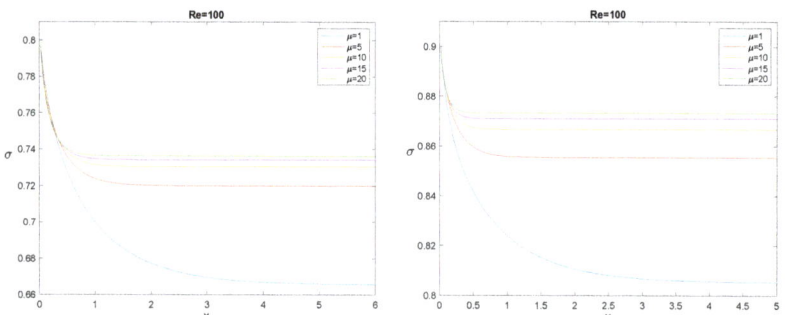

Figure 14. The evolution of $\sigma(x)$ for Re = 100, $\sigma(0) = 0.8$ (**left panel**), and 0.9 (**right panel**), and for some values of the ratio $\mu = \eta_C/\eta_A$.

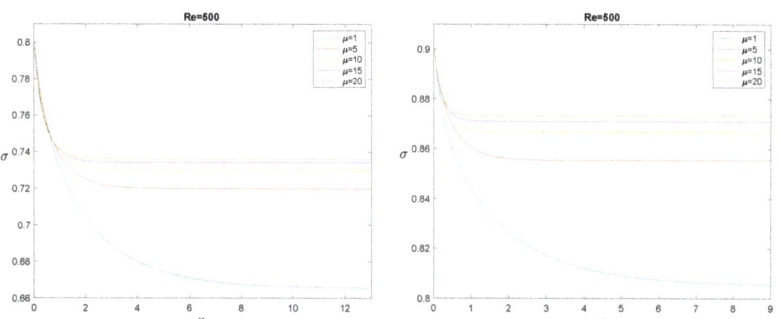

Figure 15. The evolution of $\sigma(x)$ for Re = 500, $\sigma(0) = 0.8$ (**left panel**), and 0.9 (**right panel**), and for some values of the ratio $\mu = \eta_C/\eta_A$.

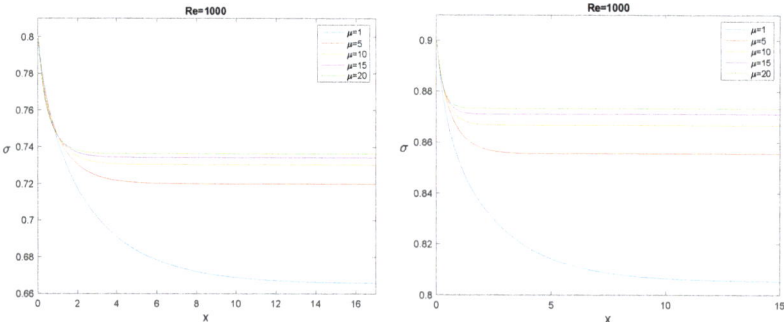

Figure 16. The evolution of $\sigma(x)$ for Re = 1000, $\sigma(0) = 0.8$ (**left panel**), and 0.9 (**right panel**), and some values of the ratio $\mu = \eta_C/\eta_A$.

4.4. The Mathematical Model versus the Experimental Data

Now, as in [37], we use formula (108), where

$$\eta_A = 1 + \alpha(\eta_C - 1), \tag{119}$$

and $\alpha = O(10^{-1})$ is a fitting parameter. Physically, this means that we consider the marginal layer *not completely free* of RBCs. A reasonable explanation may be that the "marginal exclusion effect" cannot be precisely stated (as it would be if the RBCs were rigid spheres) and it should be more understood as a statistical concept (see, for example, Ethier and Simmons, 2007). Thus, it is acceptable to think that a small percentage of hematocrit is present in the marginal layer and that this value may have some variability (Kim et al., 2007 refer to the outer layer also as a "cell–poor" region).

Now we can combine Formulas (108) and (119) with $\sigma_o = 1 - 2a/D$, where $D = 2R$ and a (the minimum outer thickness) is a fitting parameter related to the half thickness of the RBCs, so with a limited range of variability, i.e., 1–1.5 µm, since the average RBCs thickness is about 2–3 µm (see [62]). The result is a dimensional formula for the core radius s as a function of the tube diameter D, namely

$$s = \mathfrak{S}(D, \eta_C; a, \alpha),$$

where, however, a, α are "tuning" parameters with very little variability.

Figure 17 shows how the mathematical model fits the original data. The fits by means of two popular empirical formulas are also shown for comparison.

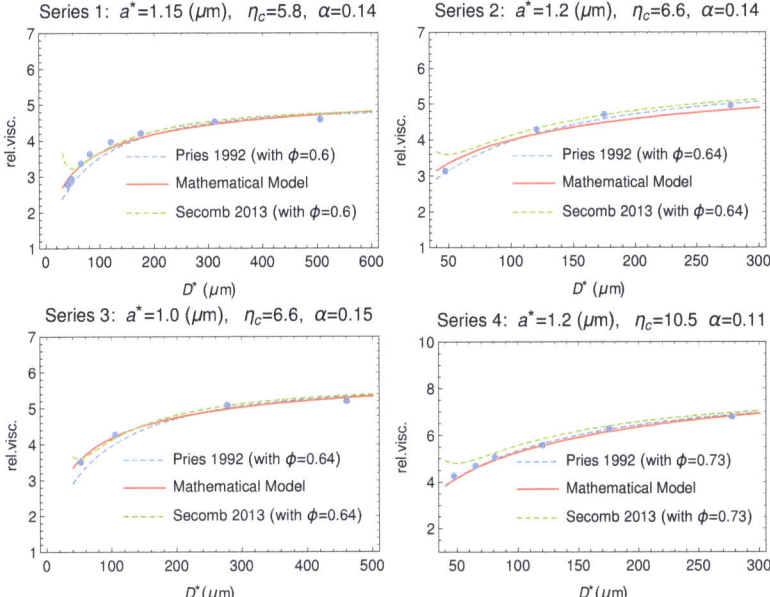

Figure 17. Comparison between the experimental series 1, 2, 3 and 4 reported in Tables at page 565 of Fåhræus and Lindqvist [35] (dots) and the theoretical model (solid curve). The fitting via the empirical formulas by Pries [63] and by Secomb [64] are also shown (dashed curves). On the top of each plot the values of a^*, α, η_C and the hematocrit ϕ used in the empirical formulas to fit the Fåhræus and Lindqvist data.

The model has been tested versus other classical experiments like those by Kümin [65] and by Zilow and Linderkamp [66]. Figures 18 and 19 show that the agreement is at least as good as the empirical formulas also in these cases.

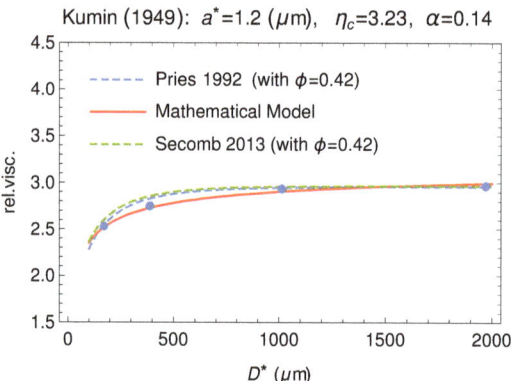

Figure 18. Comparison between our model and the experimental data by Kümin [65] (dots). Data are extracted from Figure 2, at p. 1195 of [39]. The empirical fitting via the empirical formulas by Pries and by Secomb are also shown (dashed curves).

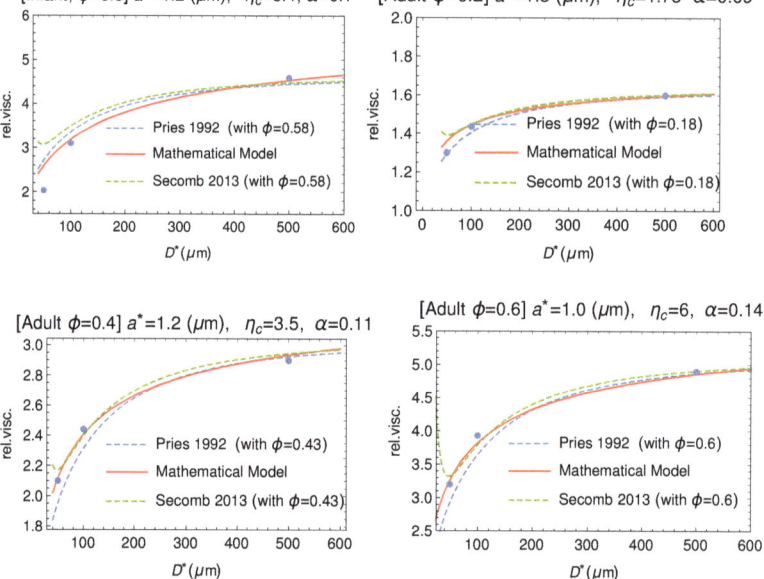

Figure 19. Comparison between our mathematical model (solid curve) and data by Zilow and Linderkamp [66] (dots). These authors considered both adult and infant blood samples at different values of the hematocrit. The empirical fitting via the empirical formulas by Pries and by Secomb are also shown (dashed curves).

4.5. The Fåhræus–Lindqvist Effect: Conclusions

Starting form the seminal work of Fåhræus and Lindqvist [35], we recalled the relevance of the Haynes' conjecture [39] in suggesting the right path to follow for a rigorous justification of the FL effect based on fundamental principles of fluid dynamics. Then we showed that this goal is achieved by relating the two recent contributions by Ascolese et al. [41] and Guadagni and Farina [53], thus solving a problem remained open for more than ninety years. To this end, the theory developed in [53] for flows in a plane symmetry has been here updated to the the case of axisymmetric flows. This relation contains, as a parameter, only the ratio between the viscosity of outer and inner layers.

Finally, following [37], we showed how this formula can be used to fit, quite reasonably, not only the original data by Fåhræus–Lindqvist, but also those of other classical experiments Zilow and Linderkamp [66], by Kümin [65], and even two well-known empirical formulas proposed by Pries [63] and Secomb [64].

Author Contributions: The authors equally contributed to this article. All authors have read and agreed to the published version of the manuscript.

Funding: This research received no external funding.

Conflicts of Interest: The authors declare no conflict of interest.

References

1. Fasano, A.; Sequeira, A. *Hemomath: The Mathematics of Blood*; Springer: Berlin/Heidelberg, Germany, 2017.
2. Robertson, A.; Sequeira, A.; Kameneva, M. Hemorheology. In *Hemodynamical Flows: Modeling, Analysis and Simulation*; Oberwolfach Seminars; Birkhäuser: Basel, Switzerland, 2008; Volume 37, pp. 63–120.
3. Robertson, A.; Sequeira, A.; Owens, R. Cardiovascular Mathematics. Modeling and Simulation of the Circulatory System. In *Hemorheology*; Springer: Berlin, Germany, 2009; pp. 211–242.
4. Pozrikidis, C. Axisymmetric motion of a file of red blood cells through capillaries. *Phys. Fluids* **2005**, *17*, 645–657. [CrossRef]
5. Farina, A.; Fasano, A.; Mizerski, J. A new model for blood flow in fenestrated capillaries with application to ultrafiltration in kidney glomeruli. *Adv. Math. Sci. Appl.* **2013**, *23*, 319–337.
6. Remuzzi, A.; Brenner, B.; Pata, V.; Tebaldi, G.; Mariano, R.; Belloro, A.; Remuzzi, G. Three-dimensional reconstructed glomerular capillary network: Blood flow distribution and local filtration. *Am. J. Physiol.* **1992**, *263*, F562–F572. [CrossRef] [PubMed]
7. Landis, E.; Pappenheimer, J. Exchange of substances through the capillary walls. In *Handbook of Physiology. Circulation*; American Physiological Society: Washington, DC, USA, 1963; Chapter 29, pp. 961–1034.
8. Borsi, I.; Farina, A.; Fasano, A. The effect of osmotic pressure on the flow of solutions through semi-permeable hollow fibers. *Appl. Math. Model.* **2013**, *37*, 5814–5827. [CrossRef]
9. Ronco, C.; Garzotto, F.; Kim, J.C.; Fasano, A.; Borsi, I.; Farina, A. Modeling blood filtration in hollow fibers dialyzers coupled with patient's body dynamics. *Rend. Lincei Mat. Appl.* **2016**, *27*, 369–412. [CrossRef]
10. Jones, T.W. Discovery that veins of the bat's wing (which are furnished with valves) are endowed with rhythmical contractility and that the onward flow of blood is accelerated by each contraction. *Philos. Trans. R. Soc. Lond.* **1852**, *142*, 131–136.
11. Reho, J.J.; Zheng, X.; Fisher, S.A. Smooth muscle contractile diversity in the control of regional circulations. *Am. J. Physiol. Heart Circ. Physiol.* **2014**, *306*, H163–H172. [CrossRef]
12. Haddock, R.E.; Hill, C.E. Rhythmicity in arterial smooth muscle. *J. Physiol.* **2005**, *566*, 645–656. [CrossRef]
13. Aalkjær, C.; Nilsson, H. Vasomotion: Cellular background for the oscillator and for the synchronization of smooth muscle cells. *Br. J. Pharmacol.* **2005**, *144*, 605–616. [CrossRef] [PubMed]
14. Parthimos, D.; Haddock, R.E.; Hill, C.E.; Griffith, T.M. Dynamics of a three-variable nonlinear model of vasomotion: Comparison of theory and experiment. *Biophys. J.* **2007**, *93*, 1534–1556. [CrossRef] [PubMed]
15. Ursino, M.; Fabbri, G.; Belardinelli, E. A mathematical analysis of vasomotion in the peripheral vascular bed. *Cardioscience* **1992**, *3*, 13–25. [PubMed]
16. Matchkov, V.V.; Gustafsson, H.; Rahman, A.; Boedtkjer, D.M.; Gorintin, S.; Hansen, A.K.; Bouzinova, E.V.; Praetoriu, H.A.; Aalkjaer, C.; Nilsson, H. Interaction between Na/K pump and Na/Ca2 exchanger modulates intercellular communication. *Circ. Res.* **2007**, *100*, 1026–1035. [CrossRef] [PubMed]
17. de Wit, C. Closing the gap at hot spots. *Circ. Res.* **2007**, *100*, 931–933. [CrossRef]
18. Haddock, R.E.; Hirst, G.D.S.; Hill, C.E. Voltage independence of vasomotion in isolated irideal arterioles of the rat. *J. Physiol.* **2002**, *540*, 219–229. [CrossRef] [PubMed]
19. Rivadulla, C.; de Labra, C.; Grieve, K.L.; Cudeiro, J. Vasomotion and neurovascular coupling in the visual thalamus. *PLoS ONE* **2011**, *6*, e28746. [CrossRef] [PubMed]
20. Koenigsberger, M.; Sauser, R.; Bény, J.L.; Meister, J.J. Effects of arterial wall stress on vasomotion. *Biophys. J.* **2006**, *91*, 1663–1674. [CrossRef]
21. Intaglietta, M. Vasomotion and flowmotion: Physiological mechanisms and clinical evidence. *Vasc. Med. Rev.* **1990**, *2*, 1101–1112. [CrossRef]
22. Gratton, R.J.; Gandley, R.E.; McCarthy, J.F.; Michaluk, W.K.; Slinker, B.K.; McLaughlin, M.K. Contribution of vasomotion to vascular resistance: A comparison of arteries from virgin and pregnant rats. *J. Appl. Physiol.* **1998**, *85*, 2255–2260. [CrossRef] [PubMed]
23. Meyer, C.; de Vries, G.; Davidge, S.T.; Mayes, D.C. Reassessing the mathematical modeling of the contribution of vasomotion to vascular resistance. *J. Appl. Physiol.* **2002**, *92*, 888–889. [CrossRef]
24. Fasano, A.; Farina, A.; Caggiati, A. Modeling vasomotion. *Rev. Vasc. Med.* **2016**, *8*, 1–4. [CrossRef]
25. Dongaonkar, R.M.; Quick, C.M.; Vo, J.C.; Meisner, J.K.; Laine, G.A.; Davis, M.J.; Stewart, R.H. Blood flow augmentation by intrinsic venular contraction. *Am. J. Physiol. Regul. Integr. Comp. Physiol.* **2012**, *302*, R1436–R1442. [CrossRef]

26. Farina, A.; Fusi, L.; Fasano, A.; Ceretani, A.; Rosso, F. Modeling peristaltic flow in vessels equipped with valves: Implications for vasomotion in bat wing venules. *Int. J. Eng. Sci.* **2016**, *107*, 1–12. [CrossRef]
27. Cardini, M.; Farina, A.; Fasano, A.; Caggiati, A. Blood flow in venules: A mathematical model including valves inertia. *Veins Lymphat.* **2019**, *8*, 7946. [CrossRef]
28. Farina, A.; Fasano, A. Incompressible flows through slender oscillating vessels provided with distributed valves. *Adv. Math. Sci. Appl.* **2016**, *25*, 33–42.
29. Caggiati, A.; Phillips, M.; Lametschwandtner, A.; Allegra, C. Valves in small veins and venules. *Eur. J. Vasc. Endovasc. Surg.* **2006**, *32*, 447–452. [CrossRef] [PubMed]
30. Caggiati, A.; Bertocchi, P. Regarding "Fact and fiction surrounding the discovery of the venous valves". *J. Vasc. Surg.* **2001**, *33*, 1317. [CrossRef] [PubMed]
31. Caggiati, A. The venous valves in the lower limbs. *Phlebolymphology* **2013**, *20*, 87–95.
32. Fusi, L.; Farina, A.; Fasano, A. Short and long wave peristaltic flow: Modeling and mathematical analysis. *Int. J. Appl. Mech.* **2015**. [CrossRef]
33. Kikuchi, N.; Oden, J.T. *Contact Problem in Elasticity: A Study of Variational Inequalities and Finite Element Methods*; SIAM: Philadelphia, PA, USA, 1988.
34. Lurie, F.; Kistner, R.L. The relative position of paired valves at venous junctions suggests their role in modulating three-dimensional flow pattern in veins. *Eur. J. Vasc. Endovasc. Surg.* **2012**, 337–340. [CrossRef] [PubMed]
35. Fåhræus, R.; Lindqvist, T. The Viscosity Of The Blood In Narrow Capillary Tubes. *Am. J. Physiol.* **1931**, *96*, 562–568. [CrossRef]
36. Copley, A.L. The rheology of blood. A survey. *J. Colloid Sci.* **1952**, *7*, 323–333. [CrossRef]
37. Farina, A.; Rosso, F.; Fasano, A. A Continuum Mechanics Model for the Fåhræus-Lindqvist Effect. *J. Biol. Phys.* **2021**. [CrossRef]
38. Poiseuille, J.L.M. Observations of blood flow. *Ann. Sci. Nat.* **1836**, *5*, 111–115.
39. Haynes, R.F. Physical Basis of the Dependence of Blood Viscosity on Tube Radius. *Am. J. Physiol.* **1960**, *198*, 1193–1200. [CrossRef]
40. Jeffery, G.B. The motion of ellipsoidal particles immersed in a viscous fluid. *Proc. Ray. Soc.* **1922**, *102*, 161–179.
41. Ascolese, M.; Farina, A.; Fasano, A. The Fåhræus-Lindqvist effect in small blood vessels: How does it help the heart? *J. Biol. Phys.* **2019**, *45*, 379–394. [CrossRef]
42. Nubar, Y. Effect of slip on the rheology of a composite fluid: Application to blood. *Biorheology* **1967**, *4*, 113–117. [CrossRef] [PubMed]
43. Krieger, I.M.; Dougherty, T.J. A mechanism for non-Newtonian flow in suspensions of rigid spheres. *Trans. Soc. Rheol.* **1959**, *3*, 137–152. [CrossRef]
44. Bingham, E.C.; White, G.F.; Amer, J. The viscosity and fluidity of emulsions, crystalline liquids and colloidal solutions. *Chem. Soc.* **1911**, *33*, 1257–1275. [CrossRef]
45. Charm, S.E.; Kurland, G.S. *Blood Flow and Microcirculation*; John Wiley: Hoboken, NJ, USA, 1974.
46. Cokelet, G.R. The Rheology of Human Blood. Ph.D. Thesis, MIT, Cambridge, MA, USA, 1963.
47. Hatschek, E. Eine Reihe von abnormen Liesegang'schen Schichtungen. *Colloid Polym. Sci.* **1920**, *27*, 225–229. [CrossRef]
48. Yeleswarapu, K.K.; Kameneva, M.V.; Rajagopal, K.R.; Antaki, J.F. The flow of blood in tubes: Theory and experiment. *Mech. Res. Commun.* **1998**, *25*, 257–262. [CrossRef]
49. Phillips, R.; Armstrong, R.; Brown, R.; Graham, A.; Abbott, J. A Constitutive Equation for Concentrated Suspensions That Accounts for Shear-induced Particle Migration. *Phys. Fluids* **1992**, *4*, 30–40. [CrossRef]
50. Secomb, T.W. Blood Flow in the Microcirculation. *Annu. Rev. Fluid Mech.* **2017**, *49*, 443–461. [CrossRef]
51. Ethier, R.C.; Simmons, C.A. *Introductory Biomechanic*; Cambridge University Press: Cambridge, UK, 2007.
52. Roselli, R.J.; Diller, K.R. *Biotransport: Principles and Applications*; Springer: Berlin/Heidelberg, Germany, 2011.
53. Guadagni, S.; Farina, A. Entrance flow of a suspension and particles migration towards the vessel center. *Int. J. Nonlinear Mech.* **2020**, *126*, 103587. [CrossRef]
54. Schlichting, H.; Gersten, K. *Boundary-Layer Theory*; Springer: Berlin/Heidelberg, Germany, 2017.
55. Maeda, N.; Suzuki, Y.; Tanaka, S.; Tateishi, N. Erythrocyte flow and elasticity of microvessels evaluated by marginal cell-free layer and flow resistance. *Am. J. Physiol. Heart Circ. Physiol.* **1996**, *271*, H2454–H2461. [CrossRef] [PubMed]
56. Kim, S.; Kong, L.R.; Popel, A.S.; Intaglietta, M.; Johnson, P.C. Temporal and spatial variations of cell-free layer width in arterioles. *Am. J. Physiol. Heart Circ. Physiol.* **2007**, *293*, H1526–H1535. [CrossRef]
57. Langhaar, H.L. Steady flow in the transitional length of a straight tube. *J. Appl. Mech.* **1942**, *64*, A55–A58. [CrossRef]
58. Sparrow, E.M.; Lin, S.H.; Lundgren, T.S. Flow developents in the hydrodynamic entrance region of tubes and ducts. *Phys. Fluids* **1964**, *7*, 338–347. [CrossRef]
59. Avula, X.J.R. Analysis of suddenly started laminar flow in the entrance region of a circular tube. *Appl. Sci. Res.* **1969**, *21*, 248–259. [CrossRef]
60. Gupta, R.C. Laminar flow in the entrance of a tube. *Appl. Sci. Res.* **1977**, *33*, 1–10. [CrossRef]
61. Campbell, W.D.; Slattery, J.C. Flow in the entrance of a tube. *J. Basic Eng.* **1963**, *81*, 41–45. [CrossRef]
62. Fung, Y.C. *Biomechanics: Mechanical Properties of Living Tissues*; Springer: New York, NY, USA, 1981.
63. Pries, A.R.; Neuhaus, D.; Gaehtgens, P. Blood viscosity in tube flow: Dependence on diameter and hematocrit. *Am. J. Physiol.* **1992**, *263*, 1770–1778. [CrossRef]

64. Secomb, T.W.; Pries, A.R. Blood viscosity in microvessels: Experiment and theory. *Comptes Rendus Phys.* **2013**, *14*, 470–478. [CrossRef]
65. Kümin, K. Bestimmung de Zähigkeitskoeffizienten für Rindeblut bei Newtonscher Strömung in Verschiden Weiten Röhren und Capillaren bei Physiologischer Temperatur. Ph.D. Thesis, Universität Bern, Friborg, Switzerland, 1949.
66. Zilow, E.P.; Linderkamp, O. Viscosity Reduction of Red Blood Cells from Preterm and Full-Term Neonates and Adults in Narrow Tubes (Fåhræus-Lindqvist effect). *Pediatr. Res.* **1989**, *25*, 595–599. [CrossRef] [PubMed]

Article

Dynamics of an Eco-Epidemic Predator–Prey Model Involving Fractional Derivatives with Power-Law and Mittag–Leffler Kernel

Hasan S. Panigoro [1,2], Agus Suryanto [1,*], Wuryansari Muharini Kusumawinahyu [1] and Isnani Darti [1]

[1] Department of Mathematics, Faculty of Mathematics and Natural Sciences, University of Brawijaya, Malang 65145, Indonesia; hspanigoro@ung.ac.id (H.S.P.); wmuharini@ub.ac.id (W.M.K.); isnanidarti@ub.ac.id (I.D.)

[2] Department of Mathematics, Faculty of Mathematics and Natural Sciences, State University of Gorontalo, Bone Bolango 96119, Indonesia

* Correspondence: suryanto@ub.ac.id

Citation: Panigoro, H.S.; Suryanto, A.; Kusumawinahyu, W.M.; Darti, I. Dynamics of an Eco-Epidemic Predator–Prey Model Involving Fractional Derivatives with Power-Law and Mittag–Leffler Kernel. *Symmetry* **2021**, *13*, 785. https://doi.org/10.3390/sym13050785

Academic Editors: Federico Papa and Carmela Sinisgalli

Received: 5 April 2021
Accepted: 29 April 2021
Published: 2 May 2021

Publisher's Note: MDPI stays neutral with regard to jurisdictional claims in published maps and institutional affiliations.

Copyright: © 2021 by the authors. Licensee MDPI, Basel, Switzerland. This article is an open access article distributed under the terms and conditions of the Creative Commons Attribution (CC BY) license (https://creativecommons.org/licenses/by/4.0/).

Abstract: In this paper, we consider a fractional-order eco-epidemic model based on the Rosenzweig–MacArthur predator–prey model. The model is derived by assuming that the prey may be infected by a disease. In order to take the memory effect into account, we apply two fractional differential operators, namely the Caputo fractional derivative (operator with power-law kernel) and the Atangana–Baleanu fractional derivative in the Caputo (ABC) sense (operator with Mittag–Leffler kernel). We take the same order of the fractional derivative in all equations for both senses to maintain the symmetry aspect. The existence and uniqueness of solutions of both eco-epidemic models (i.e., in the Caputo sense and in ABC sense) are established. Both models have the same equilibrium points, namely the trivial (origin) equilibrium point, the extinction of infected prey and predator point, the infected prey free point, the predator-free point and the co-existence point. For a model in the Caputo sense, we also show the non-negativity and boundedness of solution, perform the local and global stability analysis and establish the conditions for the existence of Hopf bifurcation. It is found that the trivial equilibrium point is a saddle point while other equilibrium points are conditionally asymptotically stable. The numerical simulations show that the solutions of the model in the Caputo sense strongly agree with analytical results. Furthermore, it is indicated numerically that the model in the ABC sense has quite similar dynamics as the model in the Caputo sense. The essential difference between the two models is the convergence rate to reach the stable equilibrium point. When a Hopf bifurcation occurs, the bifurcation points and the diameter of the limit cycles of both models are different. Moreover, we also observe a bistability phenomenon which disappears via Hopf bifurcation.

Keywords: Atangana–Baleanu; Caputo; eco-epidemiology; Rosenzweig–MacArthur

1. Introduction

The long history of mathematical biology reveals that predator–prey modeling plays an imperative role in scientific research. Since the classical Lotka–Volterra, as the fundamental predator–prey model, have been proposed [1–3], the theoretical ecology has been constantly developed. The Lotka–Volterra model has been modified by a lot of researchers to contrive the relevant model which corresponds to the actual phenomena, such as the functional response [4–9], the Allee effect [10–14], the impact of competition [15–17] and so forth. All of these modifications affect the density of populations as the result of interactions between two or more populations. From the biological point of view, the population density also depends on the epidemiological frameworks, which leads to the increment of the death rate caused by the disease in the population. Eco-epidemiology describes the occurrence of ecological and epidemiological circumstances simultaneously [18–23].

For instance, in a biotope that involves pests and its natural enemies, we observe that the eco-epidemiological problem occurs and described by the interaction between pest and its predator. One or both populations may be infected by a disease caused by microbiological pathogens such as parasites, viruses, fungi and bacteria, for further see refs. [24–28] and some references therein. For the real-world example, to suppress the growth rate of rats (*Rattus sp.*) in agricultural landscape, the farmers use barn owls (*tyto alba*) and some pathogens such as viruses (*paramyxoviridae* and *pneumovirus* family), bacterias (*klebsiella pneumoniae, mycoplasma pulmonis, citrobacter rodentium* and *streptococcus pneumoniae*), and parasites (*giardia muris, spironucleus muris, oxyuriasis* and *acariasis*) [29–33].

Regarding to the description above, some researchers have successfully constructed and studied the eco-epidemiological problem in a deterministic model. Mondal et al. [21], Wang et al. [34] and Suryanto et al. [35] study the dynamics of the interaction between two populations in a predator–prey relationship where the prey is infected by a disease and the predator is hunting the infected prey. In facts, many natural phenomena in the ecological system show that predation still occurs although the infected prey does not exist. This means both susceptible and infected prey are regarded to be predated. Based on this assumption, Sahoo [19], Saifuddin et al. [20], Panigoro et al. [23], Upadhyay et al. [36] and Nugraheni et al. [37] study the eco-epidemic model with the predation existing on both susceptible and infected prey. The fundamental differences of their models lie on the infectious transmission behavior, the predator functional response, the existence of the Allee effect and the operator of the derivative. Here, we study the eco-epidemic model formulated under the following assumptions.

(a) In the presence of disease, the prey is divided into two compartments, namely susceptible prey $S(t)$ and infected prey $I(t)$. The susceptible prey becomes infected when the individuals have contact with the infected prey. Since the density of prey and predator are assumed large enough, the infection rate due to this contact is bilinear which is symbolized by b.

(b) In the presence of the predator–prey relationship, the interaction between susceptible prey, infected prey and predator is following the Rosenzweig–MacArthur model [38] with a few adjustments. The susceptible prey growth logistically with intrinsic growth rate r and environmental carrying capacity K. The infected prey competes for food with the susceptible prey but has no contribution to the growth rate of susceptible prey. Both susceptible prey and infected prey are predated following Holling type-II with the attack rate of predator on susceptible prey m_s, the attack rate of predator on infected prey m_i, the half-saturation constant of predator for susceptible prey k_s and the half-saturation constant of predator for infected prey k_i. Since both predations contribute to the predator birth, the conversion efficiency consists of two parts, i.e., the conversion efficiency of predator on susceptible prey b_s and the conversion efficiency of predator on infected prey b_i. It is also assumed that both infected prey and predator are reduced due to mortality following exponential decay where d is the death rate of infected prey, and a is the death rate of predator.

Based on above assumptions, we have the following eco-pidemic model.

$$\begin{aligned}\frac{dS}{dt} &= rS\left(1 - \frac{S+I}{K}\right) - bSI - \frac{m_s SP}{k_s + S},\\ \frac{dI}{dt} &= bSI - dI - \frac{m_i IP}{k_i + I},\\ \frac{dP}{dt} &= \left(\frac{b_s S}{k_s + S} + \frac{b_i I}{k_i + I} - a\right)P,\end{aligned} \qquad (1)$$

For simplicity, model (1) is transformed into a non-dimensional system by introducing transformation of variables $(S, I, P, t) \to \left(\frac{S}{K}, \frac{I}{K}, \frac{m_s P}{rK}, rt\right)$ to obtain the following eco-epidemic model.

$$\frac{dS}{dt} = \left[1 - S - (1+\hat{\eta})I - \frac{P}{\kappa + S}\right]S,$$

$$\frac{dI}{dt} = \left[\hat{\eta}S - \hat{\delta} - \frac{\hat{m}P}{\omega + I}\right]I, \qquad (2)$$

$$\frac{dP}{dt} = \left[\frac{\hat{\mu}S}{\kappa + S} + \frac{\hat{\beta}I}{\omega + I} - \hat{q}\right]P,$$

where $\hat{\eta} = \frac{bK}{r}, \hat{\delta} = \frac{d}{r}, \hat{m} = \frac{m_i}{m_s}, \hat{\mu} = \frac{b_s}{r}, \hat{\beta} = \frac{b_i}{r}, \kappa = \frac{k_s}{K}, \omega = \frac{k_i}{K}$ and $\hat{q} = \frac{a}{r}$.

To approach the superlative shape of the eco-epidemiological model, the ordinary calculus is considered less effective in describing the complex ecological phenomena that involves the system memory and hereditary biological properties of complex multiple timescale dynamics, see refs. [39–41]. To overcome such problem, many researchers apply fractional calculus because it is considered to have the ability to represent biological conditions related to the memory effects more powerfully and accurately than the classical calculus [42–48]. Particularly, the fractional-order derivatives, as part of the fundamental theory of fractional calculus, have nonlocal properties which are naturally connected to the biological systems. It means that the current state of population density depends on all earlier states [49–51]. If we revisited the evolution of fractional-order derivative, the Riemann–Liouville [52] and Caputo [53] operators have been widely applied to the biological modeling. To investigate the behavior of the fractional-order dynamical system, the theoretical aspect of the Caputo operator is the most complete tool compared to others, see refs. [52,54,55]. However, the kernels of the first two definitions of fractional operators are single and local [56–59]. Therefore, Caputo operator is not sufficient enough to express better nonlocal dynamics. To cover the limitation of Caputo operator, in 2015, Caputo and Fabrizio proposed a new fractional operator, which is called the Caputo–Fabrizio derivative [60]. The non-singular and exponential kernel of this fractional derivative is the novelty of their result and has been successfully applied in several fields [40,61–63]. One year later, Atangana and Baleanu introduced a new fractional operator with a nonlocal and non-singular kernel. Such an operator is well-known as the Atangana–Baleanu operator, which has all the advantages of the Caputo–Fabrizio operator but it uses the Mittag–Leffler function as its kernel [64]. Most researchers reveal that the Atangana–Baleanu operator gives better results and claim that the effect of memory is represented efficiently, see refs. [9,40,51,65].

For a better approach in epidemiological modeling, the fractional-order derivative is utilized in a similar way with [48,66] which replace the first-order derivative $\frac{d}{dt}$ at the left-hand side of model (2) with the fractional-order derivative $\mathcal{D}_t^\alpha$. Therefore, we obtain

$$\mathcal{D}_t^\alpha S = \left[1 - S - (1+\hat{\eta})I - \frac{P}{\kappa + S}\right]S,$$

$$\mathcal{D}_t^\alpha I = \left[\hat{\eta}S - \hat{\delta} - \frac{\hat{m}P}{\omega + I}\right]I, \qquad (3)$$

$$\mathcal{D}_t^\alpha P = \left[\frac{\hat{\mu}S}{\kappa + S} + \frac{\hat{\beta}I}{\omega + I} - \hat{q}\right]P.$$

Pay close attention to the dimension of the equations in model (3), where the fractional-order derivatives have the dimensions of $(time)^{-\alpha}$ while the parameters $\hat{\eta}, \hat{\delta}, \hat{m}, \hat{\mu}, \hat{\beta}$ and $\hat{q}$ have the dimensions of $(time)^{-1}$. This circumstance means the inconsistency of physical dimensions in the model (3) and can be surmounted by rescaling the parameters as in the following model.

$$\mathcal{D}_t^\alpha S = \left[1 - S - (1 + \hat{\eta}^\alpha)I - \frac{P}{\kappa + S}\right]S,$$

$$\mathcal{D}_t^\alpha I = \left[\hat{\eta}^\alpha S - \hat{\delta}^\alpha - \frac{\hat{m}^\alpha P}{\omega + I}\right]I, \tag{4}$$

$$\mathcal{D}_t^\alpha P = \left[\frac{\hat{\mu}^\alpha S}{\kappa + S} + \frac{\hat{\beta}^\alpha I}{\omega + I} - \hat{q}^\alpha\right]P.$$

By applying new parameters $\hat{\eta} = \eta, \hat{\delta} = \delta, \hat{m} = m, \hat{\mu} = \mu, \hat{\beta} = \beta$ and $\hat{q} = q$, we achieve

$$\mathcal{D}_t^\alpha S = \left[1 - S - (1 + \eta)I - \frac{P}{\kappa + S}\right]S,$$

$$\mathcal{D}_t^\alpha I = \left[\eta S - \delta - \frac{mP}{\omega + I}\right]I, \tag{5}$$

$$\mathcal{D}_t^\alpha P = \left[\frac{\mu S}{\kappa + S} + \frac{\beta I}{\omega + I} - q\right]P.$$

We note that model (5) consists of three fractional differential equations. The order of the fractional derivative in all equations is set to be the same to maintain their symmetrical aspect.

Notice that we have to assume in model (5) that the disease transmission follows a bilinear incidence rate. Previously, Nugraheni et al. [37] have studied the same model but with saturated incidence rate. However, Nugraheni et al. [37] have only presented some numerical simulations of model (5) with Caputo sense without any analytical studies. In this article, we start our work by constructing the fractional-order eco-epidemic model consisting of the model assumptions, the first-order modeling, its non-dimensional form and the fractional-order modeling including the replacement of the first-order derivative with fractional-order derivative and the time dimension adjustment for some parameters to prevent the inconsistency of physical dimensions. Furthermore, we present the complete dynamics of model (5) with Caputo operator including the local and global stability, the existence of Hopf bifurcation and their appropriated numerical simulations. We also use the Atangana–Baleanu in Caputo sense as the fractional-order operator of model (5) numerically by previously showing the existence and uniqueness of solution of the model. We compare numerically the difference between model (5) with Caputo and Atangana–Baleanu operators, especially the difference of the dynamical behaviors when the Hopf bifurcation occurs. All of these analytical results and numerical simulations have never been done in [37], which is the novelty of our work.

This paper is organized as follows. In Section 2, we present some fundamental concepts which consist of definitions, theorems and lemmas that are associated with Caputo and Atangana–Baleanu derivatives and dynamical systems. Further, in Section 3, we investigate the dynamics of model (5) with Caputo derivative. The investigation includes the existence, uniqueness, non-negativity, boundedness of the solutions, the existence of equilibrium points, their local and global stability, as well as the occurrence of Hopf bifurcation. The existence and uniqueness of solutions of model (5) with Atangana–Baleanu derivative in Caputo sense are discussed in Section 4. To support our theoretical findings, we demonstrate some numerical simulations in Section 5. Finally, we present some conclusions in Section 6.

2. Fundamental Concepts

In this section, we present the important results from previous research such as definitions, theorems and lemmas associated with the fractional-order differential equation.

Definition 1 ([55]). *Suppose $0 < \alpha \leq 1$. The Caputo fractional derivative of order $-\alpha$ is defined by*

$$^{C}\mathcal{D}_t^\alpha f(t) = \frac{1}{\Gamma(1-\alpha)} \int_0^t (t-s)^{-\alpha} f'(s) ds, \tag{6}$$

where $t \geq 0$, $f \in C^n([0, +\infty), \mathbb{R})$, and Γ is the Gamma function.

Definition 2 ([64]). *Suppose $0 < \alpha \leq 1$. The Atangana–Baleanu fractional integral and derivative in Caputo sense of order $-\alpha$ (ABC sense) are respectively defined by*

$$^{ABC}\mathcal{I}_t^\alpha f(t) = \frac{1-\alpha}{B(\alpha)} f(t) + \frac{\alpha}{\Gamma(\alpha) B(\alpha)} \int_0^t (t-s)^{\alpha-1} f(s) ds,$$

$$^{ABC}\mathcal{D}_t^\alpha f(t) = \frac{B(\alpha)}{1-\alpha} \int_0^t E_\alpha \left[-\frac{\alpha}{1-\alpha} (t-s)^\alpha \right] f'(s) ds,$$

where $t \geq 0$, $f \in C^n([0, +\infty), \mathbb{R})$, E_α is the Mittag–Leffler function defined by $E_\alpha(t) = \sum_{k=0}^\infty \frac{t^k}{\Gamma(\alpha k + 1)}$, and $B(\alpha)$ is a normalization function with $B(0) = B(1) = 1$. In this paper, we define $B(\alpha) = 1 - \alpha + \frac{\alpha}{\Gamma(\alpha)}$.

Theorem 1 ([64]). *By using the inverse Laplace transform and convolution theorem, the unique solution of the time fractional differential equation*

$$^{ABC}\mathcal{D}_t^\alpha f(t) = \varphi(t) \tag{7}$$

can be written as

$$f(t) = \frac{1-\alpha}{B(\alpha)} \varphi(t) + \frac{\alpha}{\Gamma(\alpha) B(\alpha)} \int_0^t \varphi(s)(t-s)^{\alpha-1} ds. \tag{8}$$

Lemma 1 ([67]). *Let $0 < \alpha \leq 1$. Suppose that $f(t) \in C[a,b]$ and $^{C}\mathcal{D}_t^\alpha f(t) \in C[a,b]$. If $^{C}\mathcal{D}_t^\alpha f(t) \geq 0$, $\forall t \in (a,b)$, then $f(t)$ is a non-decreasing function for each $t \in [a,b]$. If $^{C}\mathcal{D}_t^\alpha f(t) \leq 0$, $\forall t \in (a,b)$, then $f(t)$ is a non-increasing function for each $t \in [a,b]$.*

Theorem 2 (Matignon condition [55,68]). *Consider a Caputo fractional-order system*

$$^{C}\mathcal{D}_t^\alpha \vec{x} = \vec{f}(\vec{x}); \ \vec{x}(0) = \vec{x}_0; \ \alpha \in (0,1]. \tag{9}$$

A point $\vec{x}^*$ is called an equilibrium point of Equation (9) if it satisfies $\vec{f}(\vec{x}^*) = 0$. This equilibrium point is locally asymptotically stable if all eigenvalues λ_j of the Jacobian matrix $J = \frac{\partial \vec{f}}{\partial \vec{x}}$ evaluated at $\vec{x}^*$ satisfy $|\arg(\lambda_j)| > \frac{\alpha\pi}{2}$. If there exists at least one eigenvalue that satisfies $|\arg(\lambda_k)| > \frac{\alpha\pi}{2}$ while $|\arg(\lambda_l)| < \frac{\alpha\pi}{2}$, $k \neq l$, then $\vec{x}^*$ is a saddle-point.

Lemma 2 ([69]). *Consider a Caputo fractional-order system*

$$^{C}\mathcal{D}_t^\alpha x(t) = f(t, x(t)), \ t > 0, \ x(0) \geq 0, \ \alpha \in (0,1], \tag{10}$$

where $f: (0, \infty) \times \Omega \to \mathbb{R}^n$, $\Omega \subseteq \mathbb{R}^n$. A unique solution of Equation (10) on $(0, \infty) \times \Omega$ exists if $f(t, x(t))$ satisfies the locally Lipschitz condition with respect to x.

Lemma 3 (Standard comparison theorem for Caputo fractional-order derivative [42]). *Let $x(t) \in C([0, +\infty))$. If $x(t)$ satisfies*

$$^{C}\mathcal{D}_t^\alpha x(t) + \lambda x(t) \leq \mu, \ x(0) = x_0,$$

where $\alpha \in (0,1]$, $(\lambda, \mu) \in \mathbb{R}^2$ and $\lambda \neq 0$, then

$$x(t) \leq \left(x_0 - \frac{\mu}{\lambda}\right) E_\alpha[-\lambda t^\alpha] + \frac{\mu}{\lambda}.$$

Lemma 4 ([70]). *Let $x(t) \in C(\mathbb{R}_+)$, $x^* \in \mathbb{R}_+$, and its Caputo fractional derivatives of order α exist for any $\alpha \in (0,1]$. Then, for any $t > 0$, we have*

$$^C D_t^\alpha \left[x(t) - x^* - x^* \ln \frac{x(t)}{x^*}\right] \leq \left(1 - \frac{x^*}{x(t)}\right) {}^C D_t^\alpha x(t).$$

Lemma 5 (Generalized Lasalle Invariance Principle [71]). *Suppose Ω is a bounded closed set and every solution of system*

$$^C D_t^\alpha x(t) = f(x(t)), \tag{11}$$

which starts from a point in Ω remains in Ω for all time. If $\exists V(x) : \Omega \to \mathbb{R}$ with continuous first order partial derivatives satisfies following condition:

$$^C D_t^\alpha V|_{Eq.(11)} \leq 0,$$

then every solution $x(t)$ originating in Ω tends to M as $t \to \infty$, where M is the largest invariant set of E and $E := \{x | {}^C D_t^\alpha V|_{Eq.(11)} = 0\}$.

3. Eco-Epidemic Model in the Caputo Sense

In this section, we consider a fractional-order eco-epidemic model (5) with the fractional derivative in the Caputo sense as defined in Definition 1:

$$\begin{aligned}
{}^C D_t^\alpha S &= \left[1 - S - (1+\eta)I - \frac{P}{\kappa + S}\right] S = F_1(X), \\
{}^C D_t^\alpha I &= \left[\eta S - \delta - \frac{mP}{\omega + I}\right] I = F_2(X), \\
{}^C D_t^\alpha P &= \left[\frac{\mu S}{\kappa + S} + \frac{\beta I}{\omega + I} - q\right] P = F_3(X),
\end{aligned} \tag{12}$$

where $X = (S, I, P)$. In the following sub-sections, we investigate the dynamics of model (12).

3.1. Existence and Uniqueness

In this section, we investigate the sufficient condition for the existence and uniqueness of solution of model (12).

Theorem 3. *Consider model (12) with positive initial condition $S_0 \geq 0$, $I_0 \geq 0$, $P_0 \geq 0$ and $\alpha \in (0,1]$, $F : [0, \infty) \to \mathbb{R}^3$, where $F(X) = (F_1(X), F_2(X), F_3(X))$, $X \equiv X(t)$ and $\Psi = \{(S, I, P) \in \mathbb{R}_+^3 : \max\{|S|, |I|, |P|\} \leq \gamma\}$ for sufficiently large γ. The model (12) with positive initial condition has a unique solution.*

Proof. We use a similar approach as in [8]. For any $X = (S, I, P)$, $\bar{X} = (\bar{S}, \bar{I}, \bar{P})$, $X, \bar{X} \in \Psi$, it follows from model (12) that

$$\begin{aligned}
\|F(X) - F(\bar{X})\| &= |F_1(X) - F_1(\bar{X})| + |F_2(X) - F_2(\bar{X})| + |F_3(X) - F_3(\bar{X})| \\
&= \left|(S - \bar{S}) - (S^2 - \bar{S}^2) - (1+\eta)(SI - \bar{S}\bar{I}) - \left(\frac{SP}{\kappa + S} - \frac{\bar{S}\bar{P}}{\kappa + \bar{S}}\right)\right| + \\
&\quad \left|\eta(SI - \bar{S}\bar{I}) - \delta(I - \bar{I}) - m\left(\frac{IP}{\omega + I} - \frac{\bar{I}\bar{P}}{\omega + \bar{I}}\right)\right| + \\
&\quad \left|\mu\left(\frac{SP}{\kappa + S} - \frac{\bar{S}\bar{P}}{\kappa + \bar{S}}\right) + \beta\left(\frac{IP}{\omega + I} - \frac{\bar{I}\bar{P}}{\omega + \bar{I}}\right) - q(P - \bar{P})\right|
\end{aligned}$$

$$\leq |S - \tilde{S}| + \left|S^2 - \tilde{S}^2\right| + (1+\eta)|SI - \tilde{S}\tilde{I}| + \left|\frac{SP}{\kappa + S} - \frac{\tilde{S}\tilde{P}}{\kappa + \tilde{S}}\right| +$$

$$\eta|SI - \tilde{S}\tilde{I}| + \delta|I - \tilde{I}| + m\left|\frac{IP}{\omega + I} - \frac{\tilde{I}\tilde{P}}{\omega + \tilde{I}}\right| + \mu\left|\frac{SP}{\kappa + S} - \frac{\tilde{S}\tilde{P}}{\kappa + \tilde{S}}\right| +$$

$$\beta\left|\frac{IP}{\omega + I} - \frac{\tilde{I}\tilde{P}}{\omega + \tilde{I}}\right| + q|P - \tilde{P}|$$

$$\leq L_1|S - \tilde{S}| + L_2|I - \tilde{I}| + L_3|P - \tilde{P}|$$

$$\leq L\|X - \tilde{X}\|$$

where

$$L_1 = 1 + \left(3 + 2\eta + \frac{1+\mu}{\kappa}\right)\gamma,$$

$$L_2 = \delta + \left(1 + 2\eta + \frac{m+\beta}{\omega}\right)\gamma,$$

$$L_3 = q + \left(\frac{1+\mu}{\kappa} + \frac{m+\beta}{\omega}\right)\gamma + \left(\frac{1+\mu}{\kappa^2} + \frac{m+\beta}{\omega^2}\right)\gamma^2,$$

$$L = \max\{L_1, L_2, L_3\}.$$

Hence, $F(X)$ satisfies the Lipschitz condition. According to Lemma 2, the existence and uniqueness of model (12) with initial value $S_0 \geq 0$, $I_0 \geq 0$ and $P_0 \geq 0$ is established, and the theorem is well proven. □

3.2. Non-Negativity and Boundedness

Model (12) describes an eco-epidemiological model in fractional-order differential equations. Therefore, the solution of model (12) must be bounded and non-negative, as it is performed in the following theorem.

Theorem 4. *All solutions of model (12) with non-negative initial values are non-negative and uniformly bounded.*

Proof. We start by proving that for non-negative initial condition, $S(t) \geq 0$ for $t \to \infty$. Suppose that is not true, then there exists $t_1 > 0$ such that

$$\begin{cases} S(t) > 0, & 0 \leq t < t_1, \\ S(t_1) = 0, \\ S(t_1^+) < 0. \end{cases} \quad (13)$$

Employing (13) and the first equation of model (12), we obtain

$$\left.^C\mathcal{D}_t^\alpha S(t_1)\right|_{S(t_1)=0} = 0. \quad (14)$$

Based on Lemma 1, we have $S(t_1^+) = 0$, which contradicts to the fact $S(t_1^+) < 0$. Thus, $S(t) \geq 0$ for all $t \geq 0$. Using the similar procedure, we conclude $I(t) \geq 0$ and $P(t) \geq 0$ for all $t > 0$.

Now, we show the boundedness of solutions by adopting similar manner as in [8]. We first define a function

$$V(t) = S + I + \zeta P.$$

Then, for each $\xi > 0$, we obtain

$$^C\mathcal{D}_t^\alpha V(t) + \xi V(t) = \left(S - S^2 - (1+\eta)SI - \frac{SP}{\kappa + S}\right) + \left(\eta SI - \delta I - \frac{mIP}{\omega + I}\right) +$$

$$\zeta\left(\frac{\mu SP}{\kappa+S} + \frac{\beta IP}{\omega+I} - qP\right) + \xi(S+I+\zeta P)$$

$$= (1+\xi)S - S^2 - SI + \beta\left(\zeta - \frac{m}{\beta}\right)\frac{IP}{\omega+I} + \mu\left(\zeta - \frac{1}{\mu}\right)\frac{SP}{\kappa+S} +$$

$$(\xi - \delta)I + \zeta(\xi - q)P.$$

By choosing $\xi < \min\{\delta, q\}$ and $\zeta < \min\left\{\frac{m}{\beta}, \frac{1}{\mu}\right\}$, we have

$${}^C D_t^\alpha V(t) + \xi V(t) \leq (1+\xi)S - S^2$$

$$= (1+\xi)S - S^2 - \left(\frac{1+\xi}{2}\right)^2 + \left(\frac{1+\xi}{2}\right)^2$$

$$= -\left(S^2 - (1+\xi)S + \left(\frac{1+\xi}{2}\right)^2\right) + \left(\frac{1+\xi}{2}\right)^2$$

$$\leq \frac{(1+\xi)^2}{4}.$$

The standard comparison theorem for fractional-order derivative (see Lemma 3) gives

$$V(t) \leq \left(V(0) - \frac{(1+\xi)^2}{4\xi}\right)E_\alpha[-\xi t^\alpha] + \frac{(1+\xi)^2}{4\xi},$$

from which we have that $V(t)$ is convergent to $\frac{(1+\xi)^2}{4\xi}$ for $t \to \infty$. Therefore, all solutions of model (12) with non-negative initial conditions are confined to the region Φ, where

$$\Phi := \left\{(S, I, P) \in \mathbb{R}_+^3 \;:\; V(t) \leq \frac{(1+\xi)^2}{4\xi} + \varepsilon, \varepsilon > 0\right\}. \tag{15}$$

Therefore, the proof of non-negativity and boundedness of solutions are completely presented. □

3.3. The Existence of Equilibrium Point

From model (12), we can determine the nullclines of the susceptible prey, infected prey and predator, which are respectively denoted by N_S, N_I and N_P and are defined by the following sets

$$N_S := \left\{(S, I, P) : S = 0 \vee S + (1+\eta)I + \frac{P}{\kappa+S} = 1\right\},$$

$$N_I := \left\{(S, I, P) : I = 0 \vee S = \frac{\delta}{\eta} + \frac{mP}{\eta(\omega+I)}\right\},$$

$$N_P := \left\{(S, I, P) : P = 0 \vee \frac{\mu S}{\kappa+S} + \frac{\beta I}{\omega+I} = q\right\}.$$

Since we are only interested in solutions that satisfy biological conditions, we only consider equilibrium points that satisfy $N_S \cap N_I \cap N_P \subset \mathbb{R}_+^3$. We can obviously identify that the infected prey and predator are extinct if the susceptible prey is zero. Therefore, the following lemma shows that the origin is the only equilibrium point when $N_S = \{(S, I, P) : S = 0\}$.

Lemma 6. *If $N_S := \{(S, I, P) : S = 0\}$ then the origin $E_0 = (0, 0, 0)$ is the only equilibrium point of model (12).*

Proof. For $N_S := \{(S, I, P) : S = 0\}$, the equilibrium point is defined by $N_I \cap N_P \cap \mathbb{R}^3_+$, where

$$N_I := \left\{(S, I, P) : I = 0 \vee \frac{\delta}{\eta} + \frac{mP}{\eta(\omega + I)} = 0\right\},$$

$$N_P := \left\{(S, I, P) : P = 0 \vee \frac{\beta I}{\omega + I} = q\right\}.$$

Since $\frac{\delta}{\eta} + \frac{mP}{\eta(\omega+I)} \neq 0$, then $I = 0$ is the only nullcline of I. By substituting $I = 0$ to N_P, we have $N_P = \{(S, I, P) : P = 0 \vee q = 0\}$. $P = 0$ is the only nullcline of P because $q \neq 0$. Thus, $E_0 = (0, 0, 0)$ is the only equilibrium point. □

Now, we will investigate the equilibrium point when $S \neq 0$. Notice that if $N_I := \{(S, I, P) : I = 0\}$, then $N_S \cap N_P \cap \mathbb{R}^3_+$ is the equilibrium point of model (12) where

$$N_S := \left\{(S, I, P) : S + \frac{P}{\kappa + S} = 1\right\}, \text{ and } N_P := \left\{(S, I, P) : P = 0 \vee \frac{\mu S}{\kappa + S} = q\right\}.$$

Immediately we recognize two equilibrium points as follows:

1. The extinction of infected prey and predator point: $E_1 = (1, 0, 0)$, which always exists.
2. The infected prey free point $E_2 = (\hat{S}, 0, \hat{P})$ where $\hat{S} = \frac{q\kappa}{\mu - q}$ and $\hat{P} = (1 - \hat{S})(\kappa + \hat{S})$ which exists if $\mu > (1 + \kappa)q$. The condition $\mu > (1 + \kappa)q$ is equivalent to condition that the conversion rate of susceptible prey predation into the birth rate of predator is larger than the sum of the death rate of predator and its multiplication with half-saturation constant of predation.

Furthermore, if $N_P = \{(S, I, P) : P = 0\}$, we obtain equilibrium points that satisfy $N_S \cap N_I \cap \mathbb{R}^3_+$ where

$$N_S := \{(S, I, P) : S + (1 + \eta)I = 1\}, \text{ and } N_I := \left\{(S, I, P) : I = 0 \vee S = \frac{\delta}{\eta}\right\}.$$

Thus, we have the extinction of infected prey and predator point $E_1 = (1, 0, 0)$ and the predator-free point $E_3 = \left(\tilde{S}, \frac{1-\tilde{S}}{1+\eta}, 0\right)$, where $\tilde{S} = \frac{\delta}{\eta}$. The point E_3 exists if $\tilde{S} \in (0, 1)$ or $\eta > \delta$, i.e., when the prey infection rate is greater than the infected prey death rate.

By considering the following nullclines

$$N_S := \left\{(S, I, P) : S + (1 + \eta)I + \frac{P}{\kappa + S} = 1\right\},$$

$$N_I := \left\{(S, I, P) : S = \frac{\delta}{\eta} + \frac{mP}{\eta(\omega + I)}\right\}, N_P := \left\{(S, I, P) : \frac{\mu S}{\kappa + S} + \frac{\beta I}{\omega + I} = q\right\},$$

we obtain the co-existence equilibrium point $E^* = (S^*, I^*, P^*)$ that satisfies $N_S \cap N_I \cap N_P \cap \mathbb{R}^3_+$, i.e.,

$$S^* = \frac{-a_2 \pm \sqrt{D}}{2a_1}, I^* = \frac{(1 - S^*)(\kappa + S^*)m - \omega(\eta S^* - \delta)}{(\kappa + S^*)(\eta + 1)m + (\eta S^* - \delta)}, P^* = \frac{(\eta S^* - \delta)(\omega + I^*)}{m},$$

where

$a_1 = (\beta + \mu)m - mq,$
$a_2 = ((\eta + 1)\omega + 1)mq + (\eta\omega + m\kappa)\beta - (((\eta + 1)\omega + 1)\mu + q\kappa + \beta)m$
$a_3 = ((\eta + 1)\omega + 1)mq\kappa - (m\kappa + \delta\omega)\beta$
$D = a_2^2 - 4a_1a_3$

The existence of E^* is described by the following lemma.

Lemma 7. *Suppose that*

$$S_1^* = -\frac{a_2 - \sqrt{D}}{2a_1}, \quad S_2^* = -\frac{a_2 + \sqrt{D}}{2a_1}, \quad S_3^* = -\frac{a_2}{2a_1},$$

$$S_{1,2}^* \in \left(\frac{\delta}{\eta}, 1\right), \quad m > \frac{\omega(\eta S_j^* - \delta)}{(1 - S_j^*)(\kappa + S_j^*)}, \; j = 1, 2, \quad a_1 a_2 < 0.$$

(i) *If $D < 0$, then the co-existence point does not exist.*
(ii) *if $D > 0$ and*
    (a) $a_1 a_3 > 0$ *then there are two co-existence points, i.e., $E_1^* = (S_1^*, I_1^*, P_1^*)$ and $E_2^* = (S_2^*, I_2^*, P_2^*)$.*
    (b) $a_1 a_3 \leq 0$ *then $E_1^* = (S_1^*, I_1^*, P_1^*)$ is the unique co-existence point.*
(iii) *If $D = 0$, then there is a unique co-existence point $E_3^* = (S_3^*, I_3^*, P_3^*)$.*

Proof. Notice if $S_j^* \in \left(\frac{\delta}{\eta}, 1\right)$ and $m > \frac{\omega(\eta S_j^* - \delta)}{(1-S_j^*)(\kappa+S_j^*)}$ then $I_j^* > 0$ and $P_j^* > 0, j = 1, 2$.

(i) It is clear that if $D < 0$ then $S_j^* \notin \mathbb{R}$, and thus the co-existence point does not exist.
(ii) if $D > 0$ then $S_j^* \in \mathbb{R}$. As a result that $a_1 a_2 < 0$, we have $S_1^* + S_2^* > 0$. Furthermore, if
    (a) $a_1 a_3 > 0$ then $S_1^* S_2^* > 0$. Therefore, we have $S_1^* > 0$ and $S_2^* > 0$ and $E_{1,2}^* \in \mathbb{R}_+^3$.
    (b) $a_1 a_3 \leq 0$ then $S_1^* S_2^* \leq 0$ so that $S_1^* > 0$ and $S_2^* \leq 0$.
(iii) If $D = 0$ then S_3^* is the only solution for S_j^*. Furthermore, if $a_1 a_2 < 0$ then $S_3^* > 0$.

Thus, we have the lemma. □

To illustrate the existence of equilibrium point by utilizing the nullclines, we take $\eta = 0.95, \kappa = 0.3, \delta = 0.2, m = 0.6, \omega = 0.6 \, \mu = 0.4, \beta = 0.4$ and $q = 0.1$. We note that E_0 always exists. Besides E_0, there also exist E_1 and E_2 in $\mathbb{R}_+^3$, see Figure 1a,b. If we decrease η so that $\eta = 0.5$, then model (12) has a predator-free point E_3, see Figure 1c. Next, to show the existence of co-existence point (E^*), we choose parameter values: $\eta = 0.8, \delta = 0.17, m = 0.7, \omega = 0.1, \mu = 0.5, \beta = 0.3$ and $q = 0.4$. It can be seen in Figure 1d that model (12) with $\kappa = 0.6$ has two co-existence points. If we increase κ such that $\kappa = 0.4$, then we have a unique co-existence point, see Figure 1e. However, if we take $\kappa = 1$, then model (12) does not have co-existence point (see Figure 1f).

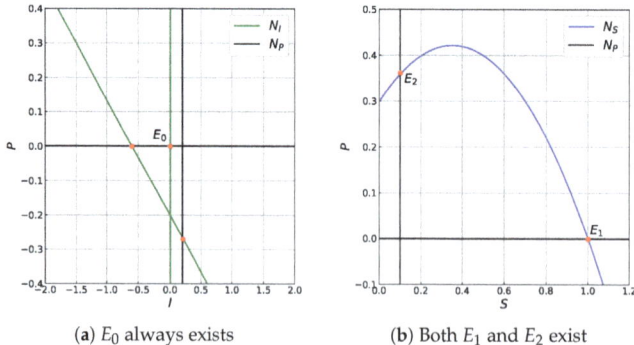

(a) E_0 always exists   (b) Both E_1 and E_2 exist

Figure 1. *Cont.*

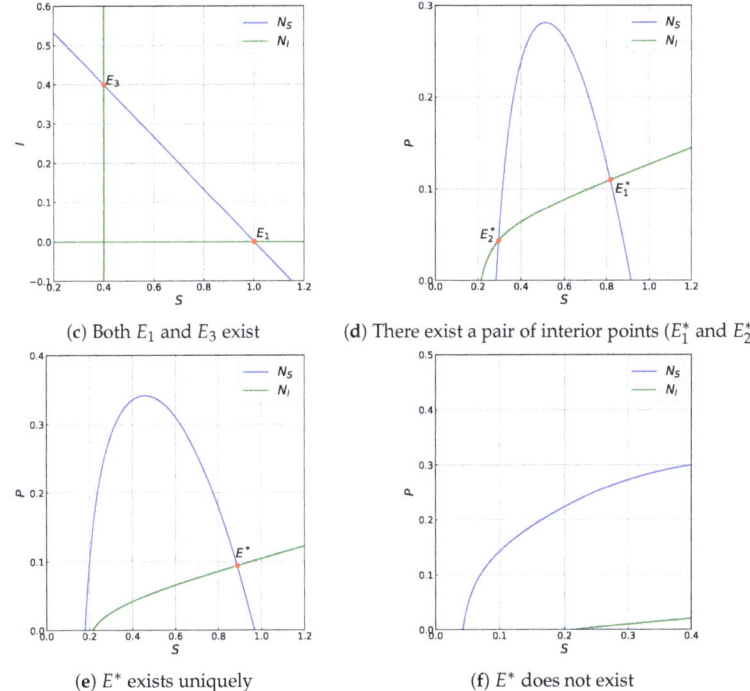

Figure 1. The existence of equilibrium point of model (12) by utilizing the intersection of nullclines.

3.4. Local Stability of Equilibrium Points

In this part, we investigate the local stability properties of each equilibrium point of model (12). The local stability properties are studied by observing the eigenvalues of the Jacobian matrix at each equilibrium points, and the results are described in the following theorems.

Theorem 5. *The equilibrium point E_0 is always a saddle point.*

Proof. The Jacobian matrix of model (12) evaluated at E_0 is

$$J(E_0) = \begin{bmatrix} 1 & 0 & 0 \\ 0 & -\delta & 0 \\ 0 & 0 & -q \end{bmatrix}.$$

The eigenvalues of this Jacobian matrix are $\lambda_1 = 1$, $\lambda_2 = -\delta$ and $\lambda_3 = -q$. Thus, $|\arg(\lambda_1)| = 0 < \frac{\alpha\pi}{2}$ and $|\arg(\lambda_2)| = |\arg(\lambda_3)| = \pi > \frac{\alpha\pi}{2}$. Based on Matignon condition in Theorem 2, we conclude that E_0 is a saddle point. □

Theorem 6. *The equilibrium point E_1 is:*
(i) *locally asymptotically stable if $\eta < \delta$ and $\mu < (1 + \kappa)q$.*
(ii) *a saddle point if $\eta > \delta$ or $\mu > (1 + \kappa)q$.*

Proof. The Jacobian matrix at E_1 is

$$J(E_1) = \begin{bmatrix} -1 & -(\eta+1) & -\frac{1}{\kappa+1} \\ 0 & \eta - \delta & 0 \\ 0 & 0 & \frac{\mu}{\kappa+1} - q \end{bmatrix}.$$

$J(E_1)$ has eigenvalues: $\lambda_1 = -1$, $\lambda_2 = \eta - \delta$ and $\lambda_3 = \frac{\mu}{\kappa+1} - q$. We have $|\arg(\lambda_1)| = \pi > \frac{\alpha\pi}{2}$. Hence, the stability of E_1 depends on $\lambda_{2,3}$.

(i) If $\eta < \delta$ and $\mu < (1+\kappa)q$, then $|\arg(\lambda_2)| = \pi > \frac{\alpha\pi}{2}$ and $|\arg(\lambda_3)| = \pi > \frac{\alpha\pi}{2}$. Due to Matignon condition at Theorem 2, E_1 is locally asymptotically stable.

(ii) If $\eta > \delta$ then $|\arg(\lambda_2)| = 0 < \frac{\alpha\pi}{2}$. In addition, if $\mu > (1+\kappa)q$ then $|\arg(\lambda_3)| = 0 < \frac{\alpha\pi}{2}$. Thus, Theorem 2 says that E_1 is a saddle point. □

Theorem 7. *Suppose that:*

$$\hat{\eta} = \frac{\delta}{\hat{S}} + \frac{m(1-\hat{S})(\kappa+\hat{S})}{\omega\hat{S}}, \qquad \hat{\Delta} = \frac{4(1-\hat{S})\mu\kappa\hat{S}}{(\kappa+\hat{S})^2} - \left(\frac{\kappa-1+2\hat{S}}{\kappa+\hat{S}}\right)^2\hat{S}^2,$$

$$\hat{\alpha} = \frac{2}{\pi}\tan^{-1}\left(\frac{(\kappa+\hat{S})\sqrt{\hat{\Delta}}}{(\kappa-1+2\hat{S})\hat{S}}\right).$$

The equilibrium point E_2 is:

(i) *locally asymptotically stable if $\eta < \hat{\eta}$ and*
  (a) $\kappa > 1 - 2\hat{S}$, *or;*
  (b) $\kappa < 1 - 2\hat{S}$, $\hat{\Delta} > 0$ and $\alpha < \hat{\alpha}$.

(ii) *a saddle point if*
  (a) $\eta > \hat{\eta}$ and $\kappa > 1 - 2\hat{S}$, *or;*
  (b) $\eta > \hat{\eta}$, $\kappa < 1 - 2\hat{S}$, $\hat{\Delta} > 0$, and $\alpha < \hat{\alpha}$, *or;*
  (c) $\eta < \hat{\eta}$, $\kappa < 1 - 2\hat{S}$, and $\alpha > \hat{\alpha}$.

Proof. The Jacobian matrix of model (12) evaluated at E_2 is

$$J(E_2) = \begin{bmatrix} -\hat{S} + \frac{(1-\hat{S})\hat{S}}{\kappa+\hat{S}} & -(1+\eta)\hat{S} & -\frac{\hat{S}}{\kappa+\hat{S}} \\ 0 & (\eta-\hat{\eta})\hat{S} & 0 \\ \frac{(1-\hat{S})\mu\kappa}{\kappa+\hat{S}} & \frac{\beta(1-\hat{S})(\kappa+\hat{S})}{\omega} & 0 \end{bmatrix},$$

which has eigenvalues: $\lambda_1 = (\eta - \hat{\eta})\hat{S}$ and $\lambda_{2,3} = -\frac{\hat{S}}{2}\left(\frac{\kappa-1+2\hat{S}}{\kappa+\hat{S}}\right) \pm \frac{\sqrt{\hat{\Delta}}}{2}$. Notice that if $\eta < \hat{\eta}$ then $|\arg(\lambda_1)| = \pi > \frac{\alpha\pi}{2}$, else if $\eta > \hat{\eta}$ then $|\arg(\lambda_1)| = 0 < \frac{\alpha\pi}{2}$. Furthermore, if $\kappa > 1 - 2\hat{S}$ then $|\arg(\lambda_{2,3})| > \frac{\alpha\pi}{2}$ for both $\hat{\Delta} \geq 0$ and $\hat{\Delta} < 0$. If $\kappa < 1 - 2\hat{S}$ and $\hat{\Delta} > 0$, then $\lambda_{2,3}$ is a pair of complex eigenvalues. Thus, $|\arg(\lambda_{2,3})| > \frac{\alpha\pi}{2}$ is attained if $\alpha < \hat{\alpha}$. When $\kappa < 1 - 2\hat{S}$, and $\alpha > \hat{\alpha}$, we have $|\arg(\lambda_{2,3})| < \frac{\alpha\pi}{2}$ for both $\hat{\Delta} \leq 0$ and $\hat{\Delta} > 0$. Therefore, by Matignon condition in Theorem 2, the theorem is completely proven. □

Theorem 8. *Suppose that:* $\tilde{q} = \frac{\mu\hat{S}}{\kappa+\hat{S}} + \frac{(1-\hat{S})\beta}{\omega(1+\eta)+(1-\hat{S})}$. *The predator-free point E_3 is locally asymptotically stable if $q > \tilde{q}$ and it is a saddle point if $q < \tilde{q}$.*

Proof. We compute the Jacobian matrix of model (12) evaluated at E_3 and obtain

$$J(E_3) = \begin{bmatrix} -\hat{S} & -(1+\eta)\hat{S} & -\frac{\hat{S}}{\kappa+\hat{S}} \\ \frac{(1-\hat{S})\eta}{1+\eta} & 0 & -\frac{(1-\hat{S})m}{\omega(1+\eta)+(1-\hat{S})} \\ 0 & 0 & \tilde{q} - q \end{bmatrix}.$$

The eigenvalues of $J(E_3)$ are $\lambda_1 = \tilde{q} - q$ and $\lambda_{2,3} = \frac{-\hat{S} \pm \sqrt{(\hat{S}-4(1-\hat{S})\eta)\hat{S}}}{2}$. If $\eta \leq \frac{\hat{S}}{4(1-\hat{S})}$, then the eigenvalues $\lambda_{2,3}$ are always real and negative. Moreover, if $\eta > \frac{\hat{S}}{4(1-\hat{S})}$, then $\lambda_{2,3}$ are a pair of complex conjugates where $\text{Re}(\lambda_{2,3}) < 0$. Hence, the eigenvalues $\lambda_{2,3}$ always satisfy $|\arg(\lambda_{2,3})| > \frac{\alpha\pi}{2}$. Finally, $|\arg(\lambda_1)| = \pi > \frac{\alpha\pi}{2}$ is achieved if $q > \tilde{q}$. Therefore, the predator-free point E_3 is locally asymptotically stable if $q > \tilde{q}$; otherwise it is a saddle point. □

Theorem 9. *Suppose that:*

$$d_1 = S^* - \left(\frac{S^*P^*}{(\kappa+S^*)^2} + \frac{mI^*P^*}{(\omega+I^*)^2}\right),$$

$$d_2 = \left[\frac{mS^*I^*(P^*)^2}{(\kappa+S^*)^2(\omega+I^*)^2} + \frac{\beta mI^*P^*}{(\omega+I^*)^2} + \frac{\mu S^*P^*}{(\kappa+S^*)^2} + (\eta+1)\eta S^*I^*\right] -$$
$$\left[\frac{mS^*I^*P^*}{(\omega+I^*)^2} + \frac{m\beta(I^*)^2P^*}{(\omega+I^*)^3} + \frac{\mu(S^*)^2P^*}{(\kappa+S^*)^3}\right],$$

$$d_3 = \left[\frac{\eta}{\kappa+S^*} + \frac{\omega m}{(\omega+I^*)^2}\right]\frac{\beta S^*I^*P^*}{\omega+I^*} - \left[\frac{\beta\eta I^*}{\omega+I^*} + \frac{(\eta+1)\mu\kappa m}{\kappa+S^*}\right]\frac{S^*I^*P^*}{(\kappa+S^*)(\omega+I^*)} -$$
$$\left[\frac{\mu\kappa}{\kappa+S^*} + \frac{\beta\omega}{\omega+I^*}\right]\frac{mS^*I^*(P^*)^2}{(\kappa+S^*)^2(\omega+I^*)^2},$$

$$\Delta^* = 18d_1d_2d_3 + (d_1d_2)^2 - 4d_3d_1^3 - 4d_2^3 - 27d_3^2.$$

The co-existence point $E^* = (S^*, I^*, P^*)$ is locally asymptotically stable if one of the following statements is satisfied.

(i) $\Delta^* > 0$, $d_1 > 0$, $d_3 > 0$, and $d_1d_2 > cd_3$.
(ii) $\Delta^* < 0$, $d_1 \geq 0$, $d_2 \geq 0$, $d_3 > 0$, and $0 < \alpha < (2/3)$.
(iii) $\Delta^* < 0$, $d_1 < 0$, $d_2 < 0$, and $(2/3) < \alpha < 1$.
(iv) $\Delta^* < 0$, $d_1 > 0$, $d_2 > 0$, $d_1d_2 = d_3$, and $0 < \alpha < 1$.

Proof. The Jacobian matrix of model (12) evaluated at E^* is,

$$J(E^*) = \begin{bmatrix} \frac{S^*P^*}{(\kappa+S^*)^2} - S^* & -(\eta+1)S^* & -\frac{S^*}{\kappa+S^*} \\ \eta I^* & \frac{mI^*P^*}{(\omega+I^*)^2} & -\frac{mI^*}{\omega+I^*} \\ \left[1 - \frac{S^*}{\kappa+S^*}\right]\frac{\mu P^*}{\kappa+S^*} & \left[1 - \frac{I^*}{\omega+I^*}\right]\frac{\beta P^*}{\omega+I^*} & 0 \end{bmatrix}.$$

The characteristic equation of $J(E^*)$ is $\lambda^3 + d_1\lambda^2 + d_2\lambda + d_3 = 0$. Using the Routh–Hurwitz condition for a fractional-order dynamical system (See Proposition 1 in [72]), the locally stability conditions of co-existence point $E^* = (S^*, I^*, P^*)$ are proven. □

3.5. Global Stability of Equilibrium Points

The global asymptotic stability of the equilibrium point of model (12) is studied. The results are presented in the following theorems.

Theorem 10. $E_1 = (1, 0, 0)$ *is globally asymptotically stable if* $\max\left\{\frac{\eta}{\delta}, \frac{\beta\kappa+\mu}{\kappa q}\right\} < 1$.

Proof. Consider a Lyapunov function $W_1(S, I, P) = [S - 1 - \ln S] + \frac{1+\eta}{\eta}I + \frac{1}{\mu}P$. By using Lemma 4, we get

$${}^CD_t^\alpha W_1(S, I, P) \leq \left(\frac{S-1}{S}\right){}^CD_t^\alpha S + \frac{1+\eta}{\eta}{}^CD_t^\alpha I + \frac{1}{\mu}{}^CD_t^\alpha P$$

$$= (S-1)\left[1 - S - (1+\eta)I - \frac{P}{\kappa+S}\right] + \frac{1+\eta}{\eta}\left[\eta S - \delta - \frac{mP}{\omega+I}\right]I$$

$$+ \frac{1}{\mu}\left[\frac{\mu S}{\kappa+S} + \frac{\beta I}{\omega+I} - q\right]P$$

$$= -(S-1)^2 - \frac{(\delta-\eta)(1+\eta)I}{\eta} + \frac{P}{\kappa+S} - \frac{(1+\eta)mIP}{(\omega+I)\eta}$$

$$+\frac{\beta IP}{(\omega+I)\mu}-\frac{qP}{\mu}$$

$$\leq -(S-1)^2-\frac{(\delta-\eta)(1+\eta)I}{\eta}+\frac{P}{\kappa}+\frac{\beta P}{\mu}-\frac{qP}{\mu}$$

$$= -(S-1)^2-\frac{(\delta-\eta)(1+\eta)I}{\eta}-\left(q-\left(\beta+\frac{\mu}{\kappa}\right)\right)\frac{P}{\mu}$$

Thus, ${}^C D_t^\alpha W_1(S,I,P) \leq 0$ when $\max\left\{\frac{\eta}{\delta}, \frac{\beta\kappa+\mu}{\kappa q}\right\} < 1$. According to Lemma 5, it follows that E_1 is globally asymptotically stable. □

Theorem 11. *If* $\hat{S} < \min\left\{\frac{\delta}{\eta}, \frac{((1+\eta)m\mu-\beta\eta)\kappa}{\beta\eta}\right\}$ *and* $\hat{P} < \kappa^2$ *then the infected prey extinction point* E_2 *is globally asymptotically stable.*

Proof. We define a Lyapunov function

$$W_2(S,I,P) = \left[S-\hat{S}-\hat{S}\ln\frac{S}{\hat{S}}\right]+\frac{1+\eta}{\eta}I+\frac{\kappa+\hat{S}}{\mu\kappa}\left[P-\hat{P}-\hat{P}\ln\frac{P}{\hat{P}}\right].$$

Based on Lemma 4, we have

$${}^C D_t^\alpha W_2(S,I,P) \leq \left(\frac{S-\hat{S}}{S}\right){}^C D_t^\alpha S+\frac{1+\eta}{\eta}{}^C D_t^\alpha I+\frac{\kappa+\hat{S}}{\mu\kappa}\left(\frac{P-\hat{P}}{P}\right){}^C D_t^\alpha P$$

$$= (S-\hat{S})\left[1-S-(1+\eta)I-\frac{P}{\kappa+S}\right]+\frac{1+\eta}{\eta}\left[\eta S-\delta-\frac{mP}{\omega+I}\right]I$$

$$+\frac{\kappa+\hat{S}}{\mu\kappa}(P-\hat{P})\left[\frac{\mu S}{\kappa+S}+\frac{\beta I}{\omega+I}-q\right]$$

$$= (S-\hat{S})\left[-(S-\hat{S})-(1+\eta)I-\frac{(\kappa+\hat{S})(P-\hat{P})-\hat{P}(S-\hat{S})}{(\kappa+S)(\kappa+\hat{S})}\right]$$

$$+\frac{1+\eta}{\eta}\left[\eta S-\delta-\frac{mP}{\omega+I}\right]I$$

$$+\frac{\kappa+\hat{S}}{\mu\kappa}(P-\hat{P})\left[\frac{\mu\kappa(S-\hat{S})}{(\kappa+S)(\kappa+\hat{S})}+\frac{\beta I}{\omega+I}\right]$$

$$= -(S-\hat{S})^2+\frac{\hat{P}(S-\hat{S})^2}{(\kappa+S)(\kappa+\hat{S})}-\left(\frac{\delta}{\eta}-\hat{S}\right)(1+\eta)I$$

$$-\left(\frac{(1+\eta)m}{\eta}-\frac{(\kappa+\hat{S})\beta}{\mu\kappa}\right)\frac{IP}{\omega+I}$$

$$\leq -\left(1-\frac{\hat{P}}{\kappa^2}\right)(S-\hat{S})^2-\left(\frac{\delta}{\eta}-\hat{S}\right)(1+\eta)I$$

$$-\left(\frac{(1+\eta)m}{\eta}-\frac{(\kappa+\hat{S})\beta}{\mu\kappa}\right)\frac{IP}{\omega+I}$$

It is clear that ${}^C D_t^\alpha W_2(E_2) \leq 0$ if $\hat{S} < \min\left\{\frac{\delta}{\eta}, \frac{((1+\eta)m\mu-\beta\eta)\kappa}{\beta\eta}\right\}$ and $\hat{P} < \kappa^2$. Consequently, Lemma 5 says that E_2 is globally asymptotically stable. □

Theorem 12. *If* $q > \beta+\frac{\mu\tilde{S}}{\kappa}+\frac{(1+\eta)\mu mI}{\eta\omega}$ *then the predator-free point* E_3 *is globally asymptotically stable.*

Proof. We first write $\tilde{I} = \frac{1-\tilde{S}}{1+\eta}$ and define a Lyapunov function

$$W_3(S, I, P) = \left[S - \tilde{S} - \tilde{S}\ln\frac{S}{\tilde{S}}\right] + \frac{1+\eta}{\eta}\left[I - \tilde{I} - \tilde{I}\ln\frac{I}{\tilde{I}}\right] + \frac{1}{\mu}P.$$

By using Lemma 4, we obtain

$$^CD_t^\alpha W_3(S, I, P) \leq \left(\frac{S-\tilde{S}}{S}\right){^CD_t^\alpha S} + \frac{1+\eta}{\eta}\left(\frac{I-\tilde{I}}{I}\right){^CD_t^\alpha I} + \frac{1}{\mu}{^CD_t^\alpha P}$$

$$= (S - \tilde{S})\left[1 - S - (1+\eta)I - \frac{P}{\kappa+S}\right] + \frac{1+\eta}{\eta}(I - \tilde{I})\left[\eta S - \delta - \frac{mP}{\omega+I}\right]$$

$$+ \frac{1}{\mu}\left[\frac{\mu S}{\kappa+S} + \frac{\beta I}{\omega+I} - q\right]P$$

$$= (S - \tilde{S})\left[\tilde{S} + (1+\eta)\tilde{I} - S - (1+\eta)I - \frac{P}{\kappa+S}\right]$$

$$+ \frac{1+\eta}{\eta}(I - \tilde{I})\left[\eta S - \eta\tilde{S} - \frac{mP}{\omega+I}\right] + \frac{1}{\mu}\left[\frac{\mu S}{\kappa+S} + \frac{\beta I}{\omega+I} - q\right]P$$

$$= -(S - \tilde{S})^2 + \frac{\tilde{S}P}{\kappa+S} - \left(\frac{(1+\eta)m}{\eta} - \frac{\beta}{\mu}\right)\frac{IP}{\omega+I} + \frac{(1+\eta)m\tilde{I}P}{(\omega+I)\eta} - \frac{qP}{\mu}$$

$$\leq -(S - \tilde{S})^2 + \frac{\tilde{S}P}{\kappa} + \frac{\beta P}{\mu} + \frac{(1+\eta)m\tilde{I}P}{\eta\omega} - \frac{qP}{\mu}$$

$$= -(S - \tilde{S})^2 - \left(\frac{q}{\mu} - \frac{\beta}{\mu} - \frac{\tilde{S}}{\kappa} - \frac{(1+\eta)m\tilde{I}}{\eta\omega}\right)P$$

If $q > \beta + \frac{\mu\tilde{S}}{\kappa} + \frac{(1+\eta)\mu m\tilde{I}}{\eta\omega}$, then we have $^CD_t^\alpha W_3(S, I, P) \leq 0$. It follows from Lemma 5 that E_3 is globally asymptotically stable. □

Theorem 13. *Suppose that*

$$\varphi_1 = \frac{qP^*}{\mu} + \frac{(1+\eta)\delta I^*}{\eta},$$

$$\varphi_2 = \min\left\{I^* + \eta I^* - 1, \frac{\delta}{\eta}, \frac{q\eta\omega - (1+\eta)m\kappa I^*}{\eta\omega}\right\}.$$

The co-existence point E^* is globally asymptotically stable if $\mu > \frac{\beta}{m}$ and $\varphi_1 < S^* < \varphi_2$.

Proof. Consider a positive Lyapunov function

$$W_4(E^*) = \left[S - S^* - S^*\ln\frac{S}{S^*}\right] + \frac{1+\eta}{\eta}\left[I - I^* - I^*\ln\frac{S}{I^*}\right] + \frac{1}{\mu}\left[P - P^* - P^*\ln\frac{P}{P^*}\right].$$

By utilizing Lemma 4, one has

$$^CD_t^\alpha W_4(E^*) \leq \left(\frac{S-S^*}{S}\right){^CD_t^\alpha S} + \frac{1+\eta}{\eta}\left(\frac{I-I^*}{I}\right){^CD_t^\alpha I} + \frac{1}{\mu}\left(\frac{P-P^*}{P}\right){^CD_t^\alpha P}$$

$$= (S - S^*)\left[1 - S - (1+\eta)I - \frac{P}{\kappa+S}\right]$$

$$+ \frac{1+\eta}{\eta}(I - I^*)\left[\eta S - \delta - \frac{mP}{\omega+I}\right] + \frac{1}{\mu}(P - P^*)\left[\frac{\mu S}{\kappa+S} + \frac{\beta I}{\omega+I} - q\right]$$

$$= -S^2 - ((1+\eta)I^* - (1+S^*))S - \left(\frac{\delta}{\eta} - S^*\right)(1+\eta)I + \frac{S^*P}{\kappa+S}$$

$$+ \frac{(1+\eta)\delta I^*}{\eta} - \left(\frac{(1+\eta)m}{\eta} - \frac{\beta}{\mu}\right)\frac{IP}{\omega+I} + \frac{(1+\eta)mI^*P}{\eta(\omega+I)} - \frac{qP}{\mu}$$

$$\begin{aligned}
&-\frac{P^*S}{\kappa+S} - \frac{\beta P^*I}{\mu(\omega+I)} - S^* + \frac{qP^*}{\mu} \\
&\leq -((1+\eta)I^* - (1+S^*))S - \left(\frac{\delta}{\eta} - S^*\right)(1+\eta)I - \left(m - \frac{\beta}{\mu}\right)\frac{IP}{\omega+I} \\
&\quad - \left(\frac{q}{\mu} - \frac{S^*}{\kappa} - \frac{(1+\eta)mI^*}{\eta\omega}\right)P - \left(S^* - \frac{qP^*}{\mu} - \frac{(1+\eta)\delta I^*}{\eta}\right).
\end{aligned}$$

Obviously, ${}^C D_t^\alpha W_4(E^*) \leq 0$ whenever $\mu > \frac{\beta}{m}$ and $\varphi_1 < S^* < \varphi_2$. Thus, by applying Lemma 5, we can conclude that E^* is globally asymptotically stable. □

3.6. The Existence of Hopf Bifurcation

One of the interesting phenomena in studying the predator–prey model is the occurrence of Hopf bifurcation. This circumstance arises when the stability of an equilibrium point changes and a limit-cycle appears simultaneously as a parameter is varied [73,74]. In a system of first order differential equations, the occurrence of Hopf bifurcation is indicated by the appearance of purely imaginary eigenvalues of the Jacobian matrix. If we vary the bifurcation parameter, then the sign of the real part of the complex eigenvalues changes [75]; and therefore the stability properties of the equilibrium point also changes. In a fractional-order system, this bifurcation also occurs when the order of fractional derivative (α) is varied [76]. It is shown in [77,78] that a 3rd-dimensional fractional-order system undergoes a Hopf bifurcation around an equilibrium point if eigenvalues $\lambda_{1,2,3}$ of its Jacobian matrix evaluated at the equilibrium point satisfy the following conditions:

1. $\lambda_1 < 0$ and $\lambda_{2,3} = \theta \pm \omega i$ where $\theta > 0$;
2. $m(\alpha^*) = \alpha^* \pi/2 - \min_{1 \leq i \leq 3} |\arg(\lambda_i)| = 0$;
3. $\left.\frac{dm(\alpha)}{d\alpha}\right|_{\alpha=\alpha^*} \neq 0$.

When α crosses $\alpha^* = (2/\pi)\tan^{-1}(\omega/\theta)$, the equilibrium point changes its stability and is accompanied by the appearance of a stable limit-cycle. Since the fractional-order system has no periodic orbits [79], the limit-cycle is not a periodic solution, but it is a nearby solution that converges to periodic signals [76,80].

4. Eco-Epidemic Model in the Atangana–Baleanu Sense

If the fractional-order eco-epidemic model (5) is expressed in the Atangana–Baleanu derivative in Caputo (ABC) sense, then we obtain

$$\begin{aligned}
{}^{ABC}D_t^\alpha S &= \left[1 - S - (1+\eta)I - \frac{P}{\kappa+S}\right]S, \\
{}^{ABC}D_t^\alpha I &= \left[\eta S - \delta - \frac{mP}{\omega+I}\right]I, \\
{}^{ABC}D_t^\alpha P &= \left[\frac{\mu S}{\kappa+S} + \frac{\beta I}{\omega+I} - q\right]P.
\end{aligned} \quad (16)$$

By Theorem 1, the solution of model (16) can be expressed in the following Volterra-type integral equation

$$\begin{aligned}
S(t) - S(0) &= \frac{1-\alpha}{B(\alpha)} G_1(t,S) + \frac{\alpha}{B(\alpha)\Gamma(\alpha)} \int_0^t (t-s)^{\alpha-1} G_1(s,S)\, ds, \\
I(t) - I(0) &= \frac{1-\alpha}{B(\alpha)} G_2(t,I) + \frac{\alpha}{B(\alpha)\Gamma(\alpha)} \int_0^t (t-s)^{\alpha-1} G_2(s,I)\, ds, \\
P(t) - P(0) &= \frac{1-\alpha}{B(\alpha)} G_3(t,P) + \frac{\alpha}{B(\alpha)\Gamma(\alpha)} \int_0^t (t-s)^{\alpha-1} G_3(s,P)\, ds,
\end{aligned} \quad (17)$$

where

$$G_1(t,S) = \left[1 - S(t) - (1+\eta)I(t) - \frac{P(t)}{\kappa + S(t)}\right]S(t),$$

$$G_2(t,S) = \left[\eta S(t) - \delta - \frac{mP(t)}{\omega + I(t)}\right]I(t),$$

$$G_3(t,S) = \left[\frac{\mu S(t)}{\kappa + S(t)} + \frac{\beta I(t)}{\omega + I(t)} - q\right]P(t).$$

The existence and uniqueness of the solutions of model (16) will be investigated in the following sub-section.

Existence and Uniqueness

To prove the existence and uniqueness of solutions of model (16), we first show that the kernels $G_i(t,S), i = 1,2,3$ satisfy the Lipschitz condition. Suppose that S, $\tilde{S}$, I, $\tilde{I}$, P and $\tilde{P}$ are functions that satisfy $\|S\| \leq a_1$, $\|\tilde{S}\| \leq a_2$, $\|I\| \leq b_1$, $\|\tilde{I}\| \leq b_2$, $\|P\| \leq c_1$ and $\|\tilde{P}\| \leq c_2$. For the kernel $G_1(t,S) = \left(1 - S - (1+\eta)I - \frac{P}{\kappa + S}\right)S$ and two functions S and $\tilde{S}$, we get

$$\begin{aligned}
&\|G_1(t,S) - G_1(t,\tilde{S})\| \\
&= \left\|S - S^2 - (1+\eta)SI - \frac{SP}{\kappa+S} - \left(\tilde{S} - \tilde{S}^2 - (1+\eta)\tilde{S}I - \frac{\tilde{S}P}{\kappa+\tilde{S}}\right)\right\| \\
&= \left\|S - S^2 - (1+\eta)SI - \frac{SP}{\kappa+S} - \tilde{S} + \tilde{S}^2 + (1+\eta)\tilde{S}I + \frac{\tilde{S}P}{\kappa+\tilde{S}}\right\| \\
&= \left\|(S-\tilde{S}) - (S^2 - \tilde{S}^2) - ((1+\eta)SI - (1+\eta)\tilde{S}I) - \left(\frac{SP}{\kappa+S} - \frac{\tilde{S}P}{\kappa+\tilde{S}}\right)\right\| \\
&= \left\|(S-\tilde{S}) - (S+\tilde{S})(S-\tilde{S}) - (1+\eta)I(S-\tilde{S}) - \left(\frac{SP(\kappa+\tilde{S}) - \tilde{S}P(\kappa+S)}{(\kappa+S)(\kappa+\tilde{S})}\right)\right\| \\
&\leq \|S-\tilde{S}\| + (a_1 + a_2)\|S-\tilde{S}\| + (1+\eta)b_1\|S-\tilde{S}\| + \frac{c_1}{\kappa}\|S-\tilde{S}\| \\
&= \left(1 + a_1 + a_2 + (1+\eta)b_1 + \frac{c_1}{\kappa}\right)\|S-\tilde{S}\| \\
&= g_1\|S-\tilde{S}\|,
\end{aligned} \tag{18}$$

where $g_1 = 1 + a_1 + a_2 + (1+\eta)b_1 + \frac{c_1}{\kappa}$. Hence, the Lipschitz condition holds for $G_1(t,S)$. In a similar manner, we can show that

$$\begin{aligned}
\|G_2(t,I) - G_2(t,\tilde{I})\| &\leq g_2\|I - \tilde{I}\|, \\
\|G_3(t,P) - G_3(t,\tilde{P})\| &\leq g_3\|P - \tilde{P}\|,
\end{aligned} \tag{19}$$

where $g_2 = a_1\eta + \delta + \frac{c_1 m}{\omega}$ and $g_3 = \frac{a_1\mu}{\kappa} + \frac{b_1\beta}{\omega} + q$. Hence, the Lipschitz condition also holds for kernels $G_2(t,I)$ and $G_3(t,P)$. Furthermore, $G_2(t,I)$ and $G_3(t,P)$ are contracted if $0 \leq g_2 < 1$ and $0 \leq g_3 < 1$, respectively.

Now, we investigate the existence of solutions of model (16) by employing the fixed-point theorem. For this purpose, we start by writing Equation (17) in the following recursive formulae

$$\begin{aligned}
S_n(t) &= \frac{1-\alpha}{B(\alpha)}G_1(t,S_{n-1}) + \frac{\alpha}{B(\alpha)\Gamma(\alpha)}\int_0^t (t-s)^{\alpha-1}G_1(s,S_{n-1})\,ds, \\
I_n(t) &= \frac{1-\alpha}{B(\alpha)}G_2(t,I_{n-1}) + \frac{\alpha}{B(\alpha)\Gamma(\alpha)}\int_0^t (t-s)^{\alpha-1}G_2(s,I_{n-1})\,ds, \\
P_n(t) &= \frac{1-\alpha}{B(\alpha)}G_3(t,P_{n-1}) + \frac{\alpha}{B(\alpha)\Gamma(\alpha)}\int_0^t (t-s)^{\alpha-1}G_3(s,P_{n-1})\,ds.
\end{aligned} \tag{20}$$

The associated initial conditions along with Equation (20) are $S_0(t) = S(0)$, $I_0(t) = I(0)$, and $P_0(t) = P(0)$. Next, from Equation (20), we have the difference expression of successive terms as follows.

$$\Phi_{1,n}(t) = S_n(t) - S_{n-1}(t)$$
$$= \frac{1-\alpha}{B(\alpha)}(G_1(t, S_{n-1}) - G_1(t, S_{n-2}))$$
$$+ \frac{\alpha}{B(\alpha)\Gamma(\alpha)} \int_0^t (t-s)^{\alpha-1}(G_1(s, S_{n-1}) - G_1(s, S_{n-2})) \, ds,$$

$$\Phi_{2,n}(t) = I_n(t) - I_{n-1}(t)$$
$$= \frac{1-\alpha}{B(\alpha)}(G_2(t, I_{n-1}) - G_2(t, I_{n-2})) \qquad (21)$$
$$+ \frac{\alpha}{B(\alpha)\Gamma(\alpha)} \int_0^t (t-s)^{\alpha-1}(G_2(s, I_{n-1}) - G_2(s, I_{n-2})) \, ds,$$

$$\Phi_{3,n}(t) = P_n(t) - P_{n-1}(t)$$
$$= \frac{1-\alpha}{B(\alpha)}(G_3(t, P_{n-1}) - G_3(t, P_{n-2}))$$
$$+ \frac{\alpha}{B(\alpha)\Gamma(\alpha)} \int_0^t (t-s)^{\alpha-1}(G_3(s, P_{n-1}) - G_3(s, P_{n-2})) \, ds.$$

Based on Equation (21), we have that

$$S_n(t) = \sum_{i=1}^n \Phi_{1,i}(t), \; I_n(t) = \sum_{i=1}^n \Phi_{2,i}(t), \text{ and } P_n(t) = \sum_{i=1}^n \Phi_{3,i}(t). \qquad (22)$$

By using (18) and (19), we can show that the norm of both sides in (21) fulfill the following relations

$$\|\Phi_{1,n}(t)\| \leq \frac{1-\alpha}{B(\alpha)} g_1 \|\Phi_{1,n-1}\| + \frac{\alpha}{B(\alpha)\Gamma(\alpha)} g_1 \int_0^t \|\Phi_{1,n-1}(s)\|(t-s)^{\alpha-1} \, ds,$$

$$\|\Phi_{2,n}(t)\| \leq \frac{1-\alpha}{B(\alpha)} g_2 \|\Phi_{2,n-1}\| + \frac{\alpha}{B(\alpha)\Gamma(\alpha)} g_2 \int_0^t \|\Phi_{2,n-1}(s)\|(t-s)^{\alpha-1} \, ds, \qquad (23)$$

$$\|\Phi_{3,n}(t)\| \leq \frac{1-\alpha}{B(\alpha)} g_3 \|\Phi_{3,n-1}\| + \frac{\alpha}{B(\alpha)\Gamma(\alpha)} g_3 \int_0^t \|\Phi_{3,n-1}(s)\|(t-s)^{\alpha-1} \, ds.$$

Now, by applying (23), the existence and uniqueness of model (16) are shown by the following theorem.

Theorem 14. *Model (16) has a unique solution if we can find t_{max} such that*

$$\frac{(1-\alpha)g_i}{B(\alpha)} + \frac{t_{max}^\alpha g_i}{B(\alpha)\Gamma(\alpha)} < 1, \; i = 1, 2, 3 \qquad (24)$$

Proof. We assume that $S(t)$, $I(t)$ and $P(t)$ are bounded functions, and hence the Lipschitz condition is satisfied. From Equation (23) we can get the following inequalities.

$$\|\Phi_{1,n}(t)\| \leq \|S_0\| \left(\frac{(1-\alpha)g_1}{B(\alpha)} + \frac{t^\alpha g_1}{B(\alpha)\Gamma(\alpha)}\right)^n,$$

$$\|\Phi_{2,n}(t)\| \leq \|I_0\| \left(\frac{(1-\alpha)g_2}{B(\alpha)} + \frac{t^\alpha g_2}{B(\alpha)\Gamma(\alpha)}\right)^n, \qquad (25)$$

$$\|\Phi_{3,n}(t)\| \leq \|P_0\| \left(\frac{(1-\alpha)g_3}{B(\alpha)} + \frac{t^\alpha g_3}{B(\alpha)\Gamma(\alpha)}\right)^n.$$

Therefore, the existence and smoothness of the solution presented in Equation (22) are proven since $\|\Phi_{1,n}(t)\| \to 0$, $\|\Phi_{2,n}(t)\| \to 0$ and $\|\Phi_{3,n}(t)\| \to 0$ as $n \to \infty$ and $t = t_{max}$. To show that the functions which satisfy Equation (17) are the solutions of Equation (16), we suppose that

$$S(t) - S(0) = S_n(t) - Y_{1,n}(t),$$
$$I(t) - I(0) = I_n(t) - Y_{2,n}(t), \qquad (26)$$
$$P(t) - P(0) = P_n(t) - Y_{3,n}(t),$$

where $Y_{i,n}(t), i = 1, 2, 3$ are the remainder terms of series solutions. The norm of $Y_{1,n}(t)$ satisfies

$$\|Y_{1,n}(t)\| \leq \frac{1-\alpha}{B(\alpha)} \|G_1(t,S) - G_1(t,S_{n-1})\|$$
$$+ \frac{\alpha}{B(\alpha)\Gamma(\alpha)} \int_0^t \|G_1(s,S) - G_1(s,S_{n-1})\|(t-s)^{\alpha-1} \, ds, \qquad (27)$$
$$\leq \|S - S_{n-1}\| \left(\frac{1-\alpha}{B(\alpha)} + \frac{t^\alpha}{B(\alpha)\Gamma(\alpha)} \right) g_1.$$

By applying this relation iteratively, we get at $t = t_{max}$

$$\|Y_{1,n}(t)\| \leq a_1 \left(\frac{1-\alpha}{B(\alpha)} + \frac{t_{max}^\alpha}{B(\alpha)\Gamma(\alpha)} \right)^{n+1} g_1^{n+1}. \qquad (28)$$

For $n \to \infty$, we obtain $\|Y_{1,n}(t)\| \to 0$. Applying the similar manner, we have $\|Y_{2,n}(t)\| \to 0$ and $\|Y_{3,n}(t)\| \to 0$. Hence, the functions which satisfy Equation (17) are the solutions of Equation (16).

Now, we show the uniqueness of solutions of Equation (16). For this aim, we suppose that $S^*(t)$, $I^*(t)$ and $P^*(t)$ are another solution of Equation (16). Then, we have

$$S(t) - S^*(t) = \frac{1-\alpha}{B(\alpha)}(G_1(t,S) - G_1(t,S^*))$$
$$+ \frac{\alpha}{B(\alpha)\Gamma(\alpha)} \int_0^t (G_1(s,S) - G_1(s,S^*))(t-s)^{\alpha-1} \, ds. \qquad (29)$$

Taking the norm for both sides and using the same procedures as in (23) and (25), we obtain

$$\|S(t) - S^*(t)\| \left(1 - \frac{(1-\alpha)g_1}{B(\alpha)} - \frac{t^\alpha g_1}{B(\alpha)\Gamma(\alpha)} \right) \leq 0. \qquad (30)$$

For $t = t_{max}$, we have (24). Hence, $\|S(t) - S^*(t)\| = 0$ and consequently $S(t) = S^*(t)$. In the same way, we can show that $I(t) = I^*(t)$ and $P(t) = P^*(t)$. Hence, the uniqueness of the solution of Equation (16) is proven. □

5. Numerical Simulations

In this section, we present some results of our numerical simulations for the fractional-order eco-epidemic models in both Caputo sense (12) and ABC sense (16). For this aim, we solve the model in Caputo sense (12) using the predictor–corrector scheme developed by Diethelm et al. [81], while the model in ABC sense (16) is solved by applying the predictor–corrector scheme proposed by Baleanu et al. [82]. Since the field data are not available, the simulations are performed by using some hypothetical parameter values.

We first perform simulation by setting the parameter values as follows:

$$\eta = 0.25, \ \kappa = 0.5, \ \delta = 0.3, \ m = 0.6, \ \omega = 0.6, \ \mu = 0.4, \ \beta = 0.4, \ q = 0.3, \ \alpha = 0.9. \qquad (31)$$

Using these parameter values, the eco-epidemic model with fractional-order derivative in both Caputo sense (12) and ABC sense (16) have two equilibrium points, i.e., E_0 and

E_1. Based on the analysis for the model in Caputo sense (12), it is shown that E_0 is a saddle point and E_1 is asymptotically stable. This behavior is confirmed by our numerical simulation shown in Figure 2. If we modify the parameter values in (31) such that $\eta = 0.35$ and $q = 0.2$, then, in addition to E_0 and E_1, the model also has equilibrium points E_2 and E_3. All of these equilibrium points are unstable except E_2. The stability of E_2 is clearly observed in Figure 3. Now, some parameter values in (31) are replaced by $\eta = 0.95$, $\delta = 0.2$ and $q = 0.4$. Under these parameter values, the model has three equilibrium points, i.e., E_0, E_1 and E_3. The previous analysis for the model in Caputo sense shows that E_0 and E_1 are unstable, while E_3 is asymptotically stable. Such stability behavior can be seen in Figure 4. Furthermore, in Figures 2–4, the numerical solutions of model in the Caputo sense are compared to those of models in ABC sense. It is observed that the phase portraits and time series of both models have similar dynamical behavior. To see the difference between the solutions of the two models, we perform some simulations using the same parameter values as in Figures 2–4, but with varying value of α. The time series of solutions obtained from those simulations are plotted in Figures 5–7. In these simulations, although the value of α does not affect the stability of the equilibrium point, Figures 5–7 show that the value of α greatly affects the rate of convergence in reaching the equilibrium point. Indeed, when $\alpha = 1$, the eco-epidemic model with fractional derivative in the Caputo sense and model with fractional derivative in the ABC sense have solutions that coincide with each other.

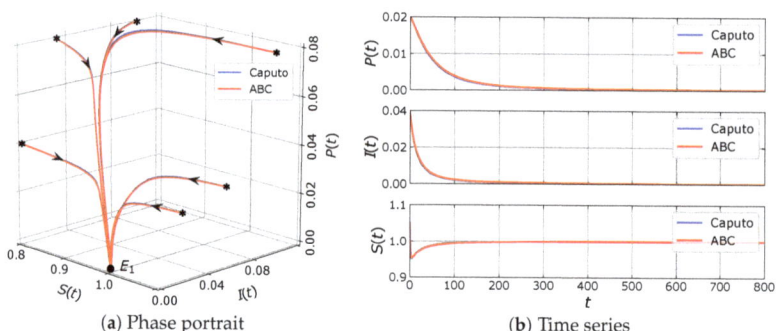

Figure 2. Numerical simulation of the eco-epidemic model with parameter values: $\eta = 0.25$, $\kappa = 0.5$, $\delta = 0.3$, $m = 0.6$, $\omega = 0.6$, $\mu = 0.4$, $\beta = 0.4$, $q = 0.3$ and $\alpha = 0.9$.

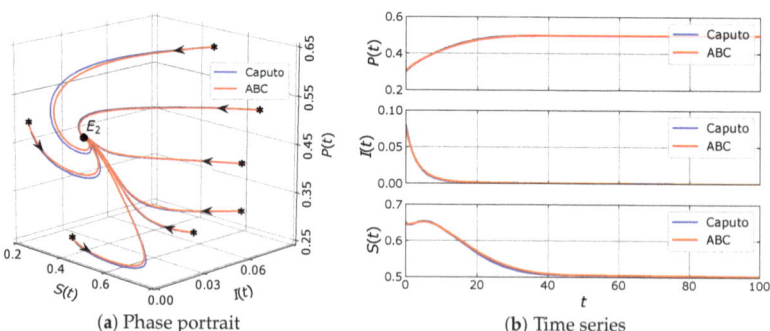

Figure 3. Numerical simulation of the eco-epidemic model with parameter values: $\eta = 0.35$, $\kappa = 0.5$, $\delta = 0.3$, $m = 0.6$, $\omega = 0.6$, $\mu = 0.4$, $\beta = 0.4$, $q = 0.2$ and $\alpha = 0.9$.

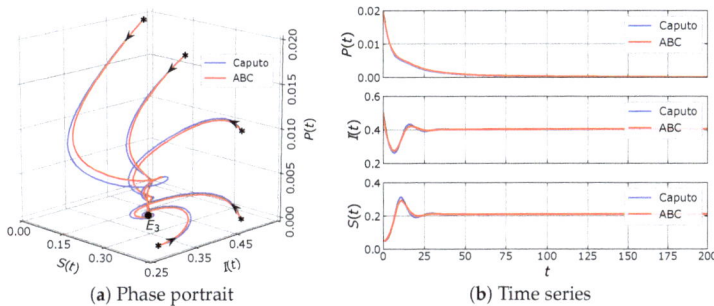

Figure 4. Numerical simulation of the eco-epidemic model with parameter values: $\eta = 0.95$, $\kappa = 0.5$, $\delta = 0.2$, $m = 0.6$, $\omega = 0.6$, $\mu = 0.4$, $\beta = 0.4$, $q = 0.4$ and $\alpha = 0.9$.

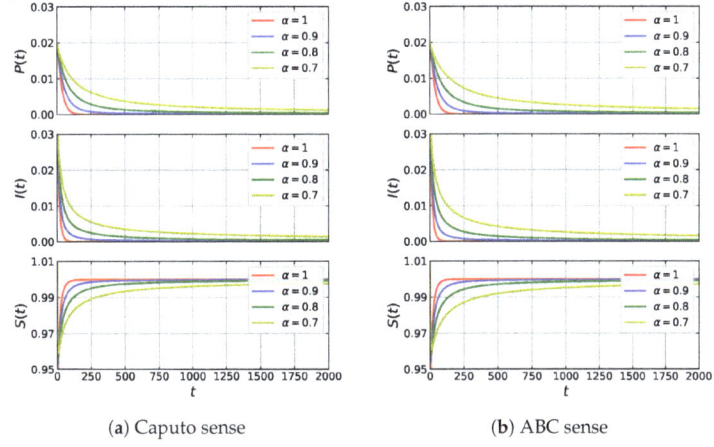

Figure 5. Time series of solutions of the eco-epidemic model (5) with fractional derivative in the Caputo sense and fractional derivative in ABC sense. The parameter values are $\eta = 0.35$, $\kappa = 0.5$, $\delta = 0.3$, $m = 0.6$, $\omega = 0.6$, $\mu = 0.4$, $\beta = 0.4$ and $q = 0.2$.

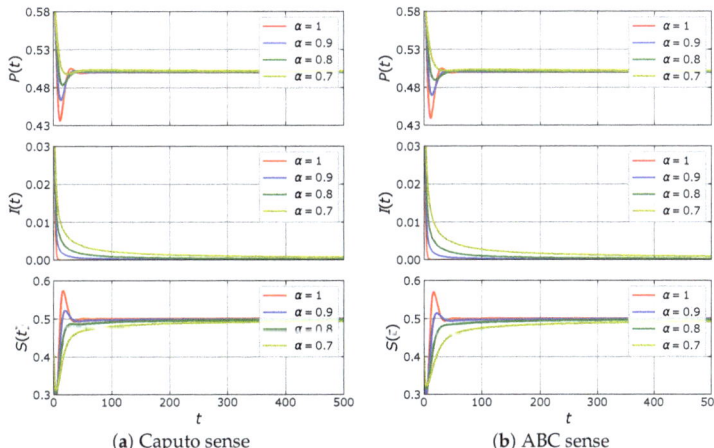

Figure 6. Time series of solutions of the eco-epidemic model (5) with fractional derivative in the Caputo sense and fractional derivative in ABC sense. The parameter values are $\eta = 0.35$, $\kappa = 0.5$, $\delta = 0.3$, $m = 0.6$, $\omega = 0.6$, $\mu = 0.4$, $\beta = 0.4$ and $q = 0.2$.

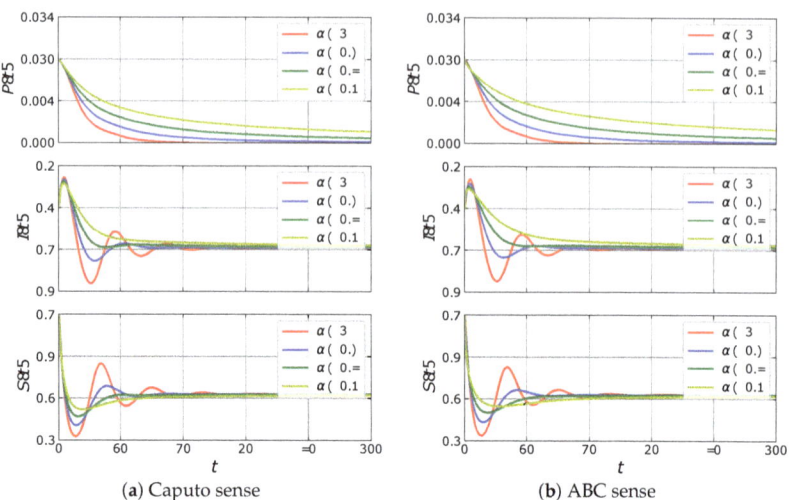

(a) Caputo sense (b) ABC sense

Figure 7. Time series of solutions of the eco-epidemic model (5) with fractional derivative in the Caputo sense and fractional derivative in ABC sense. The parameter values are $\eta = 0.95$, $\kappa = 0.5$, $\delta = 0.2$, $m = 0.6$, $\omega = 0.6$, $\mu = 0.4$, $\beta = 0.4$ and $q = 0.4$.

Next, we perform simulation using the following parameter values:

$$\eta = 0.8,\ \kappa = 0.01,\ \delta = 0.17,\ m = 0.7,\ \omega = 0.1,\ \mu = 0.2,\ \beta = 0.27,\ q = 0.3. \qquad (32)$$

Here, the model has equilibrium points: E_0, E_1, E_3 and E^*. By applying the stability analysis for the model in the Caputo sense, it can be shown that E_0, E_1 and E_3 are unstable; while the stability of E^* is determined by α. If $\alpha < \alpha^* \approx 0.85662$ then E^* is asymptotically stable. On the other hand, E^* becomes unstable if $\alpha > \alpha^*$, where in this case, the solution is convergent to a limit-cycle. In other words, there occurs a Hopf bifurcation controlled by α where the bifurcation point is at $\alpha = \alpha^*$. The Hopf bifurcation is indeed verified by our bifurcation diagram shown in Figure 8. We confirm numerically that both models with Caputo sense and ABC sense undergo the Hopf bifurcation, but with different bifurcation points. The bifurcation point of model with Caputo sense has smaller value of α than that of the model with ABC sense. To describe their dynamics, we select three values of $\alpha = 0.79, 0.86, 0.9$, each of which is denoted by the labels [a], [b], [c] in Figure 8, respectively. When $\alpha = 0.79$, both models with Caputo sense and ABC sense are convergent to E^* as in Figure 9a. From the time series in Figure 10a, the solution of model with ABC sense converges faster than model with Caputo sense. For $\alpha = 0.86$, E^* of model with Caputo sense losses its stability and the solution goes to the limit-cycle while E^* of model with ABC sense still maintains its stability, see Figures 9b and 10b. This circumstance confirms that the model with Caputo sense has undergone the Hopf bifurcation while model with ABC sense has not. When $\alpha = 0.9$, E^* of model with ABC sense losses its stability via Hopf bifurcation as in Figure 9c. The solution of both models converge to the limit-cycle where the diameter of limit-cycles obtained by model in ABC sense is smaller than those obtained by model in Caputo sense, see Figure 10c. To see the evolution of limit-cycle in more detail, we perform simulations using parameter values in (32) and $\alpha \in (0.8, 0.94)$. In Figure 11, we show the stable equilibrium point or limit-cycle in (I, P)-plane as function of α. As mentioned before the stable limit-cycle appears if $\alpha > \alpha^*$. It can be seen that the diameter of limit-cycle obtained by both models in Caputo sense and ABC sense are getting bigger when α is increased. We notice from Figure 8 that the model with Caputo sense has a smaller critical value of α. Therefore, there are situations where the model with Caputo sense has an α that passes its critical value (α^*) while the model with ABC sense does not. This situation shows that the model with the two fractional derivative operators have different biological interpretations in determining the density of prey and predators. On one hand, the density of prey and predator obtained by the model with Caputo sense fluctuates periodically, whereas those obtained by the model with ABC sense converge to a constant value.

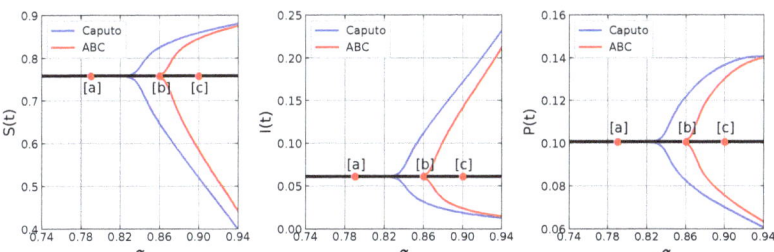

Figure 8. Bifurcation diagram of the eco-epidemic model with parameter values $\eta = 0.8$, $\kappa = 0.01$, $\delta = 0.17$, $m = 0.7$, $\omega = 0.1$, $\mu = 0.2$, $\beta = 0.27$ and $q = 0.3$.

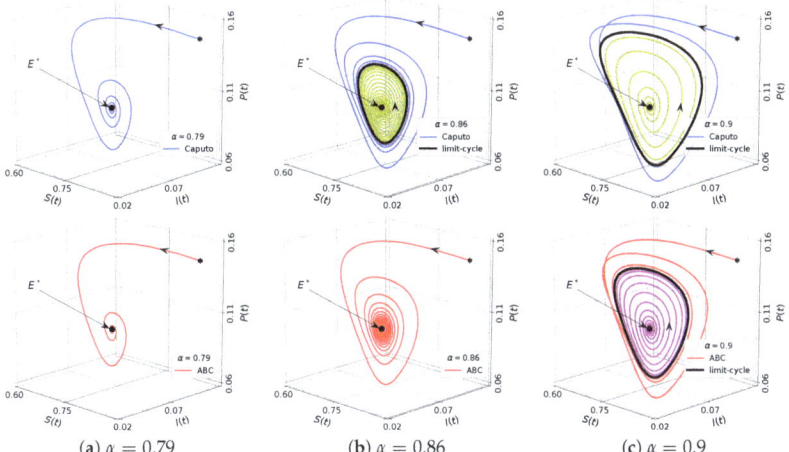

Figure 9. Phase portraits of the eco-epidemic model with parameter values: $\eta = 0.8$, $\kappa = 0.01$, $\delta = 0.17$, $m = 0.7$, $\omega = 0.1$, $\mu = 0.2$, $\beta = 0.27$ and $q = 0.3$. The top figures are solutions of model with Caputo sense while the bottom figures are ABC sense.

Finally, we take the following parameter values:

$$\eta = 0.8, \kappa = 0.6, \delta = 0.17, m = 0.7, \omega = 0.1, \mu = 0.5, \beta = 0.3, q = 0.4. \quad (33)$$

For this case, the model has five equilibrium points, namely E_0, E_1, E_3, E_1^* and E_2^*. Using the results of a previous stability analysis, it is shown that E_0, E_1 and E_2^* are unstable, while E_3 is asymptotically stable regardless of the value of α. We also check that there exists Hopf bifurcation around E_1^*. In the latter case, E_1^* is stable for $\alpha < \alpha_1^* \approx 0.84730$. If $\alpha > \alpha_1^*$ then E_1^* loses its stability and there appears a limit-cycle. Hence, the model exhibits a bistability phenomenon for $\alpha < \alpha_1^*$, where, in this case, E_3 and E_1^* are locally asymptotically stable. To illustrate the dynamics of eco-epidemic model with parameter values in (33), we plot numerical solutions with two slightly different initial values in Figure 12. When we take $\alpha = 0.83 < \alpha_1^*$ the solutions of both models are respectively convergent to different equilibrium points, namely E_3 and E_1^*, see Figure 12a,b. Furthermore, when we increase the order of fractional derivative to $\alpha = 0.95$ then E_3 remains stable but the stability of E_1^* vanishes via Hopf bifurcation as in Figure 12c,d. Thus, a captivating circumstance has been shown, where the initial condition is very sensitive in determining the limiting behavior of the system.

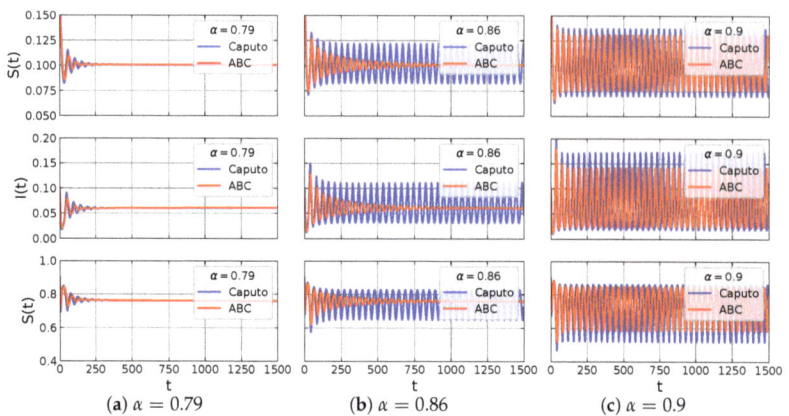

Figure 10. Time series of the eco-epidemic model with parameter values: $\eta = 0.8$, $\kappa = 0.01$, $\delta = 0.17$, $m = 0.7$, $\omega = 0.1$, $\mu = 0.2$, $\beta = 0.27$ and $q = 0.3$.

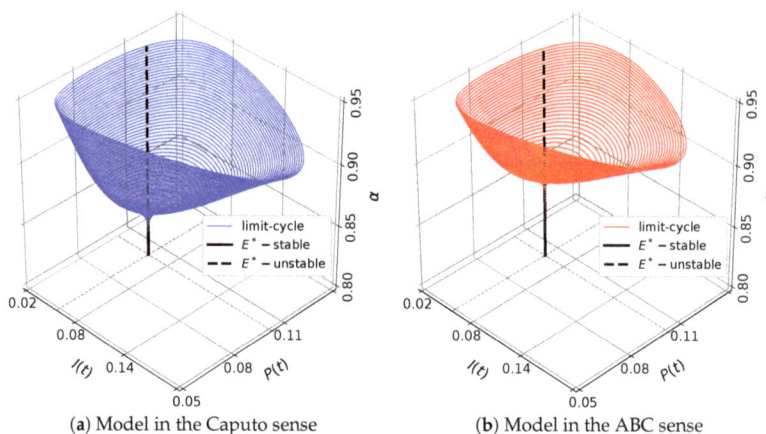

(a) Model in the Caputo sense

(b) Model in the ABC sense

Figure 11. The evolution of limit-cycle in (I, P)-plane as a function of α for eco-epidemic model with parameter values $\eta = 0.8$, $\kappa = 0.01$, $\delta = 0.17$, $m = 0.7$, $\omega = 0.1$, $\mu = 0.2$, $\beta = 0.27$ and $q = 0.3$.

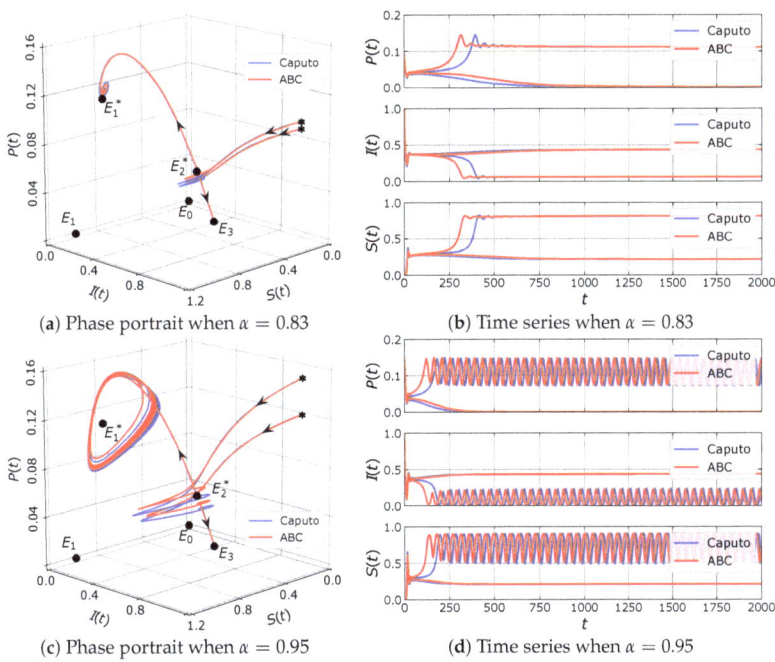

Figure 12. Numerical simulation of the eco-epidemic model with parameter values: $\eta = 0.8$, $\kappa = 0.6$, $\delta = 0.17$, $m = 0.7$, $\omega = 0.1$, $\mu = 0.5$, $\beta = 0.3$ and $q = 0.4$.

6. Conclusions

We have presented the dynamics of fractional-order Rosenzweig–MacArthur eco-epidemic model using fractional derivative in both Caputo sense and ABC-sense. We have determined conditions for the existence and uniqueness of solutions for models in both Caputo sense and ABC sense. It is also shown that all solutions are non-negative and bounded in $\mathbb{R}^3_+$. The model has at most five types of equilibrium points, i.e., the origin, the extinction of infected prey and predator point, the infected prey free point, the predator-free point and the co-existence point. Based on the stability analysis for the model in the Caputo sense, it is found that the origin is a saddle point, meaning that the extinction of all populations will never happen. We also found that the other equilibrium points are conditionally asymptotically stable. Furthermore, the conditions for the existence of Hopf bifurcation have been established, where the bifurcation is driven by the order of the fractional derivative. Our theoretical results have been confirmed by numerical solutions of the model in the Caputo sense. In this article, the eco-epidemic model in the ABC sense has also been solved numerically. The comparison of our numerical results shows that model with both Caputo sense and ABC sense have the same dynamical behavior except around the interior equilibrium point. In other words, the dynamical behavior of the proposed model with both senses are symmetric around axial equilibrium points, but it is asymmetric around the interior point when a Hopf bifurcation occurs. We confirm numerically that the interior point of both models has a different bifurcation point when Hopf bifurcation occurs. For some values of the order-α, the interior point of model with ABC sense is stable while the interior point of model with Caputo sense is unstable. Our numerical simulations also show that the proposed models may exhibit a bistable phenomenon. We finally notice that our simulations are based on some hypothetical parameter values. For further studies, it is recommended to compare the performance of both models, namely with Caputo sense and with ABC sense, by using real data of selected eco-epidemiological case.

Author Contributions: Conceptualization, A.S.; methodology, A.S. and W.M.K.; software, H.S.P. and I.D.; validation, A.S. and I.D.; formal analysis, H.S.P., A.S. and W.M.K.; investigation, H.S.P. and I.D.; resources, A.S.; data curation, H.S.P. and W.M.K.; writing—original draft preparation, H.S.P.; writing—review and editing, A.S., W.M.K. and I.D.; visualization, H.S.P.; supervision, A.S., W.M.K. and I.D.; project administration, W.M.K.; funding acquisition, A.S. All authors have read and agreed to the published version of the manuscript.

Funding: This research is funded by the Directorate of Research and Community Service. The Directorate General of Strengthening Research and Development, the Ministry of Research, Technology and Higher Education (Brawijaya University), Indonesia, via Doctoral Dissertation Research, in accordance with the Research Contract No. 037/ SP2H/ LT/ DRPM/ 2020, dated 9 March 2020.

Institutional Review Board Statement: Not applicable.

Informed Consent Statement: Not applicable.

Data Availability Statement: Not applicable.

Conflicts of Interest: The authors declare no conflict of interest in this paper.

References

1. Lotka, A.J. Elements of physical biology. *Nature* **1925**, *116* , 461. [CrossRef]
2. Volterra, V. Variations and fluctuations of the number of individuals in animal species living together. *ICES J. Mar. Sci.* **1928**, *3*, 3–51. [CrossRef]
3. Berryman, A.A. The orgins and evolution of predator-prey theory. *Ecology* **1992**, *73*, 1530–1535. [CrossRef]
4. González-Olivares, E.; Tintinago-Ruiz, P.C.; Rojas-Palma, A. A Leslie–Gower-type predator–prey model with sigmoid functional response. *Int. J. Comput. Math.* **2015**, *92*, 1895–1909. [CrossRef]
5. Wei, F.; Fu, Q. Hopf bifurcation and stability for predator-prey systems with Beddington-DeAngelis type functional response and stage structure for prey incorporating refuge. *Appl. Math. Model.* **2016**, *40*, 126–134. [CrossRef]
6. Khajanchi, S. Modeling the dynamics of stage-structure predator-prey system with Monod-Haldane type response function. *Appl. Math. Comput.* **2017**, *302*, 122–143. [CrossRef]
7. Song, Q.; Yang, R.; Zhang, C.; Tang, L. Bifurcation analysis in a diffusive predator–prey system with Michaelis–Menten-type predator harvesting. *Adv. Differ. Equ.* **2018**, *2018*, 329. [CrossRef]
8. Suryanto, A.; Darti, I.; Panigoro, H.S.; Kilicman, A. A fractional-order predator–prey model with ratio-dependent functional response and linear harvesting. *Mathematics* **2019**, *7*, 1100. [CrossRef]
9. Ghanbari, B.; Kumar, D. Numerical solution of predator-prey model with Beddington-DeAngelis functional response and fractional derivatives with Mittag-Leffler kernel. *Chaos* **2019**, *29*, 063103. [CrossRef] [PubMed]
10. Manna, D.; Maiti, A.; Samanta, G.P. A Michaelis–Menten type food chain model with strong Allee effect on the prey. *Appl. Math. Comput.* **2017**, *311*, 390–409. [CrossRef]
11. Dhiman, A.; Poria, S. Allee effect induced diversity in evolutionary dynamics. *Chaos Soliton Fract.* **2018**, *108*, 32–38. [CrossRef]
12. Elaydi, S.; Kwessi, E.; Livadiotis, G. Hierarchical competition models with the Allee effect III: Multispecies. *J. Biol. Dyn.* **2018**, *12*, 271–287. [CrossRef]
13. Zhang, J.; Zhang, L.; Bai, Y. Stability and bifurcation analysis on a predator–prey system with the weak Allee effect. *Mathematics* **2019**, *7*, 432. [CrossRef]
14. Rahmi, E.; Darti, I.; Suryanto, A.; Trisilowati; Panigoro, H.S. Stability analysis of a fractional-order Leslie-Gower model with Allee Effect in predator. *J. Phys. Conf. Ser.* **2021**, *1821*, 012051. [CrossRef]
15. Bodine, E.N.; Yust, A.E. Predator–prey dynamics with intraspecific competition and an Allee effect in the predator population. *Lett. Biomath.* **2017**, *4*, 23–38. [CrossRef]
16. Ali, N.; Haque, M.; Venturino, E.; Chakravarty, S. Dynamics of a three species ratio-dependent food chain model with intra-specific competition within the top predator. *Comput. Biol. Med.* **2017**, *85*, 63–74. [CrossRef]
17. Jana, D.; Banerjee, A.; Samanta, G. Degree of prey refuges: Control the competition among prey and foraging ability of predator. *Chaos Soliton Fract.* **2017**, *104*, 350–362. [CrossRef]
18. Sieber, M.; Malchow, H.; Hilker, F.M. Disease-induced modification of prey competition in eco-epidemiological models. *Ecol. Complex.* **2014**, *18*, 74–82. [CrossRef]
19. Sahoo, B. Role of additional food in eco-epidemiological system with disease in the prey. *Appl. Math. Comput.* **2015**, *259*, 61–79. [CrossRef]
20. Saifuddin, M.; Biswas, S.; Samanta, S.; Sarkar, S.; Chattopadhyay, J. Complex dynamics of an eco-epidemiological model with different competition coefficients and weak Allee in the predator. *Chaos Soliton Fract.* **2016**, *91*, 270–285. [CrossRef]
21. Mondal, S.; Lahiri, A.; Bairagi, N. Analysis of a fractional order eco-epidemiological model with prey infection and type 2 functional response. *Math. Methods Appl. Sci.* **2017**, *40*, 6776–6789. [CrossRef]

22. Mondal, A.; Pal, A.K.; Samanta, G.P. On the dynamics of evolutionary Leslie-Gower predator-prey eco-epidemiological model with disease in predator. *Ecol. Genet. Genom.* **2019**, *10*, 100034. [CrossRef]
23. Panigoro, H.S.; Suryanto, A.; Kusumawinahyu, W.M.; Darti, I. Dynamics of a fractional-order predator-prey model with infectious diseases in prey. *Commun. Biomath. Sci.* **2019**, *2*, 105–117. [CrossRef]
24. Wei, C.; Chen, L. Global dynamics behaviors of viral infection model for pest management. *Discrete. Dyn. Nat. Soc.* **2009**, *2009*, 1–16. [CrossRef]
25. Fu, J.; Wang, Y. The Mathematical study of pest management strategy. *Discrete. Dyn. Nat. Soc.* **2012**, *2012*, 1–19. [CrossRef]
26. Sun, K.; Zhang, T.; Tian, Y. Theoretical study and control optimization of an integrated pest management predator–prey model with power growth rate. *Math. Biosci.* **2016**, *279*, 13–26. [CrossRef]
27. Mandal, D.S.; Samanta, S.; Alzahrani, A.K.; Chattopadhyay, J. Study of a predator-prey model with pest management perspective. *J. Biol. Syst.* **2019**, *27*, 309–336. [CrossRef]
28. Suryanto, A.; Darti, I. Dynamics of Leslie-Gower pest-predator model with disease in pest including pest-harvesting and optimal implementation of pesticide. *Int. J. Math. Math. Sci.* **2019**, *2019*, 5079171. [CrossRef]
29. Connole, M.D.; Yamaguchi, H.; Elad, D.; Hasegawa, A.; Segal, E.; Torres-Rodriguez, J.M. Natural pathogens of laboratory animals and their effects on research. *Med. Mycol.* **2000**, *38*, 59–65. [CrossRef]
30. Kan, I.; Motro, Y.; Horvitz, N.; Kimhi, A.; Leshem, Y.; Yom-Tov, Y.; Nathan, R. Agricultural rodent control using barnowls: Is it profitable. *Am. J. Agric. Econ.* **2014**, *96*, 733–752. [CrossRef]
31. Kross, S.M.; Bourbour, R.P.; Martinico, B.L. Agricultural land use, barn owl diet, and vertebrate pest control implications. *Agric. Ecosyst. Environ.* **2016**, *223*, 167–174. [CrossRef]
32. Wendt, C.A.; Johnson, M.D. Agriculture, Ecosystems and Environment Multi-scale analysis of barn owl nest box selection on Napa Valley vineyards. *Agric. Ecosyst. Environ.* **2017**, *247*, 75–83. [CrossRef]
33. Solter, L.; Hajek, A.; Lacey, L. Exploration for Entomopathogens. In *Microbial Control of Insect and Mite Pests*; Lacey, L.A., Ed.; Academic Press: San Diego, CA, USA, 2017; pp. 13–23. [CrossRef]
34. Wang, J.; Qu, X. Qualitative analysis for a ratio-dependent predator-prey model with disease and diffusion. *Appl. Math. Comput.* **2011**, *217*, 9933–9947. [CrossRef]
35. Suryanto, A. Dynamics of an eco-epidemiological model with saturated incidence rate. *AIP Conf. Proc.* **2017**, *1825*, 020021. [CrossRef]
36. Upadhyay, R.K.; Roy, P. Spread of a Disease and its effect on population dynamics in an eco-epidemiological system. *Comm. Nonlinear. Sci. Numer. Simulat.* **2014**, *19*, 4170–4184. [CrossRef]
37. Nugraheni, K.; Trisilowati, T.; Suryanto, A. Dynamics of a fractional order eco-epidemiological model. *J. Trop. Life Sci.* **2017**, *7*, 243–250. [CrossRef]
38. Rosenzweig, M.L.; MacArthur, R.H. Graphical representation and stability conditions of predator–prey interactions. *Am. Nat.* **1963**, *97*, 209–223. [CrossRef]
39. Panja, P. Dynamics of a fractional order predator-prey model with intraguild predation. *Int. J. Model. Simul.* **2019**, *39*, 256–268. [CrossRef]
40. Morales-Delgado, V.F.; Gómez-Aguilar, J.F.; Saad, K.; Escobar Jiménez, R.F. Application of the Caputo-Fabrizio and Atangana-Baleanu fractional derivatives to mathematical model of cancer chemotherapy effect. *Math. Meth. Appl. Sci.* **2019**, *42*, 1167–1193. [CrossRef]
41. El-Saka, H.A.; Lee, S.; Jang, B. Dynamic analysis of fractional-order predator–prey biological economic system with Holling type II functional response. *Nonlinear Dyn.* **2019**, *96*, 407–416. [CrossRef]
42. Li, H.L.; Zhang, L.; Hu, C.; Jiang, Y.L.; Teng, Z. Dynamical analysis of a fractional-order predator-prey model incorporating a prey refuge. *J. Appl. Math. Comput.* **2017**, *54*, 435–449. [CrossRef]
43. Supajaidee, N.; Moonchai, S. Stability analysis of a fractional-order two-species facultative mutualism model with harvesting. *Adv. Differ. Equ.* **2017**, *2017*, 372. [CrossRef]
44. Shaikh, A.; Tassaddiq, A.; Nisar, K.S.; Baleanu, D. Analysis of differential equations involving Caputo–Fabrizio fractional operator and its applications to reaction–diffusion equations. *Adv. Differ. Equ.* **2019**, *2019*, 178. [CrossRef]
45. Jajarmi, A.; Yusuf, A.; Baleanu, D.; Inc, M. A new fractional HRSV model and its optimal control: A non-singular operator approach. *Phys. A* **2020**, *547*, 123860. [CrossRef]
46. Baleanu, D.; Jajarmi, A.; Mohammadi, H.; Rezapour, S. A new study on the mathematical modelling of human liver with Caputo–Fabrizio fractional derivative. *Chaos Soliton Fract.* **2020**, *134*, 109705. [CrossRef]
47. Panigoro, H.S.; Suryanto, A.; Kusumawinahyu, W.M.; Darti, I. A Rosenzweig–MacArthur model with continuous threshold harvesting in predator involving fractional derivatives with power law and Mittag–Leffler kernel. *Axioms* **2020**, *9*, 122. [CrossRef]
48. Panigoro, H.S.; Suryanto, A.; Kusumawinahyu, W.M.; Darti, I. Continuous threshold harvesting in a gause-type predator-prey model with fractional-order. *AIP Conf. Proc.* **2020**, *2264*, 040001. [CrossRef]
49. Suryanto, A.; Darti, I.; Anam, S. Stability analysis of a fractional order modified Leslie-Gower model with additive Allee effect. *Int. J. Math. Math. Sci.* **2017**, *2017*, 1–9. [CrossRef]
50. Xie, Y.; Lu, J.; Wang, Z. Stability analysis of a fractional-order diffused prey–predator model with prey refuges. *Phys. A* **2019**, *526*, 120773. [CrossRef]

51. Shah, S.A.A.; Khan, M.A.; Farooq, M.; Ullah, S.; Alzahrani, E.O. A fractional order model for Hepatitis B virus with treatment via Atangana–Baleanu derivative. *Phys. A* **2020**, *538*, 122636. [CrossRef]
52. Podlubny, I. *Fractional Differential Equations: An Introduction to Fractional Derivatives, Fractional Differential Equations, to Methods of Their Solution and Some of Their Applications*; Academic Press: San Diego, CA, USA, 1999.
53. Caputo, M. Linear models of dissipation whose Q is almost frequency independent–II. *Geophys. J. Int.* **1967**, *13*, 529–539. [CrossRef]
54. Diethelm, K. *The Analysis of Fractional Differential Equations: An Application-Oriented Exposition Using Differential Operators of Caputo Type*; Springer: Braunschweig, Germany, 2010. [CrossRef]
55. Petras, I. *Fractional-Order Nonlinear Systems: Modeling, Analysis and Simulation*; Springer: Beijing, China, 2011.
56. Atangana, A.; Koca, I. Chaos in a simple nonlinear system with Atangana–Baleanu derivatives with fractional order. *Chaos Soliton Fract.* **2016**, *89*, 447–454. [CrossRef]
57. Yadav, S.; Pandey, R.K.; Shukla, A.K. Numerical approximations of Atangana–Baleanu Caputo derivative and its application. *Chaos Soliton Fract.* **2019**, *118*, 58–64. [CrossRef]
58. Bonyah, E.; Atangana, A.; Elsadany, A.A. A fractional model for predator-prey with omnivore. *Chaos* **2019**, *29*, 013136. [CrossRef] [PubMed]
59. Tajadodi, H. A Numerical approach of fractional advection-diffusion equation with Atangana–Baleanu derivative. *Chaos Soliton Fract.* **2020**, *130*, 109527. [CrossRef]
60. Caputo, M.; Fabrizio, M. A new definition of fractional derivative without singular kernel. *Progr. Fract. Differ. Appl.* **2015**, *1*, 73–85. [CrossRef]
61. Li, H.; Cheng, J.; Li, H.B.; Zhong, S.M. Stability analysis of a fractional-order linear system described by the Caputo-Fabrizio derivative. *Mathematics* **2019**, *7*, 200. [CrossRef]
62. Khan, S.A.; Shah, K.; Zaman, G.; Jarad, F. Existence theory and numerical solutions to smoking model under Caputo–Fabrizio fractional derivative. *Chaos* **2019**, *29*, 013128. [CrossRef]
63. Atangana, A.; Khan, M.A.; Fatmawati. Modeling and analysis of competition model of bank data with fractal-fractional Caputo-Fabrizio operator. *Alex. Eng. J.* **2020**, *59*, 1985–1998. [CrossRef]
64. Atangana, A.; Baleanu, D. New fractional derivatives with nonlocal and non-singular kernel: Theory and application to heat transfer model. *Therm. Sci.* **2016**, *20*, 763–769. [CrossRef]
65. Fatmawati; Khan, M.A.; Azizah, M.; Windarto; Ullah, S. A fractional model for the dynamics of competition between commercial and rural banks in Indonesia. *Chaos Soliton Fract.* **2019**, *122*, 32–46. [CrossRef]
66. Diethelm, K. A fractional calculus based model for the simulation of an outbreak of dengue fever. *Nonlinear Dyn.* **2003**, *71*, 613–619. [CrossRef]
67. Odibat, Z.M.; Shawagfeh, N.T. Generalized Taylor's formula. *Appl. Math. Comput.* **2007**, *186*, 286–293. [CrossRef]
68. Matignon, D. Stability results for fractional differential equations with applications to control processing. *Comput. Eng. Sys. appl.* **1996**, *2*, 963–968.
69. Li, Y.; Chen, Y.; Podlubny, I. Stability of fractional-order nonlinear dynamic systems: Lyapunov direct method and generalized Mittag–Leffler stability. *Comput. Math. Appl.* **2010**, *59*, 1810–1821. [CrossRef]
70. Vargas-De-León, C. Volterra-type Lyapunov functions for fractional-order epidemic systems. *Comm. Nonlinear Sci. Numer. Simulat.* **2015**, *24*, 75–85. [CrossRef]
71. Huo, J.; Zhao, H.; Zhu, L. The effect of vaccines on backward bifurcation in a fractional order HIV model. *Nonlinear Anal. Real World Appl.* **2015**, *26*, 289–305. [CrossRef]
72. Ahmed, E.; El-Sayed, A.; El-Saka, H.A. On some Routh–Hurwitz conditions for fractional order differential equations and their applications in Lorenz, Rössler, Chua and Chen systems. *Phys. Lett. A* **2006**, *358*, 1–4. [CrossRef]
73. Baisad, K.; Moonchai, S. Analysis of stability and Hopf bifurcation in a fractional Gauss-type predator–prey model with Allee effect and Holling type-III functional response. *Adv. Differ. Equ.* **2018**, *2018*, 82. [CrossRef]
74. Deshpande, A.S.; Daftardar-Gejji, V.; Sukale, Y.V. On Hopf bifurcation in fractional dynamical systems. *Chaos Soliton Fract.* **2017**, *98*, 189–198. [CrossRef]
75. Kuznetsov, Y.A. *Elements of Applied Bifurcation Theory*, 3rd ed.; Springer: New York, NY, USA, 2004.
76. Li, X.; Wu, R. Hopf bifurcation analysis of a new commensurate fractional-order hyperchaotic system. *Nonlinear Dyn.* **2014**, *78*, 279–288. [CrossRef]
77. Moustafa, M.; Mohd, M.H.; Ismail, A.I.; Abdullah, F.A. Stage structure and refuge effects in the dynamical analysis of a fractional order Rosenzweig-MacArthur prey-predator model. *Prog. Fract. Differ. Appl.* **2019**, *5*, 49–64. [CrossRef]
78. Abdelouahab, M.S.; Hamri, N.E.; Wang, J. Hopf bifurcation and chaos in fractional-order modified hybrid optical system. *Nonlinear Dyn.* **2012**, *69*, 275–284. [CrossRef]
79. Tavazoei, M.S.; Haeri, M. A proof for non existence of periodic solutions in time invariant fractional order systems. *Automatica* **2009**, *45*, 1886–1890. [CrossRef]
80. Moustafa, M.; Mohd, M.H.; Ismail, A.I.; Abdullah, F.A. Dynamical analysis of a fractional-order eco-epidemiological model with disease in prey population. *Adv. Differ. Equ.* **2020**, *2020*, 48. [CrossRef]

81. Diethelm, K.; Ford, N.J.; Freed, A.D. A Predictor-corrector approach for the numerical solution of fractional differential equations. *Nonlinear Dyn.* **2002**, *29*, 3–22. [CrossRef]
82. Baleanu, D.; Jajarmi, A.; Hajipour, M. On the nonlinear dynamical systems within the generalized fractional derivatives with Mittag–Leffler kernel. *Nonlinear Dyn.* **2018**, *94*, 397–414. [CrossRef]

Article

On Systems of Active Particles Perturbed by Symmetric Bounded Noises: A Multiscale Kinetic Approach

Bruno Felice Filippo Flora [1], Armando Ciancio [1] and Alberto d'Onofrio [2,3,4,*]

[1] Department of Biomedical and Dental Sciences and Morphofunctional Imaging (BIOMORF), University of Messina (Italy), via Consolare Valeria c/o A.O.U. Policlinico 'G.Martino', 98126 Messina, Italy; bruno.flora@libero.it (B.F.F.F.); aciancio@unime.it (A.C.)
[2] Formerly at International Prevention Research Institute, 95 Cours Lafayette, 69006 Lyon, France
[3] Department of Mathematics and Statistics, Strathclyde University, Glasgow G4 0LN, Scotland, UK
[4] 37 Quai Gailleton, 69002 Lyon, France
* Correspondence: adonofrio1967@gmail.com

Citation: Flora, B.F.F.; Ciancio, A.; d'Onofrio, A. On Systems of Active Particles Perturbed by Symmetric Bounded Noises: A Multiscale Kinetic Approach. *Symmetry* **2021**, *13*, 1604. https://doi.org/10.3390/sym13091604

Academic Editors: Carmela Sinisgalli and Federico Papa

Received: 26 July 2021
Accepted: 20 August 2021
Published: 1 September 2021

Publisher's Note: MDPI stays neutral with regard to jurisdictional claims in published maps and institutional affiliations.

Copyright: © 2021 by the authors. Licensee MDPI, Basel, Switzerland. This article is an open access article distributed under the terms and conditions of the Creative Commons Attribution (CC BY) license (https://creativecommons.org/licenses/by/4.0/).

Abstract: We consider an ensemble of active particles, i.e., of agents endowed by internal variables $u(t)$. Namely, we assume that the nonlinear dynamics of u is perturbed by realistic bounded symmetric stochastic perturbations acting nonlinearly or linearly. In the absence of birth, death and interactions of the agents (BDIA) the system evolution is ruled by a multidimensional Hypo-Elliptical Fokker–Plank Equation (HEFPE). In presence of nonlocal BDIA, the resulting family of models is thus a Partial Integro-differential Equation with hypo-elliptical terms. In the numerical simulations we focus on a simple case where the unperturbed dynamics of the agents is of logistic type and the bounded perturbations are of the Doering–Cai–Lin noise or the Arctan bounded noise. We then find the evolution and the steady state of the HEFPE. The steady state density is, in some cases, multimodal due to noise-induced transitions. Then we assume the steady state density as the initial condition for the full system evolution. Namely we modeled the vital dynamics of the agents as logistic nonlocal, as it depends on the whole size of the population. Our simulations suggest that both the steady states density and the total population size strongly depends on the type of bounded noise. Phenomena as transitions to bimodality and to asymmetry also occur.

Keywords: bounded noises; kinetic theory; active particles; statistical mechanics; population dynamics; Fokker–Planck equation; mathematical oncology; ecology; noise induced transitions

1. Introduction

Two of the more active fields of application of statistical physics to biology are theoretical population dynamics, mathematical epidemiology (including behavioral aspects [1,2]), sociophysics [3–5] and mathematical oncology [6,7]. In these fields, the importance of multiscale phenomena has been recognized in the last twenty years. Many important approaches are based on individual based models [8–10]. Another very important approach is based on classical and recent development of nonlinear statistical physics: the theory of active particles [11–20]. This is a multiscale mean field theory that allows us to link the dynamics of internal variables, named activity, to the macroscale of the interactions between large sets of agents [12–17]. Bellomo and coworkers stressed in particular two concepts are of the utmost relevance in applying theory of active particles to living matter: (i) new agents that are generated can have an activity different than the one of their parent agent; (ii) non destructive interactions between two agents of the same or of different species (e.g., tumor cells and immune system effectors) can induce a change of activity level in both agents. Among the most recent developments of the Bellomo theories we cite: (i) the theory of thermostatted active particles, which allows to impose physically backgrounded constraints to the activity of individuals, developed by Bianca and Menale [21–23]; (ii) the stochastic evolutionary theory of tumor adaptation developed by Clairambault, Delitala,

Lorenzi and coworkers [24–29]. Finally, it is worth mentioning the mathematical modeling of Darwinian species emergence by Volpert and colleagues that represent the evolution of active particles uniquely subject to a Brownian force and logistic non-local growth [30–32].

In the framework of Bellomo's theories, Firmani, Preziosi and Guerri (FPG) [33] (see also [34]) first modeled in a detailed way how to pass from the deterministic dynamics of the activity variable of single individual agent to the dynamics of the densities of interacting populations. In the FPG model the dynamics of the agent's activity was assumed to be deterministic. This led the authors to define a generalization of the Liouville's equation to model the temporal evolution of the densities (w.r.t. the agents' activities) of the interacting populations.

However important this approach may be, it constitutes an approximation of the real world behavior. Indeed, on the one hand it has been stressed that fundamental biological phenomena arise from the microscale presence of internal additive noise, i.e., infinitesimal spontaneous stochastic fluctuations of the activity [24–29]. In the case where the activity represents phenotypic defining variables, this represents the spontaneous phenotypic changes [24–29]. On the other hand, individual agent activities are perturbed by many unknown internal and external interaction, which can only be statistically known.

Modeling such stochastic extrinsic perturbations is less straightforward than one could think. Namely, one could be tempted to extend a deterministic model by including multiplicative Gaussian white or colored perturbations. Although allowing nice analytical or semi-analytical inferences, this approach can lead to artifacts, most often hidden. A major example is the following [35,36] modeling in the above-mentioned way the perturbations affecting an anti-tumor cytotoxic therapy implies that for a substantial part of time therapy adds tumor cells instead of killing them. A second 'hidden' but equally important artifact is also induced: an excessive instantaneous killing of tumor cells. Finally, Gaussian White noise perturbations cannot be applied to parameters on which a system depends nonlinearly, and often even Gaussian colored perturbation cannot.

These and other critical issues imply that bounded stochastic processes ought to be used in most case in biophysics: an increasingly important approach [36]. In last twenty years about, a large body of scientific work has been devoted to the application of bounded stochastic processes in statistical physics and to biophysics. Some key application can be listed: noise-induced transitions [37], stochastic and parametric resonance [38], bifurcation theory [39], fractional and nonlinear mechanics [40–42], mathematical oncology [43,44], cell biology [45], ecology and environment [46,47] and neurosciences [48].

As a consequence, the above mentioned interplays can be modeled by assuming that the dynamics is affected by bounded stochastic perturbations. This is our key assumption here, which will lead us to define a family of partial integro-differential models that extends hypo-elliptic nonlinear Fokker–Planck equation. Similar but not identical since, duty to the presence of nontrivial non–local birth and death terms, in our case the integral of the population density is the time-varying population size, and not the unity, as in the nonlinear FP equation. The above-mentioned hypoellipticity is a key point since it is implied from the assumption that the perturbations are symmetric bounded stochastic processes.

This work is organized in three parts. In the first part, we summarize and slightly extend the FPG model in Section 2 and we extend it to take into the account stochastic white noise perturbations acting on the dynamic of all agents in Section 3. The second part of the work starts in Section 4, where we stress pitfalls that can occur by an acritical use of Gaussian white or colored noises. In the following Section 5 we derive the main family of models of this work, which models the dynamics of ensembles of active particles perturbed by realistic stochastic processes of bounded nature, and in Section 6 we briefly stress the possible occurrence, in specific models, of phase transitions. Finally, in Section 7 we formulate a specific model (belonging to the general family of models defined in Section 5) where the dynamics of the population of agents are given by a nonlocal generalized logistic model. The third part of this work is devoted to numerical simulations. First (Section 8) we summarize two 'recipes' to define and simulate three types of bounded stochastic processes. Then in Section 9 we briefly model the perturbations at level of each single agent as a logistic dynamics and in Section 10 we parameterize the various adopted functions. In Section 11, we numerically infer the steady state probability distribution of the FPE that described the collective dynamics of particles in absence of generation, death and interplay: this allows us to stress some interesting noise induced transitions phenomena. The steady state solution of the FPE is used in the following Section 12 as initial value of the full logistic non–local dynamics.

At the best of our knowledge, this work has some novelties of potential interest in statistical physics: it is the first kinetic model where the impact of bounded stochastic processes is included (resulting in hypo-ellictic integro-differential equations) and it is investigated its interplay with logistic non-local birth–death dynamics. Moreover, noise induced transition to bimodality and asymmetry are also observed.

2. A Slight Generalization of the FPG Model

In this section, we briefly summarize and slightly extend the FPG model [33,34] in case of a single population, and we frame it in the classical statistical mechanics. To start, let us suppose that the activity of an idealized agent is of the type

$$u' = f(u), \tag{1}$$

where the state variable is called *activity* of the agent. In the general case u is vectorial but here for the sake of the notation simplicity we will suppose it scalar. Just to give some examples of activities we can mention: the level of proteins defining the degree of immunogenicity and 'abnormality' of a tumor cell [49], the level of activation for an immune system effector [49], the 'level of effectiveness in performing the job that a species is expected to do' in a multi species environment [50], the pair (opinion, connectivity) in models of opinion formation in social networks [51], the viral load for a subject during an epidemics [20]. Of course, a very important class of activities is the couple position–velocity (x, v) [52].

We denote by

$$\rho(t, u)$$

the density of agents w.r.t. the time and to the activity variable u.

Let us now preliminary consider the very idealized case where the agents do not interplay and do not reproduce and die. In such a case, the dynamics of the ensemble of agent is nothing else than the dynamics of the distribution of an ensemble of particles in their phase space [53]. Thus, given the initial distribution of agents w.r.t. the activity u

$$\rho(0, u) = \rho_0(u),$$

the evolution for $t > 0$ of the ensemble of agents is given by the Liouville's Equation [53]:

$$\partial_t \rho + \partial_u (f(u)\rho) = 0. \tag{2}$$

The physical interpretation of the term $f(u)\rho$ is straightforward: since $f(u)$ is the velocity in the activity state space, then $J = f(u)\rho$ is the current of active particles in that space, and Equation (2) is nothing else than the conservation law:

$$\partial_t \rho + Div(J) = 0.$$

Note that at variance to [33,34], where the FPG model is derived by a conservation law approach, here we focused on a probabilistic approach in view of the stochastic extension of next sections. Indeed, the Liouville equation is a particular case of the Fokker–Planck Equation [53].

The inclusion of the proliferation, death and inter-agents interaction gives the full model

$$\partial_t \rho + \partial_u(f(u)\rho) = \mathcal{H}(\rho(.); N(.)), \qquad (3)$$

where $\mathcal{H}(\rho(.); N(.))$ is an integro-differential nonlinear operator that models: (i) agents' birth, interaction and death; (ii) how the generation and interaction of agents modify their activity. For example, if the mother agent before asexual reproduction has an activity level $\hat{u}$ then its m daughter agents, let us call them $D_1, D_2, \ldots, D_m$, may have different activity levels $\hat{u}_{D_1} \neq \hat{u}, \ldots, \hat{u}_{D_m} \neq \hat{u}$. We will later specify some noteworthy cases.

An important difference between the FPG model and the family of models (3) is that, at variance with the FPG model, the generation and destruction of agents here can be independent of agents interaction, as in the above example of asexual reproduction of agents.

Finally, we mention that the total size of the cellular population is given by the following integral:

$$N(t) = \int_{D_u} \rho(t, u) du. \qquad (4)$$

As far as the domain of the activity we will consider (as in [33]) a finite interval, for example

$$D_u = [0, u_M].$$

3. Impact of the Stochastic Fluctuations of the Activity

In this section, we introduce the study of the impact at the population scale of the stochastic perturbations acting on the dynamics of the activity u of each single agents. This is an important matter since in many complex systems composed by ensemble of individuals there can be the onset of emergent phenomena [54–58].

Due to unavoidable interactions with the external world and with the myriad of other internal processes (e.g., for cells: intra-cellular biomolecular networks) a far more realistic model of the evolution of the activity of the single agent is apparently

$$u' = f(u) + g(u)\xi(t), \qquad (5)$$

where $\xi(t)$ is a white noise and the stochastic differential equation is in the Ito interpretation (but one could consider the Stratonovich interpretation). A more realistic model will be considered in the next section.

In the absence of generation, death and of inter–agents interplay yields the dynamics of $\rho(t, u)$ is given by the following linear Fokker–Planck equation:

$$\partial_t \rho + \partial_u(f(u)\rho) = \partial_{uu}\left(\frac{g^2(u)}{2}\rho\right). \qquad (6)$$

Note that at variance with the classical Fokker–Planck equation here it is

$$\int_{D_u} \rho(t, u) du \neq 1$$

since it holds that

$$N(t) = \int_{D_u} \rho(t, u) du = N_0,$$

where $N_0 = N(0)$ is the initial size of the population (unchanged due to a assumption of no modification of the number of agents). Indeed, the total size of the population remains constant because of the lack of birth and of death events.

In presence of birth and death events and of inter-agents interactions, the Fokker–Planck-like Equation (2) becomes as follows:

$$\partial_t \rho + \partial_u(f(u)\rho) = \partial_{uu}\left(\frac{g^2(u)}{2}\rho\right) + \mathcal{H}(\rho(.); N(.)), \quad (7)$$

where $\mathcal{H}$ is an operator acting on the (present and past) agents' distribution $\rho(.)$ and that can depend on the (present and past) population size $N(t)$.

Note that specific models where it holds that

$$g(u) = \text{Constant},$$

i.e., the activity u has spontaneous stochastic fluctuations; have been investigated by Clairambault, Delitala, and Lorenzi and coworkers in a series of works (e.g., [24–29]) where the activity u represent phenotype variables and thus the additive noise represent spontaneous infinitesimal changes of phenotype.

4. Realistic Bounded Stochastic Perturbations of Agent's Activity

Let us more closely analyze from the biological viewpoint the microscopic model (5). Namely, consider a model of the activity linearly depending on a positive parameter q:

$$u' = a(u) + qb(u).$$

The stochastic fluctuations of the parameter q could be modeled as a white noise perturbations

$$u' = a(u) + (q + q\xi(t))b(u), \quad (8)$$

where $\xi(t)$ is a white noise, characterized by $\mathcal{E}[\xi(t)]$ and $\mathcal{E}[\xi(t)\xi(t+\tau)] = \delta(\tau)$.

Thus, according to our previous the notation, corresponds to $f(u) = a(u) + qb(u)$ and $g(u) = qb(u)$. The fact is that writing in the Ito form [59]

$$du = a(u)dt + (qdt + qdB)b(u), \quad (9)$$

where $B(t)$ is a Brownian stochastic process [59], it immediately follow that in the realization

$$\text{Prob}(qdt + qdB < 0) > 0$$

(note that since dB scales as $dt^{0.5}$ it follow that the occurrence of the event $qdt + qdB < 0$ is quite frequent). In other words, the unbounded nature of the Gauss distribution renders negative the perturbed parameter q. Moreover, there is a second more subtle problem: the unbounded Gauss perturbation can also make the perturbed parameter q excessively large.

Both these two problems persists also if one uses a colored Gaussian perturbation instead of a Gauss white noise, or other non Gaussian unbounded perturbations.

A third and equally important problem is that if one has a general model nonlinearly depending on a parameter q

$$u' = c(u; q),$$

then one cannot use white noise perturbations, and often one cannot use colored unbounded perturbations.

The solution is to use bounded stochastic perturbations [36]: $z(t)$ such that

$$z(t)q + q > 0$$

and

$$z(t)q + q \leq Q_{max} < \infty.$$

In turn $z(t)$ can depend on a (bounded or unbounded) noise y (which we will call *support noise*) by means of the following *link function*:

$$z(t) = \zeta(y(t)).$$

If y is unbounded, then $\zeta(y)$ is a bounded function, otherwise if y is itself bounded we assume $\zeta(y) = y$.

The problem of modeling the activity of a single agents becomes slightly more complex than in the case of white noise perturbations since at level of the individual agent one has two stochastic equations: the equation of the activity perturbed by the bounded noise y:

$$u' = f(u,y), \tag{10}$$

where no white noise appears, and a model for the noise

$$y' = k(y) + n(y)\eta(t), \tag{11}$$

which is independent of u, and where $\eta(t)$ is a white noise.

5. Macro-Scale Implication of the Boundedness of the Perturbations

The use of more realistic white noise perturbations implies that the resulting population-level model for the evolution of the density is quite more complex than in the case of Gaussian perturbations.

Indeed, in absence of generation, death and interplay we obtain a bidimensional Fokker–Planck equation because of the two stochastic state variables—(u, y)—which reads as follows:

$$\partial_t \rho + \partial_u(f(u,y)\rho) + \partial_y(k(y)\rho) = \partial_{yy}\left(\frac{n^2(y)}{2}\rho\right). \tag{12}$$

Note that the above equation is a degenerate diffusion-transport PDE since the u variable does not appear in the diffusion equation. The reason is that the microscopic equation for u does not contain a white noise term.

Finally, taking into the account the vital dynamics of the agents and their interactions yields the following model:

$$\partial_t \rho + \partial_u(f(u,y)\rho) + \partial_y(k(y)\rho) = \partial_{yy}\left(\frac{n^2(y)}{2}\rho\right) + \mathcal{H}(\rho(.); N(.)). \tag{13}$$

Remark 1. *Although the full density $\rho(t, u, y)$ is of interest, what in the practice really matters is the density $\rho^{eff}(t, u)$ unconditional to y, which is given by the following integral:*

$$\rho^{eff}(t, u) = \int_{-B}^{B} \rho(t, u, y)dy. \tag{14}$$

6. Possibility of First and Second-Order Phase Transitions

The presence of $N(t)$ in the above-defined models has deep implications. Indeed, let us consider the search for steady state concentrations $\varrho_{ss}(u)$ (uniquely for the sake of the notation simplicity here we consider Gaussian perturbations):

$$\partial_u(f(u)\varrho_{ss}(u)) = \partial_{uu}\left(\frac{g^2(u)}{2}\varrho_{ss}(u)\right) + \mathcal{H}(\varrho_{ss}(.); N_{ss}). \tag{15}$$

Let us treat N_{ss} as it *were* a parameter, and suppose now that we can find an analytical solution that will be denoted as follows:

$$\varrho_{ss}(u, N_{ss}; p),$$

where p denotes other parameters of the system.

This solution will have to verify the following self-consistency equation

$$N_{ss} = \int_{D_u} \varrho_{ss}(u, N_{ss}, p) du. \tag{16}$$

The above equation could have one or more solution, depending also on the values of the parameters p. The case of multiple solutions means that there are multiple steady state solutions. Thus, the dynamics of the system depend on the initial conditions and that by varying the parameter p first and second order phase transitions can be observed, with the switch from a scenario where the system has two (or more) stochastic attractors to a scenario with a unique stochastic attractors, which is the genuine landmark of phase transitions, as stressed by Shiino [60]. This is not surprising since the *exact* self-consistency Equation (16) is similar to the self-consistency equation of the *approximated* mean field Curie–Weiss theory [61,62].

7. A Generalized Logistic Growth of Agents

Up to now, we kept unspecified the functional $\mathcal{H}$, because we wanted to define a general family of models. In view of the simulations, here we consider the death and birth of agents in presence of competition for nutrients and space. As it happens in the reality we assume that the competition is not direct, i.e., two agents do not start a deadly battle for the last glass of water, but indirect. As such, in our specific example there are no interaction terms. This leads to decompose the operator $\mathcal{H}$ in two components, namely a birth component and a death component:

$$\mathcal{H}(\rho(.); N(.)) = \mathcal{B}_0(\rho(.); N(t)) - \mathcal{D}_0(\rho(.); N(t)), \tag{17}$$

where we will call $\mathcal{B}_0$ the generation operator, and $\mathcal{D}_0$ the death operator

$$\partial_t \rho + \partial_u (f(u)\rho) = \partial_{uu}\left(\frac{g^2(u)}{2}\rho\right) + \mathcal{B}_0(\rho(.); N(t)) - \mathcal{D}_0(\rho(.); N(t)); \tag{18}$$

or in case of bounded perturbations:

$$\partial_t \rho + \partial_u (f(u,y)\rho) + \partial_y (k(y)\rho) = \partial_{yy}\left(\frac{n^2(y)}{2}\rho\right) + \mathcal{B}_0(\rho(.); N(t)) - \mathcal{D}_0(\rho(.); N(t)). \tag{19}$$

As far as the death operator is concerned, a reasonable assumption is to set:

$$\mathcal{D}_0(\rho(.); N(t)) = \mu(u, N(t))\rho(t, u, y), \tag{20}$$

i.e., agents with activity u dies with a death rate μ that may depend on u and that, due to competition effects, depend on $N(t)$. since the dependence on $N(t)$ is due to competition effects, it yields that

$$\partial_N \mu(u, N) > 0.$$

For the sake of the simplicity, henceforward, we will only consider the following simple form for the death rate :

$$\mu(u, N(t)) = \mu_0(u) + \mu_1(u) N^a(t), \tag{21}$$

where $a > 0$.

The operator $\mathcal{B}_0$ is less straightforward. First we suppose that agents around a value w of the activity have a reproduction rate $\alpha(w, N(t)) > 0$ that depends on the activity w and that, due to the competition with other agents (causing lack of nutrients and of space), the rate is a decreasing function of the population size:

$$\partial_N \alpha(w, N) < 0.$$

The generated agents will have an activity u with a given probability density $\vartheta(u,w)$. More specifically, we will assume that $\vartheta(u,w)$ will has either mode or mean at w.
As far as the transition probability $\vartheta(u,w)$ is concerned, in case of a finite range of activities, $D_u = [0, u_M]$, one can employ a beta distribution

$$\vartheta(u,w) = \frac{1}{u_M B(p,q)} \left(\frac{u}{u_M}\right)^{p-1} \left(1 - \frac{u}{u_M}\right)^{q-1}. \tag{22}$$

As far as the relationship between the value of the activities of mother and daughter agents, a natural choice could be the following:

(i) The average of the activity u of a daughter agent is equal to the activity w of the mother agent, which implies:

$$p = \left(\frac{w}{u_M - w}\right) q; \tag{23}$$

(ii) The mode of the activity u of a daughter agent is equal to the activity w of the mother agent, which implies:

$$p - 1 = \left(\frac{w}{u_M - w}\right)(q - 1). \tag{24}$$

Finally, a particular but important case is the case where the daughter agents have the same activity of the mother agent:

$$\vartheta(u,w) = \delta_{Dirac}(u - w).$$

Based on the above premises, we define:

$$\mathcal{B}_0(\rho(.); N(t)) = \int_{D_u} \vartheta(u,w)\alpha(w, N(t))\rho(t,w,y)dw. \tag{25}$$

Formula (25) is particularly suited to the represent cell proliferation, which is characterized by an unequal division of metabolic constituents to daughter cells [63–66]. As far as the specific form of $\alpha(w, N(t))$ are concerned, one can consider

$$\alpha(w, N) = \left(\alpha_0(w) - \alpha_1(w)N^b(t)\right)_+, \tag{26}$$

or

$$\alpha(w, N) = \frac{\alpha_0(w)}{1 + \alpha_1(w)N^b(t)}. \tag{27}$$

8. 'Recipes' to Model Bounded Noises

In this section, we shortly summarize two of the main methodologies used in the literature to generate bounded stochastic processes [36,67].

The first and most easy recipe to model a bounded stochastic perturbation consists of applying a bounded function, say $\beta(y)$, to an colored unbounded noise, for example the Orenstein–Uhlenbeck noise. This means

$$k(y) = -\frac{1}{\tau}y;$$

$$n(y) = \frac{\sqrt{2\sigma}}{\sqrt{\tau}};$$

$$f(u,y) = h(u, \zeta(y)). \tag{28}$$

Namely here we use the arctan noise, introduced in [67,68], in which:

$$\zeta(y) = B\frac{2}{\pi}Arctan\left(\frac{y}{Q}\right). \quad (29)$$

The rationale underlying the arctan noise defined by (29) is very simple: (i) the *Arctan* function is bounded by the values $M = \pm\pi/2$; (ii) thus $(2/\pi)Arctan$ is bounded by ± 1 and, as a consequence, $(2/\pi)Arctan$ is bounded by $\pm B$; (iii) the parameter Q 'tunes' the bounded noise: if $Q << \sigma$ then (roughly speaking) $\zeta(y(t))$ assumes mostly the two values $\pm B$, whereas if $Q >> \sigma$ then $\zeta(y(t))$ is mostly proportional to y: $\zeta(y(t)) \approx 2By/(\pi Q)$.

Another and very general family of bounded stochastic processes, introduced in [69], can be obtained by assuming that

$$k(y) = -\frac{1}{\tau}y,$$

and imposing the condition

$$n(\pm 1) = 0. \quad (30)$$

Condition (30) implies that

$$y'|_{y=1} < 0 \text{ AND } y'|_{y=-1} > 0,$$

which in turn yields that if $y(0) \in [-1,1]$ then it $y(t)$ is bounded

$$y(t) \in [-1,1].$$

In this case the link function $\zeta(y)$ is simply $\zeta(y) = By$ An instance of this class of noises is the Doering–Cai–Lin noise, introduced in [69,70] and whose properties where studied in [71] where

$$n(y) = \sqrt{\frac{1}{(1+\delta)\tau}(1-y^2)}, \quad (31)$$

where

$$\delta > -1,$$

whose stationary PDF is

$$p(y) = C(1-y^2)^\delta.$$

Note that in in [71] it was shown that if $\delta = -1/2$ then the DCL noise is equal in law to the well-known and widely adopted sine-Wiener noise, introduced in [72], and defined by setting $k(y) = 0$ and $z(y) = Bsin(y)$.

9. Agents Activity Dynamics Perturbed by a Bounded Noise

Until now we left unspecified the dynamics of the activity of the agents. In view of the numerical simulations, we give here a noteworthy example. Namely, we consider the case where the unperturbed dynamics of the activity u is ruled by a simple logistic-like law:

$$u' = \lambda u - u^2.$$

Considering a white noise perturbation of λ yields:

$$u' = (\lambda + \sigma\xi(t))u - u^2;$$

$$u \geq 0.$$

The statistical behavior of the solutions of the white-noise perturbations of the logistic models is well known from other fields of applications of statistical mechanics [55,73]: the model shows a noise-induced transition that depends on the value assumed by the noise strength σ. Namely [55]: (i) for $\sigma^2 > 2\lambda$ then $u(t) \to 0$, i.e., $\rho_{ss}(u) = \delta(u)$; (ii) For $\sigma^2 < 2\lambda$ the stationary density is

$$\rho_{ss}(u) = \frac{C}{u^{2(-1+\lambda/\sigma^2)}} e^{-2u/\sigma^2},$$

which for $\lambda < \sigma^2 < 2\lambda$ has a vertical asymptote at $u = 0$ and it is decreasing; (iii) Finally for $\sigma^2 < \lambda$ the density $\rho_{ss}(u)$ is unimodal and its mode is at

$$u_{Max} = \frac{\lambda - \sigma}{2}.$$

If instead we impose realistic bounded fluctuations of λ, this yields:

$$u' = h(u,z) = (\lambda + z(t))u - u^2;$$

$$u \geq 0,$$

where $z \in [-B, B]$ and

$$B \leq \lambda.$$

This has the noteworthy consequence that if $u(0) > 0$ the dynamics of $u(t)$ remains bounded, and asymptotically:

$$u(t) \in (\lambda - B, \lambda + B).$$

As an example of nonlinear perturbation, we again refer to the logistic model, where this time we consider stochastic fluctuations of the carrying capacity

$$u' = h(u,z) = \lambda u - \frac{u^2}{K(1+z(t))};$$

$$u \geq 0,$$

where the bound of the noise z is smaller than one:

$$B < 1.$$

We will use the above single-agent model with bounded perturbations in the rest of this work.

10. Parametrization

10.1. Initial Condition

We assume that at $t = 0$ all agents are close to equilibrium and the noise distribution is such that y is close to zero

$$p(0, u, y) = A(u)\Phi(y),$$

where

$$A(u) = \frac{1}{\epsilon_1 \sqrt{\lambda}} \left(H(u - \sqrt{\lambda}(1 - \epsilon_1)) - H(u - \sqrt{\lambda}(1 + \epsilon_1)) \right)$$

and

$$\Phi(y) = \frac{1}{\sqrt{2\pi}\sigma_1} Exp\left(\frac{-y^2}{2\sigma_1^2}\right).$$

Values of the parameters used: $\epsilon_1 = 0.05$; $\sigma_1 = 0.0218$; $\lambda = 1$.

10.2. Logistic Activity Dynamics

We assume that, in absence of stochastic perturbations, the agents' activity follows a logistic dynamics. We consider the two bounded perturbations of such logistic dynamics illustrated in the previous section, namely: (i) Stochastic fluctuation of the growth rate λ:

$$u' = (\lambda + \zeta)u - \frac{u^2}{K},$$

which we will call *linear perturbation*, because the noise is in linear position w.r.t. the differential equation for u (ii) Stochastic fluctuations of the carrying capacity K:

$$u' = \lambda u - \frac{u^2}{K(1+\zeta)},$$

which we will call *hyperbolic perturbation*, because the noise z is in nonlinear hyperbolic position w.r.t. the differential equation for u. We adopted the following values for the parameters: $\lambda = 1, K = 1$.

10.3. Birth and Death Rate

As far as the birth and death rate we consider the functionals defined in (26) and in (27) but but with parameters that are independent of w

$$\alpha(N(t)) = \left(\alpha_0 - \alpha_1 N(t)^b\right)_+$$

(where we set $\alpha_0 = 2$, $\alpha_1 = 0.5$, $b = 0.5$) and

$$\alpha(N(t)) = \frac{\alpha_0}{1 + \alpha_1 N(t)^b}$$

(where we set)

As far as the death rate is concerned, we employed the simple rate defined in (21) with

$$\mu_0(u) = 1 - \zeta H(u - 0.9)$$

and

$$\mu_1(u) = 0.5 \mu_0(u),$$

where we set $a = 0.5$, $\zeta \in \{0, 0.3, 0.65, 0.8\}$ (although, as illustrated in next sections, we will mainly use the value $\zeta = 0$). Although this work is mainly a mathematical physics work inspired by biology and we do not have the pretension to be fully realistic, the choice of the parameters values is not covered by the current literature. First, the ratio $\alpha_0/\mu_0 = 2$ represent a system that if the competition for resources was null then it would have a Malthusian growth where the proliferation rate is the double of the death rate. This could be the scenario of a population in rapid growth. As per the parameters b and a, which are both set to 0.5: this reminds of a generalized logistic growth of an unstructured population of size $X(t)$: $X' = R(X)X$ with convex specific growth rate $R(X) = \alpha(X) - \mu(X) = 1 - X^{1/2}$, in agreement with the theoretical analysis of [74].

10.4. Transition Probability

As probability transition we used the beta PDF (Formula (22)), where we set $u_M = 2$ and $q \in \{2, 3\}$. We considered the two cases where (i) the average activity u of the daughter agents is equal to the activity w of the mother agent (Formula (23)); (ii) the mode of the activity u of the daughter agents is equal to the activity w of the mother agent (Formula (24)).

10.5. Parameterization of the Bounded Noises

In all cases we set $B = 0.9$ and $\tau = 1$.

We considered three cases:
- Arctan Noise : $Q = 0.2$, $\sigma = 1$. As far as the domain D_y is concerned, we approximately considered the bounded interval $D_y = [-3.71\sigma, 3.71\sigma]$;
- DCL noise with $\delta = 0.5$;
- DCL noise with $\delta = -0.5$, where the noise is equal in law to the Sine-Wiener noise.

10.6. Boundary Conditions

We imposed zero flow boundary conditions since no agents can flow out.

10.7. Temporal Behaviour

Our simulations have two aims:
- N, i.e., numerically exploring the steady state behavior of the system in absence of birth and death, i.e., assessing the steady state of the hypoelliptic Fokker–Planck equation;
- Assessing the steady state of the full model, assuming in the phase where birth and deaths occur that the system in absence of vital dynamics was at its equilibrium, i.e., at the steady state of the above mentioned Fokker–Planck equation.

This was done splitting he simulation in two phases:
1. For $t \in [0, t^*]$ the vital dynamics is null, where t^* is sufficiently large to safely assume that the solution of Fokker–Planck equation is at its steady state;
2. For $t \in [t^*, t_{Stop}]$ is non null, where t_{Stop} is sufficiently marge to stop the simulation because the system is at the steady state.

By a number of preliminary simulation we set

$$(t^*, t_{Stop}) = (20, 45),$$

but probably smaller values could be adequate as well.

10.8. Numerical Methods

The simulations were obtained by applying the finite element method. We used the scientific software COMSOL ver.5.6, and in particular its Multifrontal Massively Parallel Sparse direct solver (MUMPS) [75–77] with a Newton automatic termination method.

The discretization was performed using triangular elements and the quadratic order Lagrange form function.

We solved the problem by imposing zero flow boundary condition.

In the case Arctan and Sine-Wiener, when the noise perturbs the carrying capacity term of the logistic activity equation, it is necessary to apply 8 boundary layers near the edges $u = 0$ and $u = 2$, with a thickness of 0.1 for the Arctan case, and 0.05 for Sine-Wiener case.

11. Numerical Solution for the Bidimensional Fokker–Planck Hypo-Elliptic Equation

In this section, we consider the numerical study of the time evolution and steady state of the Fokker Planck equation describing the dynamics of the agents populations in absence of birth and death effects. This problem is interesting in itself since at the best of our knowledge there is no work on the numerical investigation of Bidimensional Hypo-elliptic Fokker–Planck (BHFP) equations.

In our simulations we compared the impact of different type and parameters of the bounded noises, showing that to different noises it correspond a very different steady state behavior.

In all simulations the Steady State of the BHFP Equation (SSBHFPE) is reached relatively soon, so that we stropped our simulation at time $t = 20$. For the sake of the simplicity, in this section and in the following ones, we sill use the following acronyms: (i) case where the noise is of the Arctan type with $Q = 0.2$ is denoted as ATAN case; (ii) case where the noise is DCL and $\delta = 0.5$ is denoted as DCLpos case; (iii) case where the noise is DCL and $\delta = -0.5$ is denoted as DCLneg case

First, in Figure 1 we show the SSBHFPE and the associated marginal steady state distribution in the case where the bounded noise acts on the linear term of the logistic equation defining the activity of agents. In the left panels it is shown the ATAN case. The SSBHFPE (Upper left panel) is in this case characterized by two modes that, are asymmetric with respect to the noise-related variable y. This is surprisingly since the adopted stochastic perturbation is *symmetric*. In the lower left panel, we can observe again bimodality. Since the distribution of the model in absence of generation/destruction has a unique deterministic equilibrium at $u = 1$ equal for all agents, this means that (adopting the terminology introduced in [55]) the bounded stochastic symmetric perturbation has induced a noise-induced-transition. In the central panel it is shown the impact of DCLpos noise: the PDF is a curved surface apparently convex everywhere but again it is asymmetric with respect to y despite the symmetric nature of the bounded stochastic perturbations. Finally, the right panels shown the impact of DCLneg noise. The bidimensional PDF is strongly asymmetric and it is characterized by a large number of peaks. The related marginal PDF (see right lower panels) is also multimodal and, roughly speaking, its envelope is reminiscent of the marginal distribution obtained in the case of arctan noise. In other words, also in this case NIT occurred. None of PDFs is symmetric, neither w.r.t. u nor w.r.t. y.

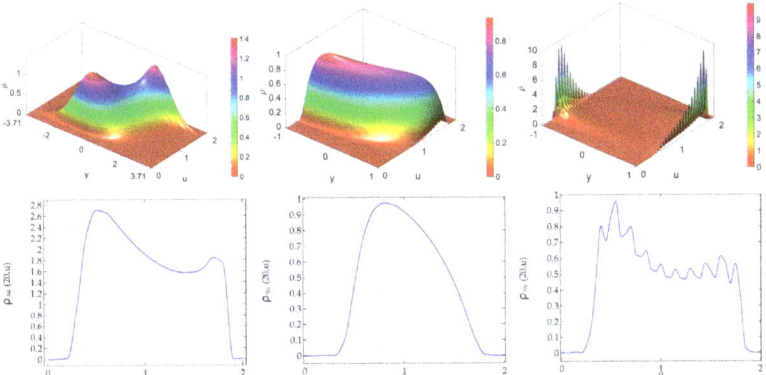

Figure 1. Bidimensional and marginal PDF in absence of births and deaths. Noise perturbing the linear term of the logistic activity equation. (**Upper panel**): steady state PDF of the Bidimensional Hypo-elliptic Fokker–Planck equation. (**Lower panels**): the corresponding marginal distribution. Role of the type of noise. In all panels the noise amplitude is set to $B = 0.9$. (**Left panels**): arctan noise with $Q = 0.2$; (**Central panels**): DCL noise with $\delta = 0.5$; (**Right panels**): DCL noise with $\delta = -0.5$ (equivalent to the Sine-Wiener noise).

Instead, in Figure 2 we show the steady state of the BHFP equation in the case where the bounded noise acts on the carrying capacity of the logistic equation defining the activity of agents. In other words, we study the case where the action of the symmetric bounded noise is nonlinear. In the left panels it is shown the ATAN case. The SSBHFPE is in this case is unimodal with a portion fairly flat. The associated marginal PDF is unimodal and its mode is remarkably smaller than one. In the central panel it is shown the impact of DCLpos noise: the PDF is a curved surface. The associated marginal distribution is unimodal and its mode is at about 0.8. Finally, the right panel shows the impact of DCLneg case: the PDF is strongly asymmetric and characterized by a large number of peaks. The associated marginal PDF has a large number of small peaks, but its envelope is reminiscent of a unimodal PDF, where the mode is about at $u = 0.2$. None of PDFs is symmetric, neither w.r.t. u and y. All the SSBHFPE are strongly asymmetric w.r.t of both u and y.

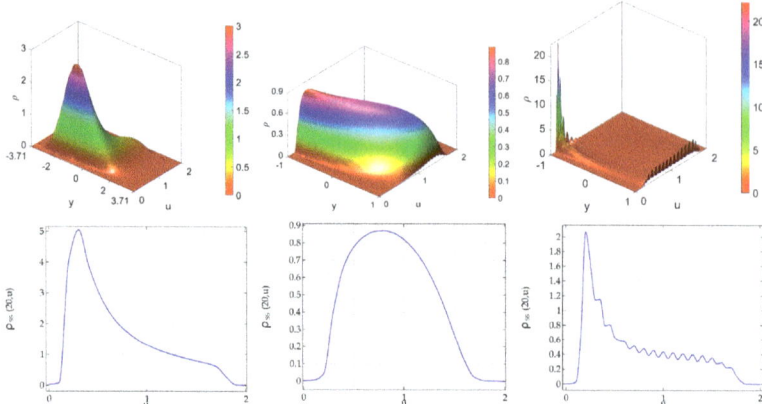

Figure 2. Noise perturbing the carrying capacity of the logistic activity equation: steady state PDF of the Bidimensional Hypoelliptic Fokker–Planck equation. Role of the type of noise. In all panels the noise amplitude is set to $B = 0.9$. (**Left panel**): arctan noise with $Q = 0.2$; (**Central panel**): DCL noise with $\delta = 0.5$; (**Right panel**): DCL noise with $\delta = -0.5$ (equivalent to the Sine-Wiener noise).

12. Numerical Solution of the Full Birth Death System

In this section, we investigate the dynamics of the full birth death kinetic system by assuming as initial conditions the steady state solutions of the bidimensional hypoelliptic Fokker–Planck equation described in the previous section.

12.1. Noise Acting Linearly

In this subsection we consider the impact of a bounded noise acting on the linear term of the logistic equation.

In Figure 3, it is shown the case where the mean of the activity of daughter agents is located at the activity of mother agent (w). As far as the bidimensional steady state densities, a new mode at zero is observed for both the ATAN and the DCLpos cases. As far as the marginal distributions is concerned, for all three types of noises that we considered the density of the population has a mode at zero. This implies that in the DCLpos case the birth and death terms implied the onset of a noise induced transition. Interestingly, although the birth and death terms are the same for all the three series of simulations, there is a remarkable quantitative difference in the steady state value of the population: the arctan noise is associated to a two steady state population, equal to about 0.3. In the DCLpos case the steady state population is about 0.87, whereas for DCLneg noise the steady state population is about 0.67.

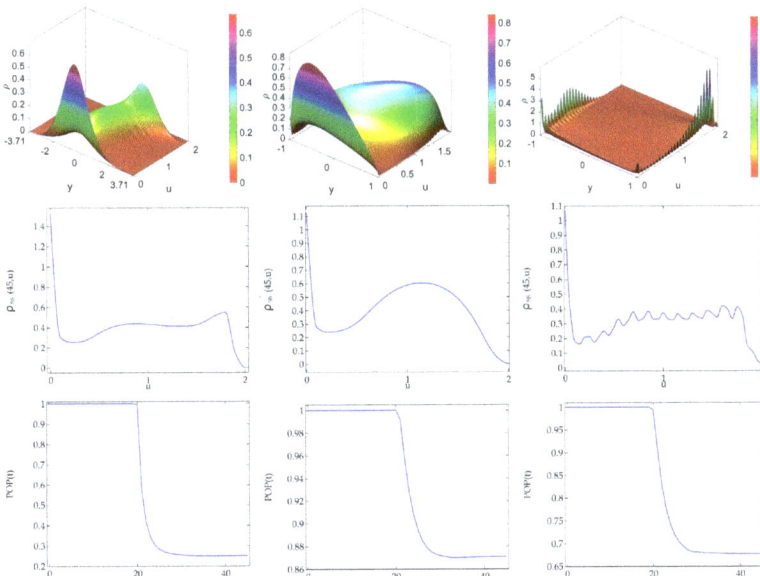

Figure 3. Mean of the activity of daughter agents is located at the activity of mother agent (w). Bidimensional density, marginal density and total population in presence of births and deaths. Noise perturbing the linear term of the logistic activity equation. (**Upper panel**): steady state PDF of the system. Central panels: the corresponding marginal distribution. (**Lower panels**): the corresponding total population (normalized). Role of the type of noise. In all panels the noise amplitude is set to $B = 0.9$. (**Left panels**): arctan noise with $Q = 0.2$; (**Central panels**): DCL noise with $\delta = 0.5$; (**Right panels**): DCL noise with $\delta = -0.5$ (equivalent to the Sine-Wiener noise).

In Figure 4, it is shown the case where the mode of the activity of daughter agents is located at the activity of mother agent (w). As far as the steady state bidimensional densities, they are: (i) bimodal for the ATAN case but associated to a unimodal marginal density; (ii) unimodal for the DCLpos case; (iii) multimodal characterized by a large number of peaks for DCLneg noise. As far as the population dynamics we observe, quite interestingly, that in the DCLpos case about a 10% increase of the population is observed.

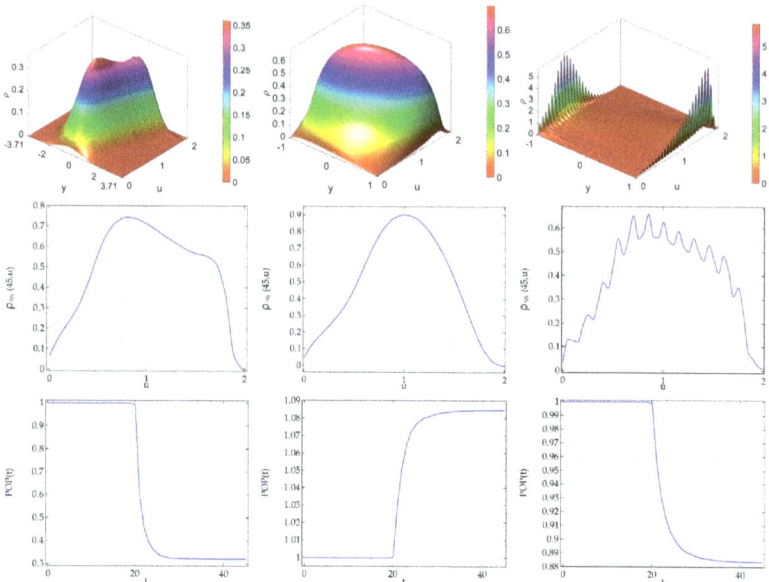

Figure 4. Mode of the activity of daughter agents located at the activity of mother agent (w). Bidimensional density, marginal density and total population in presence of births and deaths. Noise perturbing the linear term of the logistic activity equation. (**Upper panel**): steady state PDF of the system. Central panels: the corresponding marginal distribution. (**Lower panels**): the corresponding total population (normalized). Role of the type of noise. In all panels the noise amplitude is set to $B = 0.9$. (**Left panels**): arctan noise with $Q = 0.2$; (**Central panels**): DCL noise with $\delta = 0.5$; (**Right panels**): DCL noise with $\delta = -0.5$ (equivalent to the Sine-Wiener noise).

12.2. Noise Acting Nonlinearly

In this subsection we consider the impact of a bounded noise acting on the carrying capacity term of the logistic equation, i.e., acting nonlinearly.

In Figure 5, (mean value of the daughter agents' activities at the activity of the mother agent) we note that: (i) the ATAN case is characterized by trimodality in both the bidimensional and the marginal steady state densities, with one mode at zero; (ii) The DCLneg is characterized by a multi peaks strongly asymmetric bidimensional steady state density to which it is associated a trimodal like (plus manu local peaks) steady state density (iii) the DCLpos case is characterized by a curve bidimensional steady state density associated to a unimodal marginal density. As far as the dynamics of the total population, and in the previous subsection, the DCLpos case shows a moderate increase of the steady state value.

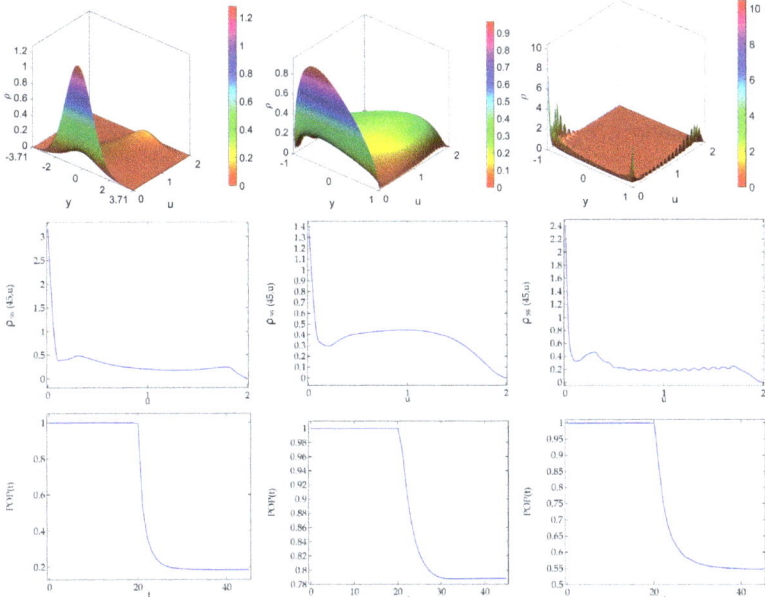

Figure 5. Mean of the activity of daughter agents located at the activity of mother agent (w). Noise perturbing the (nonlinear) carrying capacity term of the logistic activity equation. Bidimensional density, marginal density and total population in presence of births and deaths. (**Upper panel**): steady state PDF of the system. Central panels: the corresponding marginal distribution. (**Lower panels**): the corresponding total population (normalized). Role of the type of noise. In all panels the noise amplitude is set to $B = 0.9$. (**Left panels**): arctan noise with $Q = 0.2$; (**Central panels**): DCL noise with $\delta = 0.5$; (**Right panels**): DCL noise with $\delta = -0.5$ (equivalent to the Sine-Wiener noise).

In Figure 6 (mode of the daughters agents' activities at the activity of the mother agent) we note that (i) both in ATAN and in the DCLpos cases the bidimentional and the marginal densities are unimodal; (ii) as usual the DCLneg case is characterized bu a large number of peaks asymmetrically distributed. The most interesting phenomenon concerns the total population: here not only it is observed the 10% of increase previously observed, but also in the case ATAN a increase of the steady state population, and this increase is large: the 30%.

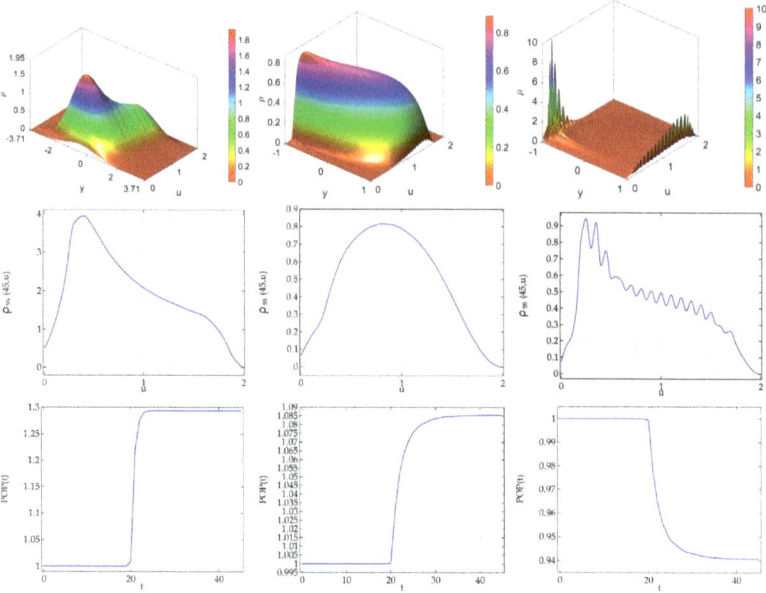

Figure 6. Mode of the activity of daughter agents located at the activity of mother agent (w). Noise perturbing the (nonlinear) carrying capacity term of the logistic activity equation. Bidimensional density, marginal density and total population in presence of births and deaths. (**Upper panel**): steady state PDF of the system. Central panels: the corresponding marginal distribution. (**Lower panels**): the corresponding total population (normalized). Role of the type of noise. In all panels the noise amplitude is set to $B = 0.9$. (**Left panels**): arctan noise with $Q = 0.2$; (**Central panels**): DCL noise with $\delta = 0.5$; (**Right panels**): DCL noise with $\delta = -0.5$ (equivalent to the Sine-Wiener noise).

13. Impact of the Death and Birth Rates

Int their section we numerically show and example of the impact of both the birth and the death rates. Namely we set:

$$\alpha(N) = \frac{\alpha_0}{1+\alpha_1 N^b}; \tag{32}$$

$$\mu_0(u) = 1 - \xi H(u - 0.9); \tag{33}$$

$$\mu_1(u) = 0.5\mu_0(u). \tag{34}$$

As shown in Figure 7, which for the sake of the simplicity refers only to the ATAN case, the one system dynamics impact of the type of birth rate and of the parameter ξ is remarkable, as it was expected.

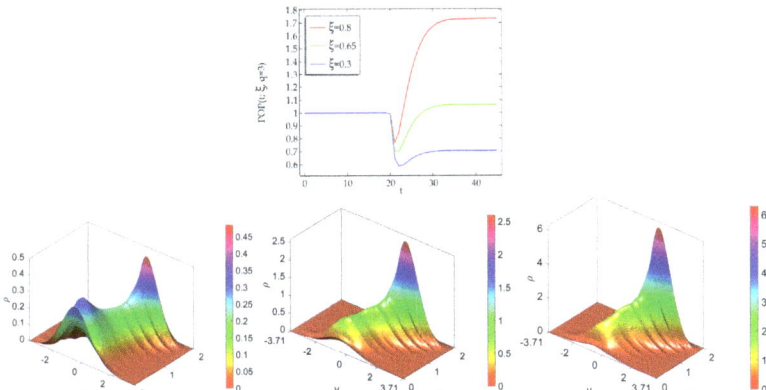

Figure 7. Impact of the birth and death rates. Influence of the death rate-related parameter $\check{\zeta}$ on the dynamics of the total population. Upper panel: the dynamics of the total population. Lower panels: the bidimensional steady state density for : $\check{\zeta} = 0.3$ (**left panel**), $\check{\zeta} = 0.65$ (**central panel**), $\check{\zeta} = 0.8$ (**right panel**).

14. Concluding Remarks

In this work, we considered a system of active particles, i.e., of agents (such as cells, animals in a flock, etc.) endowed by an internal variable u whose evolution is known and stochastic. Namely we assume that the dynamics of u is ruled by a nonlinear dynamical systems perturbed by realistic bounded symmetric stochastic perturbations: $u' = f(u, p(t))$ where the dependence of the rhs on p can be nonlinear. In absence of birth and death of the agents the system evolution is ruled by a multidimensional hypo-elliptical Fokker–Plank equation.

However, we assume that each individual agent can reproduce by generating other agents whose activity is a stochastic variable related to the activity of the mother, animals in a flock. The agents can die. Both birth and death depend on the available resources, i.e., on the whole population. The resulting model is thus an Partial Integro-differential Equation with hypo-elliptical terms. If also a white noise perturbation act on agents, $u' = f(u, p(t)) + g(u)\xi(t)$, then the resulting model is a FPE with fully elliptical terms.

In the numerical simulations we focus on a simple case where the unperturbed dynamics of the agents is of logistic type and then we consider the presence of bounded symmetric stochastic perturbations acting in a linear and non-linear way. As far as the bounded perturbations are concerned, we consider the Doering–Cai–Lin noise and a new bounded noise, obtained by applying and arctan function to the well known Orenstein–Uhlenbeck Gaussian noise. We then numerically find the evolution and the steady state of the above—mentioned hypo-elliptical bidimensional Fokker–Plank equation to be used as initial state for the system in study.

We observed a number of phenomena that depends on the type of noise and on the interplay between noise and birth and death of agents.

First, since the unperturbed model in absence of birth and death has a unique equilibrium at $u = 1$ (monostability), and since in both ATAN and DCLneg cases the bidimensional and the marginal densities are multimodal, this means that the bounded symmetric perturbations can induce noise induced transitions. However, this occurs (in our simulations) only in the case where the noise perturbs the linear term of the logistic equation.

The presence of the birth and deaths may induce, in turn; transitions from unimodality to bimodality even when the steady state of the FP equation is unimodal.

Moreover the total population can be in some cases quantitatively and qualitatively (decreasing vs. increasing time patterns) influenced in a noise-depending manner.

An important effect observed could be roughly described as a symmetry to asymmetry effect since despite the symmetric nature of the stochastic perturbations in some cases the distribution is asymmetric.

Finally, although in our simulations we did not find genuine phase transitions, notwithstanding that we pointed out that the nonlocality could result in some specific models in the onset of first or second order phase transitions.

Limitation and Specificity This study, eminently theoretical, has a number of limitations, real and apparent. The first and most important limitation is that here we study a prototypicalgeneric population of agents that is not directly derived by a specific biological problem. However, this is not a so strong limitation because we apply general principles common to many areas of cellular biology and ecology. Thus, this study could be classified as *statistical biophysics/biomathematics inspired by biology*.

The key novelty here is the fact that our multiscale mean field model explicitly included the presence of realistic bounded stochastic perturbations. This kind of stochastic perturbations have two classes of advantages. The first, largely discussed in the literature on bounded stochastic processes, is that bounded noises preserves the positivity of the parameters and impeded their excessive expansion. The second is that, at variance with white or colored Gaussian perturbations, even parameters that nonlinearly impact on the system can be perturbed.

The second limitation is that the proposed model is a mean field model. Furthermore, here two observations are useful to mitigate the nature of limitations. First, we qualitatively describe a problem that easily could be implemented by means of an individual based model. However populations of some types of agents such as cells rarely are of small medium size, and most often are of very large huge sizes, for which a mean field description are the one we propose here is well suited.

A third limitation is that we have chosen, for the sake of the simplicity, to focus on the behavior of a single population. However, also in this case intra-population interactions are biologically observed, leading to complex integro-differential terms in our model. the inclusion of multiple interplaying population can be easily be integrated by following the large body of research by Belomo and coworkers.

A final limitation is the use of bounded activities. The case of unbounded activities is important for two reasons: (i) this allows in a straightforward way the inclusion of the space is straightforward, since position and velocity it can be considered as a component of a generalized vectorial activity u; (ii) this could allow the possibility of the onset of traveling waves and solutions, a key topic in theoretical and applied mathematical physics [30,78–82] that have extremely interesting synergies with possible noisy perturbations [83].

Author Contributions: Conceptualization, A.d.; methodology, A.d., B.F.F.F. and A.C.; simulations, B.F.F.F.; validation, A.d., B.F.F.F. and A.C.; investigation, A.d., B.F.F.F. and A.C.; writing—original draft preparation, A.d., B.F.F.F. and A.C.; writing—review and editing, A.d., B.F.F.F. and A.C. All authors have read and agreed to the published version of the manuscript.

Funding: This research received no external funding.

Institutional Review Board Statement: Not Applicable.

Informed Consent Statement: Not Applicable.

Data Availability Statement: Not Applicable.

Acknowledgments: The authors thank Carmela Sinisgalli and Federico Papa for their kind invitation to contribute to this Special Issue of *Symmetry*, as well as the three Anonymous Referees for their important suggestions.

Conflicts of Interest: The authors declare no conflict of interest.

References

1. Wang, Z.; Bauch, C.T.; Bhattacharyya, S.; d'Onofrio, A.; Manfredi, P.; Perc, M.; Perra, N.; Salathé, M.; Zhao, D. Statistical physics of vaccination. *Phys. Rep.* **2016**, *664*, 1–113. [CrossRef]
2. Shang, Y. Modeling epidemic spread with awareness and heterogeneous transmission rates in networks. *J. Biol. Phys.* **2013**, *39*, 489–500. [CrossRef]
3. Schweitzer, F. Sociophysics. *Phys. Today* **2018**, *71*, 40. [CrossRef]
4. Sen, P.; Chakrabarti, B.K. *Sociophysics: An Introduction*; Oxford University Press: Oxford, UK, 2014.
5. Shang, Y. Lie algebraic discussion for affinity based information diffusion in social networks. *Open Phys.* **2017**, *15*, 705–711. [CrossRef]
6. Adam, J.A.; Bellomo, N. *A Survey of Models for Tumor-Immune System Dynamics*; Springer Science & Business Media: Basel, Switzerland, 1997.
7. d'Onofrio, A.; Gandolfi, A. *Mathematical Oncology 2013*; Springer Science+Business Media:Birkhäuser: New York, NY, USA, 2014.
8. Drasdo, D.; Höhme, S. Individual-based approaches to birth and death in avascular tumors. *Math. Comput. Model.* **2003**, *37*, 1163–1175. [CrossRef]
9. Drasdo, D.; Höhme, S. A single-cell-based model of tumor growth in vitro: Monolayers and spheroids. *Phys. Biol.* **2005**, *2*, 133. [CrossRef]
10. Krinner, A.; Hoffmann, M.; Loeffler, M.; Drasdo, D.; Galle, J. Individual fates of mesenchymal stem cells in vitro. *BMC Syst. Biol.* **2010**, *4*, 1–9. [CrossRef]
11. Bellomo, N.; Degond, P.; Tadmor, E. *Active Particles, Volume 1: Advances in Theory, Models, and Applications*; Birkhäuser: Basel, Switzerland, 2017.
12. Bellomo, N.; Bellouquid, A.; Gibelli, L.; Outada, N. *A Quest towards a Mathematical Theory of Living Systems*; Springer: Birkhäuser, Basel, 2017.
13. Bianca, C.; Bianca, C.; Bellomo, N. *Towards a Mathematical Theory of Complex Biological Systems*; World Scientific: Singapore; Hackensack, NJ, USA, 2011.
14. Bellomo, N. *Modeling Complex Living Systems*, 1st ed.; Modeling and Simulation in Science, Engineering and Technology; Birkhauser: Basel, Switzerland, 2008.
15. Arlotti, L.; Bellomo, N. Population dynamics with stochastic interaction. *Transp. Theory Stat. Phys.* **1995**, *24*, 431–443. [CrossRef]
16. Arlotti, L.; Bellomo, N. Solution of a new class of nonlinear kinetic models of population dynamics. *Appl. Math. Lett.* **1996**, *9*, 65–70. [CrossRef]
17. Bellomo, N.; Preziosi, L.; Forni, G. On a kinetic (cellular) theory for competition between tumors and the host immune system. *J. Biol. Syst.* **1996**, *4*, 479–502. [CrossRef]
18. Delitala, M.; Lorenzi, T. Asymptotic dynamics in continuous structured populations with mutations, competition and mutualism. *J. Math. Anal. Appl.* **2012**, *389*, 439–451. [CrossRef]
19. Cattani, C.; Ciancio, A. Hybrid two scales mathematical tools for active particles modelling complex systems with learning hiding dynamics. *Math. Model. Methods Appl. Sci.* **2007**, *17*, 171–187. [CrossRef]
20. Marca, R.D.; Loy, N.; Tosin, A. An SIR-like kinetic model tracking individuals' viral load. *arXiv* **2021**, arXiv:2106.14480.
21. Bianca, C. Thermostatted kinetic equations as models for complex systems in physics and life sciences. *Phys. Life Rev.* **2012**, *9*, 359–399. [CrossRef] [PubMed]
22. Bianca, C.; Menale, M. On the convergence toward nonequilibrium stationary states in thermostatted kinetic models. *Math. Methods Appl. Sci.* **2019**, *42*, 6624–6634. [CrossRef]
23. Bianca, C.; Menale, M. On the interaction domain reconstruction in the weighted thermostatted kinetic framework. *Eur. Phys. J. Plus* **2019**, *134*, 1–13. [CrossRef]
24. Lorz, A.; Lorenzi, T.; Hochberg, M.E.; Clairambault, J.; Perthame, B. Populational adaptive evolution, chemotherapeutic resistance and multiple anti-cancer therapies. *ESAIM Math. Model. Numer. Anal.* **2013**, *47*, 377–399. [CrossRef]
25. Lorenzi, T.; Chisholm, R.H.; Clairambault, J. Tracking the evolution of cancer cell populations through the mathematical lens of phenotype-structured equations. *Biol. Direct* **2016**, *11*, 1–17. [CrossRef]
26. Chisholm, R.H.; Lorenzi, T.; Lorz, A.; Larsen, A.K.; de Almeida, L.N.; Escargueil, A.; Clairambault, J. Emergence of drug tolerance in cancer cell populations: An evolutionary outcome of selection, nongenetic instability, and stress-induced adaptation. *Cancer Res.* **2015**, *75*, 930–939. [CrossRef]
27. Chisholm, R.H.; Lorenzi, T.; Clairambault, J. Cell population heterogeneity and evolution towards drug resistance in cancer: Biological and mathematical assessment, theoretical treatment optimisation. *Biochim. Biophys. Acta (BBA) Gen. Subj.* **2016**, *1860*, 2627–2645. [CrossRef] [PubMed]
28. Ardaševa, A.; Gatenby, R.A.; Anderson, A.R.; Byrne, H.M.; Maini, P.K.; Lorenzi, T. Evolutionary dynamics of competing phenotype-structured populations in periodically fluctuating environments. *J. Math. Biol.* **2020**, *80*, 775–807. [CrossRef] [PubMed]
29. Fiandaca, G.; Delitala, M.; Lorenzi, T. A mathematical study of the influence of hypoxia and acidity on the evolutionary dynamics of cancer. *Bull. Math. Biol.* **2021**, *83*, 1–29. [CrossRef] [PubMed]
30. Volpert, V.; Petrovskii, S. Reaction–diffusion waves in biology. *Phys. Life Rev.* **2009**, *6*, 267–310. [CrossRef] [PubMed]
31. Banerjee, M.; Vougalter, V.; Volpert, V. Doubly nonlocal reaction–diffusion equations and the emergence of species. *Appl. Math. Model.* **2017**, *42*, 591–599. [CrossRef]

32. Volpert, V. Pulses and waves for a bistable nonlocal reaction–diffusion equation. *Appl. Math. Lett.* **2015**, *44*, 21–25. [CrossRef]
33. Firmani, B.; Guerri, L.; Preziosi, L. Tumor/immune system competition with medically induced activation/deactivation. *Math. Model. Methods Appl. Sci.* **1999**, *9*, 491–512. [CrossRef]
34. Ambrosi, D.; Bellomo, N.; Preziosi, L. Modelling tumor progression, heterogeneity, and immune competition. *J. Theor. Med.* **2002**, *4*, 51–65. [CrossRef]
35. d'Onofrio, A. 'Noisy oncology': Some caveats in using gaussian noise in mathematical models of chemotherapy. In *Aspects of Mathematical Modelling*; Hosking, R., Venturino, E., Eds.; Birkhauser: Basel, Switzerland, 2008; pp. 229–234.
36. d'Onofrio, A. *Bounded Noises in Physics, Biology, and Engineering*; Modeling and Simulation in Science, Engineering and Technology; Springer: New York, NY, USA, 2013.
37. Wio, H.S.; Toral, R. Effect of non-Gaussian noise sources in a noise-induced transition. *Physics D* **2004**, *193*, 161–168. [CrossRef]
38. Bobryk, R.; Chrzeszczyk, A. Stability regions for Mathieu equation with imperfect periodicity. *Phys. Lett. A* **2009**, *373*, 3532–3535. [CrossRef]
39. Botts, R.T.; Homburg, A.J.; Young, T.R. The Hopf bifurcation with bounded noise. *Discret. Contin. Dyn. Syst. Ser. A* **2012**, *32*, 2997. [CrossRef]
40. Zhu, J.; Wang, X.; Xie, W.C.; So, R.M. Flow-induced instability under bounded noise excitation in cross-flow. *J. Sound Vib.* **2008**, *312*, 476–495. [CrossRef]
41. Deng, J.; Xie, W.C.; Pandey, M.D. Stochastic stability of a fractional viscoelastic column under bounded noise excitation. *J. Sound Vib.* **2014**, *333*, 1629–1643. [CrossRef]
42. Domingo, D.; d'Onofrio, A.; Flandoli, F. Boundedness vs unboundedness of a noise linked to Tsallis q-statistics: The role of the overdamped approximation. *J. Math. Phys.* **2017**, *58*, 033301. [CrossRef]
43. d'Onofrio, A.; Gandolfi, A.; Gattoni, S. The Norton–Simon hypothesis and the onset of non-genetic resistance to chemotherapy induced by stochastic fluctuations. *Phys. A Stat. Mech. Appl.* **2012**, *391*, 6484–6496. [CrossRef]
44. Guo, W.; Mei, D.C. Stochastic resonance in a tumor–immune system subject to bounded noises and time delay. *Phys. A Stat. Mech. Appl.* **2014**, *416*, 90–98. [CrossRef]
45. de Franciscis, S.; d'Onofrio, A. Cellular polarization: Interaction between extrinsic bounded noises and the wave-pinning mechanism. *Phys. Rev. E* **2013**, *88*, 032709. [CrossRef] [PubMed]
46. Naess, A.; Dimentberg, M.F.; Gaidai, O. Lotka-Volterra systems in environments with randomly disordered temporal periodicity. *Phys. Rev. E* **2008**, *78*, 021126. [CrossRef]
47. Ridolfi, L.; D'Odorico, P.; Laio, F. *Noise-Induced Phenomena in the Environmental Sciences*; Cambridge University Press: Cambridge, UK, 2011.
48. Yao, Y.; Cao, W.; Pei, Q.; Ma, C.; Yi, M. Breakup of Spiral Wave and Order-Disorder Spatial Pattern Transition Induced by Spatially Uniform Cross-Correlated Sine-Wiener Noises in a Regular Network of Hodgkin-Huxley Neurons. *Complexity* **2018**, *2018*, 8793298. [CrossRef]
49. Bellomo, N.; Forni, G. Complex multicellular systems and immune competition: New paradigms looking for a mathematical theory. *Curr. Top. Dev. Biol.* **2008**, *81*, 485–502.
50. Conte, M.; Groppi, M.; Spiga, G. Qualitative analysis of kinetic-based models for tumor-immune system interaction. *Discret. Contin. Dyn. Syst.-B* **2018**, *23*, 2393. [CrossRef]
51. Toscani, G.; Tosin, A.; Zanella, M. Opinion modeling on social media and marketing aspects. *Phys. Rev. E* **2018**, *98*, 022315. [CrossRef]
52. Bellomo, N.; Piccoli, B.; Tosin, A. Modeling crowd dynamics from a complex system viewpoint. *Math. Model. Methods Appl. Sci.* **2012**, *22*, 1230004. [CrossRef]
53. Nicolis, G.; Nicolis, C. *Foundations of Complex Systems: Emergence, Information and Prediction*; World Scientific: River Edge, NJ, USA, 2012.
54. Nicholis, G.; Prigogine, I. *Self-Organization in Nonequalibrium Systems*; John Wiley & Sons: New York, NY, USA, 1977
55. Horsthemke, W.; Lefever, R. *Noise-Induced Transitions: Theory and Applications in Physics, Chemistry, and Biology (Springer Series in Synergetics)*; Springer: Berlin/Heidelberg, Germany, 1984.
56. Cucker, F.; Smale, S. Emergent behavior in flocks. *IEEE Trans. Autom. Control* **2007**, *52*, 852–862. [CrossRef]
57. Cucker, F.; Mordecki, E. Flocking in noisy environments. *J. Math. Pures Appl.* **2008**, *89*, 278–296. [CrossRef]
58. Shang, Y. Emergence in random noisy environments. *Int. J. Math. Anal.* **2009**, *4*, 1205–1215.
59. Gardiner, C.W. *Handbook of Stochastic Methods*; Springer: Berlin/Heidelberg, Germany, 2012.
60. Shiino, M. Dynamical behavior of stochastic systems of infinitely many coupled nonlinear oscillators exhibiting phase transitions of mean-field type: H theorem on asymptotic approach to equilibrium and critical slowing down of order-parameter fluctuations. *Phys. Rev. A* **1987**, *36*, 2393. [CrossRef] [PubMed]
61. Müller, R.; Lippert, K.; Kühnel, A.; Behn, U. First-order nonequilibrium phase transition in a spatially extended system. *Phys. Rev. E* **1997**, *56*, 2658. [CrossRef]
62. Van den Broeck, C.; Parrondo, J.; Toral, R. Noise-induced nonequilibrium phase transition. *Phys. Rev. Lett.* **1994**, *73*, 3395. [CrossRef]
63. Kimmel, M.; Darzynkiewicz, Z.; Arino, O.; Traganos, F. Analysis of a cell cycle model based on unequal division of metabolic constituents to daughter cells during cytokinesis. *J. Theor. Biol.* **1984**, *110*, 637–664. [CrossRef]

64. Marciniak-Czochra, A.; Stiehl, T.; Ho, A.D.; Jäger, W.; Wagner, W. Modeling of asymmetric cell division in hematopoietic stem cells—Regulation of self-renewal is essential for efficient repopulation. *Stem Cells Dev.* **2009**, *18*, 377–386. [CrossRef] [PubMed]
65. Dolbniak, M.; Kimmel, M.; Smieja, J. Modeling epigenetic regulation of PRC1 protein accumulation in the cell cycle. *Biol. Direct* **2015**, *10*, 1–15. [CrossRef] [PubMed]
66. Wodarz, A.; Gonzalez, C. Connecting cancer to the asymmetric division of stem cells. *Cell* **2006**, *124*, 1121–1123. [CrossRef] [PubMed]
67. Han, X.; Kloeden, P.E. *Random Ordinary Differential Equations and Their Numerical Solution*; Springer: Singapore, 2017.
68. Asai, Y.; Kloeden, P.E. Numerical schemes for random ODEs via stochastic differential equations. *Commun. Appl. Anal.* **2013**, *17*, 521–528.
69. Cai, G.Q.; Lin, Y.K. Generation of non-Gaussian stationary stochastic processes. *Phys. Rev. E* **1996**, *54*, 299–303. [CrossRef] [PubMed]
70. Doering, C.R. A stochastic partial differential equation with multiplicative noise. *Phys. Lett. A* **1987**, *122*, 133–139. [CrossRef]
71. Domingo, D.; d'Onofrio, A.; Flandoli, F. Properties of bounded stochastic processes employed in biophysics. *Stoch. Anal. Appl.* **2020**, *38*, 277–306. [CrossRef]
72. Dimentberg, M.F. *Statistical Dynamics of Nonlinear and Time-Varying Systems*; Research Studies Press: Chichester, UK, 1988.
73. Shang, Y. The limit behavior of a stochastic logistic model with individual time-dependent rates. *J. Math.* **2013**, *2013*, 502635. [CrossRef]
74. d'Onofrio, A. Fractal growth of tumors and other cellular populations: Linking the mechanistic to the phenomenological modeling and vice versa. *Chaos Solitons Fractals* **2009**, *41*, 875–880. [CrossRef]
75. Anonymous. MUltifrontal Massively Parallel Solver (MUMPS 5.4.1) User's Guide. Available online: http://mumps.enseeiht.fr/doc/userguide_5.4.1.pdf (accessed on 17 August 2021).
76. Amestoy, P.R.; Duff, I.S.; L'Excellent, J.Y.; Koster, J. A fully asynchronous multifrontal solver using distributed dynamic scheduling. *SIAM J. Matrix Anal. Appl.* **2001**, *23*, 15–41. [CrossRef]
77. Amestoy, P.R.; Buttari, A.; L'excellent, J.Y.; Mary, T. Performance and scalability of the block low-rank multifrontal factorization on multicore architectures. *ACM Trans. Math. Softw. (TOMS)* **2019**, *45*, 1–26. [CrossRef]
78. Drazin, P.G.; Johnson, R.S. *Solitons: An Introduction*; Cambridge University Press: Cambridge, UK, 1989.
79. Volpert, A.; Volpert, V.; Volpert, V. *Traveling Wave Solutions of Parabolic Systems*; American Mathematical Soc.: 1994. Available online: https://books.google.com.hk/books/about/Traveling_Wave_Solutions_of_Parabolic_Sy.html?id=1qP--BRsLAwC&redir_esc=y (accessed on 19 August 2021).
80. Baskonus, H.; Cattani, C.; Ciancio, A. Periodic, complex and kink-type solitons for the nonlinear model in microtubules. *Appl. Sci.* **2019**, *21*, 34–45.
81. Ciancio, A.; Ciancio, V.; Farsaci, F. Wave propagation in media obeying a thermoviscoanelastic model. *UPB Sci. Bull. Ser. A* **2007**, *69*, 69–79
82. Bellomo, N.; Dogbe, C. On the modeling of traffic and crowds: A survey of models, speculations, and perspectives. *SIAM Rev.* **2011**, *53*, 409–463. [CrossRef]
83. Panja, D. Effects of fluctuations on propagating fronts. *Phys. Rep.* **2004**, *393*, 87–174. [CrossRef]

Article

An Entropic Gradient Structure in the Network Dynamics of a Slime Mold

Vincenzo Bonifaci

Dipartimento di Matematica e Fisica, Università degli Studi Roma Tre, 00154 Rome, Italy; vincenzo.bonifaci@uniroma3.it

Abstract: The approach to equilibrium in certain dynamical systems can be usefully described in terms of information-theoretic functionals. Well-studied models of this kind are Markov processes, chemical reaction networks, and replicator dynamics, for all of which it can be proven, under suitable assumptions, that the relative entropy (informational divergence) of the state of the system with respect to an equilibrium is nonincreasing over time. This work reviews another recent result of this type, which emerged in the study of the network optimization dynamics of an acellular slime mold, *Physarum polycephalum*. In this setting, not only the relative entropy of the state is nonincreasing, but its evolution over time is crucial to the stability of the entire system, and the equilibrium towards which the dynamics is attracted proves to be a global minimizer of the cost of the network.

Keywords: dynamical systems; network optimization; stability analysis; global attractor; relative entropy; information geometry

MSC: 92B05; 93D05; 90C25

1. Introduction

Information-theoretic concepts, such as negative entropy, and the related notion of free energy have long been recognized as relevant to natural and living systems [1–4]. It turns out that the approach to equilibrium in some classes of dynamical systems can be usefully studied from an information-theoretic perspective. Baez and Pollard [5] give an excellent overview of such an approach. Consider, for example, a system modeled as a continuous-time Markov process on K distinct states, where the probability of the state of the system at time t being $i \in \{1, 2, \ldots, K\}$ is denoted by $p_i(t)$. Such a system is ruled by the so-called master equation:

$$\frac{d}{dt} p(t) = \mathcal{H}\, p(t) \tag{1}$$

where $p(t) = (p_1(t), p_2(t), \ldots, p_K(t))$ and $\mathcal{H}$ is an appropriate $K \times K$ matrix. Drawing from information theory, one can consider the relative entropy (informational divergence) between the evolving distribution $p(t)$ and another probability distribution $q = (q_1, q_2, \ldots, q_K)$ on the set of states; this is defined as

$$D(q, p(t)) := \sum_{i=1}^{K} q_i \log \frac{q_i}{p_i(t)}. \tag{2}$$

If one chooses q as a steady state distribution (that is, $\mathcal{H} q = 0$), then one can show that

$$\frac{d}{dt} D(q, p(t)) \leq 0,$$

and if the steady state distribution is unique, this can in turn be used to argue that $p(t)$ is attracted to q over time. In other words, by proving monotonicity of the relative entropy (2) over time, one can conclude that the steady state distribution q is also a global attractor. This approach is not limited to continuous-time Markov processes and the linear ordinary differential equation system (1), but extends to other types of models such as discrete-time Markov chains, chemical reaction networks, and several models of population dynamics, such as the replicator dynamics [5–9].

This work discusses a different, nonlinear, class of systems for which the information-theoretic approach is successful: a family of dynamical systems modeling the network dynamics of the slime mold *Physarum polycephalum* [10,11].

The slime mold *Physarum polycephalum* is an acellular slime mold (myxogastrid) [12]. In its plasmodium stage, it forms a tubular network that reshapes and adapts to the environmental stimuli. The reshaping is driven by the streaming of cytoplasm through the network; tubes not sustained by cytoplasmic streaming eventually decay and dissolve. This reshaping mechanism has been experimentally observed to be remarkably effective at optimizing the use of resources [13,14]. In particular, in one laboratory experiment, the slime mold network is distributed uniformly over a maze, and two food sources are positioned in two points A and B of the maze. Over time, the slime mold retracts all tubes except those corresponding to the shortest path between A and B.

A mathematical model of the network dynamics of *P. polycephalum*'s plasmodium has been first proposed by Tero, Kobayashi and Nakagaki [10], who also showed how the model implied, for certain values of the parameters and for very simple networks, convergence to the optimal equilibrium point represented by the shortest path in the network. Subsequently, variations of this model have been proved to converge to the optimal network configuration for arbitrary network topologies for a wide range of model parameters [15–18]. The goal of this paper is to give a gentle introduction to *Physarum polycephalum*'s network modeling and to its analysis, and to explain how such analysis can be seen as another example of the information-theoretic approach to dynamical systems. Thus, the significance of the results is that they widen the scope and applicability of the information-theoretic approach in dynamical systems.

Structure of this article. Section 2 introduces one possible mathematical model for *Physarum polycephalum*'s network dynamics. This model is analyzed in Section 3. Section 4 discusses related works and extensions of the model. Some conclusions are drawn in Section 5.

2. Flow Constraints and Network Dynamics

2.1. Some Notation

For a vector $x \in \mathbb{R}^m$, $\mathrm{diag}(x)$ is used to denote the $m \times m$ diagonal matrix with the coefficients of x along the diagonal. The standard inner product of two vectors $x, y \in \mathbb{R}^m$ is denoted by $\langle x, y \rangle := x^\top y$. For a vector $x \in \mathbb{R}^m$, $\|x\|_p$ denotes the ℓ_p-norm of x ($1 \leq p < \infty$), that is, $\|x\|_p := (x_1^p + x_2^p + \ldots + x_m^p)^{1/p}$.

2.2. Cytoplasmic Flow and Kirchhoff's Laws

In the experiments of Nakagaki et al. [10,13], *P. polycephalum*'s plasmodium forms an evolving tubular network, in which the transport capacity of the edges, that is, the tubular channels routing the cytoplasm, changes over time (see [19] for a video illustration). This network is modeled mathematically as a connected weighted undirected graph G, with node set $N = \{v_1, v_2, \ldots, v_n\}$ and edge set $E = \{e_1, e_2, \ldots, e_m\}$. Edges represent the tubular channels, and nodes represent junctions between the tubes. Two special nodes in $s_0, s_1 \in N$ are distinguished; they correspond to the location of the food sources in the experiments. Node s_0 is called the *source* of the cytoplasmic flow, node s_1 the *sink*; the choice of which node is the source and which the sink is purely conventional.

The weight of an edge of G encodes the capacity of the corresponding tubular channel, which is directly related (as detailed below) to the radius and length of the tube. The capacity is a dynamic quantity, since as food is absorbed by the slime mold, and cytoplasm flows through the network, the radius of the tubular channels will respond to the flow; this is discussed in the next section. For now, let us focus on the situation at a specific instant in time.

At any time, the cytoplasmic flow through the network will be entirely determined by the capacity of the edges. Fix an arbitrary orientation of the edges, and let $B \in \mathbb{R}^{N \times E}$ be the incidence matrix of G under this orientation, that is,

$$B_{ve} := \begin{cases} +1 & \text{if node } vs. \text{ is the tail of edge } e \\ -1 & \text{if node } vs. \text{ is the head of edge } e \\ 0 & \text{otherwise} \end{cases} \quad (v \in N, e \in E).$$

Let $N' = N - \{s_1\}$ and let $A \in \mathbb{R}^{N' \times E}$ be obtained from B by removing the row corresponding to the sink s_1. Moreover, let $b \in \mathbb{R}^{N'}$ be the vector defined by

$$b_v := \begin{cases} 0 & \text{if } vs. \neq s_0, \\ 1 & \text{if } v = s_0, \end{cases} \quad (v \in N').$$

A *flow* (flux) q is represented by a vector in $\mathbb{R}^E$ that expresses, for each oriented edge $e \in E$, the amount of flow along the positive direction of that edge at a given time. Any fluid flow from the source to the sink should obey *flow conservation*; this is expressed by the linear system of equations

$$Aq = b. \tag{3}$$

This is nothing but *Kirchhoff's current law* which, in words, requires that the flow has zero divergence everywhere except at nodes s_0 and s_1, where it has divergence, respectively, $+1$ and -1 [20] (Chapter IX).

Example 1. *Consider the network of Figure 1a. It holds $N = \{v_1, v_2, v_3\}$ with source $s_0 = v_1$, sink $s_1 = v_3$, and $E = \{e_1, e_2, e_3\}$. If the network is oriented as in Figure 1b, then B, A and b are, respectively,*

$$B = \begin{pmatrix} 1 & 0 & 1 \\ -1 & 1 & 0 \\ 0 & -1 & -1 \end{pmatrix}, \quad A = \begin{pmatrix} 1 & 0 & 1 \\ -1 & 1 & 0 \end{pmatrix}, \quad b = \begin{pmatrix} 1 \\ 0 \end{pmatrix}.$$

Note that matrix A is simply matrix B with row 3 dropped (since the sink is v_3). Kirchhoff's current law for a flow $q = (q_1, q_2, q_3) \in \mathbb{R}^3$ through the edges (e_1, e_2, e_3) corresponds to the constraints:

$$\begin{cases} q_1 + q_3 = 1 \\ -q_1 + q_2 = 0 \end{cases}$$

Two examples of valid flows in this case are $q = (1, 1, 0)$ (all the flow goes through the upper path) and $q' = (1/2, 1/2, 1/2)$ (half of the flow goes through the upper path, and half goes through the lower path). In general, any vector $q \in \mathbb{R}^m$ such that $Aq = b$ encodes a valid flow.

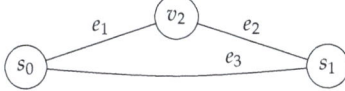

(a) An example network.

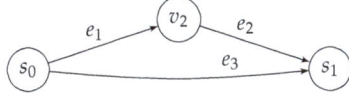

(b) A corresponding oriented network.

Figure 1. Example network.

An additional assumption is that the cytoplasmic flow q satisfies *Kirchhoff's potential law* (Section II.1) [20], which says that there exist real values $\{p_v\}_{v \in N}$ (the *pressure potentials* at the nodes) satisfying the hydrodynamic analogue of Ohm's law (*Poiseuille's law*). For an edge e between nodes u and v, Poiseuille's law states that

$$q_e = \frac{\pi R_e^4(t)}{8\eta} \frac{(p_u - p_v)}{l_e}, \qquad \text{for every } e = (u,v) \in E \qquad (4)$$

where $R_e(t)$ is the radius of the tube at time t, and η is a viscosity constant. Thus, if the *capacity* of edge e is defined as $x_e(t) := \pi R_e^4(t)/8\eta l_e$ and the *resistance* as $r_e := 1/x_e$, these are directly related to the length and radius of the tube at time t, and one can simply write

$$q_e = (p_u - p_v) x_e = \frac{p_u - p_v}{r_e}, \qquad \text{for every } e = (u,v) \in E. \qquad (5)$$

It is a standard fact from electrical network theory that, given a capacity vector $x \in \mathbb{R}_{>0}^E$ (or equivalently, a resistance vector $r \in \mathbb{R}_{>0}^E$), the flow q satisfying (3) and (5) is unique (Chapter IX) [20]; this will be called the *cytoplasmic flow*, and is analogous to the electrical flow in electrical networks. In fact, such a flow is also the unique valid flow from s_0 to s_1 of *least dissipation*, that is, the unique optimal solution to the following optimization problem:

$$\text{minimize } q^\top X^{-1} q \qquad (6)$$
$$\text{subject to } Aq = b.$$

Here, $X \in \mathbb{R}^{E \times E}$ is the diagonal matrix with the capacities $x_{e_1}, \ldots, x_{e_m}$ along the main diagonal. The quantity $\mathcal{E} := q^\top X^{-1} q = \sum_{e \in E} r_e q_e^2$ is called the *energy* of the flow q. The energy of the flow equals the difference between the source and sink potentials, times the value of the flow, which in the setting of this paper is unitary (Corollary IX.4) [20]:

$$\mathcal{E} = b^\top p = (p_{s_0} - p_{s_1}) b_{s_0} = p_{s_0} - p_{s_1}. \qquad (7)$$

Hence, in this setting $\mathcal{E}$ is also the potential difference between source and sink.

An alternative, equivalent way to express the cytoplasmic flow arises from the Laplacian operator of the network [21]. The (reduced) *Laplacian* of G is the symmetric and positive semidefinite matrix $L := AXA^\top$. If one represents the potential vector of all nodes except the sink by $p \in \mathbb{R}^{N'}$, assuming without loss of generality $p_{s_1} = 0$, then (5) can be written in matrix form as

$$q = XA^\top p. \qquad (8)$$

Multiplying both sides by A yields the discrete Poisson equation $Lp = b$, with solution $p = L^{-1}b$. Substituting this in (8), one gets a direct expression for the cytoplasmic flow in terms of the network structure and edge capacities:

$$q = XA^\top L^{-1} b. \qquad (9)$$

This also allows us to express each q_e as a (nonlinear) function of the capacity vector $x \in \mathbb{R}_{>0}^E$. Using the Laplacian matrix, the energy of the cytoplasmic flow can also be expressed as

$$\mathcal{E} = b^\top p = b^\top L^{-1} b. \qquad (10)$$

Example 2. *Continuing the same example from above, for a given vector $x = (x_1, x_2, x_3) \in \mathbb{R}_{>0}^3$ of edge capacities, the capacity matrix X and the reduced Laplacian matrix L are, respectively,*

$$X = \text{diag}(x) = \begin{pmatrix} x_1 & 0 & 0 \\ 0 & x_2 & 0 \\ 0 & 0 & x_3 \end{pmatrix}, \qquad L = AXA^\top = \begin{pmatrix} x_1 + x_3 & -x_1 \\ -x_1 & x_1 + x_2 \end{pmatrix},$$

with the latter having determinant $\det(L) = x_1 x_2 + x_1 x_3 + x_2 x_3$. Hence,

$$L^{-1} = \frac{1}{\det(L)} \begin{pmatrix} x_1 + x_2 & x_1 \\ x_1 & x_1 + x_3 \end{pmatrix}, \quad p = L^{-1} b = \frac{1}{\det(L)} \begin{pmatrix} x_1 + x_2 \\ x_1 \end{pmatrix}$$

and the cytoplasmic flow is

$$q = X A^\top L^{-1} b = \frac{1}{\det(L)} \begin{pmatrix} x_1 x_2 \\ x_1 x_2 \\ x_1 x_3 + x_2 x_3 \end{pmatrix} = \frac{1}{x_1 x_2 + x_1 x_3 + x_2 x_3} \begin{pmatrix} x_1 x_2 \\ x_1 x_2 \\ x_1 x_3 + x_2 x_3 \end{pmatrix}. \tag{11}$$

The energy of the cytoplasmic flow is $\mathcal{E} = p_{s_0} - p_{s_1} = p_{s_0} = (x_1 + x_2)/\det(L)$.

Notice that $q_1 = q_2$ and $q_1 + q_3 = 1$, as one expects due to flow conservation. Equation (11) also clearly shows that the cytoplasmic flow along an edge e_j is a function of the capacities of the entire network, not just of the capacity x_j of the same edge.

2.3. Response Dynamics on an Edge

A dynamics on the edge capacities will now be introduced. This represents the slime mold's positive feedback mechanism, which relates the pressure gradient along a tubular channel to the rate of increase or decrease of the capacity of the tube. The underlying idea is simple: tubes along which there is a strong pressure tend to increase their capacity, while tubes along which there is a weak pressure tend to decrease their capacity. Namely, the following will be assumed:

$$\dot{x}_e = x_e \left(\varphi\left(\frac{|q_e|}{x_e} \right) - 1 \right) \quad \text{for all } e \in E. \tag{12}$$

Here, q_e is (as before) the cytoplasmic flow along edge e, and $\varphi : \mathbb{R}_{\geq 0} \to \mathbb{R}_{\geq 0}$ is some strictly increasing, differentiable function such that $\varphi(1) = 1$. This function models the physical response of the tube to the flow. Some observations:

1. By Poiseuille's law (5), $|q_e|/x_e = |p_u - p_v|$, thus the larger the potential difference along edge e, the larger $\dot{x}_e$ will be.
2. For a given value of the potential difference, a tube tends to expand less if it is smaller, due to the dependency on x_e in (12).
3. Because of the absolute value in (12), the actual direction of the flow has no influence on the dynamics. In particular, exchanging the role of the source and sink nodes (thus reversing the flow) does not alter the tubes' dynamics. This is the reason why one can arbitrarily select any food source as the flow source and the other one as the flow sink.
4. A tube $e \in E$ is in equilibrium if and only if $|q_e| = x_e$, that is, $q_e = \pm x_e$.

In the remaining sections, the response function $\varphi(z) = z^2$ will be assumed, which is the mathematically most convenient. However, the qualitative evolution of the dynamics under other response functions appears to be (and in some cases, it provably is) similar; see the discussion in Section 4.1.

2.4. The Dynamics as an Ode

The adaptation Equation (12) can be given a natural interpretation as a local feedback mechanism: the flow q_e and the capacity x_e jointly determine the rate of change of the capacity x_e of the tube.

However, as seen in Section 2.2 the amount of flow on an edge is a function of the capacities of the entire network, due to Equation (9). This means that each q_e can be expressed as a (nonlinear) function of all the capacities of the network, that is, one can—at least in principle—rewrite Equation (12) as

$$\dot{x}_1 = F_1(x_1, x_2, \ldots, x_m)$$

$$\dot{x}_2 = F_2(x_1, x_2, \ldots, x_m)$$
$$\vdots$$
$$\dot{x}_m = F_m(x_1, x_2, \ldots, x_m)$$

for some appropriate nonlinear functions $F_1, \ldots, F_m$. In this way, one obtains an autonomous system of coupled, nonlinear ordinary differential equations, describing the evolution of the edge capacities.

In practice, writing down explicitly the functions $F_1, \ldots, F_m$ is inconvenient but for the smallest networks, and it turns out to be unnecessary for the stability analysis. In the following, the algebraic-differential formulation of Equations (9) and (12) will be used:

$$\dot{x}_e = x_e \left(\varphi\left(\frac{|q_e|}{x_e} \right) - 1 \right) \quad \text{for all } e \in E, \tag{13}$$
$$q = XA^\top (AXA^\top)^{-1} b.$$

Note that the singularity of (13) when some $x_e = 0$ can be removed: from the expression $q = XA^\top(AXA^\top)^{-1}b$ it can be seen that $q_e/x_e = (A^\top(AXA^\top)^{-1}b)_e$, a rational function of x that is well-defined as long as the Kirchhoff polynomial $\det(AXA^\top)$ of the network does not vanish (which it cannot when the edges corresponding to nonzero x_e's form a connected graph [22]).

In particular, with the quadratic response function $\varphi(z) = z^2$, one obtains

$$\dot{x}_e = x_e \left(\frac{q_e^2}{x_e^2} - 1 \right) \quad \text{for all } e \in E, \tag{14}$$
$$q = XA^\top(AXA^\top)^{-1}b.$$

The initial condition $x(0)$ of the dynamics can be any point in the positive orthant $\mathbb{R}^m_{>0}$. System (14) will be called the *quadratic-response Physarum system*. The question of whether this system has a solution $x(t)$ defined over all $t \geq 0$ is postponed until Section 3.3.

2.5. Equilibria

What are the equilibrium points of (14)? Any state x such that $\dot{x}_1 = \dot{x}_2 = \ldots = \dot{x}_m = 0$ should satisfy, for each $e \in E$, either $x_e = 0$ or $q_e = \pm x_e$. It turns out that equilibrium points are directly related to the paths connecting the source node to the sink node in the network. Specifically, for a source-sink path P, let its *characteristic vector* $\chi^P \in \mathbb{R}^E$ be defined as

$$\chi^P_e := \begin{cases} 1 & \text{if } e \in P, \\ 0 & \text{if } e \notin P. \end{cases} \tag{15}$$

Then one can prove the following fact.

Lemma 1. *If P is any source-sink path in the network, then χ^P is an equilibrium point of (14). Conversely, any equilibrium point of (14) is a convex combination of characteristic vectors of source-sink paths. Moreover, if each source-sink path has a distinct length, then any equilibrium point is the characteristic vector χ^P of some source-sink path P, and the energy of the corresponding cytoplasmic flow equals the length of the path.*

Proof. Let P be a source-sink path, and χ^P its characteristic vector. Consider the state $x = \chi_P$ and let q be the cytoplasmic flow with respect to x. By definition of the cytoplasmic flow $Aq = b$, and q_e can be nonzero only when x_e is nonzero (due to $q = XA^\top L^{-1}b$). In fact, $q_e = \pm 1$ for each $e \in P$, and $q_e = 0$ for each $e \notin P$, since a unit flow is sent from source to sink and the only path with nonzero capacity (due to the choice of x) is P. This means that $q_e = \pm x_e$ for all $e \in E$, and hence $x = \chi^P$ is an equilibrium point.

Conversely, consider any equilibrium point x, satisfying either $x_e = 0$ or $q_e = \pm x_e$ for all $e \in E$. By orienting the edges of E as necessary, one can assume $q \geq 0$ and thus $q = x$. Since $q = XA^\top L^{-1}b$, this implies that $(A^\top L^{-1}b)_e = 1$ whenever $x_e > 0$. In other words, along any edge $e = (u,v)$ with positive capacity, the potential difference $p_u - p_v$ is 1 (recall that $L^{-1}b = p$, hence $(A^\top L^{-1}b)_e$ is the potential difference along edge e). However, the potential difference along any path only depends on the difference between the potentials of the endpoints of the path. Hence, all paths with positive capacity from source to sink have the same length, $p_{s_0} - p_{s_1}$. Since the cytoplasmic flow can only be nonzero on paths with positive capacity, this means that q is a convex combination of characteristic vectors of source-sink paths, all of the same length. Moreover, when each source-sink path has a distinct length, there can be only one nonzero-flow path in the convex combination, with length $p_{s_0} - p_{s_1} = \mathcal{E}$ by (7). □

In the following, for the sake of exposition it will be assumed that different source-sink paths have distinct length in the network. This implies a finite set of isolated equilibrium points for the autonomous system (14), one for each source-sink path. If the assumption is not satisfied, convergence towards the convex set of minimum-energy equilibrium points can still be argued, although one cannot argue convergence towards a specific point of that set.

Example 3. *Let us continue the example from above. The autonomous system (14) is*

$$\dot{x}_j = x_j \left(\frac{q_j^2}{x_j^2} - 1 \right) \quad j = 1,2,3,$$

$$q = \frac{1}{x_1 x_2 + x_1 x_3 + x_2 x_3} \begin{pmatrix} x_1 x_2 \\ x_1 x_2 \\ x_1 x_3 + x_2 x_3 \end{pmatrix}.$$

In this case there are only two source-sink paths: $P_1 = (e_1, e_2)$, and $P_2 = (e_3)$. They have distinct lengths, hence there is one isolated equilibrium for each of P_1 and P_2. The first corresponds to the vector of capacities $x^{(1)} = \chi^{P_1} = (1,1,0)$ and cytoplasmic flow $q^{(1)} = (1,1,0)$. The second corresponds to the vector of capacities $x^{(2)} = \chi^{P_2} = (0,0,1)$ and cytoplasmic flow $q^{(2)} = (0,0,1)$. Note that the energy of the first cytoplasmic flow is 2, while the energy of the second cytoplasmic flow is 1. A linear stability analysis around each equilibrium reveals that the first equilibrium point is unstable, while the second equilibrium point is stable.

The situation in Example 3 is not accidental: in the following, a general result will be shown implying that the equilibrium of minimum energy attracts the entire positive orthant, and hence all equilibria of non-minimal energy must be unstable.

3. Stability Analysis: An Optimization Perspective

Both the experimental results of Nakagaki et al. [13] and the toy example considered above suggest that, perhaps, the stability of equilibrium points of (14) is related to the minimality of the corresponding paths in the network. Hence, in order to study the stability of the system (14), it might be useful to adopt an optimization perspective. In this section, it will be shown that this is indeed the case.

3.1. The Shortest Path Problem

In particular, let us consider the *shortest path problem* in the given network, where one wants to construct a source-sink path that uses as few edges as possible. Formally, the shortest path problem can be formulated as follows:

$$\text{minimize } \|f\|_1 \tag{16}$$

$$\text{subject to } Af = b, \quad f \in \mathbb{R}^E,$$

where $\|f\|_1 := \sum_{e \in E} |f_e| = |f_1| + |f_2| + \ldots + |f_m|$. In transportation terminology: find a way to ship a unit of a commodity from the source to the sink, while minimizing the total amount of commodity shipped along the edges of the network. The quantity f_e encodes the amount of commodity shipped along edge e; thus a vector f satisfying $Af = b$ satisfies flow conservation.

Note that at this point, the only obvious relation between shortest path flows f, which solve the shortest path problem (16), and cytoplasmic flows q, which solve the least dissipation problem (6), is that they are both unit flows, that is, they satisfy Kirchhoff's current law ($Aq = b$, $Af = b$). Apart from this, in general they could be very different vectors. For instance, in Example 3, the equilibrium flow $(1,1,0)$ is a cytoplasmic flow, but not a shortest path flow. Moreover, a cytoplasmic flow is defined only after a capacity vector x has been specified, while in the shortest path problem (16) there are no capacities to speak of.

3.2. A Variational Reformulation of the Shortest Path Objective

Interestingly, however, the shortest path problem can be related to a modified least dissipation problem. To see this, first observe that for any real number a,

$$|a| = \inf_{x>0} \frac{1}{2}\left(\frac{a^2}{x} + x\right).$$

Hence, the ℓ_1-norm of any vector $f \in \mathbb{R}^m$ can be equivalently expressed as

$$\|f\|_1 = \inf_{x \in \mathbb{R}^m_{>0}} \frac{1}{2} \sum_{j=1}^m \left(\frac{f_j^2}{x_j} + x_j\right). \tag{17}$$

Therefore

$$\begin{aligned}
\min_{\substack{f \in \mathbb{R}^m \\ Af=b}} \|f\|_1 &= \min_{\substack{f \in \mathbb{R}^m \\ Af=b}} \inf_{x \in \mathbb{R}^m_{>0}} \frac{1}{2} \sum_{j=1}^m \left(\frac{f_j^2}{x_j} + x_j\right) \\
&= \inf_{x \in \mathbb{R}^m_{>0}} \left(\frac{1}{2}\left(\min_{\substack{f \in \mathbb{R}^m \\ Af=b}} f^\top X^{-1} f\right) + \frac{1}{2} \mathbf{1}^\top x\right) \\
&= \inf_{x \in \mathbb{R}^m_{>0}} \left(\frac{1}{2} b^\top L(x)^{-1} b + \frac{1}{2} \mathbf{1}^\top x\right),
\end{aligned} \tag{18}$$

with the last identity following from (10). Let us define, for any positive vector x,

$$\mathcal{F}(x) := b^\top L(x)^{-1} b + \mathbf{1}^\top x. \tag{19}$$

If one interprets x as a vector of capacities, then the term $b^\top L(x)^{-1} b$ is the energy of the cytoplasmic flow induced by x. Thus, the function $\mathcal{F}$ is built from two terms: the first can be interpreted as the cost of transport, which is proportional to the dissipated energy, and the second as the cost of maintaining the transport infrastructure. For shortness, $\mathcal{F}(x)$ will be called the *dissipation potential* of the vector x. By (18), finding a flow f minimizing $\|f\|_1$ (a shortest path flow) is equivalent to finding an assignment x of capacities to the edges of the network that minimizes the dissipation $\mathcal{F}(x)$. The following can be concluded.

Theorem 1 ([16,23]). *The value of the optimization problem*

$$\text{minimize } \|f\|_1$$
$$\text{subject to } Af = b, \quad f \in \mathbb{R}^m$$

equals the value of the optimization problem

$$\text{minimize } \frac{1}{2}\mathbf{1}^\top x + \frac{1}{2}b^\top (AXA^\top)^{-1}b \quad (=\frac{1}{2}\mathcal{F}(x))$$
$$\text{subject to } x \in \mathbb{R}_{>0}^m$$

where $X = \mathrm{diag}(x)$.

The dissipation function $\mathcal{F}$ is defined on the positive orthant and, importantly, is convex.

Lemma 2 ([23]). *The dissipation function $\mathcal{F}$ is positive, convex and differentiable on $\mathbb{R}_{>0}^m$.*

Proof. Positivity follows from Equation (10). For convexity, it suffices to show that the mapping $x \mapsto b^\top L^{-1}(x)b$ is convex on $\mathbb{R}_{>0}^m$. This mapping can be seen as the composition of two other mappings: the first is the matrix-valued map $x \mapsto AXA^\top$, which is linear since each of the entries of $AXA^\top$ is a linear function of x, and yields a positive definite matrix $Y = AXA^\top = (AX^{1/2})(AX^{1/2})^\top$; the second is the matrix to scalar map $Y \mapsto b^\top Y^{-1}b$, which is convex on the cone of positive definite matrices, for any $b \in \mathbb{R}^n$ (see for example [24] Section 3.1.7). It follows that the composed mapping $x \mapsto b^\top (AXA^\top)^{-1}b$ is convex, and hence so is $\mathcal{F}$. Finally, since the entries of $L(x)$ are linear functions of x, the dissipation function $\mathcal{F}$ is a rational function with no poles in $\mathbb{R}_{>0}^m$, hence differentiable. □

The dissipation function can even be defined on the boundary of the positive orthant by convex closure (that is, by posing $\mathcal{F}(x) = \liminf_{x' \to x} \mathcal{F}(x')$ when x is on the boundary; see [23] for details). The extension is convex on the nonnegative orthant and differentiable in its interior, and attains its minimum, although the minimizer x^* might lie on the boundary of the positive orthant. Theorem 1 allows us to identify this minimizer.

Corollary 1. *The minimizer of $\mathcal{F}$ over $\mathbb{R}_{\geq 0}^m$ is the characteristic vector χ^{P^*} of the shortest path P^* of the network. The corresponding cytoplasmic flow is an equilibrium flow.*

Proof. Let us consider the characteristic vector χ^{P^*} and interpret it as a vector of capacities $x^* := \chi^{P^*}$. Since the capacity x_e^* is zero for any edge $e \notin P^*$, by Poiseuille's law the resulting cytoplasmic flow $q = X^* A^\top (AX^* A^\top)^{-1}b$ will also satisfy $q_e = 0 = x_e^*$ for all $e \notin P^*$. Thus, the support of flow q is contained in the path P^*, which by the flow constraints $Aq = b$ implies that along any edge of P^* there is a unit amount of flow $|q_e| = 1 = x_e^*$. This implies that $|q_e| = x_e^*$ for all edges $e \in E$. The flow q is thus an equilibrium cytoplasmic flow, since $\varphi(|q_e|/x_e^*) = \varphi(1) = 1$. Moreover, its energy is, by (10), $b^\top L^{-1}b = q^\top X^{*-1}q = \sum_{j=1}^m q_j^2/x_j^* = \|x^*\|_1$. Therefore,

$$\frac{1}{2}\mathcal{F}(x^*) = \frac{1}{2}b^\top L^{-1}b + \frac{1}{2}\mathbf{1}^\top x^* = \frac{1}{2}\|x^*\|_1 + \frac{1}{2}\|x^*\|_1 = \|x^*\|_1.$$

Since by construction x^* was chosen to minimize $\|x^*\|_1$, by Theorem 1 it also minimizes $\mathcal{F}(x^*)$. □

3.3. Physarum Dynamics as a Hessian Gradient Flow

Let us set aside Physarum's autonomous system (14) for a moment, and consider how one could set up a dynamical system in $\mathbb{R}_{>0}^m$, the solutions of which converge, over time, to the characteristic vector of the shortest path. Given Corollary 1, one possibility is to aim at minimizing the differentiable convex function $\mathcal{F}$ over the positive orthant. To minimize a generic differentiable convex function $\mathcal{F}$ over the positive orthant, one might set up the following set of ordinary differential equations:

$$\dot{x}_j = -x_j \frac{\partial \mathcal{F}(x)}{\partial x_j}, \quad j = 1, \ldots, m, \tag{20}$$

with initial condition $x(0) = x^0$ for some $x^0 \in \mathbb{R}^m_{>0}$. This is an instance of the *mirror descent dynamics*, a well-studied dynamics in convex optimization theory [25,26]. The intuition behind (20) is simple: to approach a global minimum, one should follow the (negative) gradient of $\mathcal{F}$, but the rate of change of the j-th component should be reduced the smaller x_j is, in order not to violate the constraint $x_j \geq 0$.

When $\mathcal{F}$ is the dissipation potential (19), what does one get from (20)? Let us compute the gradient of the dissipation potential.

Lemma 3 ([23]). *Let $x \in \mathbb{R}^m_{>0}$. For any $j = 1, \ldots, m$,*

$$\frac{\partial \mathcal{F}(x)}{\partial x_j} = 1 - (a_j^\top L^{-1}(x)b)^2 = 1 - \frac{q_j^2}{x_j^2},$$

where a_j stands for the jth column of matrix A.

Proof. Let us start by observing that, by definition, $L(x) = AXA^\top = \sum_{j=1}^m x_j a_j a_j^\top$ and thus $\partial L/\partial x_j = a_j a_j^\top$. Applying the following identity for the derivative of a matrix inverse (Section 8.4) [27]:

$$\frac{\partial L^{-1}}{\partial x_j} = -L^{-1} \frac{\partial L}{\partial x_j} L^{-1}, \tag{21}$$

yielding

$$\frac{\partial b^\top L^{-1} b}{\partial x_j} = -b^\top L^{-1} \frac{\partial L}{\partial x_j} L^{-1} b = -b^\top L^{-1} a_j a_j^\top L^{-1} b = -(a_j^\top L^{-1} b)^2.$$

By (9), $a_j^\top L^{-1} b = q_j/x_j$. The claim now follows by the definition of $\mathcal{F}$, (19), since $\partial(1^\top x)/\partial x_j = 1$. □

Plugging Lemma 3 into (20) yields the dynamics

$$\dot{x}_j = x_j \left(\frac{q_j^2}{x_j^2} - 1 \right), \quad j = 1, \ldots, m, \tag{22}$$

which is nothing but the Physarum system (14)!

In other words, the quadratic-response Physarum system (14) can be reformulated as a *Hessian gradient flow* [28]: it can be written in the form

$$\dot{x} = -H^{-1}(x) \nabla \mathcal{F}(x) \tag{23}$$

where $H(x) = \nabla^2 h(x)$ is the Hessian of a convex function h; namely, here $H(x) = X^{-1}$, and $h : \mathbb{R}^m_{>0} \to \mathbb{R}$ is the *negative entropy* function

$$h(x) := \sum_{j=1}^m x_j \log x_j - \sum_{j=1}^m x_j. \tag{24}$$

The Hessian gradient form immediately implies the existence of a solution to system (14) for all $t \geq 0$, using standard arguments [28].

System (23) can also be expressed as

$$\frac{d}{dt} \frac{\partial h(x)}{\partial x_j} = -\frac{\partial \mathcal{F}(x)}{\partial x_j}, \quad j = 1, \ldots, m,$$

or more succinctly,
$$\frac{d}{dt}\nabla h(x) = -\nabla \mathcal{F}(x), \tag{25}$$
another form of the mirror descent dynamics, also known as *natural gradient flow* [29].

The equivalent formulations (23) and (25) of the Physarum dynamics (14) show that the dynamics follows the gradient of the dissipation function $\mathcal{F}$, under the geometry dictated by the negative entropy function h, defined by (24). It is thus reasonable to expect convergence to the minimum of the dissipation function, i.e., to an equilibrium point where the resulting cytoplasmic flow is the shortest path flow. To rigorously prove this, thanks to Corollary 1 it is sufficient to show that the solutions of system (23) indeed converge to a minimizer of the convex function $\mathcal{F}$.

3.4. Basin of Attraction

The fact that any solution of the mirror descent dynamics (20) with initial condition in $\mathbb{R}^m_{>0}$ converges to a minimizer of a convex function $\mathcal{F}$ is, in fact, a result already established in the optimization literature [28,30]. A self-contained proof is presented here. Let us start with a straightforward lemma showing that $\mathcal{F}$ is monotonically nonincreasing along the trajectories of the dynamical system.

Lemma 4. *The values $\mathcal{F}(x(t))$ with $x(t)$ a solution of (20) are nonincreasing in t.*

Proof. By the multivariable chain rule and (20),
$$\frac{d}{dt}\mathcal{F}(x(t)) = \sum_{j=1}^{m}\frac{\partial \mathcal{F}}{\partial x_j}(x)\,\dot{x}_j = -\sum_{j=1}^{m} x_j \left(\frac{\partial \mathcal{F}}{\partial x_j}(x)\right)^2 \leq 0. \quad \square$$

A key role in the analysis of the mirror descent dynamics is played by the notion of Bregman divergence of a convex function h. This measures the distance between the value of h at a point x, and the approximate value of h at x predicted by a linear model of the function constructed at another point y; see Figure 2 for an illustration.

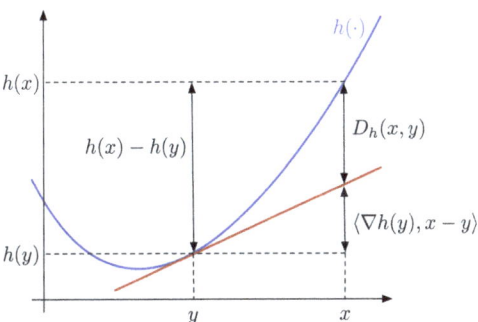

Figure 2. Illustration of the Bregman divergence $D_h(x,y)$.

Definition 1. *The Bregman divergence of a convex function $h : \mathbb{R}^m \to (-\infty, +\infty]$ is defined by $D_h(x,y) := h(x) - h(y) - \langle \nabla h(y), x - y \rangle$.*

Convexity of h implies the nonnegativity of $D_h(x,y)$. When h is the negative entropy, D_h is the *relative entropy*:
$$D_h(x,y) = \sum_{j=1}^{m} x_j \log \frac{x_j}{y_j} - \sum_{j=1}^{m}(x_j - y_j),$$

which boils down to (2) when x and y are probability distributions (since $\sum_j x_j = \sum_j y_j = 1$). The relative entropy satisfies $D_h(x,y) = 0$ if and only if $x = y$ [29].

Using the notion of Bregman divergence, let us prove that the solutions of the mirror descent dynamics converge to the minimizer of the convex function $\mathcal{F}$.

Theorem 2. *Let $x(0) \in \mathbb{R}_{>0}^m$ and let $x^* \in \mathbb{R}_{\geq 0}^m$ be the minimizer of $\mathcal{F}$ (assumed unique). Then any solution $x(t)$ of (20) satisfies, for all $t \geq 0$,*

$$\mathcal{F}(x(t)) - \mathcal{F}(x^*) \leq \frac{1}{t} D_h(x^*, x(0)). \tag{26}$$

In particular, as $t \to \infty$, the values $\mathcal{F}(x(t))$ converge to $\mathcal{F}(x^*)$ and hence $x(t)$ converges to x^*.

Proof. A proof will be given that streamlines that in [30]. In the following, to shorten notation let us write x in place of $x(t)$. Since $(d/dt)\nabla h(x) + \nabla \mathcal{F}(x) = 0$ by (25), for any y one has $\langle (d/dt)\nabla h(x) + \nabla \mathcal{F}(x), x - y \rangle = 0$. This is equivalent to

$$\langle \frac{d}{dt} \nabla h(x), x - y \rangle + \langle \nabla \mathcal{F}(x), x - y \rangle = 0. \tag{27}$$

On the other hand, since $(d/dt)h(x) = \langle \nabla h(x), \dot{x} \rangle$, Definition 1 yields

$$\frac{d}{dt} D_h(y, x) = -\frac{d}{dt} h(x) + \frac{d}{dt} \langle \nabla h(x), x - y \rangle \tag{28}$$

$$= -\langle \nabla h(x), \dot{x} \rangle + \langle \frac{d}{dt} \nabla h(x), x - y \rangle + \langle \nabla h(x), \dot{x} \rangle$$

$$= \langle \frac{d}{dt} \nabla h(x), x - y \rangle.$$

Combining (27) and (28), and plugging in $y = x^*$,

$$\frac{d}{dt} D_h(x^*, x) = -\langle \nabla \mathcal{F}(x), x - x^* \rangle. \tag{29}$$

The proof is concluded by a Lyapunov argument. Define $\Phi : [0, \infty) \to \mathbb{R}$ by

$$\Phi(t) := D_h(x^*, x) + t(\mathcal{F}(x) - \mathcal{F}(x^*)).$$

Its time derivative is, by (29),

$$\frac{d}{dt} \Phi(t) = -\langle \nabla \mathcal{F}(x), x - x^* \rangle + \mathcal{F}(x) - \mathcal{F}(x^*) + t \frac{d}{dt} \mathcal{F}(x),$$

where the last summand is nonpositive by Lemma 4 and the other terms sum to, by definition, $-D_{\mathcal{F}}(x^*, x) \leq 0$ (by the convexity of $\mathcal{F}$, Lemma 2. Hence, $\Phi(t) \leq \Phi(0)$ for all $t \geq 0$, which is equivalent to

$$D_h(x^*, x) + t(\mathcal{F}(x) - \mathcal{F}(x^*)) \leq D_h(x^*, x(0)),$$

proving (26) since $D_h(x^*, x) \geq 0$.

Because $x(0) \in \mathbb{R}_{>0}^m$ by assumption, the divergence $D_h(x^*, x(0))$ is a finite constant and (26) implies convergence of $\mathcal{F}(x(t))$ to $\mathcal{F}(x^*)$. Convergence of $x(t)$ to x^* follows from the uniqueness of the minimizer x^*. □

Corollary 2. *In the quadratic-response Physarum system (14), the basin of attraction of the shortest path equilibrium $x^* = x^{P^*}$ contains $\mathbb{R}_{>0}^m$.*

Proof. It was already argued in Section 3.3 that the Physarum system (14) can be written in the mirror descent form (20). The minimizer x^* is unique because of the assumption that each source-sink path has a distinct length. Thus, for any $x(0) \in \mathbb{R}^m_{>0}$, Theorem 2 guarantees attraction to x^*. □

Note that, with essentially the same proof, Theorem 2 can be partially extended to the case where there is more than one minimizer of $\mathcal{F}$, in the following sense: as $t \to \infty$, the values $\mathcal{F}(x(t))$ converge to the minimum of $\mathcal{F}$ over $\mathbb{R}^m_{\geq 0}$. However, when the minimizer is no longer unique, one cannot directly conclude that $x(t)$ converges against any specific minimizer.

4. Related Work and Generalizations of the Model

4.1. Beyond the Quadratic Response Function

Going back to the general formulation of the Physarum system (13), it is natural to ask whether the stability result of Corollary 2 can be extended to other response functions, beyond the quadratic response $\varphi(z) = z^2$.

Indeed, initial work on the Physarum dynamics considered the linear response $\varphi(z) = z$. Tero et al. [10] were the first to introduce such a model, and proved an analogue of Corollary 2 when the network is a simple cycle, with two nodes and two edges of different lengths. The analysis of the linear-response Physarum system was later extended to certain planar networks [31], and ultimately to all networks [15]. The latter stability proofs are substantially more involved than in the case of the quadratic response, because the system cannot in those cases be expressed as a Hessian gradient system, as it was done in (23). Nevertheless, Lyapunov arguments are still the essential ingredients of the stability proofs.

Tero et al. [10] also considered nonlinear response functions, but in a formulation that is somewhat different from (13); they assume that the tubular response of edge e is controlled by the sheer amount of flow $|q_e|$, as opposed to the pressure $|q_e|/x_e$:

$$\dot{x}_e = \varphi(|q_e|) - x_e. \tag{30}$$

When the response is linear, that is, $\varphi(z) = z$, formulation (30) by Tero et al. is equivalent to (13). However, when the response is not linear, the two models are qualitatively different. In particular, the model by Tero et al. has multiple stable equilibria when $\varphi(z) = z^\mu$ with $\mu > 1$. In contrast, the model (13) has a unique stable equilibrium even in those cases [11].

Formulation (13) was first proposed in [11], where it was shown that on a network topology consisting of parallel links, the analogue of Corollary 2 holds for all strictly increasing, differentiable functions $\varphi : \mathbb{R}_{\geq 0} \to \mathbb{R}_{\geq 0}$ such that $\varphi(1) = 1$. In fact, such a result holds even when each edge e of the network has a distinct response function φ_e. This result was later extended to all network topologies by Karrenbauer, Kolev and Mehlhorn (Theorem 3) [17], under the following additional assumption for the response functions:

$$\varphi_e(z) \geq 1 + \alpha_e(z - 1) \text{ for some } \alpha_e > 0 \text{ and all } z \geq 0. \tag{31}$$

Condition (31) is satisfied, in particular, by all convex increasing functions (to see this, take $\alpha_e = \varphi'_e(1)$). As mentioned in [17], it is an open problem whether condition (31) can be relaxed.

4.2. Beyond the Network Setting

Although the Physarum dynamics (13) and (30) originated in the context of mathematical biology, as seen in Section 3 it can also be understood from an optimization perspective. From such a more abstract view, the same dynamics can be shown to converge to the solution of optimization problems that substantially generalize the shortest path problem (16).

Namely, if instead of defining the constraint matrix A in terms of a network, one allows any full-rank matrix $A \in \mathbb{R}^{n' \times m}$, then the dynamics (13) is still well-defined, and under mild technical conditions it converges to an optimal solution of the following ℓ_1-norm minimization problem:

$$\min \|f\|_1 \tag{32}$$
$$\text{s.t. } Af = b, \quad f \in \mathbb{R}^m.$$

This looks formally the same as the shortest path formulation (16), but represents a more general problem, since A is not restricted to be a network matrix and b can be an arbitrary vector in $\mathbb{R}^{n'}$. Problem (32) is sometimes called *basis pursuit* and is an important problem in signal processing and statistics: it can yield sparse signals (f) that explain the observations (b) from a set of linear measurements (A) (see for example [32]). This abstract viewpoint on the Physarum dynamics has been explored in several works of the networks and optimization community [16,18,23,33].

4.3. Multiple Sources of Food

Finally, let us note that food-foraging experiments have been carried out in which the slime mold is provided with more than two sources of food [14]. Instead of collapsing into a path, the slime mold in this case eventually connects the sources of food into a complex network structure. One can ask how such a scenario could be modeled effectively, and what functional (if any) is optimized by the network adaptation process in this case.

In this context, a key modeling issue is to strike a balance between tractability and plausibility of the proposed model. In particular, in order for the model to be biologically plausible, it should preserve the symmetry between the sources of food. In the case of two sources of food, this symmetry is guaranteed by the absolute value in Equation (12), which makes the dynamics oblivious to the direction of the flow. In the case of more than two sources, however, it is unclear how to guarantee the same property with a conceptually simple model; the original proposal by Tero et al. [14], for example, involves a periodic random selection of the flow sink node, which seems rather challenging to analyze formally.

The formal model (13) can certainly be extended by allowing the cytoplasmic flow to have multiple sources $s_1, \ldots, s_k$ and sinks $t_1, \ldots, t_l$, each with a different supply/demand of flow; interestingly, in this case, the functional optimized is the so-called *transshipment cost* [33,34], yielding a connection with optimal transport theory [35,36]. However, symmetry with respect to the food locations is lost: exchanging the role of a source s_i with that of a sink t_j will generally result in a different set of dynamical equations, with incompatible solutions. Therefore, such a model does not appear to be plausible from a biological point of view, despite certainly being interesting from an optimization perspective. All in all, development of a plausible, yet tractable, mathematical model of *P. polycephalum*'s network dynamics with multiple sources of food remains a challenging problem for future research.

5. Conclusions

A mathematical model of the network dynamics of *P. polycephalum* was presented that exhibits, from a qualitative standpoint, a behavior compatible with that observed in the laboratory food foraging experiments. The analysis of the model reveals at least two interesting aspects.

The first is the fact that the stable equilibrium point of the dynamics provably minimizes a combination of the infrastructural cost of the network—the term $\mathbf{1}^\top x$ in (19), which corresponds to the total capacity of the network—and of the transport cost–the term $b^\top L^{-1}(x)b$ in (19), which corresponds to the energy of the cytoplasmic flow. The fact that an organism like *P. polycephalum* achieves a convenient tradeoff between transport efficiency and infrastructural cost of the network should not be surprising, since after all it presumably yields an evolutive advantage. Nevertheless, it is somewhat remarkable that this optimization objective emerges so clearly from the simple positive feedback response (12) of the tubular channels to the flow.

A second remarkable fact is the central role of information-theoretic concepts in the stability analysis. It was shown that the quadratic-response dynamics can be interpreted as a gradient descent in the non-Euclidean geometry dictated by the negative entropy function $h(x)$, and that the corresponding relative entropy $D_h(x^*, x)$ plays a crucial role in the stability proof, as it is able to track the symmetry breaking from (for example) an initially uniform configuration towards the optimal network configuration. In fact, even for response functions that are not quadratic, relative entropy makes an appearance, whether implicitly or explicitly, in all known stability proofs. Thus, information-theoretic concepts emerge as very relevant, and perhaps indispensable, mathematical tools in this context.

Funding: This research received no external funding.

Institutional Review Board Statement: Not applicable.

Informed Consent Statement: Not applicable.

Acknowledgments: This work was carried out in association with Istituto di Analisi dei Sistemi ed Informatica, Consiglio Nazionale delle Ricerche, Italy.

Conflicts of Interest: The author declares no conflict of interest.

References

1. Schrödinger, E. *What Is Life?* Cambridge University Press: Cambridge, UK, 1944.
2. Johnson, H.A. Information Theory in Biology after 18 Years. *Science* **1970**, *168*, 1545–1550. [CrossRef]
3. Gatenby, R.; Frieden, B. Information theory in living systems, methods, applications, and challenges. *Bull. Math. Biol.* **2007**, *69*, 635–657. [CrossRef]
4. Friston, K. The free-energy principle: A unified brain theory? *Nat. Rev. Neurosci.* **2010**, *11*, 127–138. [CrossRef] [PubMed]
5. Baez, J.C.; Pollard, B.S. Relative Entropy in Biological Systems. *Entropy* **2016**, *18*, 46. [CrossRef]
6. van Kampen, N. *Stochastic Processes in Physics and Chemistry*; North-Holland: Amsterdam, The Netherlands, 2007.
7. Hofrichter, J.; Host, J.; Tran, T.D. *Information Geometry and Population Genetics*; Springer: Berlin/Heidelberg, Germany, 2017.
8. Guberman, J.M. Mass Action Reaction Networks and The Deficiency Zero Theorem. Master's Thesis, Harvard University, Cambridge, MA, USA, 2003.
9. Harper, M.; Fryer, D.E.A. Lyapunov Functions for Time-Scale Dynamics on Riemannian Geometries of the Simplex. *Dyn. Games Appl.* **2015**, *5*, 318–333. [CrossRef]
10. Tero, A.; Kobayashi, R.; Nakagaki, T. A mathematical model for adaptive transport network in path finding by true slime mold. *J. Theor. Biol.* **2007**, *244*, 553–564. [CrossRef]
11. Bonifaci, V. A revised model of fluid transport optimization in *Physarum polycephalum*. *J. Math. Biol.* **2017**, *74*, 567–581. [CrossRef] [PubMed]
12. Alim, K.; Andrew, N.; Pringle, A. Physarum. *Curr. Biol.* **2013**, *23*, R1082–R1083. [CrossRef]
13. Nakagaki, T.; Yamada, H.; Tóth, Á. Maze-solving by an amoeboid organism. *Nature* **2000**, *407*, 470. [CrossRef] [PubMed]
14. Tero, A.; Takagi, S.; Saigusa, T.; Ito, K.; Bebber, D.P.; Fricker, M.D.; Yumiki, K.; Kobayashi, R.; Nakagaki, T. Rules for Biologically Inspired Adaptive Network Design. *Science* **2010**, *327*, 439–442. [CrossRef] [PubMed]
15. Bonifaci, V.; Mehlhorn, K.; Varma, G. Physarum Can Compute Shortest Paths. *J. Theor. Biol.* **2012**, *309*, 121–133. [CrossRef]
16. Facca, E.; Cardin, F.; Putti, M. Physarum Dynamics and Optimal Transport for Basis Pursuit. *arXiv* **2019**, arXiv:1812.11782v1.
17. Karrenbauer, A.; Kolev, P.; Mehlhorn, K. Convergence of the non-uniform Physarum dynamics. *Theor. Comput. Sci.* **2020**, *816*, 260–269. [CrossRef]
18. Straszak, D.; Vishnoi, N.K. Iteratively reweighted least squares and slime mold dynamics: Connection and convergence. *Math. Program.* **2021**. [CrossRef]
19. YouTube Video. 2011. Available online: https://youtu.be/czk4xgdhdY4 (accessed on 20 May 2021).
20. Bollobás, B. *Modern Graph Theory*; Springer: New York, NY, USA, 1998.
21. Strang, G. A framework for equilibrium equations. *SIAM Rev.* **1988**, *30*, 283–296. [CrossRef]
22. Biggs, N. *Algebraic Graph Theory*; Cambridge University Press: Cambridge, UK, 1974.
23. Bonifaci, V. A Laplacian Approach to ℓ_1-Norm Minimization. *Comput. Optim. Appl.* **2021**. [CrossRef]
24. Boyd, S.; Vandenberghe, L. *Convex Optimization*; Cambridge University Press: Cambridge, UK, 2004.
25. Nemirovski, A.S.; Yudin, D.B. *Problem Complexity and Method Efficiency in Optimization*; Wiley: Chichester, UK, 1983.
26. Bubeck, S. Convex Optimization: Algorithms and Complexity. *Found. Trends Mach. Learn.* **2015**, *8*, 231–357. [CrossRef]
27. Magnus, J.R.; Neudecker, H. *Matrix Differential Calculus with Applications in Statistics and Econometrics*; Wiley: Chichester, UK, 2019.
28. Alvarez, F.; Bolte, J.; Brahic, O. Hessian Riemannian Gradient Flows in Convex Programming. *SIAM J. Control Optim.* **2004**, *43*, 477–501. [CrossRef]
29. Amari, S. *Information Geometry and Its Applications*; Springer: Berlin/Heidelberg, Germany, 2016.

30. Wilson, A. Lyapunov Arguments in Optimization. Ph.D. Thesis, University of California at Berkeley, Berkeley, CA, USA, 2018.
31. Miyaji, T.; Ohnishi, I. Physarum can solve the shortest path problem on Riemannian surface mathematically rigourously. *Int. J. Pure Appl. Math.* **2008**, *47*, 353–369.
32. Chen, S.S.; Donoho, D.L.; Saunders, M.A. Atomic Decomposition by Basis Pursuit. *SIAM Rev.* **2001**, *43*, 129–159. [CrossRef]
33. Ito, K.; Johansson, A.; Nakagaki, T.; Tero, A. Convergence Properties for the Physarum Solver. *arXiv* **2011**, arXiv:1101.5249v1.
34. Straszak, D.; Vishnoi, N.K. Natural Algorithms for Flow Problems. In Proceedings of the 27th ACM-SIAM Symposium on Discrete Algorithms, Arlington, VA, USA, 10–12 January 2016; SIAM: Philadelphia, PA, USA, 2016; pp. 1868–1883.
35. Facca, E.; Cardin, F.; Putti, M. Towards a Stationary Monge–Kantorovich Dynamics: The Physarum Polycephalum Experience. *SIAM J. Appl. Math.* **2018**, *78*, 651–676. [CrossRef]
36. Cardin, F. Trasporto ottimo, sistemi viventi (in Italian). *Mat. Cult. Soc. Riv. Dell'Unione Mat. Ital.* **2017**, *2*, 327–341.

Article

Primary Model for Biomass Growth Prediction in Batch Fermentation

Yolocuauhtli Salazar [1,*], Emmanuel Rodriguez [1], Paul A. Valle [2,*] and Blanca E. Garcia [3]

[1] Postgraduate Program in Engineering, Tecnológico Nacional de México/IT Durango, Blvd. Felipe Pescador 1830 ote., Durango 34080, Mexico; 10040780@itdurango.edu.mx
[2] BioMath Research Group, Postgraduate Program in Engineering Sciences, Tecnológico Nacional de México/IT Tijuana, Blvd. Alberto Limón Padilla s/n, Tijuana 22454, Mexico
[3] Department of Chemical and Biochemical Engineering, Tecnológico Nacional de México/IT Durango, Blvd. Felipe Pescador 1830 ote., Durango 34080, Mexico; bgarcia@itdurango.edu.mx
* Correspondence: ysalazar@itdurango.edu.mx (Y.S.); paul.valle@tectijuana.edu.mx (P.A.V.)

Abstract: Predictive models may be considered a tool to ensure food quality as they provide insights that support decision making on the design of processes, such as fermentation. Objective: To formulate a mathematical model that describes the growth of lactic acid bacteria (LAB) in batch fermentation. Methodology: Based on real-life experimental data from eight LAB strains, we formulated a primary model in the form of a third-degree polynomial function that successfully describes the four phases observed in LAB growth, i.e., lag, exponential, stationary, and death. Our cubic mathematical model allows us to understand the fundamental nonlinear dynamics of LAB as well as its time-variant dependencies. Parameters of the model are written in terms of initial biomass, maximum biomass, maximum growth rate, and lag phase duration. Further, a statistical analysis was performed to compare our cubic primary model with the ones proposed by Gompertz, Baranyi, and Vázquez-Murado by computing the coefficient of determination (R^2), the residual sum of squares (RSS), and the Akaike Information Criterion (AIC). Results: The average statistical results from the cubic model are as follows: $R^2 = 0.820$ providing a better fit than the other three models, $RSS = 0.658$ and $AIC = -6.499$, where both values are lower than the other models considered in this study. Conclusion: The cubic primary model formulated in this work describes the behavior of biomass as it accurately represents the four phases of biomass growth in batch fermentation process.

Keywords: predictive microbiology; lactic acid bacteria; batch fermentation; primary mathematical model; bacterial growth

1. Introduction

Lactic Acid Bacteria (LAB) refer to a group of microorganisms that share certain morphological, physiological, and metabolic characteristics. They have the peculiarity of producing lactic acid from several carbohydrates through a process known as microbial fermentation. They are normally found in cultures such as milk, whey, and pickles [1,2]. The Danish microbiologist Orla-Jensen said that *"True lactic acid bacteria are a large group of cocci and Gram positive, immobile, spore free bacilli, which produce lactic acid in the fermentation of sugar"* [3]. Currently, LAB have a primary role in the food industry, as they are used to acidify and preserve food. Further, they contribute to texture, taste, smell, and scent development in all kinds of fermented foods [4,5].

In the industry, most fermentation is carried out through batch culture. This means that only a culture medium with the necessary nutrients is added to the fermenter, and this is incubated for the growth of bacteria and the production of its primary metabolite. During the time of incubation, nothing other than oxygen is added [6]. Hence, the bacterial growth follows an asymmetric cell division (ACD), which is a conserved mechanism evolved to generate cellular diversity. A key principle of ACD is the establishment of distinct sibling cell fates by mechanisms linked to mitosis [7]. ACD also occurs in the development and physiology of unicellular organisms ranging from bacterial species to yeasts and flagellates [8,9]. In these organisms, ACD underlies replicative aging as a means of maintaining the immortality of the mitotically proliferating population [10].

LAB are very demanding microorganisms and need a set of growing factors, including sugars such as carbohydrates, as well as amino acids and vitamins. Therefore, LAB can only grow in a medium that supplies these nutrients [3]. The interest in the physiology of LAB has been studied by its industrial importance and potential use of genetic engineering in strain optimization. For example, in the particular case of *Lactococcus lactis* spp. *lactis*, a minimal growth medium should contain glucose, acetate, vitamins, and amino acids [11]. Milk is the medium that contains all these nutrients. For this reason, LAB are used as starter cultures for the preparation and preservation of dairy products, such as acidified milk, yogurt, butter, cream, and cheese [1]. In batch fermentation, bacteria cannot grow exponentially indefinitely. The latter due to bacteria depleting nutrients as it grows, changes in the chemical composition of the medium (pH), and toxic compounds that are accumulated. The characteristic curve of bacterial growth is composed by four phases: (i) lag, (ii) exponential, (iii) stationary, and (iv) death. Lactic acid production occurs during the reproduction of LAB; the accumulation of this and other organic acids decrease the pH of the medium, which made culture conditions become more selective; hence, the more acid-tolerant bacterium will prevail.

The total number of cells in fermentation are usually represented by a logarithmic scale, and normally, at the end of this process, one can see values from 10^8 up to 10^9 CFU/mL (Cell-Forming Units per milliliter) [2]. In addition to nutritional requirements, temperature is one of the most important factors in LAB growth. Furthermore, there is an optimal temperature and other environmental conditions for which these microorganisms present a higher growth rate [4]. LAB are acid-tolerant and may grow either at pH values as low as 3.2 or as high as 9.6. Usually, most of LAB strains grow at pH values between 4 and 4.5 [1].

In microbiology, several mathematical models have been developed to predict the behavior of microorganisms on the influence of different factors in culture. This branch is known as predictive microbiology, and it aims to study the response of bacteria to environmental factors that can be controlled, such as temperature, pH, and water volume, among others. In this sense, a tool may be formulated to ensure both quality and safety of products to estimate their useful lifetime and to make decisions regarding the composition and design of fermented products [12]. Mathematical models that relate biomass production and time are called primary models, while those that describe the relationship between primary models parameters and environmental conditions are known as secondary models [13]. Some of these models are discussed below.

The Gompertz equation, formulated in 1825, is one of the most used in predictive microbiology. It is based on an exponential relationship between the growth rate and the density of a population. This equation was formulated to describe the law of human mortality. However, years later, it was adapted and re-parametrized for its use in microbiology [14]. Giraud et al. [15] observed that pH variations resulted in a decrease in the growth rate when measuring the fermentation performance of *L. plantarum* at a controlled pH between 4.0 and 8.0. Baranyi et al. [16] applied a non-autonomous differential equation to describe the dynamics of growing bacterial cultures. Based on more than 500 growth curves, the statistical properties of this equation were compared to the Gompertz approach, which is the most commonly used in food microbiology. After these results, Baranyi and Roberts [17] proposed a growth model where a single variable represents the physiological state of cells. The lag phase period is determined by the value of this variable at inoculation and by the post-inoculation environment. The model was able to describe bacterial growth in an environment where factors, such as temperature and pH, change over time. Nicolai et al. [18] constructed a dynamical model for the growth of LAB in vacuum-packed meat. The model was divided into two parts: one part describing the fermentation and the other describing the pH evolution in the liquid surface layer. These models were given as two differential equations and two algebraic equations, respectively. Passos et al. [19] developed an unstructured model to describe bacterial growth, substrate utilization, and lactic acid production by L. plantarum in cucumber juice. They also developed an equation that relates the specific mortality rate and the sodium chloride ($NaCl$) concentration. Drosinos et al. [20] formulated an empirical model to describe the growth and production of bacteriocin by Leuconostoc mesenteroides E131 under different conditions of pH and temperature. Further, a De Man, Rogosa, and Sharpe (MRS) broth was used as a growth medium in the fermenter. Vázquez and Murado [21] proposed a model based on the re-parametrized logistic equation to describe fermentation kinetics of lactic acid production by Lactococcus lactis and Pediococcus acidilactici in a batch system. Da Silva et al. [22] studied the growth of L. plantarum, W. viridescens, and L. sakei under different isothermal culture conditions at temperatures of 4, 8, 12, 16, 20, and 30 °C. They determined that LAB growth was strongly influenced by the culture temperature and created new models that allowed them to predict growth at temperatures ranging from 4 to 30 °C. Dalcanton et al. [23] built a response model of the growth rate of L. plantarum as a function of temperature, pH, and concentrations of $NaCl$ and sodium lactate ($NaC_3H_5O_3$).

Despite the existence of several mathematical models in the literature that describe the behavior of LAB during the fermentation process in its three phases, i.e., lag, exponential, and stationary phases, they do not include the death phase in these models. In batch fermentation, after the stationary state, the depletion of nutrients in the culture medium occurs, and therefore, the death phase begins and should be considered in these models. By not taking the death phase into account, a problem arises when trying to fit real-life experimental data with the models usually used in predictive microbiology. Therefore, the objective of this research is to formulate a time-variant mathematical model that describes the growth of LAB, including its death phase in batch fermentation.

The remainder of this paper proceeds as follows. In Section 2, we present the real-life experimental data concerning biomass growth for eight LAB strains; we formulate our cubic mathematical and explain each parameter; and the most important kinetic models identified in the literature are explored. In Section 3, a statistical analysis is performed to establish which model better fits the experimental data, and these results are illustrated by means of several numerical simulations. Finally, discussions are described in Section 4, and conclusions are given in Section 5.

2. Materials and Methods

2.1. Experimental Data

Eight LAB strains were investigated in the present study; all of them isolated from autochthonous fermented milk. This process was performed based on certain desirable characteristics and against microbial spoilage [24]. LAB strains were incubated for 48 h at a temperature of 37 °C in reconstituted 10% milk powder to produce acidification. Biomass production was measured every 6 h by means of the Neubauer cell counting chamber. Two repetitions were performed for each strain, and the average was calculated as the final concentration value at each corresponding hour. The total biomass concentration was written on a logarithmic scale with units given in $\log_{10}(CFU/mL)$. Furthermore, the experimental data were conditioned by a moving mean filter to minimize noisy measurements in the biomass concentration and to better illustrate LAB growth in each of its four phases, which we mentioned before as lag, exponential, stationary, and death. The results are illustrated in Figure 1, and the overall dynamics allow us to formulate a third-degree polynomial that will be discussed in the following section.

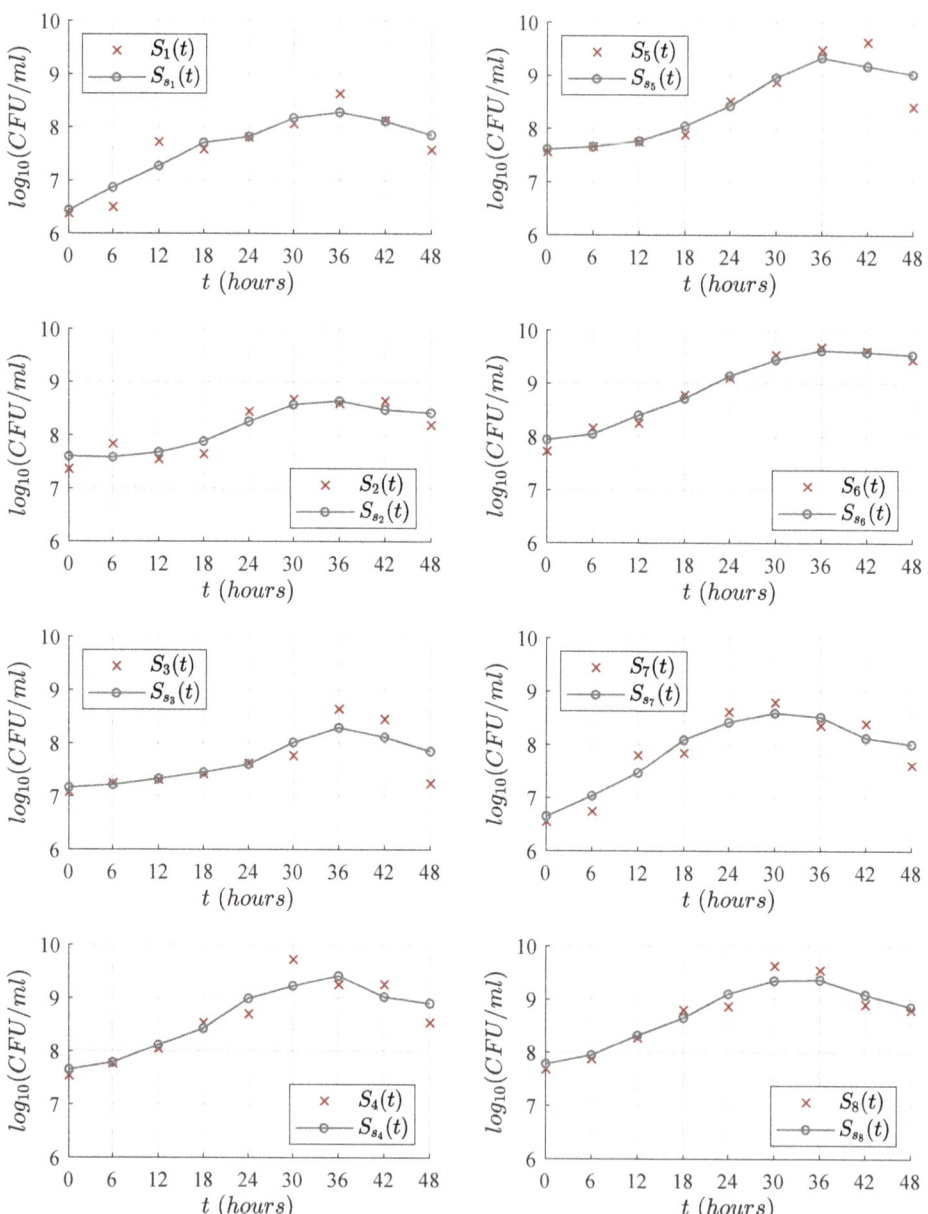

Figure 1. Time-evolution for the eight LAB strains, each × mark represents the average value of the two measurements made with Neubauer cell counting chamber on each strain. The ○ mark represents the results obtained when applying a moving mean filter to smooth the experimental data.

2.2. Mathematical Modelling: Cubic Polynomial Model

In order to formulate a mathematical model to describe the time-evolution for the eight different strains of LAB in the 48 h of the process (see Figure 1), we proposed the following third-degree polynomial

$$x_\beta(t) = x_0 + at^2 - bt^3, \qquad (1)$$

where $x_\beta(t)$ describes biomass growth dynamics in $\log_{10}(\text{CFU/mL})$ as a function of time, x_0 is the initial biomass in each experiment, and coefficients $a, b > 0$ represent the relationships between maximum biomass, lag phase time, and maximum growth rate. Differential calculus concepts were applied to write coefficients as functions of the desired set of parameters. Now, let us compute the first derivative, as it represents growth rate as follows

$$\dot{x}_\beta(t) = 2at - 3bt^2, \qquad (2)$$

to find the maximum increase in biomass, which is denoted as $x_{\max}$, we calculate the local extremums as indicated below

$$t(2a - 3bt) = 0,$$

from the latter, it is evident that at $t = 0$, there is a minimum. Therefore, the time when the maximum biomass increase occurs is given at

$$t = \frac{2a}{3b}. \qquad (3)$$

Then, by the substitution of Equation (3) into Equation (1), one can calculate $x_{\max}$ as follows

$$x_{\max} = x_0 + \frac{4}{27}\frac{a^3}{b^2}. \qquad (4)$$

Now, by computing the second derivative of Equation (1), which is given below

$$\ddot{x}_\beta(t) = 2a - 6bt, \qquad (5)$$

and the time to the inflection point is computed as follows from Equation (5)

$$T_{IP} = \frac{1}{3}\frac{a}{b}, \qquad (6)$$

then, this value is evaluated in Equation (2) to calculate the maximum growth rate, which is denoted as $\mu_{\max}$. This parameter represents the slope of the tangent at the inflection point, and its value is given by the next result

$$\mu_{\max} = \frac{1}{3}\frac{a^2}{b}. \qquad (7)$$

The total amount of biomass at the inflection point, which is given as h, is obtained by evaluating Equation (6) into Equation (1), and the corresponding result is given below

$$h = x_0 + \frac{2}{27}\frac{a^3}{b^2} = \frac{x_0 + x_{\max}}{2}, \qquad (8)$$

therefore, the inflection point is located at the following coordinate

$$\left(\frac{a}{3b}, \frac{x_0 + x_{\max}}{2}\right).$$

Now, in order to find the lag time-period (L), the intersection of the tangent line on the inflection point at the t-axis was calculated, as illustrated in Figure 2.

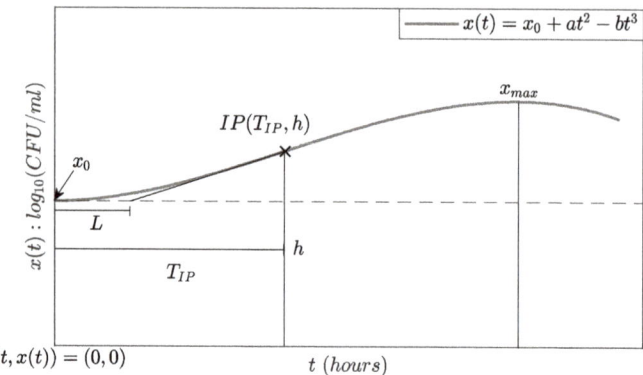

Figure 2. A graphic representation to compute the lag time-period parameter L.

Hence, by applying the point-slope equation, we formulate the following

$$x_0 - h = \mu_{max}(L - T_{IP}), \qquad (9)$$

and by isolating L from Equation (9), the following result is obtained

$$L = T_{IP} + \frac{x_0 - h}{\mu_{max}}, $$

then, replace T_{PI} and h with Equations (6) and (8), respectively. Thus, L is rewritten as follows

$$L = \frac{a}{3b} - \frac{x_{max} - x_0}{2\mu_{max}}. \qquad (10)$$

Equations (4) and (10) relate parameters of interest with coefficients a and b of Equation (1). Therefore, one can isolate a from Equation (10) as follows

$$a = 3b\left(L + \frac{x_{max} - x_0}{2\mu_{max}}\right), \qquad (11)$$

and substitute it into Equation (4) to find the value of b as indicated below

$$b = \frac{x_{max} - x_0}{4\left(L + \frac{x_{max} - x_0}{2\mu_{max}}\right)^3}, \qquad (12)$$

then, Equation (12) should be replaced by Equation (11) to determine the final value of coefficient a; hence

$$a = \frac{3}{4} \frac{x_{max} - x_0}{\left(L + \frac{x_{max} - x_0}{2\mu_{max}}\right)^2}. \qquad (13)$$

Values of a and b, given by Equations (12) and (13), respectively, are replaced into Equation (1) to formulate the model in terms of parameters x_{max}, μ_{max} and L. Therefore, our cubic polynomial model to describe the four phases of LAB growth is shown below

$$x_\beta(t) = x_0 + \frac{3}{4} \frac{x_{max} - x_0}{\left(L + \frac{x_{max} - x_0}{2\mu_{max}}\right)^2} t^2 - \frac{1}{4} \frac{x_{max} - x_0}{\left(L + \frac{x_{max} - x_0}{2\mu_{max}}\right)^3} t^3. \qquad (14)$$

2.3. Primary Models

Numerical simulations were made to illustrate and analyze the time-evolution of our model and the other three chosen from the literature. These models are presented below. First, let us introduce the Gompertz model [14]:

$$x_G(t) = x_0 + (x_{max} - x_0) \exp\left(-\exp\left(1 + \frac{\mu_{max} e}{x_{max} - x_0}(L+t)\right)\right). \tag{15}$$

Then, the Baranyi model [17], which is given as follows:

$$x_B(t) = x_0 + \mu_{max} A(t) - \ln\left(1 + \frac{e^{\mu_{max} A(t)} - 1}{e^{(x_{max} - x_0)}}\right), \tag{16}$$

where $A(t)$ and h_0 may be written as indicated below [25]:

$$A(t) = t + \frac{1}{\mu_{max}} \ln\left(e^{-\mu_{max} t} + e^{-h_0} - e^{-\mu_{max} t - h_0}\right) \text{ with } h_0 = \mu_{max} L.$$

Now, the model from Vázquez-Murado [21]:

$$x_V(t) = x_0 + \frac{x_{max} - x_0}{1 + \exp\left(2 + \frac{4\mu_{max}}{x_{max} - x_0}(L-t)\right)}. \tag{17}$$

In each model, x_0 represents the initial biomass, x_{max} the maximum biomass, μ_{max} the maximum growth rate, and L the lag phase time. Further, these three models were selected because they are among the most cited in predictive microbiology, and their parameters are the same as in our cubic primary model (14). Parameter values were calculated from the smoothed data of the eight LAB strains (see in Figure 1). Parameters x_0 and x_{max} are, respectively, the initial and the maximum biomass values. The value of the parameter μ_{max} is computed as shown below

$$\mu_{max} = \max\left\{\frac{S_{i+1} - S_i}{\Delta t}\right\},$$

where S_{i+1} and S_i are taken from the smoothed experimental data, i.e., a given value and its previous one. The latter is divided by the time interval of the measurements, which, in this particular case, $\Delta t = 6$ h, and since we have nine measurements, then $i = 0, \ldots, 8$. Furthermore, it should be noted that Equation (10) was used to calculate the Lag time period, L. The results concerning all necessary parameter values are shown in Table 1.

Table 1. The results concerning all parameter values for the four mathematical models under study respecting each LAB strain illustrated in Figure 1.

Strains	x_0	x_{max}	μ_{max}	L
$S_1(t)$	6.442	8.279	0.073	5.374
$S_2(t)$	7.602	8.638	0.062	9.696
$S_3(t)$	7.163	8.125	0.055	9.371
$S_4(t)$	7.651	9.412	0.093	8.571
$S_5(t)$	7.612	9.337	0.089	8.323
$S_6(t)$	7.942	9.614	0.071	6.262
$S_7(t)$	6.646	8.547	0.086	7.005
$S_8(t)$	7.779	9.364	0.075	7.461

3. Results

In order to validate our model, a statistical analysis was performed to calculate and compare the descriptive capacity of the cubic model (14) and models (15)–(17). The statistic used was the coefficient of determination (R^2), which measures the goodness of fit of a non-linear model according to experimental data. Its calculation is made based on the sum of squared residuals (RSS), and the explanatory capacity of a model is better the closer R^2 is to 1, see Section 11-8.2 [26].

Figures 3–6 illustrate the dynamics of the cubic model and its comparison with analyzed models from the literature concerning the experimental data of eight LAB strains, $S_i(t), i = 1, \ldots, 8$. One can see in Figure 3 that the cubic model describes the four expected growth phases in batch fermentation, while the Gompertz model, see Figure 4; the Baranyi model, see Figure 5; and Vázquez-Murado model, see Figure 6; only describe up to the stationary phase, which caused the RSS value to be higher for these models, and therefore, the results concerning R^2 and AIC indicate a poorer fit. The lag phase time was around 5 to 9 h. The maximum biomass growth was reached between 30 and 36 h for each of the strains, and from that time, the death phase begins.

According to our numerical simulations, one can observe that the proposed cubic model (14) and the other primary models (15)–(17) have a good adjustment in the lag phase, as is shown by each solution and the corresponding experimental data. Concerning the exponential phase, the Baranyi model is slightly above the others. However, this model has a lower growth rate, which causes a delay when reaching the maximum concentration, approximately at 48 h, while other models reach this value at around 30 or 36 h. Regarding the maximum biomass growth, the three primary models remain in the stationary phase, while the experimental data goes to the death phase. Therefore, the RSS of these models is higher than the cubic model, as this one better fits the observed data in this last phase. Table 2 shows the results of R^2 and RSS for the cubic, Gompertz, Baranyi, and Vázquez-Murado models with respect to the experimental data illustrated in Figure 1.

Table 2. The results of R^2 and RSS for each mathematical model.

Strains	Cubic Model		Gompertz		Baranyi		Vázquez-Murado	
	R^2	RSS	R^2	RSS	R^2	RSS	R^2	RSS
$S_1(t)$	0.805	0.843	0.669	1.431	0.556	1.920	0.678	1.392
$S_2(t)$	0.793	0.437	0.722	0.586	0.641	0.760	0.723	0.587
$S_3(t)$	0.637	0.899	0.435	1.400	0.392	1.508	0.428	1.419
$S_4(t)$	0.924	0.324	0.742	1.102	0.705	1.262	0.741	1.106
$S_5(t)$	0.800	0.977	0.677	1.578	0.685	1.539	0.654	1.693
$S_6(t)$	0.912	0.373	0.957	0.178	0.836	0.698	0.960	0.167
$S_7(t)$	0.792	1.049	0.590	2.064	0.491	2.561	0.614	1.944
$S_8(t)$	0.898	0.365	0.756	0.871	0.640	1.285	0.766	0.835

Now, concerning strain 1, the cubic model presented an RSS of 0.843 and, consequently, a higher value of R^2 given by 0.805 compared to Gompertz, Baranyi and Vázquez-Murado models, which obtained an RSS equal to 1.431, 1.920, and 1.392 and an R^2 equal to 0.669, 0.556, and 0.678, respectively. For strain 2, the highest R^2 value was for the cubic model with 0.793, followed closely by the Vázquez-Murado and Gompertz models with 0.723 and 0.722, respectively, while the Baranyi model had a result of 0.641. In the particular case of strain 3, all models had a lower adjustment when comparing them with the other seven strains. However, the best fit was for the cubic model with an R^2 of 0.637, while the Gompertz model obtained a value of 0.435, Baranyi obtained 0.392, and Vázquez-Murado 0.428. For strain 4, very similar R^2 values were obtained for Gompertz, and Vázquez-Murado models, 0.742 and 0.741, respectively, while the cubic model obtained a result of 0.924, and Baranyi got a value of 0.705. In strain 5, the cubic model had an R^2 value of 0.800, which was higher than the Gompertz 0.677, Baranyi 0.685, and Vazquez-Murado

0.654. Strain 6 had a better fit for all models. The Vázquez-Murado model had an R^2 of 0.960, Gompertz 0.957, cubic model 0.912, and the lowest value was for Baranyi, with 0.836. These higher R^2 values are due to fact that the experimental data for this strain have fewer outliers, as seen in Figure 1, and its death phase is lower compared to the other strains. Strain 7 had a better fit for the cubic model, with an R^2 of 0.792, than the Gompertz (0.590), Baranyi (0.491), and Vázquez-Murado (0.614) models. Finally, as in most cases, the cubic model had the best fit for strain 8 with an R^2 value of 0.898, while Gompertz and Vázquez-Murado obtained, respectively, 0.756 and 0.766. In general, the cubic model had higher values of R^2 than the rest of the models, except in strain 6, where the Vázquez-Murado model had the better fit to the experimental data. The latter was due to the data not yet presenting the death phase as the other strains in the 48 h of the experiment.

Furthermore, the Akaike Information Criterion (AIC) test was performed, which allows us to determine which model better fits the observed data. To calculate this value, the goodness of fit between predictions of models and experimental data is considered through the RSS while penalizing models that have a greater number of parameters due to these becoming more complex for its practice [27]. Table 3 shows results for every mathematical model.

Table 3. AIC results for each mathematical model.

Strains	Cubic Model	Gompertz	Baranyi	Vázquez-Murado
$S_1(t)$	−3.310	+1.453	+4.097	+1.205
$S_2(t)$	−9.213	−6.570	−4.242	−6.573
$S_3(t)$	−2.735	+1.256	+1.921	+1.377
$S_4(t)$	−11.921	−0.898	+0.317	−0.868
$S_5(t)$	−1.980	+2.335	+2.098	+2.963
$S_6(t)$	−10.650	−17.293	−5.079	−17.845
$S_7(t)$	−1.342	+4.750	+6.688	+4.209
$S_8(t)$	−10.844	−3.019	+0.481	−3.398

By taking the latter into account, the model that better fits the experimental data is the one with the lowest AIC value. For strain 1, the lowest AIC was for the cubic model with a value of −3.310, while Gompertz, Baranyi, and Vázquez-Murado models obtained values of 1.453, 4.097, and 1.205, respectively. In strain 2, the cubic model had the lowest AIC, with a value of −9.213, and the Gompertz model and the Vázquez-Murado model had similar results, −6.570 and −6.573 respectively, while the Baranyi had a value of −4.242. The cubic model fitted better to the experimental data of strain 3 with an AIC of −2.735, followed by Gompertz with 1.256, Vázquez-Murado with 1.377, and finally, Baranyi with 1.921. Again, for strain 4, according to the AIC values, the cubic model (−11.921) was better than the Gompertz (−0.898), Baranyi (0.317), and Vázquez-Murado (−0.868) models. In strain 5, the best AIC value was for the cubic model (−1.980), while Gompertz obtained 2.335, Baranyi 2.098, and Vázquez-Murado 2.963. In strain 6, very close AIC values were obtained for Vazquez-Murado −17.845 and Gompertz −17.293, but the Vázquez-Murado model was slightly better. The cubic model had a value of −10.650. On the other hand, Baranyi model had a lower fit with an AIC of −5.079. For strain 7, the lowest AIC value was obtained for the cubic model −1.342, while Gompertz had a value of 4.750, Baranyi 6.688, and Vázquez-Murado 4.209. Finally, regarding strain 8, the cubic model had the better fit to the experimental data based on its AIC value (−10.844), and Baranyi had the worst fit (0.481), while Gompertz and Vázquez-Murado obtained results of −3.019 and −3.398, respectively.

After analyzing the statistical results, it is evident that our formulated cubic primary model better fits the experimental data because it was the one that presented the lowest RSS in general and therefore had higher values for the R^2 in all LAB strains but number 6, which had a higher value with the Vázquez-Murado model (0.960). However, the result for the cubic model was of 0.912, which is still a good value concerning this parameter.

Therefore, based on the results for the RSS, R^2, and the AIC, we can establish that the cubic primary model (14) better represents the overall dynamics of the experimental data for the eight LAB strains under study in this research.

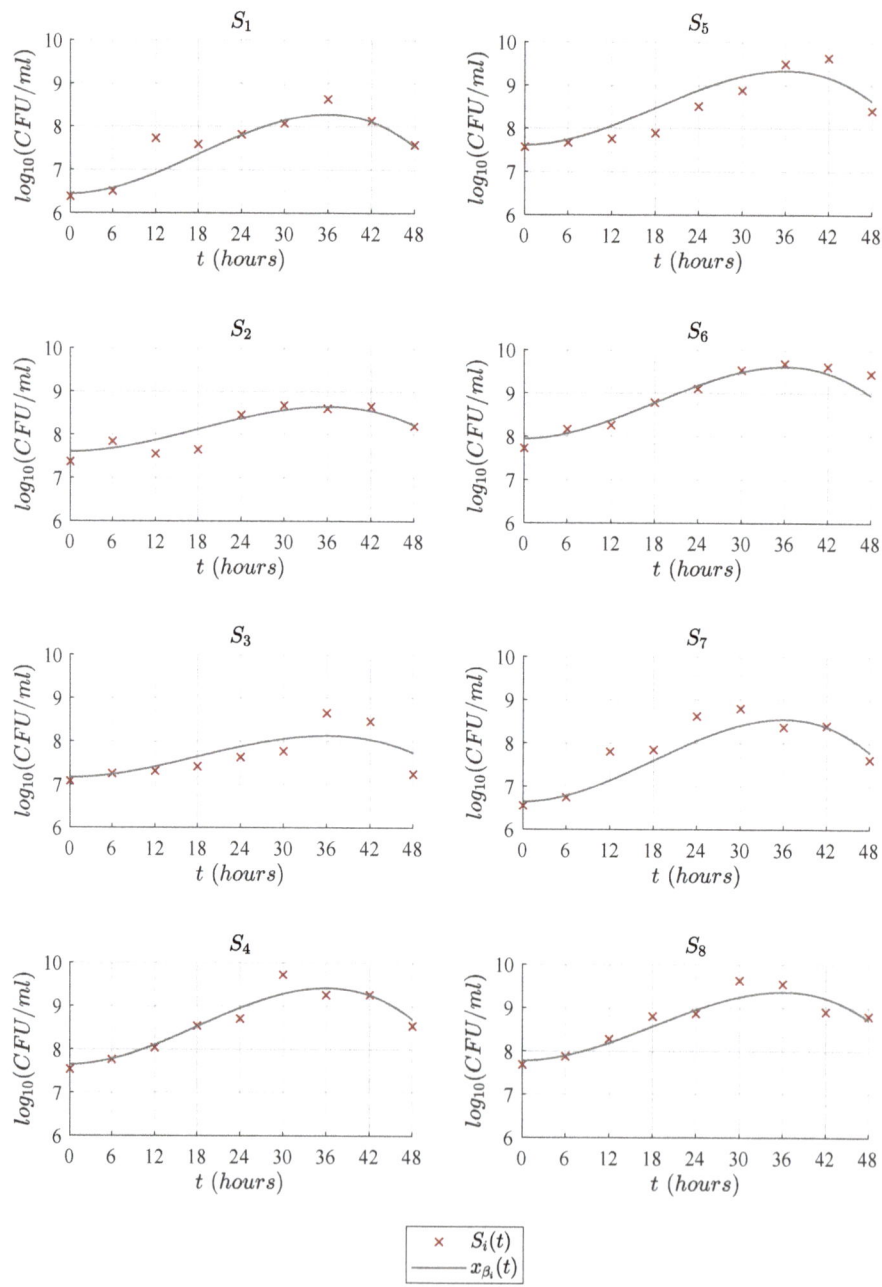

Figure 3. Predictions of the cubic model $x_\beta(t)$ compared with the experimental data $S_i(t)$.

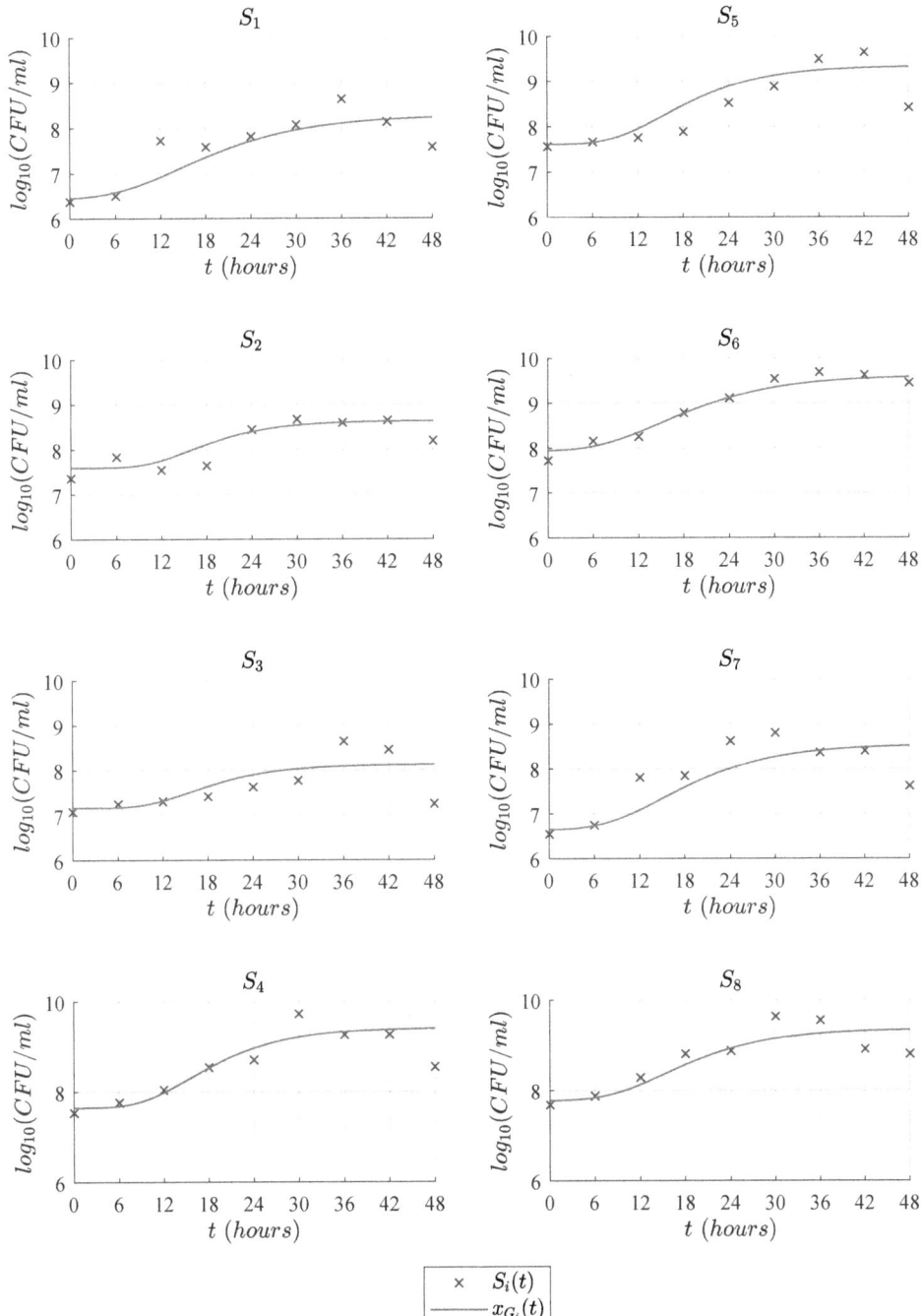

Figure 4. Predictions of Gompertz model $x_G(t)$ compared with the experimental data $S_i(t)$.

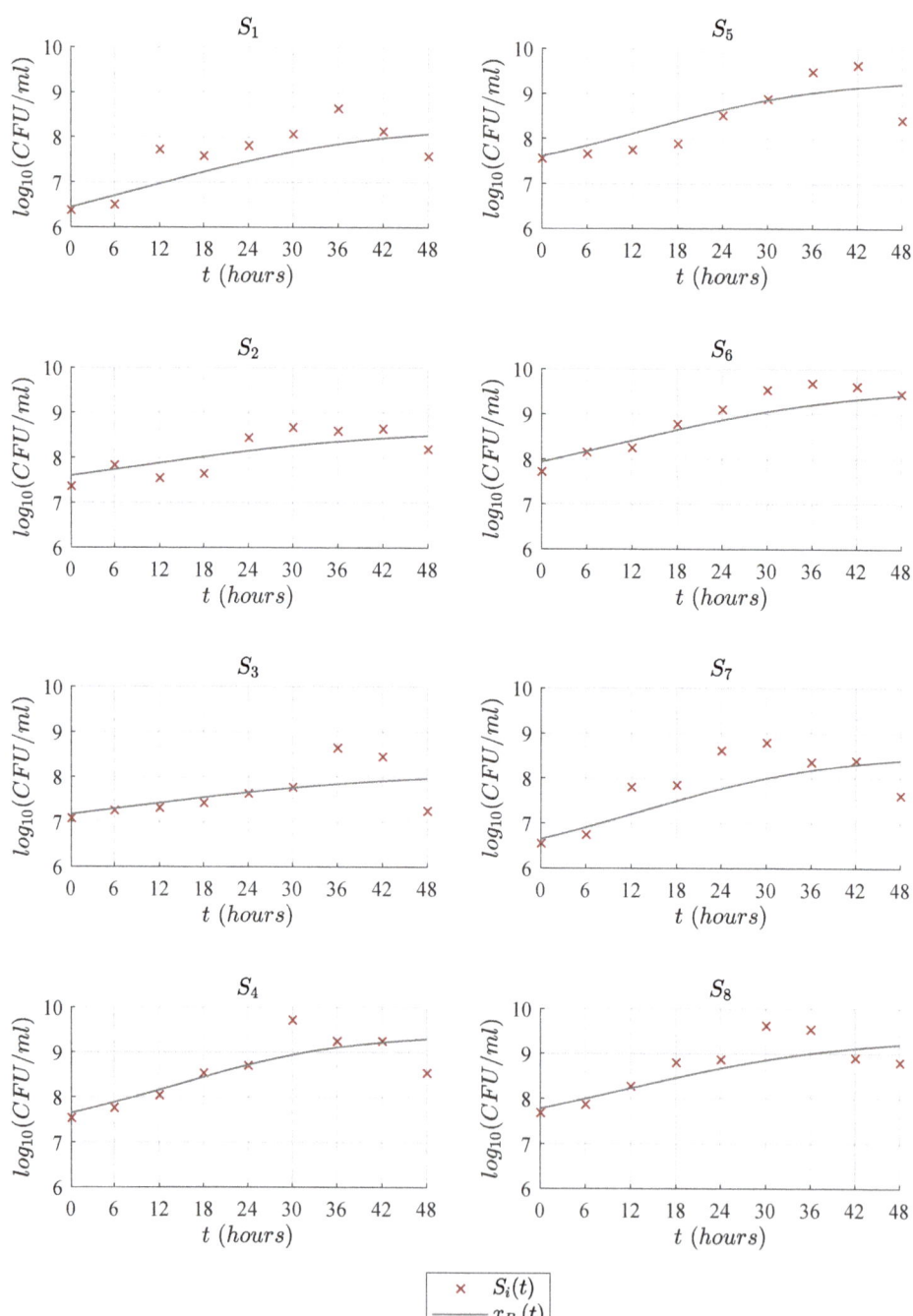

Figure 5. Predictions of the Baranyi model $x_B(t)$ compared with the experimental data $S_i(t)$.

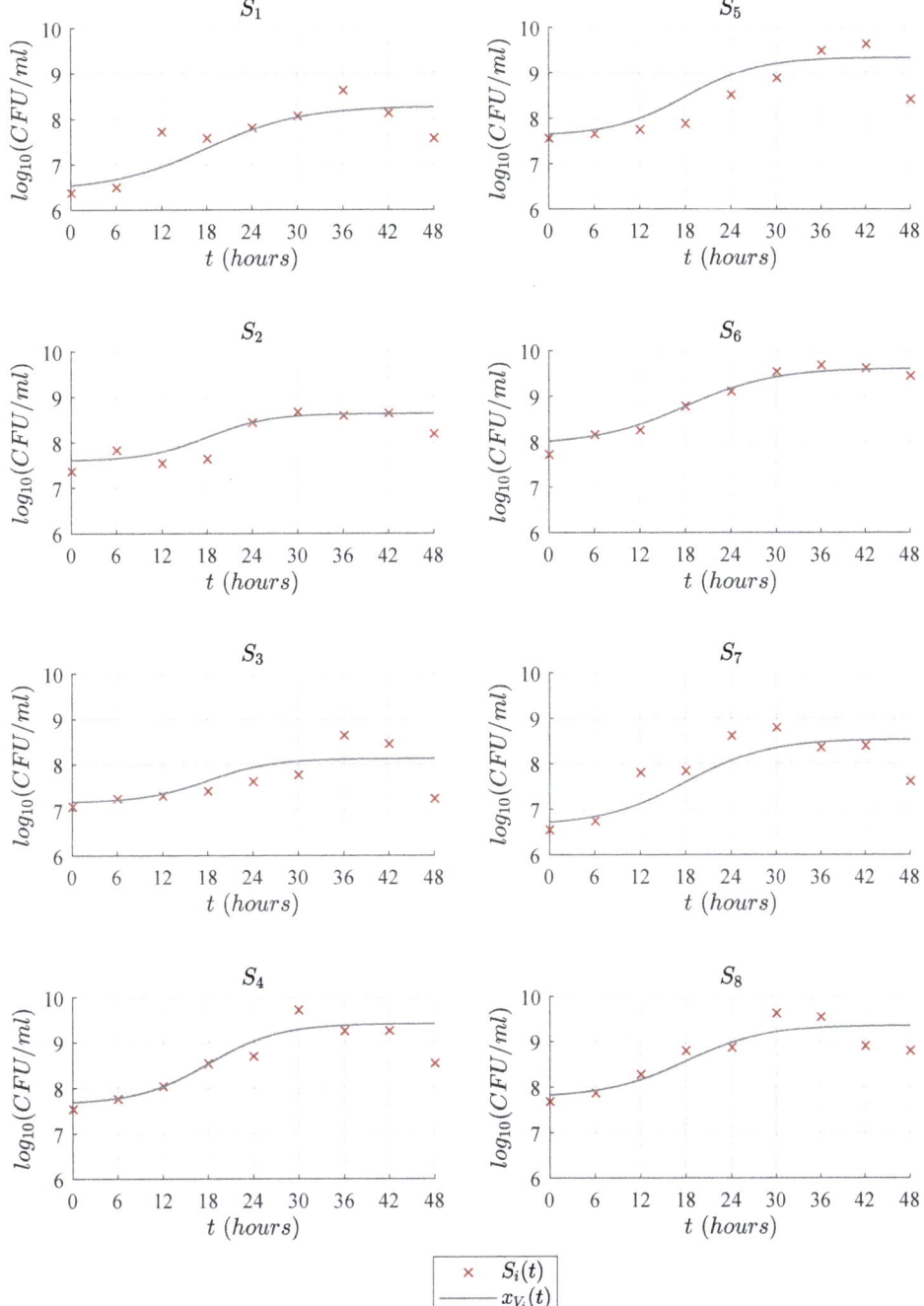

Figure 6. Predictions of the Vázquez-Murado $x_V(t)$ compared with the experimental data $S_i(t)$.

4. Discussion

In predictive microbiology, primary models based on sigmoidal functions are usually used. Among the most common models, we have the Gompertz [14], the Baranyi [17], and the Vázquez-Murado [21] models. Nonetheless, the latter only describe the first three growth phases, i.e., lag phase, exponential growth, and the stationary state. According to Buchanan et al. [28] and Garre et al. [29], these phases are sufficient to fit experimental data for growth models. However, according to Mandigan et al. [6], in batch fermentation, the bacterial population presents a death phase due to nutrient depletion in the culture medium. Therefore, when adjusting these models to observed data in this kind of fermentation, values of greater discrepancy are found in the death phase between the experimental data and approximated values. Chatterjee et al. [30] incorporated the death phase into the Gompertz model to better describe the behavior of *E. coli* and *S. aureus*. Studies by Bevilacqua et al. [31] were focused on demonstrating the importance of the death phase of microorganisms and its impact on the shelf life of food. Solano et al. [32] evaluated the capacity of five models, including the Gompertz, Baranyi, and Vázquez-Murado, to predict acid production in lactic fermentation of fishing products, and they found that models with the lowest residual variance were those of Gompertz and Baranyi. Further, this study shows that the Vázquez-Murado model failed to give an adequate adjustment for lactic fermentation. In the same way, Zwietering et al. [33] managed to describe the behavior of *L. plantarum* in an MRS medium with the Gompertz model, while the Vázquez-Murado logistic model was not suitable to accurately approximate the experimental data. In contrast, Kedia et al. [34] obtained a good fit with the Vázquez-Murado model for *L. reuteri*, *L. plantarum*, and *L. acidophilus* in oat fractions. Da Silva et al. [22] studied the growth of *L. plantarum*, *W. viridescens*, and *L. sakei* in vacuum-packed meats, and, as well as Baty and Delignette [35] who studied different growth models for various LAB, all authors in these two works found that the Baranyi model has a slightly better fit than the Gompertz model.

According to the R^2 and AIC values, it can be established that the cubic model has a better fit to the experimental data with average values of $R^2 = 0.820$ and $AIC = -6.499$. There was not enough difference between the average values for the Gompertz model with $R^2 = 0.693$ and $AIC = -2.248$, while the Vázquez-Murado had average results of $R^2 = 0.695$ and $AIC = -2.366$. Regarding the Baranyi model, the average results were as follows $R^2 = 0.618$ and $AIC = 0.785$. Further, the overall adjustment to the experimental data for the four primary models under study is illustrated in Figures 3–6.

In this research, the four primary models presented a good adjustment in the lag phase (L) and reached the maximum growth (x_{max}) registered in the experimental data. However, the maximum growth rate value (μ_{max}) had a greater impact on the adjustment of the exponential growth phase, in which the cubic model was the one that had the better fit. Nonetheless, in order to get a good fit with primary models, it is necessary to measure the largest amount of experimental data with the greatest possible continuity, which will ensure a better prediction by the models. In the batch fermentation process performed for this work, the eight LAB strains showed outliers, which could be due to the method applied for the measurements. Therefore, the experimental data had to be smoothed to calculate all required parameters for each mathematical model. It is important to consider that outliers are present in all real-life data measurements, such as biomass growth.

In the cubic model, the parameter μ_{max} also influences the death phase of the biomass. The latter because a higher growth rate implies that the maximum biomass concentration will be reached, and due to the inherit dynamics of this kind of function, after reaching this maximum point, the biomass begins to decline. It is important to consider that if this mathematical model is simulated at time values further than 70 h, biomass will take negative values, which is not biologically feasible in real-life scenarios. However, this can be neglected because the fermentation process to produce acidified milk generally takes around 48 h, and it is not necessary to predict the behavior of this variable beyond this time, as this is the final desired product. Predictive models aim to ensure food quality and provide a tool that supports decision-making on fermentation design. Therefore, based on the results and as it is illustrated in Figures 3–6, a decision can be made to perform a fermentation process under the same culture conditions only up to 36 h, i.e., when the maximum biomass growth is reached for this type of fermented milk.

5. Conclusions

A time-variant mathematical model given in the form of a third-order polynomial was formulated to describe the growth dynamics over a period of 48 h for eight LAB strains. Our so-called cubic primary model (Equation (14)) was constructed with the parameters that are frequently used in other primary models, i.e, biomass initial concentration, (x_0); lag phase time, (L); maximum growth rate, (μ_{max}); and maximum growth, (x_{max}). Furthermore, both the numerical simulations and the statistical results concerning RSS, R^2, and the AIC support our statement that the cubic model $x_\beta(t)$ accurately represents the four biomass growth phases in the batch fermentation process when comparing it with three other models that are among the most cited in predictive microbiology literature.

Author Contributions: Conceptualization, Y.S. and E.R.; methodology, Y.S. and E.R.; software, P.A.V.; validation, Y.S., B.E.G. and P.A.V.; formal analysis, Y.S. and P.A.V.; investigation, E.R.; resources, B.E.G.; data curation, B.E.G.; writing—original draft preparation, Y.S. and E.R.; writing—review and editing, P.A.V.; visualization, Y.S. and P.A.V.; supervision, Y.S. and P.A.V.; project administration, Y.S. All authors have read and agreed to the published version of the manuscript.

Funding: This research received no external funding.

Institutional Review Board Statement: Not applicable.

Informed Consent Statement: Not applicable.

Data Availability Statement: Data are contained within the article.

Acknowledgments: This work was supported by TecNM Projects: Modelizado de la dinámica de crecimiento de microorganismos durante la fermentación de leche fresca with number 10083.21-P (Y.S.); Modelizado computacional y experimentos in silico aplicados al análisis y control de sistemas biológicos with number 9951.21-P (P.A.V.); and Jocoque un producto lácteo fermentado tradicional y sus características microbiológicas, fisicoquímicas y sensoriales with number 6075.17-P (B.E.G.). Further, E.R. and B.E.G. express their recognition to the National Council of Science and Technology of Mexico (CONACyT) for financial support during her postgraduate studies under their scholarship agreement.

Conflicts of Interest: The authors declare no conflict of interest.

Abbreviations

The following abbreviations and symbols are used in this manuscript:

LAB	Lactic Acid Bacteria
ACD	Asymmetric Cell Division
MRS	De Man, Rogosa and Sharpe
R^2	Coefficient of determination
RSS	Residual Sum of Squares
AIC	Akaike Information Criterion

References

1. Axelsson, L. Lactic Acid Bacteria: Classification and Physiology. In *Lactic Acid Bacteria: Microbiology and Functional Aspects*, 2nd ed.; Marcel Dekker, Inc.: New York, NY, USA, 1998; pp. 1–72.
2. Sheeladevi, A.; Ramanathan, N. Lactic acid production using lactic acid bacteria under optimized conditions. *Int. J. Pharm. Biol. Arch.* **2011**, *2*, 1686–1691.
3. Axelsson, L.; Ahrné, S. Lactic acid bacteria. In *Applied Microbial Systematics*; Springer: Berlin/Heidelberg, Germany, 2000; pp. 367–388. [CrossRef]
4. Carr, F.J.; Chill, D.; Maida, N. The Lactic Acid Bacteria: A Literature Survey. *Crit. Rev. Microbiol.* **2002**, *28*, 281–370. [CrossRef]

5. Novik, G.; Meerovskaya, O.; Savich, V. Waste degradation and utilization by lactic acid bacteria: Use of lactic acid bacteria in production of food additives, bioenergy and biogas. In *Food Additive*; InTech: London, UK, 2017; p. 105. [CrossRef]
6. Mandigan, M.; Martinko, J.; Bender, K.; Buckley, D.; Stahl, D. *Brock Biology of Microorganisms*, 14th ed.; Pearson: Boston, MA, USA, 2015.
7. Sunchu, B.; Cabernard, C. Principles and mechanisms of asymmetric cell division. *Development* **2020**, *147*, dev167650. [CrossRef]
8. Bi, E.; Park, H.O. Cell polarization and cytokinesis in budding yeast. *Genetics* **2012**, *191*, 347–387. [CrossRef]
9. Rotureau, B.; Subota, I.; Buisson, J.; Bastin, P. A new asymmetric division contributes to the continuous production of infective trypanosomes in the tsetse fly. *Development* **2012**, *139*, 1842–1850. [CrossRef] [PubMed]
10. Li, R. The art of choreographing asymmetric cell division. *Dev. Cell* **2013**, *25*, 439–450. [CrossRef] [PubMed]
11. Jensen, P.R.; Hammer, K. Minimal requirements for exponential growth of Lactococcus lactis. *Appl. Environ. Microbiol.* **1993**, *59*, 4363–4366. [CrossRef] [PubMed]
12. Guillier, L. Predictive microbiology models and operational readiness. *Procedia Food Sci.* **2016**, *7*, 133–136. [CrossRef]
13. Stavropoulou, E.; Bezirtzoglou, E. Predictive Modeling of Microbial Behavior in Food. *Foods* **2019**, *8*, 654. [CrossRef] [PubMed]
14. Gompertz, B. XXIV. On the nature of the function expressive of the law of human mortality, and on a new mode of determining the value of life contingencies. In *a letter to Francis Baily, Esq. FRS & c*; Philosophical Transactions of the Royal Society of London: London, UK, 1825; Volume 1, pp. 513–583. [CrossRef]
15. Giraud, E.; Lelong, B.; Raimbault, M. Influence of pH and initial lactate concentration on the growth of Lactobacillus plantarum. *Appl. Microbiol. Biotechnol.* **1991**, *36*, 96–99. [CrossRef]
16. Baranyi, J.; Roberts, T.; McClure, P. A non-autonomous differential equation to model bacterial growth. *Food Microbiol.* **1993**, *10*, 43–59. [CrossRef]
17. Baranyi, J.; Roberts, T.A. A dynamic approach to predicting bacterial growth in food. *Int. J. Food Microbiol.* **1994**, *23*, 277–294. [CrossRef]
18. Nicolai, B.; Van Impe, J.; Verlinden, B.; Martens, T.; Vandewalle, J.; De Baerdemaeker, J. Predictive modelling of surface growth of lactic acid bacteria in vacuum-packed meat. *Food Microbiol.* **1993**, *10*, 229–238. [CrossRef]
19. Passos, F.V.; Fleming, H.P.; Ollis, D.F.; Felder, R.M.; McFeeters, R. Kinetics and modeling of lactic acid production by Lactobacillus plantarum. *Appl. Environ. Microbiol.* **1994**, *60*, 2627–2636. [CrossRef] [PubMed]
20. Drosinos, E.; Mataragas, M.; Metaxopoulos, J. Modeling of growth and bacteriocin production by Leuconostoc mesenteroides E131. *Meat Sci.* **2006**, *74*, 690–696. [CrossRef] [PubMed]
21. Vázquez, J.A.; Murado, M.A. Unstructured mathematical model for biomass, lactic acid and bacteriocin production by lactic acid bacteria in batch fermentation. *J. Chem. Technol. Biotechnol.* **2008**, *83*, 91–96. [CrossRef]
22. Silva, A.P.R.d.; Longhi, D.A.; Dalcanton, F.; Aragão, G.M.F.d. Modelling the growth of lactic acid bacteria at different temperatures. *Braz. Arch. Biol. Technol.* **2018**, *61*. [CrossRef]
23. Dalcanton, F.; Carrasco, E.; Pérez-Rodríguez, F.; Posada-Izquierdo, G.D.; Falcão de Aragão, G.M.; García-Gimeno, R.M. Modeling the combined effects of temperature, pH, and sodium chloride and sodium lactate concentrations on the growth rate of Lactobacillus plantarum ATCC 8014. *J. Food Qual.* **2018**, *2018*, 1726761. [CrossRef]
24. Leroy, F.; De Vuyst, L. Lactic acid bacteria as functional starter cultures for the food fermentation industry. *Trends Food Sci. Technol.* **2004**, *15*, 67–78. [CrossRef]
25. Powell, C.D.; López, S.; France, J. New Insights into Modelling Bacterial Growth with Reference to the Fish Pathogen Flavobacterium psychrophilum. *Animals* **2020**, *10*, 435. [CrossRef] [PubMed]
26. Montgomery, D.C.; Runger, G.C. *Applied Statistics and Probability for Engineers*, 6th ed.; John Wiley and Sons: Hoboken, NJ, USA, 2013; p. 920.
27. Burnham, K.P.; Anderson, D.R. Multimodel inference: Understanding AIC and BIC in model selection. *Sociol. Methods Res.* **2004**, *33*, 261–304. [CrossRef]
28. Buchanan, R.L.; Whiting, R.C.; Damert, W.C. When is simple good enough: A comparison of the Gompertz, Baranyi, and three-phase linear models for fitting bacterial growth curves. *Food Microbiol.* **1997**, *14*, 313–326. [CrossRef]
29. Garre Pérez, A.; Egea Larrosa, J.; Fernández Escámez, P. Modelos matemáticos para la descripción del crecimiento de microorganismos patógenos en alimentos. *Anuario de Jóvenes Investigadores* **2016**, *9*, 160–163.
30. Chatterjee, T.; Chatterjee, B.K.; Majumdar, D.; Chakrabarti, P. Antibacterial effect of silver nanoparticles and the modeling of bacterial growth kinetics using a modified Gompertz model. *Biochim. Biophys. Acta Gen. Subj.* **2015**, *1850*, 299–306. [CrossRef]
31. Bevilacqua, A.; Speranza, B.; Sinigaglia, M.; Corbo, M.R. A Focus on the Death Kinetics in Predictive Microbiology: Benefits and Limits of the Most Important Models and Some Tools Dealing with Their Application in Foods. *Foods* **2015**, *4*, 565–580. [CrossRef]
32. Solano-Cornejo, M.A.; Vidaurre-Ruiz, J.M. Application of unstructured kinetic models in the lactic fermentation modeling of the fishery by-products. *Sci. Agropecu.* **2017**, *8*, 367–375. [CrossRef]
33. Zwietering, M.; Jongenburger, I.; Rombouts, F.; Van't Riet, K. Modeling of the bacterial growth curve. *Appl. Environ. Microbiol.* **1990**, *56*, 1875–1881. [CrossRef] [PubMed]
34. Kedia, G.; Vázquez, J.A.; Pandiella, S.S. Evaluation of the fermentability of oat fractions obtained by debranning using lactic acid bacteria. *J. Appl. Microbiol.* **2008**, *105*, 1227–1237. [CrossRef]
35. Baty, F.; Delignette-Muller, M.L. Estimating the bacterial lag time: Which model, which precision? *Int. J. Food Microbiol.* **2004**, *91*, 261–277. [CrossRef] [PubMed]

Article

A Control Based Mathematical Model for the Evaluation of Intervention Lines in COVID-19 Epidemic Spread: The Italian Case Study

Paolo Di Giamberardino, Rita Caldarella and Daniela Iacoviello *

Department of Computer, Control and Management Engineering Antonio Ruberti, Sapienza University of Rome, Via Ariosto 25, 00185 Rome, Italy; paolo.digiamberardino@uniroma1.it (P.D.G.); caldarella.1640339@studenti.uniroma1.it (R.C.)
* Correspondence: daniela.iacoviello@uniroma1.it

Citation: Di Giamberardino, P.; Caldarella, R.; Iacoviello, D. A Control Based Mathematical Model for the Evaluation of Intervention Lines in COVID-19 Epidemic Spread: The Italian Case Study. *Symmetry* **2021**, *13*, 890. https://doi.org/10.3390/sym13050890

Academic Editor: Dalibor Štys

Received: 12 April 2021
Accepted: 10 May 2021
Published: 17 May 2021

Publisher's Note: MDPI stays neutral with regard to jurisdictional claims in published maps and institutional affiliations.

Copyright: © 2021 by the authors. Licensee MDPI, Basel, Switzerland. This article is an open access article distributed under the terms and conditions of the Creative Commons Attribution (CC BY) license (https://creativecommons.org/licenses/by/4.0/).

Abstract: This paper addresses the problem of describing the spread of COVID-19 by a mathematical model introducing all the possible control actions as prevention (informative campaign, use of masks, social distancing, vaccination) and medication. The model adopted is similar to SEIQR, with the infected patients split into groups of asymptomatic subjects and isolated ones. This distinction is particularly important in the current pandemic, due to the fundamental the role of asymptomatic subjects in the virus diffusion. The influence of the control actions is considered in analysing the model, from the calculus of the equilibrium points to the determination of the reproduction number. This choice is motivated by the fact that the available organised data have been collected since from the end of February 2020, and almost simultaneously containment measures, increasing in typology and effectiveness, have been applied. The characteristics of COVID-19, not fully understood yet, suggest an asymmetric diffusion among countries and among categories of subjects. Referring to the Italian situation, the containment measures, as applied by the population, have been identified, showing their relation with the government's decisions; this allows the study of possible scenarios, comparing the impact of different possible choices.

Keywords: epidemic ODE model; COVID-19 spread in Italy; system control and identification

1. Introduction

In this paper, the spread of COVID-19 is discussed with a particular focus on the application of the containment measures, referring to the Italian situation.

Officially defined as a pandemic in March 2020, the disease induced by the SARS-CoV-2 virus, called COVID-19, has influenced and changed human life all over the world [1]. Some of its peculiarities represent a complication in the identification of the epidemic outbreaks; one of them is the significant number of asymptomatic subjects, able to infect other people. An additional interesting characteristic of COVID-19 is the asymmetric increase in the number of hospitalised patients with age; in fact, while for young people the virus is almost harmless, for the elderly population, especially in association with pre-existing pathologies, it is extremely dangerous; the mean age of patients dead in Italy for COVID-19 is 81, counting more than 10^5 deaths and over than 3 million infected patients [2–4]. Moreover, the reasons for the asymmetric increase in cases and case fatality rate among countries are still not evident [5]; after a deep analysis of various factors that could justify the differences among countries, it seems that the density of the population plays an important role, suggesting a fast implementation of active control measures (as quarantine, the tracking of infections and testing) and a low case fatality rate.

The virus spreads through individuals' movements and the most effective containment measure is the reduction in contacts among people, from mild public recommendations to strict lockdowns, with the use of masks everywhere; no specific medication is available and in severe cases, oxygen support is required [1]. For a fast recognition of the infection (and therefore to prevent the spread of the virus), suitable swab tests are performed on subjects who are suspected to have had a dangerous contact or before entering the hospital or starting some activities. For example, a swab test campaign has been promoted by some Italian universities for their students [6].

Despite all the containment measures applied, three epidemic waves can be recognised after a year of pandemic and to date, the most dangerous has been the second one, in November 2020.

In a few months, some vaccines have become available and countries are trying to immunise their population as quickly as possible; in fact, after some initial problems with the supply of doses, the vaccination campaign has the ambition of immunising more than 70% of the European population by the end of next summer.

Since the beginning of the pandemic, many researchers have focused their works on studying the evolution of the virus spread, trying to predict future trends in the number of infected patients, in order to adequately set up suitable containment measures. Nevertheless, the unknown diffusion of asymptomatic subjects makes the challenge very difficult [7,8]; a possible estimation of the number of non-diagnosed subjects has been obtained by testing entire (small) communities, such as the case of the Italian city of Vo', one of the first studies of this kind [7], or by means of serological test campaign, as the one conducted in Italy during the period May–July 2020 [9], which evidenced a significant number of subjects (a mean value of 2.5% of the population, not equally distributed in the country) that were infected by SARS-CoV-2 during the first months of the pandemic without knowing.

Some papers have been devoted to the analysis of real data trying to determine the modalities of the spread among nations, as in the early work [10], or in a homogeneous population [11–14]. In the latter paper, a quite rich model composed by eight different classes is proposed: in addition to the usual susceptible (S), exposed (E), infectious with symptoms (I) and recovered (R) compartments, there are also the groups of pre-symptomatic infectious (A), the hospitalised (H), the quarantined susceptible (Sq), the isolated exposed (Eq) and the isolated infected (Iq) compartments.

Due to the specificity of the virus, interesting works have focused on age-compartmental models, as in [15], where the role of quarantined subjects is emphasised, referring in particular to residential care homes, or as in [16], in which the initial contagion step was distinguished among age-classes.

Sometimes, previously studied models for other epidemic emergencies are adapted to the specificity of COVID-19, like in [17], where a short time forecast is provided, on the basis of the few data initially available. On the other hand, the current COVID-19 emergency has been the inspiration for a more general analysis as in [18], in which the problem of how to face the next wave of infectious disease is studied by analysing the global symmetries of the system under suitable time rescaling. It shows the importance of controlling the arrival of the next wave when the number of infections grows linearly, i.e., during the period between waves.

As already noted in the cited papers, the model structure that appears suitable to describe the COVID-19 evolution inside a population is the $SEIR$ one (referring to the four classes of subjects in which the population is partitioned: *Susceptible–Exposed–Infected–Removed*), enriched with the classes specific for this emergency, like the asymptomatic individuals and the quarantined ones.

All the proposed models must consider the containment measures applied since the beginning of the pandemic, including social distancing, the use of masks, medication, the swab test, informative campaigns and the vaccination. In [19], the importance of using masks is studied, even in the case of non-totally effective protection; it models both the inward and outward efficiency of the mask, disaggregating the population variables into those that do and do not use masks. The results show how the use of masks decreases the effective transmission rate, especially with other interventions, such as social distancing and hygienic measures. In particular, social distancing and informative campaigns are discussed in [20,21]. The social distancing measure is modelled by means of a nonlinear function influencing the contact rate; numerical simulations show the impact of this specific containment measure on the virus spread. The importance of general awareness in regard to the dangers of COVID-19 infection was investigated in [21], in which the impact of the media campaign is studied, along with the rapid testing; the class of susceptible individuals is partitioned depending on the careful application of preventive behaviours, and the test campaign was modelled by improving the transfer of subjects from the asymptomatic (and dangerous) condition to the infected diagnosed one.

The identification of the model is therefore influenced by these actions, the consequences of the governments' choices and of personal behaviours; as previously mentioned, the strict lockdown is the most effective action to contain the spread. Nevertheless, it cannot be the solution for long periods, for both social and economic reasons; therefore, there have been attempts to propose proper and balanced containment measures, depending on the evolution of the pandemic [22]. It is worth noting that awareness of the impact of the containment measures can also modify people's behaviours and therefore the trend of pandemic itself.

In this paper, starting from the model proposed in [23], the problem of identifying the applied containment measures is faced, studying the model under the realistic condition of the implementation of these actions since the very beginning of the health emergency. The consequence is the possibility of identifying the restrictions as they were really applied by the population and by the healthcare system, observing on one hand an increase in the awareness of people in the application of social distancing (also depending on the specific period under study) and, on the other hand, a general improvement in the capability of the sanitary system to face the emergency. This identification, corresponding to a sort of transducer of the government's measures, is useful when one wants to predict what would happen by applying the same kind of control measures already applied or a combination of them.

The paper is organised as follows; in the second section, the mathematical model was recalled and studied, determining the equilibrium points, the effective reproduction number and discussing the identification of the containment measures by proposing a suitable cost index. In the numerical results section, after showing the effectiveness of the identification procedure as well as the fitting ability, interesting scenarios are studied.

2. Materials and Methods

In this section, the mathematical model proposed in [23] is enriched with the introduction of the possible control actions, the test campaign, the quarantine, the medication and the vaccination, as shown in Section 2.1. The model is studied in Sections 2.2 and 2.3, determining the equilibrium points and proposing a stability analysis, calculating the expression of the basic reproduction number and studying its relation with the equilibrium points. In Section 2.4, the identification of the applied containment measures is proposed.

2.1. The Mathematical Model Proposed and Introduction of the Containment Measures

In the model adopted and briefly recalled in this subsection, all the typologies of controls that can be put in place for containing the spread of COVID-19 and for the reduction of its mortality are introduced. The state space dimension is kept as low as possible to maintain the simplicity and immediacy of a SEIR model, but including those classes specific to the main characteristics of COVID-19, thus allowing to determine the effects of the controls introduced. The six-dimensional system proposed is:

$$\dot{S} = B - \beta(1-u_2)SI_u + bnQ + cnu_5Q - au_1S - d_SS - vu_6S \tag{1}$$
$$\dot{E} = \beta(1-u_2)SI_u - au_1E - kE - d_EE \tag{2}$$
$$\dot{I}_u = kE - au_1I_u - h_1I_u - h_2I_u - d_{I_u}I_u \tag{3}$$
$$\dot{I}_d = h_1I_u + h_1(1-n)Q + c(1-n)u_5Q - (\gamma + \eta u_3)I_d$$
$$\quad - d_{I_d}(1-u_4)I_d \tag{4}$$
$$\dot{Q} = au_1(S + E + I_u) - bnQ - h_1(1-n)Q - cu_5Q - d_QQ \tag{5}$$
$$\dot{R} = h_2I_u + (\gamma + \eta u_3)I_d - d_RR + vu_6S \tag{6}$$

where:

- S is the class of susceptible individuals;
- E is the class of infected patients in the incubation phase; they cannot infect other subjects;
- I_u is the class of the infected patients without symptoms; they are infective and then are responsible for the disease spread. They can remain asymptomatic for all the illness course or can start to have some symptoms;
- I_d is the class including the diagnosed infected patients which are isolated and then cannot transmit the virus even if infective. Patients in this class are the ones that can receive medical treatment both for the infection and for secondary diseases or complications;
- Q is the class of the suspected infected individuals which are temporarily isolated and tested for positivity of the SARS-CoV-2, or simply quarantined for security reasons;
- R is the class of the recovered individuals, the ones which healed spontaneously or after therapy, which are supposedly no longer infected.

The parameters introduced in (1)–(6) have been extensively described in [23]. The death rates in each class are denoted by the d_* terms. The constant rate B of new incoming individuals was only added in the susceptible class, considering the negligible time of permanence in the other classes with respect to the population growth. Parameter β is the contact rate. The parameters k, h_1, h_2 and γ denote the natural transition rates between classes; b and c are related to the results of the tests on the suspected cases in Q. More precisely, b is the rate of return from quarantine of the supposedly healthy people, while c denotes the rate of transition from Q to the class corresponding to the results of the test, healthy with probability $n = \frac{S(t)}{S(t)+E(t)+I_u(t)}$ (test negative), or infected for the remaining $1-n$, defined according to the average time required for the tests.

As far as the control actions u_i, $i = 1,\ldots,6$, are concerned with reducing the spread of the virus and to take care of medical issues, respectively, the following functions are introduced:

- u_1, with an efficacy coefficient a, which denotes the action aiming to stimulate or force a test campaign on the population, even without any suspect of infection. The goal is to recognise infected individuals as early as possible to reduce the contact rates;
- u_2 models the isolation indications, aiming to reduce the interaction with other people. This isolation acts on the factor β for the part responsible of the frequency of individual contacts; it is bounded between zero and one, with $u_2 = 1$ corresponding to an ideal total individual isolation;
- u_3 represents the therapy action devoted directly to counteract the virus by means of antiviral drugs; the associated coefficient η denotes the effectiveness of the therapy;
- u_4 is the therapy action aiming at reducing the side-effects, typically the induced cardio–respiratory diseases. Its effect is introduced as a direct contribution to reduce the mortality rate and it is bounded between zero and one, corresponding, respectively, to no therapy and to the desirable condition of all individuals kept alive during the course of the infection;

- u_5 models all the constraints (medical, political and economical) influencing the tests policy and the consequent effects;
- u_6 regards the vaccination strategy, possible since the end of 2020. The coefficient v denotes the efficiency of the vaccination, depending on the individual response and on the type of vaccine used.

2.2. Model Analysis

In this section, the qualitative analysis of the system behaviour is proposed, choosing to include the control actions u_i, $i = 1, \ldots, 6$; the reason for this is that it can be assumed that there is a lack of any containment measure only in the very first period of the epidemic, until January 2020, when nobody, at least in Europe, was sufficiently aware of the danger of the situation.

Aiming at the unified analysis in which all potentially active control actions are naturally included in the system evolution, the following positions are assumed:

- $\tilde{a}(t) = au_1(t)$
- $\tilde{\beta}(t) = \beta(1 - u_2(t))$
- $\tilde{\eta}(t) = \eta u_3(t)$
- $\tilde{\gamma}(t) = \gamma + \eta u_3(t)$
- $\tilde{d}_{I_d}(t) = d_{I_d}(1 - u_4(t))$
- $\tilde{c}(t) = cu_5(t)$
- $\tilde{v}(t) = vu_6(t)$

Moreover, for the sake of simplicity in the formulation, the following non-negative functions are introduced:

- $m_1(t) = \tilde{a}(t) + d_S + \tilde{v}(t)$
- $m_2(t) = \tilde{a}(t) + k + d_E$
- $m_3(t) = \tilde{a}(t) + h_1 + h_2 + d_{I_u}(t)$
- $m_4(t) = bn + \tilde{c}(t)n$
- $m_5(t) = bn + h_1(1 - n) + \tilde{c}(t) + \tilde{d}_Q(t)$
- $m_6(t) = d_S + \tilde{v}(t)$

The model analysis was performed, as usual, by assuming constant controls u_i, which correspond to constant values for m_i; the equilibrium points are determined by equating the second members of the Equations (1)–(6) to zero, that is, by using the notations introduced above, by solving the system:

$$0 = B - \tilde{\beta}SI_u + m_4 Q - m_1 S \quad (7)$$
$$0 = \tilde{\beta}SI_u - m_2 E \quad (8)$$
$$0 = kE - m_3 I_u \quad (9)$$
$$0 = h_1 I_u + (h_1 + \tilde{c})(1 - n)Q - \tilde{\gamma}I_d - \tilde{d}_{I_d} I_d \quad (10)$$
$$0 = \tilde{a}(S + E + I_u) - m_5 Q \quad (11)$$
$$0 = h_2 I_u + \tilde{\gamma}I_d - d_R R + \tilde{v}S \quad (12)$$

Observing that in absence of infection, $n = 1$ (being equal to 1 the probability of having negative COVID-19 test), it is easily verified that the disease-free equilibrium (DFE), always present, is given by

$$P_1^e = \begin{pmatrix} S_1^e & E_1^e & I_{u1}^e & I_{d1}^e & Q_1^e & R_1^e \end{pmatrix}^T$$
$$= \begin{pmatrix} \dfrac{Bm_5}{m_4 m_6 + \tilde{d}_Q m_1} & 0 & 0 & 0 & \dfrac{B\tilde{a}}{m_4 m_6 + \tilde{d}_Q m_1} & \dfrac{B\tilde{v}m_5}{d_R(m_4 m_6 + \tilde{d}_Q m_1)} \end{pmatrix}^T \quad (13)$$

once the solution with $E = I_d = I_u = 0$ is taken. Note that, as will be used later, when $n = 1$, the following identity holds $m_4 m_6 + \tilde{d}_Q m_1 = m_1 m_5 - \tilde{a}m_4$.

A second equilibrium point:

$$P_2^e = \begin{pmatrix} S_2^e & E_2^e & I_{u2}^e & I_{d2}^e & Q_2^e & R_2^e \end{pmatrix}^T \qquad (14)$$

the endemic one, can be found in (7)–(12). In particular, from (9) and (8), it can be obtained that:

$$S_2^e = \frac{m_2 m_3}{k\bar{\beta}} \qquad (15)$$

$$E_2^e = \frac{m_3}{k} I_{u2}^e \qquad (16)$$

By substituting in (11), it results:

$$Q_2^e = \frac{\bar{a} m_2 m_3}{k\bar{\beta}} + \frac{\bar{a}}{m_5}\left(\frac{m_3}{k} + 1\right) I_{u2}^e \qquad (17)$$

and I_{d2}^e is obtained, as function of Q_2^e, from (10):

$$I_{d2}^e = \frac{1}{\bar{\gamma} + \bar{d}_{I_d}}(h_1 I_{u2}^e + (1-n)(h_1 + \bar{c}) Q_2^e) \qquad (18)$$

All these quantities, with the exception of S_2^e, definitely depend on I_{u2}^e, and are well defined once I_{u2}^e is defined. Its expression is obtained from (7) by

$$I_{u2}^e = \frac{\bar{a} m_2 m_3 m_4 + k\bar{\beta} m_5 B - m_1 m_2 m_3 m_5}{\bar{\beta}(\bar{\beta} m_2 m_3 m_5 k - \bar{a} m_3 m_4 - \bar{a} k m_4)} \qquad (19)$$

This solution can be accepted only if positive; by substituting the definitions of m_i, $i = 1, \ldots, 5$, it can be easily shown that the denominator is always positive, whereas the sign of the numerator depends on the condition:

$$\frac{\bar{\beta} k B m_5}{m_2 m_3 (m_1 m_5 - \bar{a} m_4)} - 1 = \frac{\bar{\beta} k P_1^e}{m_2 m_3} - 1 = \mathcal{R} - 1 > 0 \qquad (20)$$

The meaning of the herein defined expression $\mathcal{R}$ will be discussed in the next subsection, when determining the *Effective Reproduction Number* [24].

As far as the analysis of the stability property of P_1^e is concerned, the following result can be stated.

Proposition 1. *The disease-free equilibrium point P_1^e is asymptotically stable if and only if:*

$$\mathcal{R} - 1 = \frac{\bar{\beta} k B m_5}{m_2 m_3 (m_1 m_5 - \bar{a} m_4)} - 1 < 0 \qquad (21)$$

In fact, by writing the Jacobian of the controlled system (1)–(6) and using the introduced notations with the m_i quantities, it is obtained that:

$$J = \begin{pmatrix} -m_1 & 0 & -\bar{\beta} S_1^e & 0 & m_4 & 0 \\ 0 & -m_2 & \bar{\beta} S_1^e & 0 & 0 & 0 \\ 0 & k & -m_3 & 0 & 0 & 0 \\ 0 & 0 & h_1 & -(\bar{\gamma} + \bar{d}_{I_d}) & (1-n)(h_1 + \bar{c}) & 0 \\ \bar{a} & \bar{a} & \bar{a} & 0 & -m_5 & 0 \\ \bar{v} & 0 & h_1 & \bar{\gamma} & 0 & -d_R \end{pmatrix} \qquad (22)$$

Due to the special structure of the Jacobian J, its characteristic equation evaluated in P_1^e has two negative roots, $-d_R$ and $-(\tilde{\gamma}+\tilde{d}_{I_d})$, found considering the sixth and the fourth columns; the other roots are obtained from the four degrees polynomial:

$$P(\lambda) = \lambda^4 + N_3\lambda^3 + N_2\lambda^2 + N_1\lambda + N_0 \qquad (23)$$

whose coefficients N_i, $i = 0,\ldots,3$ contain the defined quantity $\mathcal{R}$ previously introduced:

$$N_3 = m_1 + m_2 + m_3 + m_5 \qquad (24)$$

$$N_2 = m_2 m_3(1-\mathcal{R}) + (m_2+m_3)(m_1+m_5) + m_1 m_5 - \tilde{a}m_4 \qquad (25)$$

$$N_1 = m_2 m_3(1-\mathcal{R})(m_1+m_5) + (m_2+m_3)(m_1 m_5 - \tilde{a}m_4) \qquad (26)$$

$$N_0 = m_2 m_3(1-\mathcal{R})(m_1 m_5 - \tilde{a}m_4) \qquad (27)$$

To study the sign of the real part of the roots of the $P(\lambda)$, Routh's arguments are used [25]; first of all, it can be noted that, since $m_i > 0$, $i = 1,\ldots,6$, it results that the sign of the N_i is the same as $1-\mathcal{R}$, as it can be easily shown by substituting the definitions of m_i, $i = 1,4,5$ in $m_1 m_5 - \tilde{a}m_4$, always positive. By applying Routh's rule to $P(\lambda)$, the sign of the two quantities must be studied:

$$N_3 N_2 - N_1 \qquad N_1(N_2 N_3 - N_1) - N_3^2 N_0 \qquad (28)$$

From the definitions (24)–(27), and substituting the expressions of m_i, $i = 1,\ldots,6$, it can be deduced that they are positive if $1-\mathcal{R} > 0$. Therefore, it is possible to conclude that in this case, the disease-free equilibrium is stable. When the second equilibrium point exists, see condition (20), the point P_1^e becomes unstable.

2.3. The Effective Reproduction Number

As already stated, the model analysis is performed assuming constant controls, thus obtaining the equilibrium points that depend on those values of the containment measures. In the contest of coping with the pandemic, these actions are generally kept constant for a period of at least two weeks, to be able to see their effects and provide suitable adjustments of the containment measurements, if needed. In this sense, both P_1^e and P_2^e (when the latter equilibrium point exists) depend on the applied controls, and therefore, on the period during which the chosen actions are applied. The DFE, P_1^e, in particular, has a special meaning; if a population is in that condition by means of the (constant) control actions introduced during a specific period and for the model parameters, and if the quantity $1-\mathcal{R}$ is positive, then the evolution of the population will remain near P_1^e, without allowing the spread of the epidemic. Referring to COVID-19 (and therefore assuming fixed model parameters) and to the definition of $\mathcal{R}$, a suitable application of social distancing (thus acting on $\tilde{\beta}$), of swab tests and quarantine (thus acting on $\tilde{a}$ and $\tilde{c}$), medication (acting on $\tilde{\gamma}$) and vaccination (control $\tilde{v}$) would lead the population to the DFE.

The quantity $\mathcal{R}$ introduced in (20) is related to the *effective reproduction number*, the actual average number of secondary cases per primary case at calendar time t [26]. More precisely, this indicator, when evaluated in absence of any control action (i.e., at the beginning of the epidemic), is the well-known $\mathcal{R}_0$, the *basic reproduction number* that can be estimated from data or by using the *next-generation matrix approach* [24,27].

The introduction of the containment measures aims to reduce the incidence of the epidemic; in this case, the *effective reproduction number* is an indicator of the epidemic evolution and of the effectiveness of the applied control actions. Generally, it is determined from data, that by using a statistical approach [28], or by adapting the previously cited *next-generation matrix approach*, as proposed in [24,29,30]. The difference between the methods proposed in the above-cited papers relies on the points in which the next-generation matrix is evaluated; according to the approach in [30], the reproduction number will be herein evaluated by using the disease-free equilibrium (13), which includes the vaccination, when possible, and the tests campaign, with all controls assumed constant when the $\mathcal{R}$ evaluation is performed.

The computation starts by considering in the dynamics (1)–(6) the classes directly involved in the spread of infection, E, I_u, I_d and Q, and therefore only the Equations (2)–(5). By using the notations with the m_i, $i = 1,\ldots,6$ quantities, the reduced system (2)–(5) may be written and enhance the contributions due the infection, $\mathcal{F}$, and the ones due to changing the health condition, $\mathcal{V}$:

$$\begin{pmatrix} \dot{E} \\ \dot{I}_u \\ \dot{I}_d \\ \dot{Q} \end{pmatrix} = \begin{pmatrix} \bar{\beta} S I_u \\ 0 \\ 0 \\ 0 \end{pmatrix} - \begin{pmatrix} m_2 E \\ -kE + m_3 I_u \\ -h_1 I_u - [(h_1 + \bar{c})(1-n)Q] + (\bar{\gamma} + \bar{d}_{I_d}) I_d \\ -\bar{a}(S + E + I_u) + m_5 Q \end{pmatrix} = \mathcal{F} - \mathcal{V} \qquad (29)$$

The variations of these vectors with respect to the variables E, I_u, I_d and Q, evaluated in the disease-free equilibrium, yield the matrices F and V, respectively:

$$F = \left. \frac{\partial \mathcal{F}}{\partial (E, I_u, I_d, Q)} \right|_{P_e^1} = \begin{pmatrix} 0 & \bar{\beta} S_e^1 & 0 & 0 \\ 0 & 0 & 0 & 0 \\ 0 & 0 & 0 & 0 \\ 0 & 0 & 0 & 0 \end{pmatrix} \qquad (30)$$

and:

$$V = \left. \frac{\partial \mathcal{V}}{\partial (E, I_u, I_d, Q)} \right|_{P_e^1} = \begin{pmatrix} m_2 & 0 & 0 & 0 \\ -k & m_3 & 0 & 0 \\ 0 & -h_1 & \bar{\gamma} + d_{I_d} & 0 \\ -\bar{a} & -\bar{a} & 0 & m_5 \end{pmatrix} \qquad (31)$$

Under these positions, the effective reproduction number is given by the dominant eigenvalue of the matrix FV^{-1}, given in this case by its $\{(1,1)\}$ element; its computation easily yields the same expression defined in (20), $\mathcal{R} = \frac{\bar{\beta} k P_1^e}{m_2 m_3}$.

Therefore, also in the proposed approach that includes the control actions, it can be deduced that if the effective the reproduction number $\mathcal{R}$ is smaller than 1, there exists a unique equilibrium point, the disease-free equilibrium one that is stable; otherwise, the equilibrium points are two and the disease-free one is no longer stable.

2.4. Containment Measures Identification

The approach adopted in this paper was to consider the model evolution influenced by the application of the containment measures since the very beginning of the analysis; this is reasonable as the data only started to be collected at the end of February 2020 with the introduction of measures of increasing severity [1]. All the actions u_i, $i = 1,\ldots,6$, are assumed between 0 and 1. Note that for the controls, the value 0 corresponds to the absence of any action, whereas 1 represents the maximum effort. The controls are multiplied by factors representing the effectiveness of the control; therefore, the identification of the containment measures is obtained once the evolutions of the quantities $\bar{a}(t)$, $\bar{\beta}(t)$, $\bar{\gamma}(t)$, $\bar{d}_{I_d}(t)$, $\bar{c}(t)$ and $\bar{v}(t)$ are determined. Note that the meaning of the evolution of $\bar{\beta}$ is opposite with respect to the corresponding one of u_2: when the control $u_2(t)$ is maximum (ideally equal to 1), the quantity $\bar{\beta}$ has its minimum value (corresponding to the absence of contacts); similar consideration holds for the control $u_4(t)$ and the quantity $\bar{d}_{I_d}(t)$.

The data that will be used for identification regard the Italian situation; they were downloaded from the Civil Protection website [2]. More precisely, there are considered:

- The number of newly diagnosed infections $I_{real}^N(t)$ obtained considering the sum of the variation of the number of infected patients, of the recovered and the deaths between two consecutive days; $I_{model}^N(t)$ is the corresponding quantity evaluated from the model;
- The number of positive patients I_{real} corresponding to the I_d ones of this model;

- The number of subjects officially recovered R_{real} from COVID-19, corresponding to:

$$R_{I_d}(t) = (\gamma + \eta u_3(t))I_d(t) \tag{32}$$

- The number of patients deceased from direct effects of the virus—D_{real}—corresponding to the following function obtained from the model:

$$D(t) = d_{I_d}(1 - u_4(t))I_d(t) \tag{33}$$

- The number of subjects vaccinated with the two doses $V_{real}(t)$ corresponding to the quantity $V(t) = \bar{v}S(t)$ of the model.

The following cost index is proposed, aiming to fit the available real data, by minimizing the errors between measured quantities and the corresponding outputs of the model:

$$\begin{aligned} J\ (\bar{\alpha},\bar{\beta},\bar{\gamma},\bar{d}_{I_d},\bar{c},\bar{v}) &= \int_{t_0}^{t_f} [w_1(I_{real}^N(t) - I_{model}^N(t))^2 \\ &+ w_2(I_{real}(t) - I_d(t))^2 + w_3(R_{real}(t) - R_{I_d}(t))^2 \\ &+ w_4(D_{real}(t) - D(t))^2 + w_5(V_{real}(t) - V(t))^2]dt \end{aligned} \tag{34}$$

where the parameters w_i, $i = 1,\ldots,5$, weight the relevance of each term in the optimisation procedure.

All the available information will be used to improve the numerical identification of the quantities $\bar{\alpha}, \bar{\beta}, \bar{\gamma}, \bar{d}_{I_d}, \bar{c}, \bar{v}$. For example, it is well known that the vaccination campaign only started in January 2021; therefore, in the first period, it could be assumed $\bar{v} = 0$. Another possible simplification regards the relation between the two controls u_3 and u_4. In Equation (4), the two contributions related to healing and to death are assumed to be separated since they correspond to different therapy actions. Nevertheless, in some ways, they refer to the same kind of resources, referring to the medication aspects; therefore, for the sake of simplification, to better match the real data available, it can be reasonably assumed that there is a relation among u_3 and u_4:

$$\tilde{\gamma}(t) = \gamma + \eta u_3(t) = h_3 u_4(t) \tag{35}$$

where parameter h_3 is related to the rate of healing for infected patients. This implies that a simplified choice for the cost index (34) can be assumed, leading to the identification of $\bar{\alpha}, \bar{\beta}, \bar{\gamma}, \bar{c}$ up to the end of December 2020, with the addition of $\bar{v}$ starting from January 2021.

3. Numerical Results

In the model introduced in Section 2, the parameters can be distinguished on the basis of their dependence on the characteristics of the considered population or of those of SARS-CoV-2. Difficulties in this system identification arise from different causes. One is related to the real data collection; especially during the first period of the pandemic, when the data were not collected as a consistent modality, not even in the same nation. Moreover, the importance of retrieving some information was not evident since the beginning of the emergency; also, the official communication of the updated numbers of infected patients or of dead subjects was in some cases delayed, thus producing unexpected spikes, hardly predictable, in the corresponding data evolution. Another difficulty in the identification is related to the non-measurability of the important category on asymptomatic subjects (the ones modelled in the I_u class) and consequently, of the total removed ones in R.

Moreover, it is worth stressing what inspired the approach of this work: that is, the presence of control actions since the very beginning of data collection. During the period considered, of March 2020–April 2021, different and complementary containment measures were adopted by all governments all over the world, without coordination among nations, at least at the very beginning.

In the following, the main containment measures at the Italian national level are summarised, indicating the period of application:

- From 23 February 2020 to 8 March 2020: introduction of increasing measures aimed at containing the diffusion in the north of Italy;
- From 9 March 2020 to 25 April 2020: strict lockdown in the entire nation; all the "non-essential" activities were suspended, distanced learning was introduced for both schools and universities, and whenever possible, smart working was introduced. It was possible to leave home only for emergencies. This period was called "Phase 1";
- From 26 April 2020 to 10 June 2020: almost all activities started again, but it was not possible to travel between regions. This period is "Phase 2";
- From 11 June 2020 to 12 October 2020: it was the period with less restrictions, even with the suggestion of preserving cautions; it was also allowed to travel, always respecting social distancing; this was the "Phase 3";
- From 13 October 2020 to 2 November 2020: introduction of increasing containment measures common to all the nation with restaurants closed at 18:00 and a mandatory use of masks also outside closed places;
- From 3 November 2020 to 21 December 2020: a curfew from 10 p.m. to 5 a.m. was introduced; moreover, a classification mechanism was adopted, classifying each region into three classes indicated by colours (yellow, orange, red) depending on the diffusion of the virus and on the sanitary situation at territorial level. Briefly speaking, in this *phase of colours*, the red condition corresponds to a strict lockdown, with restriction in personal mobility also inside the cities; in the orange situation, it was not possible to move among regions with bars and restaurant open only for take-away. In the yellow regions, bars and restaurants were open until 18:00; teaching was allowed at schools/universities with restrictions on the number of students allowed in classrooms;
- From 22 December 2020 to 6 January 2021: the strategy based on the colours was reinforced; all of Italy was at the orange level, but these became red on the day before and after the 25 and 31 December and 6 January, respectively;
- From 7 January 2021 to 30 April 2021: the strategy with colours during the period 3 November–12 December was adopted with reinforced rules, making it more difficult to pass from a higher danger level, red and orange, to the lower one, orange and yellow, respectively.

This representation of the control actions applied by the Italian Government, as well as their time scheduling, is of course simplified; the consistency of the evolutions of the control actions identified will be discussed considering the real control actions.

As mentioned previously, some model parameters could be chosen on the basis of medical information or related to the characteristics of the population, as can be seen in Table 1 for the numerical values of the fixed model parameters and the corresponding references. Note that the values referring to the medical characteristics of the disease must be considered mean values, also depending on the generally healthy condition of the patient.

Table 1. Numerical values of the fixed model parameters.

Parameter	Value	Reference
k	$\frac{1}{4}$	[1,31]
h_1	$\frac{1}{5}$	[31]
h_2	$\frac{1}{21}$	[3]
h_3	$\frac{1}{40}$	[32]
B	1.69×10^3	[9]
$d_S = d_E = d_Q = d_{I_u} = d_R$	2.81×10^{-5}	[9]
b	$\frac{1}{14}$	[3]

The other parameters of the model can be identified by minimising the cost index (34) or a simplified version, if (35) is assumed, thus yielding the evolutions of $\bar{a}(t)$, $\bar{\beta}(t)$, $\bar{\gamma}(t)$, $\bar{c}(t)$, $\bar{v}(t)$ and indirectly, of $\bar{d}_{I_d}(t)$. The corresponding non-controlled constant values a, β, γ, c and $d_{I_d}(t)$ can be deduced, if needed, from the first values of the quantities with the bar sign, recalling that the controls u_i, $i = 1, \ldots, 6$ are assumed between 0 and 1. By using the @Matlab software and the function *fmincon*, the fitting between real data and the model output was performed. The minimisation of the cost index during the period February–December 2020 was obtained, after a *trial and error* procedure, with the following choice of the weights: $w_1 = 0.4$, $w_i = 0.2$, $i = 2, 3, 4$, with $w_5 = 0$, being the vaccination campaign not started at that time; from January 2021, the weights are chosen as equal to $w_1 = 0.4$, $w_2 = 0.2$, $w_3 = w_4 = 0.15$, $w_5 = 0.1$. In Figures 1–3, the evolutions of the diagnosed infected patients, of the recovered individuals and of the dead subjects are shown along with the corresponding real data; a good fit can be appreciated, in some way overcoming the not completely satisfactory data collection of the first period of the pandemic; in particular, in Figure 1, the three waves of pandemic can be noted, in April 2020, in November 2020 and March 2021. In Figures 4–8, the identified control actions are shown; in each figures the dotted vertical lines correspond to the significant changes in the adoption of the containment measures previously recalled. Particularly interesting is the evolution of $\bar{\beta}(t) = \beta(1 - u_2(t))$ in Figure 4: a general decrease in the evolution of $\bar{\beta}$ can be noted until July, due to the effects of the strict lockdown of Phase 1; then, an increase can be noted until the middle of October, with the re-opening of schools and of many activities. New increasing containment measures were then applied with the "phase of colours" starting in November, thus obtaining a decrease in the values of $\bar{\beta}$ until March. The evolutions of $\bar{a}$ and $\bar{c}$ are quite similar, as shown in Figures 5 and 6, corresponding to an increase in the capability of isolating subjects for a quarantine period and the improvements in the swab testing, respectively, with two decreasing periods in June 2020 and December 2020. As far as the $\bar{\gamma}$ evolution is concerned as desirable, it has been increasing since the very beginning of the pandemic, showing a general resilience capability in the sanitary system, as shown in Figure 7. The vaccination action, represented by $\bar{v}$, only started in January 2021; its evolution, to date over less than three months, shows an oscillatory increase until the middle of February, and then an increasing trend, as shown in Figure 8. To evaluate the goodness of the identification step, the evolutions of the percentage of the normalised errors, in absolute values, indicated, respectively, with Error 1, Error 2 and Error 3, between the real numbers of diagnosed infected patients, of recovered individuals and of deaths and the corresponding quantities obtained from the model, are shown in Figures 9–11. Note that, after the first few days of the identification period, the maximum error was always less than 5% and in general, after July, less than 3%. The identification of the evolutions $\bar{\beta}$, $\bar{a}$, $\bar{c}$, $\bar{\gamma}$ is important since it allows to determine a connection between the decisions about the containment measures and how they have been applied by the population; for example, the strict lockdown of Phase 1 was not applied by the population as an *on–off* control: it required some weeks to adapt to the new condition. Therefore, on the basis of this consideration, it is possible to study some scenarios determining what could have happened if different choices were made. Five scenarios are considered:

- Scenario 1: Instead of the applied containment measures (phase of colours), the adoption of the strict lockdown was assumed, starting in November 6; the trends of $I_d(t)$, $R_{I_d}(t)$ and $D(t)$ were obtained using the evolution of the $\bar{\beta}$ identified during the lockdown period (Figure 4);
- Scenario 2: Instead of ending the strict lockdown at the beginning of May 2020, it is hypothesised that there was an extension until 13 May;
- Scenario 3: Same as Scenario 2, but with the extension of the strict lockdown until 31 May;
- Scenario 4: Regards the vaccination campaign associated with different containment measures from 14 March 2021; in this scenario, it is assumed that the strict lockdown associated with the higher vaccination effort was already applied at the end of January;

- Scenario 5: Same as Scenario 4, but the containment measures applied were those of November 2020 (phase of colours).

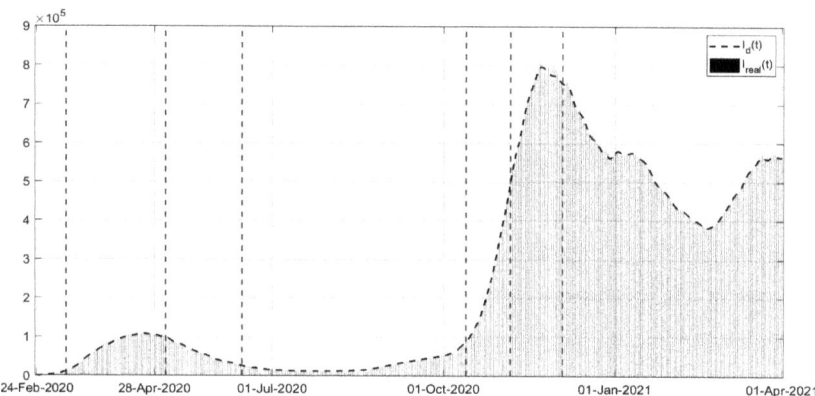

Figure 1. Infected patients $I_d(t)$ estimated from the model versus the corresponding real data.

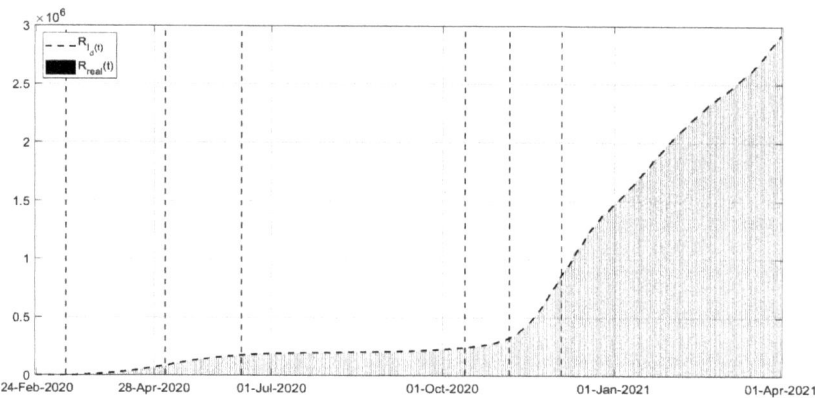

Figure 2. Recovered subjects $R_{I_d}(t)$ estimated from the model versus the corresponding real data.

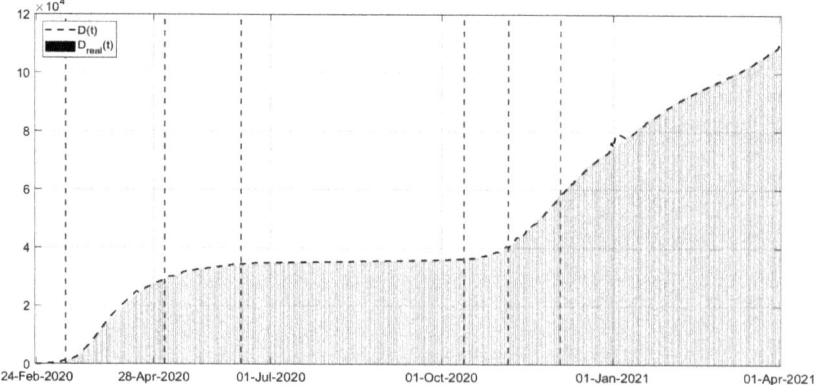

Figure 3. Deceased patients $D(t)$ estimated from the model versus the corresponding real data.

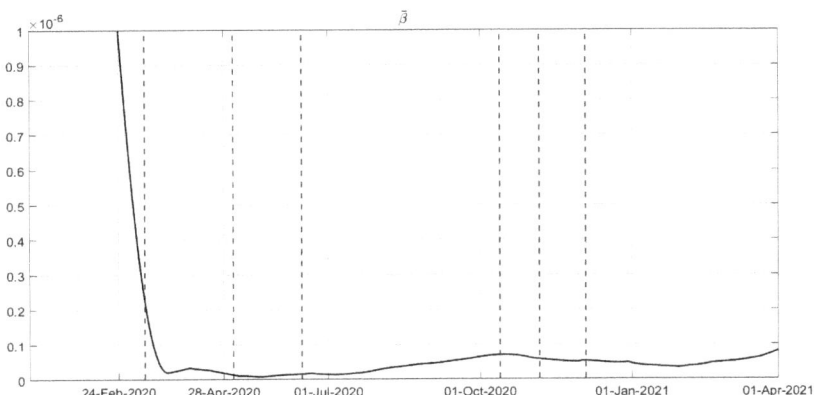

Figure 4. Reconstructed evolution of $\bar{\beta}(t) = \beta(1 - u_2(t))$.

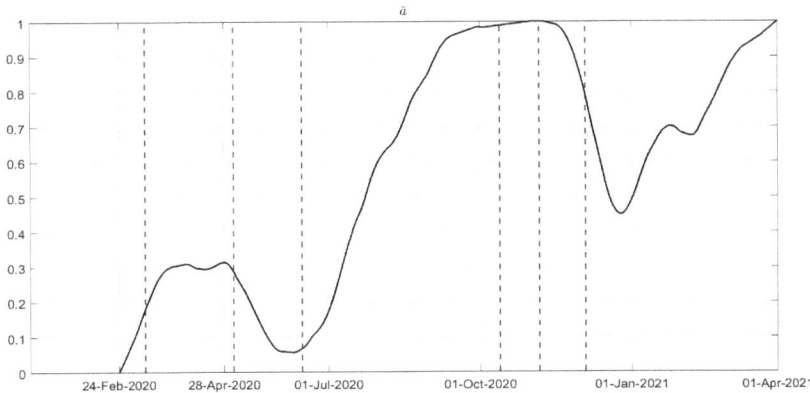

Figure 5. Reconstructed evolution of $\bar{a}$ related to the control action $u_1(t)$.

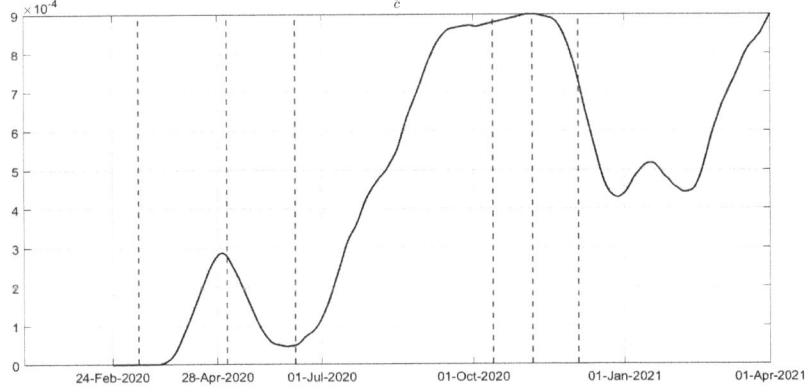

Figure 6. Reconstructed evolution of $\bar{c}(t)$ corresponding to the control action $u_5(t)$.

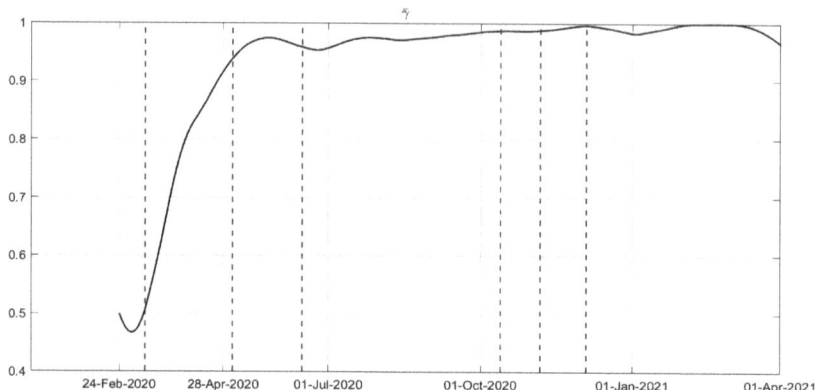

Figure 7. Reconstructed evolution of $\hat{\gamma}$ regarding the control action $u_3(t)$ and $u_4(t)$ according to the simplification in (35).

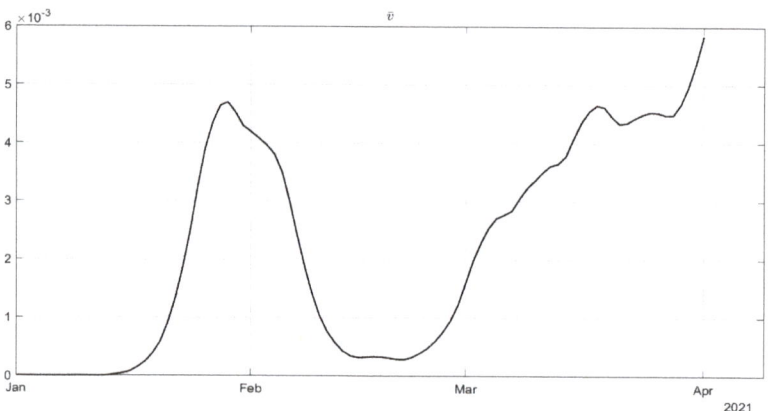

Figure 8. Reconstructed evolution of $\bar{v}$ corresponding to the control action $u_6(t)$.

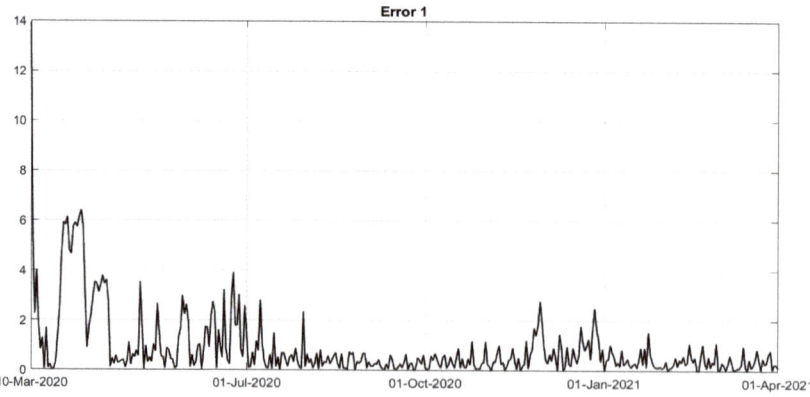

Figure 9. Error $1 = \frac{|I_{real}(t) - I_d(t)|}{I_{real}(t)}$.

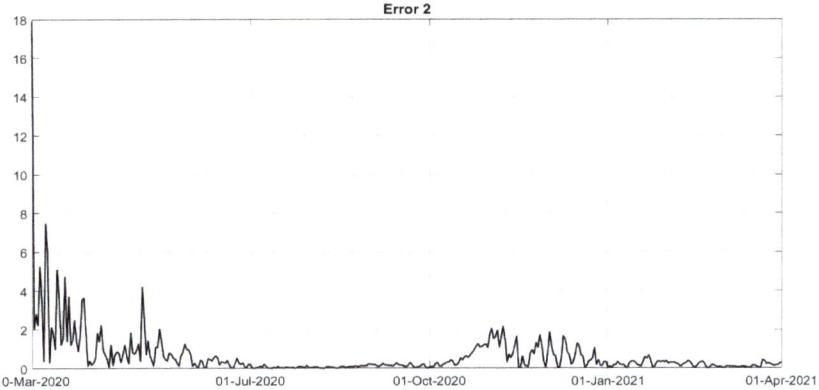

Figure 10. Error 2 = $\frac{|R_{real}(t) - R_{I_d}(t)|}{R_{real}(t)}$.

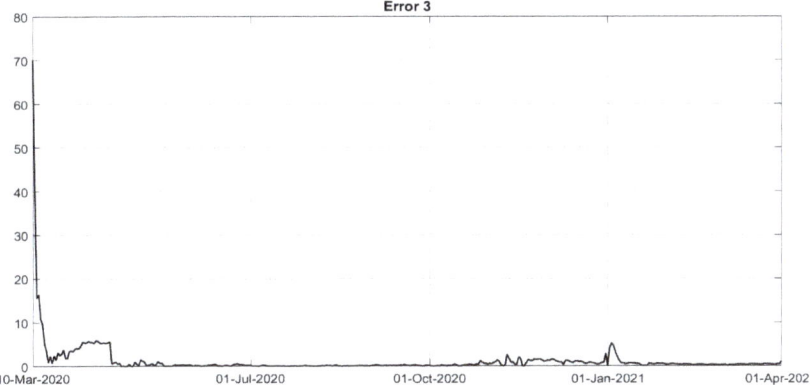

Figure 11. Error 3 = $\frac{|D_{real}(t) - D(t)|}{D_{real}(t)}$.

In Scenario 1 (Figures 12–14), it is evident that there is fast decrease in the number of infected patients in Figure 12, and deaths in Figure 14; obviously, the number of recovered subjects also decreases, as shown in Figure 13, having less patients to heal. Therefore, the adoption of a strict lockdown starting in 6 November 2020 implies a more efficient measure in contrasting the virus spread with respect to milder actions, avoiding many victims, more than 9000. In general, the choice of the containment strategy takes into account different goals and constraints, including social and economic requirements, that in this paper are not considered (Figures 12–14).

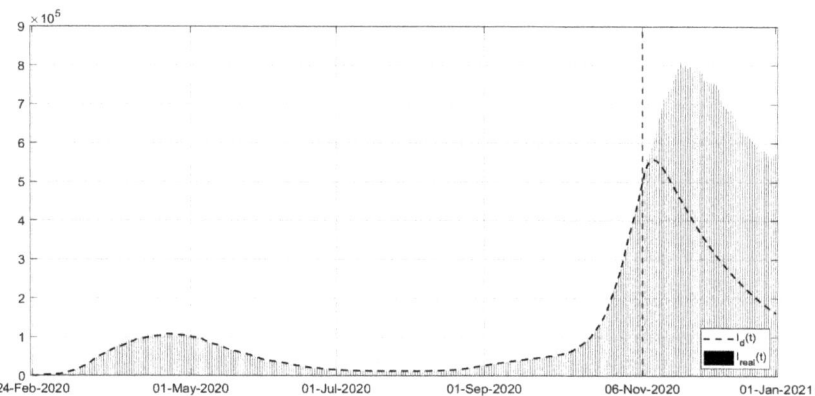

Figure 12. Scenario 1: evolution of $I_d(t)$ versus the corresponding real data.

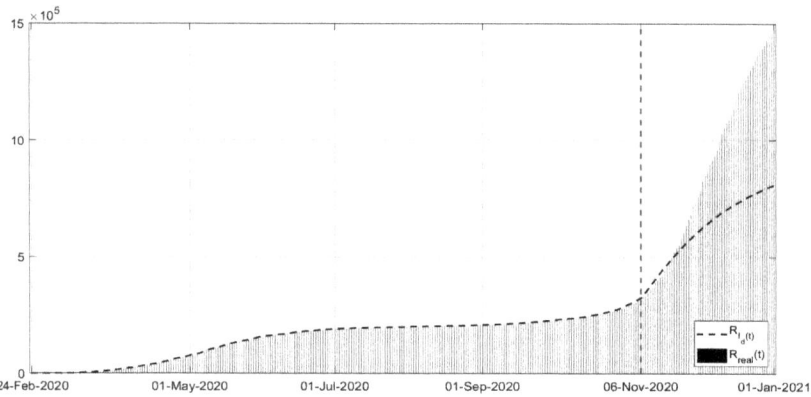

Figure 13. Scenario 1: evolution of the $R_{I_d}(t)$) versus the corresponding real data.

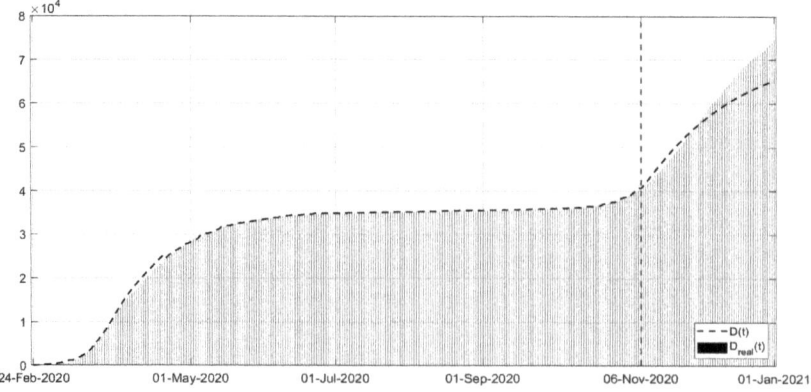

Figure 14. Scenario 1: evolution of the $D(t)$) versus the corresponding real data.

Scenarios 2 and 3 are studied together, as shown in Figures 15–17; they regard the decision of ending the strict lockdown of Phase 1 not at the beginning of May 2020 (as really happened) but in the middle and at the end of May, respectively. It can be noted that, also with an extension of only two weeks of Phase 1 restrictions, the peak of the second COVID-19 wave would have been sensibly lower also with respect to the peak of the first wave. The number of deceased patients remains almost constant in these scenarios, sensibly lower when compared with the real evolution. The results are evident especially in the Scenario 3, if the Phase 1 would have been extended until the end of May. These scenarios confirm the importance of stabilising the infection curves at low levels before re-opening; for example, in Australia, the current approach is even to apply the strict lockdown also with a few dozen cases. Due to the high contagiousness of SARS-CoV-2, it was observed that the increase in the general trend of infected patients was faster than the decrease due the containment measures and to lower the curve requires stronger effort as the number of infected patients is higher.

Scenarios 4 and 5 regard the management of the vaccination phase, Figures 18–20; all governments are trying to accelerate the vaccination campaign, in the meantime limiting the spread of virus to avoid the development of new variants. In some cases, such as in the UK, the vaccination campaign was associated with a strict lockdown obtaining a rapid decrease in the number of infected patients and deaths. In Scenario 4, a fast decrease in the number of infected patients can be noted, whereas the application of the phase of colour containment measures, shown in Scenario 5, yields a less evident decrease in the infections, Figure 18. In particular, the simulation results in Figures 18–20 were compared with the real data representing what is currently happening; it can be observed that the currently applied containment measures allowed a decrease in the number of new infections, slower than in the simulated scenarios, probably also for the new unknown variants of the virus. Nevertheless, it must be stressed that, as seen, any new action or behaviour influences the evolution of the spread, and in particular, the number of infected patients. The increased number of infected patients implies an increased number of deaths, as can be seen in Figure 20.

From the analysis of these scenarios, it can be confirmed that a severe reduction in mobility strongly reduces the infection; the effects are even more evident when the contact reduction is associated with a fast vaccination campaign; nevertheless, social and economic considerations are influencing, as expected, the decisions about containment measures, often in contrast with the suggestion of epidemiologists.

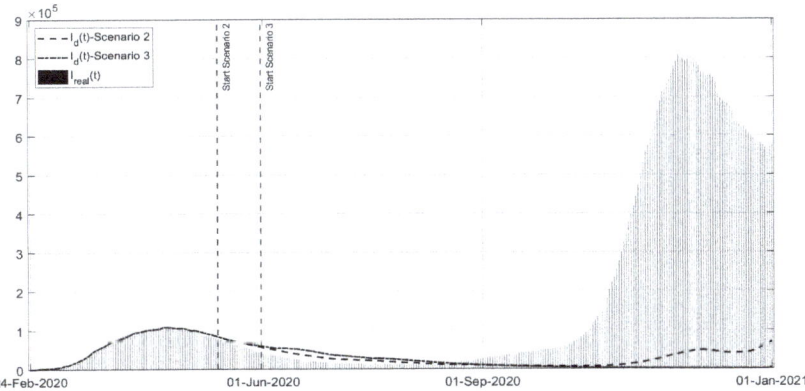

Figure 15. Scenarios 2 and 3: evolution of $I_d(t)$ in the two scenarios versus the corresponding real data.

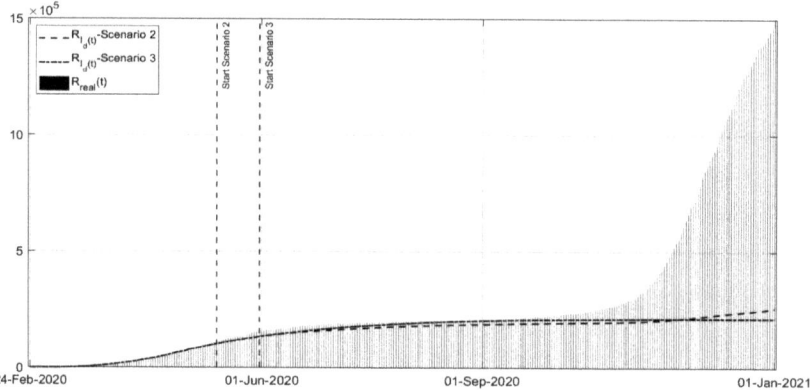

Figure 16. Scenarios 2 and 3: evolution of the $R_{I_d}(t)$ in the two scenarios versus the corresponding real data.

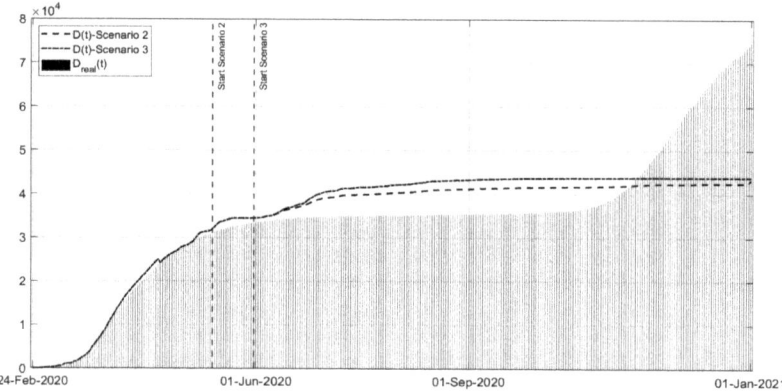

Figure 17. Scenarios 2 and 3: evolution of the $D(t)$ in the two scenarios versus the corresponding real data.

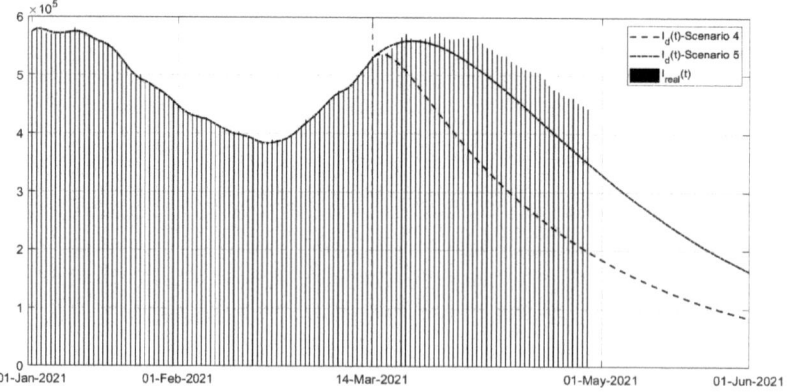

Figure 18. Scenarios 4 and 5: evolution of $I_d(t)$ in the two scenarios versus the corresponding real data.

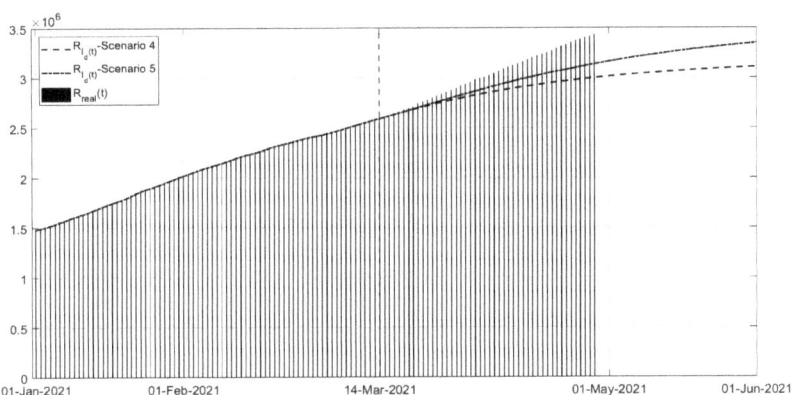

Figure 19. Scenarios 4 and 5: evolution of the $R_{I_d}(t)$) in the two scenarios versus the corresponding real data.

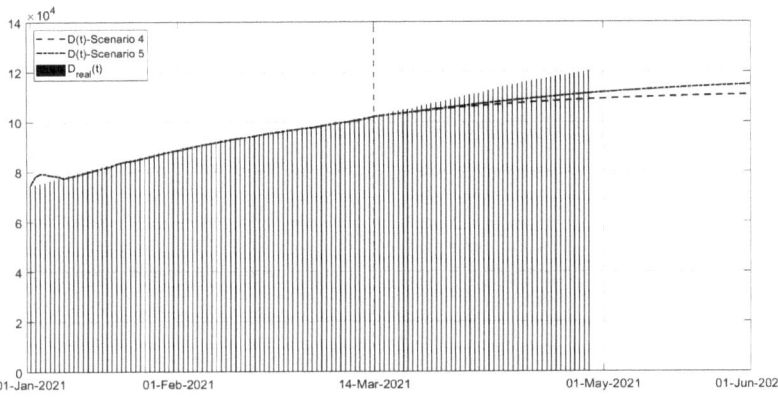

Figure 20. Scenarios 4 and 5: evolution of the $D(t)$ in the two scenarios versus the corresponding real data.

4. Conclusions

The reduction in the impact of COVID-19 in terms of the number of infected patients and deaths depends on the choice of containment measures, from the strict lockdown to vaccination, possibly applied in a coordinated way. Mathematical modelling allows to describe the epidemic spread, introducing all the controls available until now. In this paper, referring to the Italian pandemic conditions, taking into account some of the peculiarities of COVID-19, a suitably enriched $SEIR$ model is proposed, including the effective control actions available to date. Considering the real data regarding the number of infected patients, deaths and vaccinated subjects, the main result of the paper consists in the identification of the applied control actions, enabling a direct correlation between the government's decisions, as they were really applied by the population, and the numerical evolution of the functions representing the control actions. By means of this identification, the estimated effects of the containment measures, associated to the different periods of the pandemic, could be used to study the possible scenarios, in order to understand the effects of different choices, and their impact, also suggesting time scheduling and severity. In particular, the advantages of strict measures have been evidenced, such as those of the lockdown, that, while difficult for the population and the economy, could have accelerated the reduction in the spread. The importance of studying the possible scenarios depending on different control actions relies on the consideration that in a globalised world, a pandemic is not an exception and *mutatis mutandis*, the experience of facing COVID-19 should be useful in similar situations. Future developments regard the possibility of studying the effects of re-infection after vaccination and/or after being infected and healed; the proposed model and approach could be useful to determine the best control actions, also considering the new information about the available vaccines, the duration of the immunity, and specific medication.

Author Contributions: Conceptualisation, P.D.G., R.C. and D.I.; methodology, P.D.G., R.C. and D.I.; software, P.D.G., R.C. and D.I.; validation, P.D.G., R.C. and D.I.; formal analysis, P.D.G., R.C. and D.I.; investigation, P.D.G., R.C. and D.I.; resources, P.D.G., R.C. and D.I.; data curation, P.D.G., R.C. and D.I.; writing—original craft preparation, P.D.G., R.C. and D.I.; writing—review and editing, P.D.G., R.C. and D.I.; visualisation, P.D.G., R.C. and D.I.; supervision, P.D.G., R.C. and D.I.; project administration, P.D.G., R.C. and D.I.; funding acquisition, P.D.G., R.C. and D.I. All authors have read and agreed to the published version of the manuscript.

Funding: This research was funded by Sapienza grant No. 885-009-20.

Informed Consent Statement: Not applicable.

Data Availability Statement: Not applicable.

Conflicts of Interest: The authors declare no conflict of interest.

References

1. World Health Organization. 2021. Available online: https://www.who.int/ (accessed on 10 April 2021).
2. Protezione Civile. 2021. Available online: http://www.protezionecivile.gov.it/ (accessed on 10 April 2021).
3. Ministero della Salute. 2021. Available online: http://www.salute.gov.it/portale/home.html (accessed on 10 April 2021).
4. Istituto Superiore di Sanità. 2021. Available online: https://www.iss.it/ (accessed on 10 April 2021).
5. Iype, E.; Gulati, S. Understanding the asymmetric spread and case fatality rate (CFR) for COVID-19 among countries. *medRxiv* **2021**. [CrossRef]
6. Sapienza University of Rome. 2021. Available online: https://www.uniroma1.it/en/notizia/covid-19-free-swabs-students (accessed on 10 April 2021).
7. Di Giamberardino, P.; Iacoviello, D.; Papa, F.; Sinisgalli, C. Dynamical Evolution of COVID-19 in Italy with an Evaluation of the Size of the Asymptomatic Infective Population. *IEEE J. Biomed. Health Inform.* **2021**, *25*, 1326–1332. [CrossRef] [PubMed]
8. Mahajan, A.; Solanki, R.; Sivadas, N. Estimation of undetected symptomatic ans asymptomatic cases of COVID-19 infection and prediction of its spread in the USA. *J. Med. Virol.* **2021**, *93*, 3201–3210. [CrossRef]
9. Istituto Nazionale di Statistica. 2021. Available online: https://www.istat.it/en/ (accessed on 10 April 2021).
10. Wu, J.T.; Leung, K.; Leung, G.M. Nowcasting and forecasting the potential domestic and international spread of the 2019-nCoV outbreak originating in Wuhan, China: A modelling study. *Lancet* **2020**, *395*, 689–697. [CrossRef]
11. Giordano, G.; Blanchini, F.; Bruno, R.; Colaneri, P.; De Filippo, A.; Colaneri, M. Modeling the COVID-19 epidemic an implementation of population wide interventions in Italy. *Nat. Med.* **2020**, *26*, 855–860. [CrossRef] [PubMed]
12. Yang, Z.; Zeng, Z.; Wang, K.; Wong, S.S.; Liang, W.; Zanin, M.; Liu, P.; Cao, X.; Gao, Z.; Mai, Z.; et al. Modified SEIR and AI prediction of the epidemics trend of COVID-19 in China under public health interventions. *J. Thorac. Dis.* **2020**, *12*, 165–174. [CrossRef]
13. Villaverde, J.F.; Jones, C.J. Estimating and Simulating a SIRD Model of COVID-19 for Many Countries, States, and Cities. *NBER Work. Paper SERIES* **2020**, *15*, 1–60.
14. Tang, B.; Bragazzi, N.L.; Li, Q.; Tang, S.; Xiao, Y.; Wu, J. An updated estimation of the risk of transmission of the novel coronavirus 2019-nCov. *Infect. Dis. Model.* **2020**, *5*, 248–255. [CrossRef] [PubMed]
15. Colombo, R.M.; Garavello, M.; Marcellini, F.; Rossi, E. An age and space structured SIR model describing the Covid-19 pandemic. *J. Math. Ind.* **2020**, *10*, 1–20. [CrossRef] [PubMed]
16. Di Giamberardino, P.; Iacoviello, D.; Albano, F.; Frasca, F.T. Age based modelling of SARS-CoV-2 Contagion: The Italian case. In Proceedings of the 24th International Conference on System Theory, Control and Computing, ICSTCC 2020—Proceedings, Sinaia, Romania, 8–10 October 2020; Volume 9259749, pp. 274–279.
17. Roosa, K.; Lee, Y.; Luo, R.; Kirpich, A.; Rothenberg, R.; Hyman, J.M.; Yan, P.; Chowell, G. Real-time forecasts of the COVID-19 epidemic in China from February 5th to February 24th, 2020. *Infect. Dis. Model.* **2021**, *5*, 256–263. [CrossRef] [PubMed]
18. Cacciapaglia, G.; Cot, C.; Sannino, F. Multiwave pandemic dynamics explained: How to tame the next wave of infectious diseases. *Sci. Rep.* **2021**, *11*, 1–8. [CrossRef] [PubMed]
19. Eikenberry, S.E.; Mancuso, M.; Iboi, E.; Phan, T.; Eikenberry, K.; Kuang, Y.; Kostelich, E.; Gumel, A.B. To mask or not to mask: Modeling the potential for face mask use by the general public to curtail the COVID-19 pandemic. *Infect. Dis. Model.* **2020**, *5*, 293–308. [CrossRef]

20. Gounane, S.; Barkouch, Y.; Atlas, A.; Bendahmane, M.; Karami, F.; Meskine, D. An adaptive social distancing SIR model for COVID-19 disease spreading and forecasting. *Epidemiol. Methods* **2021**, *10*, 1–14. [CrossRef]
21. Aldila, D. Analyzing the impact of the media campaign and rapid testing for COVID-19 as an optimal control problem in East Java, Indonesia. *Chaos Solitons Fractals* **2020**, *141*, 1–14. [CrossRef]
22. Aleta, A.; Corral, M.D.; Piontti, P.; Ajelli, M.; Litvinova, M.; Chinazzi, M.; Dean, N.E.; Halloran, M.E.; Longini, I.M.; Merler, S.; et al. Modelling the impact of testing, contact tracing and household quarantine on second waves of COVID-19. *Nat. Hum. Behav.* **2020**, *4*, 964–971. [CrossRef] [PubMed]
23. Di Giamberardino, P.; Iacoviello, D. Evaluation of the effect of different policies in the containment of epidemic spreads for the COVID-19 case. *Biomed. Signal Process. Control* **2021**, *102325*, 1–15.
24. Martcheva, M. *An Introduction to Mathematical Epidemiology. Text Applied Mathematics*; Springer: Berlin/Heidelberg, Germany, 2015; Volume 61. [CrossRef]
25. Dorf, R.C.; Bishop, R.H. *Modern Control Systems*; Pearson: London, UK, 2001.
26. Nishiura, H.; Chowell, G. The Effective Reproduction Number as a Prelude to Statistical Estimation of Time-Dependent Epidemic Trends. In *Mathematical and Statistical Estimation Approaches in Epidemiology*; Springer: Dordrecht, The Netherlands, 2009; pp. 103–121.
27. Van Den Driessche, P.; Watmough, J. Reproduction numbers and sub-threshold endemic equilibria for compartmental models of disease transmission. *Math. Biosci.* **2002**, *180*, 29–48 [CrossRef]
28. *Reproduction Number (R) and Growth Rate (r) of the COVID-19 Epidemic in the UK: Methods of Estimation, Data Sources, Causes of Heterogeneity, and Use as a Guide in Policy Formulation*; The Royal Society: London, UK, 2020; pp. 1–86.
29. Zhao, S.; Musa, S.S.; Hebert, J.T.; Cao, P.; Ran, J.; Meng, J.; He, D.; Qin, J. Modeling the effective reproduction number of vector-borne diseases: The yellow fever outbreak in Luanda, Angola 2015–2016 as an example. *PeerJ* **2020**, *8*, e8601. [CrossRef] [PubMed]
30. Gumel, A.B.; Iboi, E.A.; Ngonghala, C.N.; Elbasha, E.H. A primer on using mathematics to understand COVID-19 dynamics: Modeling, analysis and simulations. *Infect. Dis. Model.* **2021**, *6*, 148–168. [PubMed]
31. Lu, R.; Zhao, X.; Li, J.; Niu, P.; Yang, B.; Wu, H.; Wang, W.; Song, H.; Huang, B.; Zhu, N.; et al. Genomic characterisation and epidemiology of 2019 novel coronavirus: Implications for virus origins and receptor binding. *Lancet* **2020**, *395*, 565–574. [CrossRef]
32. Epicentro. Available online: https://www.epicentro.iss.it (accessed on 10 April 2021).

Article

SARS-COV-2: SIR Model Limitations and Predictive Constraints

Charles Roberto Telles [1,*], Henrique Lopes [2] and Diogo Franco [2]

1. Intern Control Center, Secretary of State for Education and Sport of Paraná, Curitiba, Paraná 80240-900, Brazil
2. Public Health Unit, Health Sciences Institute, Catholic University of Portugal, Palma de Cima, 1649-023 Lisbon, Portugal; henrique.lopes@ucp.pt (H.L.); diogofrancosharen@gmail.com (D.F.)
* Correspondence: charlestelles@seed.pr.gov.br

Abstract: Background: The main purpose of this research is to describe the mathematical asymmetric patterns of susceptible, infectious, or recovered (SIR) model equation application in the light of coronavirus disease 2019 (COVID-19) skewness patterns worldwide. Methods: The research modeled severe acute respiratory syndrome coronavirus 2 (SARS-COV-2) spreading and dissemination patterns sensitivity by redesigning time series data extraction of daily new cases in terms of deviation consistency concerning variables that sustain COVID-19 transmission. The approach opened a new scenario where seasonality forcing behavior was introduced to understand SARS-COV-2 non-linear dynamics due to heterogeneity and confounding epidemics scenarios. Results: The main research results are the elucidation of three birth- and death-forced seasonality persistence phases that can explain COVID-19 skew patterns worldwide. They are presented in the following order: (1) the environmental variables (Earth seasons and atmospheric conditions); (2) health policies and adult learning education (HPALE) interventions; (3) urban spaces (local indoor and outdoor spaces for transit and social-cultural interactions, public or private, with natural physical features (river, lake, terrain). Conclusions: Three forced seasonality phases (positive to negative skew) phases were pointed out as a theoretical framework to explain uncertainty found in the predictive SIR model equations that might diverge in outcomes expected to express the disease's behaviour.

Keywords: COVID-19 seasonality; S.I.R. models; mathematical modeling; forced seasonality; confounding variables; uncertainty

Citation: Roberto Telles, C.; Lopes, H.; Franco, D. SARS-COV-2: SIR Model Limitations and Predictive Constraints. *Symmetry* **2021**, *13*, 676. https://doi.org/10.3390/sym13040676

Academic Editors: Federico Papa and Carmela Sinisgalli

Received: 8 March 2021
Accepted: 9 April 2021
Published: 14 April 2021

Publisher's Note: MDPI stays neutral with regard to jurisdictional claims in published maps and institutional affiliations.

Copyright: © 2021 by the authors. Licensee MDPI, Basel, Switzerland. This article is an open access article distributed under the terms and conditions of the Creative Commons Attribution (CC BY) license (https://creativecommons.org/licenses/by/4.0/).

1. Introduction

This research's main focus is to point, as noted in Grassly and Fraser [1], to the consequences of seasonality for endemic R_0 stability in order to understand and obtain an endemic equilibrium for coronavirus disease 2019 (COVID-19) involving mixing patterns such as environmental driving factors, policy interventions, and urban spaces [2–8]. These latter three variables might pose challenges for the outcomes of the SIR (susceptible, infectious, or recovered) predictive analysis [9] of severe acute respiratory syndrome coronavirus 2 (SARS-COV-2) spreading and dissemination patterns. This can be verified in the time series data regarding daily new COVID-19 cases where the type of spreading patterns in daily quantitative outcomes present a high degree of uncertainty (skewness asymmetric patterns) expressed by fluctuations and mainly random distributions [8].

By observing time series data of daily new COVID-19 cases worldwide [10], the epidemics birth and death persistence present different probabilistic distributions for each sample (country) of observation, with many delays and fluctuations for the outbreak, peak and control phases due to no initial predefined conditions within the overall samples (countries). These data with distinct outcomes among countries originate false phenomenon observations in terms of positive and negative skew to allow predictive analysis based on SIR models and derivations [11]. This is due to these models relying upon a predefined type of health policies interventions, pre-assumed human behavior and predefined spatial or temporal analysis towards outbreaks, peak and control phases. These pre-assumptions were investigated theoretically although stability to instability patterns generated by the variables that sustain the disease occurrence.

The research divided data of daily new COVID-19 cases into three phases of forced seasonality, demonstrated by a mathematical model of skewness presented in the phenomenon derived from a brief topological analysis and the confounding variables that sustain the disease transmission. Consequently it suggests specific data extraction from time series in order to make predictive analysis with SIR models. This approach aims to provide a more robust understanding of the scientific results concerning these topics of study and worldwide strategies to reduce SARS-COV-2 dissemination patterns of daily new COVID-19 cases to control infection spreading and dissemination patterns. The three main birth and death seasonality persistence (ε') phases found in this research are in the following order: (1) the environmental variables (Earth seasons and atmospheric conditions); (2) health policies and adult learning education (HPALE) interventions; (3) urban spaces (local indoor and outdoor spaces for transit and social-cultural interactions, public or private, with natural physical features (river, lake, terrain).

2. Materials and Methods

2.1. Earth Seasons: From Stable Mean to Asymptotic Patterns of Susceptible, Infectious, or Recovered (SIR) Modeling Equation

To better understand the terms used in this article, spreading patterns is considered as the type of transmission that COVID-19 may assume, be it airborne or physical contact. In contrast, dissemination patterns are understood as the cumulative daily new COVID-19 cases worldwide caused by the existent transmission forms.

To set COVID-19 dissemination patterns under the Earth seasonality aspect of analysis, the endemic free-equilibrium of COVID-19 needs to be applied to Floquet Theory, currently employed in many other infectious diseases with a defined time period (T) of Earth seasonality (ε). To perform this task from a mathematical view of the problem, it is necessary to meet an oscillation to predict endemic R_0 under periodic and defined $A(t)$ criteria, even for time-varying environments with no heterogeneity forces, thus assuming a linear force of infection with homogeneity as $F(T) = B(t)\frac{I}{N}$. This would allow stablishing a reasonable R_0^τ periodical stability for COVID-19 worldwide, as observed by Bacaër [12].

The stability point pre-assumed, if COVID-19 worldwide would be seasonal in winter as flu, could be defined as $p(t+1) = (A(t) + B(t))p(t)$ [12], with p representing the spectral matrix of periodicity $A(t)$ and $B(t)$ the environment of compartments S, I, and R of the SIR model (ecological variables such as biotic and abiotic of each country). Following this definition, the seasonality of COVID-19 at S, I, and R compartments are assumed to be dependent on deterministic outcomes for immunity, forms of transmission, healthcare interventions, and public policies under atmospheric triggering conditions (Earth seasons ε) as found, for example, in common flu. Considering this condition, the ODE (ordinary differential equations) could be easily observed in linear time series, as pointed in Sietto [13] as $y(t) = a + bt + \sum_{i=1}^{m} c_i \cos \theta + \sum_{i=1}^{m} d_i \sin \theta + e(t)$, where the proposition of periodicity θ as linear in time as $B(t+T) = B(t)$ would be possible and consistent in its fluctuations in terms of daily new infections with seasonal sinusoidal patterns as $\theta(t) = \theta_0[1 \pm \varepsilon \sin(2\pi t)]$ [14]. This could also be considered for stochastic expressions over time, considering seasonal fluctuations defined as hidden Markovian chains as $P(Y(t) = y(t)|Y(t-1) = y(t-1), Y(t-2) = y(t-2), \ldots, Y(1) = y(1))$ [13] and its many derivations, found in many studies [15–17]. This deterministic approach for the worldwide event would lead to the seasonal Fourier transform fluctuations of COVID-19 outbreaks, control, and over determined periodic cycles with no confounding scenarios. Fourier analysis would then be possible to perform considering time-periodic fluctuations as noted in Mari et al. [14]. Therefore, the use of Markovian chains to obtain the phase shifts of regularities would be a true approach to predict how SARS-COV-2 dissemination patterns are formed, regardless of spreading patterns. The main issue is when the stochastic process $Y(t)$ assumes a lack of synchrony due to random worldwide delays and uncertainty [8,18,19] due to spreading patterns and characteristics of each country, region, and place. This situation generates a stochastic form with unknown seasonality of infection, defined as $R'_0 = D \int_0^1 B(t) dt$ [18], and thus not assuming seasonality dissemination for ε and the outbreak of local epidemics. At this point, it was observed that there are several discrepant (heterogeneous) time series of daily new infection cases in countries during 2019 and 2021 that were entering winter in the southern hemisphere and summer in the northern hemisphere. No great difference was verified at Earth dissemination seasonality influencing those localities [2,8,9,11].

The lack of dissemination pattern formation for COVID-19, as not found in common flu [20,21], creates an undefined T over defined $A(t)$, as well as, a mean μ over periodicity θ criteria as a pre-assumption of analysis in Fourier's perspective transform. This confirms an unexpected seasonality forcing behavior ε' in which each sample (countries, regions, places) presents a different SARS-COV-2 dissemination pattern not only concerning the Earth seasonality but other components included in ε'.

2.2. Skewness Validation and SIR Model Limitation

What can be observed in many results [2] is an asymptotic unstable behavior of SARS-COV-2 dissemination patterns towards atmospheric conditions (temperature, humidity, ultraviolet (UV), and wind speed), policies and urban spaces that for this latter feature, differ greatly around the globe; and therefore not following only the Earth environmental seasonal forces as found in common flu [22–24]. The asymptotic feature of the phenomena relies on how virus transmission can be associated with a mixture of variables that sustain an indeterminate pattern of growing or reduction among countries. Worldwide, countries are facing daily new COVID-19 cases and the reason for countries to reduce its dissemination patterns are caused mainly due to HPALE on population [2–8] than a well-defined Earth seasonal period of COVID-19 transmission, as it is known that individual behavior and government policies are a major determinant for the pandemic peak reduction. This overall pandemic scenario could be observed in late March and starting in April 2020 when China and South Korea were the unique countries with the lowest rates of exponential growth of infection cases due to the type and strength of adopted HPALE [3,6], while Europe was in its fully active growing pattern. However, this does not mean that environmental variables such as atmosphere properties or Earth seasonality do not present causation of the event. It implies that HPALE influences the phenomenon at its beginning and end with a persistent pattern [2–8] rather than what was expected to be addressed only by the environmental factors as the main driving force of seasonality during winter periods. For this reason, constant COVID-19 dissemination is expected during all Earth seasons and HPALE can be one of the main seasonality driven force observed worldwide.

To add to this scenario, it is possible to identify one more important feature of pandemics, the urban spaces found in every city which present specific potential to influence local epidemics and mathematical simulations of SIR equations, namely the S and R compartments. This impact is due to the effects on each country/city/locality's capability to deal with the outcomes of susceptibility, immunity, spreading patterns, and public health control measures, thus making COVID-19 predictive models assume data that do not correspond to reality. For each predictive model that fails to address urban spaces heterogeneity, HPALE interventions subjectivity, and environmental non-homology of data, the uncertainty degree grows. This leads to SARS-COV-2 emerging under unknown contagion patterns as observed in Billings et al. [19] and with a similar example of measles in Grenfell et al. [25].

2.3. Mathematical Framework of Three Seasonality Forcing Behavior of Coronavirus Disease 2019 (COVID-19) Worldwide and SIR Model Variants Needed

The unexpected seasonality ε' under heterogeneity forcing behavior explain the exponential behavior of infection spreading patterns among countries an unpredictable sinusoidal expression such as $\beta(t) = \beta_0(1 + \varepsilon\varnothing(t))$, as modelled by Buonuomo et al. [26]

with a possibility of using Fourier transforms use, considering finite time lengths of analysis (seasons) equally distributed over the period T within samples (countries). This mathematical framework of analysis applies to the data series of daily new cases when these data present high-amplitude noise, often related to the lower spectral density and lower frequency that makes the analysis imprecise as a sinusoidal stable behavior in the basis form of Earth dissemination seasonality as $\int_{-\infty}^{+\infty} |f(\varepsilon)| d(t)$. In this sense, the sinusoidal behavior does not exist regarding how countries might present default oscillations within seasonal periods of Earth, as represented schematically in Figure 1.

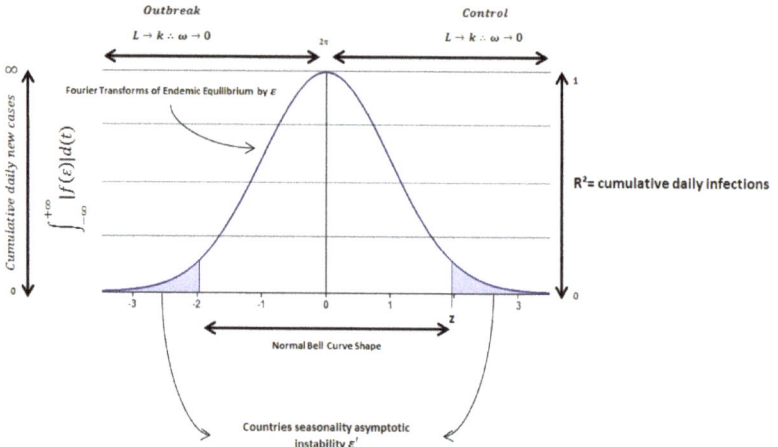

Figure 1. General framework of coronavirus disease 2019 (COVID-19) seasonality under the view of Fourier transform use limitations.

Considering the aspects mentioned before, it is possible to observe that each sample can be understood as the lack of spreading and dissemination patterns towards the confident interval and standard deviation under default periods T from 31 December 2019, to 3 March 2021, resulting in a stochastic maximum exponential form of daily new infections as $Y(t)$ changes over time, as already observed in the literature [2,8,27,28].

However, despite this scheme pointing to the weaker Earth seasonality forcing behavior of SARS-COV-2 dissemination patterns, it can still influence the overall hidden transmission patterns due to HPALE interventions, environmentally driven seasonality, and urban spaces. This point can be addressed as a pattern formation ε', of each sample, of confounding forced seasonality that dismantles S and R compartments of SIR predictive model over time [1,27–34], caused by environmental driven factors, urban spaces [35–37], and health HPALE intervention [2–8]. Then, it is possible to observe that each country might respond differently to the same initial conditions [8], influenced by the three components mentioned above, thus generating multiple patterns formation over time T for SARS-CoV-2 forms of transmission and periodicity.

2.4. SIR Model Redefinition from the Original Equation to Skewness Patterns and Global Sensitivity

Concerning a theoretical desired worldwide SIR model normal distribution that most mathematical models imply for infection spreading and dissemination patterns with shape behavior $k = 1$ or $k > 1$ (Weinbull parameterization) of the exponential "regular" distributions of SARS-CoV-2 infection within time intervals t and with defined periodicity T (possible seasonality forms among countries) [38], the original defined form of I compartment of SIR modeling equation is given as $\frac{dI}{dt} = \beta \frac{SI}{N} - gI$. However, the high asymptotic instability [27–34] of infected individuals (I) and the confounding scenario lead to redefining the equation's basic fundaments to make the skewness analysis. Following this sense, the I compartment of the SIR model was modeled to support confounding data as

$$I = \left(\frac{\omega}{\lambda}\right)^k \quad (1)$$

where the infected I is influenced by the unpredictable scale of infection λ (N) for each sample with inconsistent behavior of variables for S term of the equation, thus influencing the transition rate (βSI) defined as ω dissemination patterns (no global solution). Also it is not assumed for gI in the original form of R compartment, that there is a normal distribution output for this virus spreading and dissemination patterns. This new dissemination pattern formation of the epidemic behavior was also described by Duarte et al. [39] when the contact rate does not encompass weather conditions and time-varying aspects of epidemics. Therefore, an unpredictable shape k of probabilistic outcomes (close to reality shapes) was used, mainly defining this shape caused λ and ω asymptotic instabilities generated by S and R compartments over time [1,27–34], among the environmental- and urban space-driven factors [35–37] and HPALE interventions [2–8]. This equation represents the presence of confounding and heterogeneous environmental variables ω with an unknown predictive scale of $exp\lambda$ or maximum likelihood estimator for λ due to non-linear inputs for S and R compartments over time as a global proposition (urban spaces, HPALE, and environmental conditions influence), thus generating nonlinear outputs k (asymptotic instability) [40,41]. If it is considered that most models are searching for a normality behavior among countries, hence, implying that the k distributions are non-complex and not segmented by its partitions, thus resulting in linearity for the virus infection I over Y and t, then the overall equation as described by Dietz $\beta(t) = \beta m(1 + A \cos(\omega t))$ [40] would not be reachable for any given period of analysis considering the seasonality forcing behavior of SARS-CoV-2.

The outputs with heteroscedasticity and non-homologous form for k and λ can be modified to reach stable points of analysis, as modelled by Dietz $\beta(t) = \beta m(1 + A \cos(\omega t))$ for each of the three seasonality forces influencing SARS-CoV-2 spreading patterns. These three stable points of the asymptotic structure mentioned before can be observed in Figure 2.

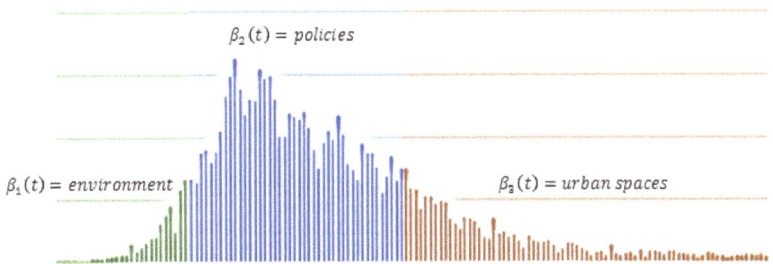

Figure 2. Severe acute respiratory syndrome coronavirus 2 (SARS-COV-2) spreading and dissemination patterns filtered and stated as expressing within the three phases of the epidemic: environmental spreading and dissemination patterns, health policies and adult learning education (HPALE), and the urban spaces dissemination patterns.

To remove heteroscedasticity and non-homologous form for k and λ from occurring in the three phases mentioned in Figure 2, as far as the $\kappa < 1$ Weibull parameterization aspect [42] (Bell curve shape) of distribution is chosen as the most reliable region of analysis (attractive orientation) for any given T periods within any sample (countries daily new cases time series), it is necessary to modify the first Equation (1) to

$$I = I = \left(\frac{Y(t)}{T}\right)^{k<1} - \left(\frac{\omega}{\lambda}\right)^k \quad (2)$$

hence with the new SIR model proposition as $I = I' - (S + R)$, where I is asymptotic stable to I' and S and R considered in its original form $\theta(t) = \theta_0[1 \pm \varepsilon \sin(2\pi t)]$ [14]. This is a mandatory redesign since many scientific breakthroughs point to health policies as the best approach to reduce COVID-19 [2–8]. Starting with this redesign of the equation, it is possible to find one of the first regions of analysis and stability that is health policy intervention, found in the slope (peak) of daily cases over time.

2.5. Birth and Death Persistence of COVID-19 Dissemination Patterns: From Positive to Negative Skew

Considering the new scope of analysis regarding time-series data mentioned before, it is now necessary to uncover the graphic regions in which confounding scenarios can be dismantled with a more robust relation of cause and effect according to Equation (2). It is important to address this birth and death persistence homology for this research, in which the desired mean function $Y(t)$ of topological space $\mathbb{X} \to \mathbb{R}$ over $\beta(t) = \beta m(1 + A\cos(\omega t))$ indicated at (2) can be found as a persistence diagram existence [43] by mapping each adjacent pair to the point $(f(Y), f(t))$ local minimum and maximum observations, due to worldwide epidemic growth behaviour and subtle reduction due to HPALE measures. This step results in critical points of Y function over time t, not in adjacent form globally but regionally triangularly space as $d(D(Y_t), D(t)) \leq \|Y_t - t\|_\infty$ [44] with a given mean region, thus expressing random critical values (dissemination patterns) defined by $I' = \left(\frac{Y(t)}{T}\right)^{k<1}$ in the real-life form of the event. However, since it is necessary to filter $f(Y_n) - f(t_n) = y_n$ unstable critical points (oscillatory instability of seasonality for S and R, HPALE, environmental driven variables, and urban spaces) to an attractive minimum behavior with normal distribution, these regions of analysis must be situated between $\pi < y_n < \frac{\pi}{2}$ for every $A(t) \to T$ asymptote period. Following this path, and roughly modelling it, the mean $\mu(A(t))$ is obtainable as the size of birth and death persistence diagram and triangulable diagonal (Δ) like $D(Y_t, t - \Delta) = \sum_{\pi < y_n < \frac{\pi}{2}} \mu_t^{Y_t}$ with multiplicity pairing regions (t, Y_t) for each desired triangulation as $0 \leq t < Y_t \leq n + 1$, resulting in the general equation for any assumed region as $\mu_t^{Y_t} = \beta(t)_{\varepsilon_{t-1}}^{\varepsilon Y_t} - \beta(t)_{\varepsilon_t}^{\varepsilon Y_t} + \beta(t)_{\varepsilon_t}^{\varepsilon Y_t - 1} - \beta(t)_{\varepsilon_{t-1}}^{\varepsilon Y_t - 1}$ [44]. Note that each mean function $\mu_t^{Y_t}$ will be given by regions defined as $\beta(t) = \beta m(1 + A\cos(\omega t))$, being $\beta(t)$ the covariance function of seasonality forcing behavior of dissemination patterns formed by $\mu(A(t))$ under each $\beta(t)$ form with ε' partitions, hence without a global mean value for the event in terms of infection and time, or in other words, spreading and dissemination patterns. Further derivations and formulations regarding this persistence diagram will not be addressed for this research. However, it is recommended that future research keep this formulation defined for predictive and monitoring analysis of epidemic seasonality forcing behavior.

It is necessary to understand that this new design of seasonality regions can now be adapted adequately to Fourier transform analysis under the amplitude of waves with the equation $e^{-i\omega t} = \cos(2\pi t) + i\sin(2\pi t)$ where angular momentum was drawn in the limits of $\beta(t) = \beta m(1 + A\cos(\omega t))$, giving $\omega = \pi < y_n < \frac{\pi}{2}$ and generally defining it with sinusoidal reduced form as $f(\varepsilon') = \int_{-\infty}^{+\infty} Y(t) e^{-2\pi i \omega t} d\omega$ to reach a sinusoidal approach of time series data extraction and analysis over periods ε' and given analysis regions.

Beyond the limitation of periods for predictive analysis and monitoring as a Gaussian process in the overall data of the given epidemics, the design in this article introduces one main point of analysis that is the lack of a global mean and covariance function $\mu(Y(t))$ over fluctuations as a global homomorphism and a decomposition form of wave signals similar to Fourier transforms. This occurs since spreading patterns of infection find heterogeneity within the type of HPALE interventions influenced by the confounding scenario created by the environment and urban spaces where persistent homology and homotopy cannot be found for $t \therefore \kappa < 1$ Weibull reliability to be situated globally for the overall times series data of epidemics in the oscillation-pairing regions of $\sin(\pi) = 1$ and $\cos(\pi) = 0$ for T desired coordinates of persistent fluctuations in $(f(Y_n), f(t_{k<1})) = y_n$ of stability can differ over an extended time of analysis. HPALE range of influence is no longer stable (weak boundaries points of persistence), and therefore assuming $t+1$ discrete form, defined as $y_n = f(f(Y_n), f(t_{k<1})) \int_{\frac{\pi}{2}}^{\pi} \mu \Sigma(Y_0, \ldots, Y_n) dt$. However, by contrast, it can be found with continuous form as $\delta = f(Y_t, t) \int_{\frac{\pi}{2}}^{\pi} \mu \Sigma(Y_0, \ldots, Y_n) d\mu$ [9], thus assuming the shape and limit to $\kappa < 1$ as small partitions ε' to the desired analysis or without a derivative form for the overall analysis within the whole epidemics behavior observed. Considering the new partitions ε', for the discretized view of Y_t, t as pointed out in the results of Roberts et al. [9], it is now possible to obtain a sample mean as a mode like $\bar{\mu} = \frac{1}{n}\sum_i^n Y_t, t$. Further results of this approach can be visualized at [9] Roberts et al. reference.

By rejecting the persistence diagram's unstable critical points generated globally, a local minimum of the event as an average mean ε' can be obtained by having $Y(t)$ with the higher number of samples Y (daily infections) that finds a condition roughly described in the nonlinear oscillations within the exponential growth epidemic behavior of event as limited between maximum local growth defined by $\frac{\pi}{2}$ by its half curvature oscillations π as a local minimum being non-periodic as 2π in a global homomorphism sense due to $\kappa < 1$. In this sense, the new sinusoidal approach offers a new mean function as an angular momentum of $= \pi < y_n < \frac{\pi}{2}$, hence the wave-signal necessary to perform the Fourier transforms in each ε' of data. This scheme can be observed for HPALE intervention on SARS-CoV-2 spreading and dissemination patterns [27] in Figure 3.

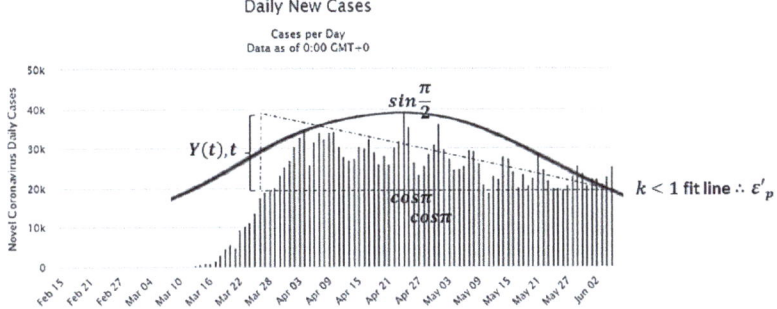

Figure 3. HPALE stable region ε' of analysis on SARS-CoV-2 dissemination patterns. Image data source: Worldometer—Italy on 8 July 2020.

Therefore, $Y(t), t$ assumes the desired oscillations samples and region conditions ε' as $\pi < y_n < \frac{\pi}{2}$ where birth and death persistent homology can be found for t ∴ $\kappa < 1$ to be situated in the oscillations pairing region of $\sin(\pi) = 0$ and $\cos(\pi) = Y(t)$ for $Y(t), t$ desired coordinates $(f(Y(t)), f(t))$ of stability with discrete form as $t+1$ as $Y(t) = f(Y(t)) \int_{\frac{\pi}{2}}^{\pi} \mu \Sigma(Y_0, \ldots, Y_n) dt$ or vice-versa for $t = f(t) \int_{\frac{\pi}{2}}^{\pi} \mu \Sigma(t_0, \ldots, t_n) dY_t$, thus assuming the shape and limit to $\kappa < 1$. Considering samples' time lengths, it is designed as $t(\delta + 1) \leq f(Y(t)) \mu \Sigma(Y_0, \ldots, Y_n) dt$ starting from $t_0, \ldots, t_n \leq \sin(\frac{\pi}{2})$ results in the desired data distribution with a conditional shape of Weibull parameterization $\kappa < 1$ for the analysis with a normal distribution, thus rejecting any critical value beyond $\cos(\pi) = \varepsilon'_p$ and under $\sin(\pi) = \varepsilon'_p$, being ε'_p the seasonality forcing behavior of HPALE intervention over SARS-CoV-2 among countries' data sets. Concerning time lengths of samples, designed as $t(y_n + 1) \leq f(Y_n) \mu \Sigma(Y_0, \ldots, Y_n) dt$ starting from $t_0, \ldots, t_n \leq \sin(\pi)$ results in the desired data distribution, thus rejecting any critical value beyond $\cos(\pi) = 0$ and under $\sin(\pi) = 1$. The main reason to ignore S and R local solutions, or to not use SIR models globally, is also the same reason to adopt a region of analysis in the time series data for I' and HPALE. This also remains for the other two important inputs of the system derivatives (environmental factors that influence COVID-19 dissemination and urban spaces) of which for each country the aforementioned confounding scenario of analysis is shown in Figure 4.

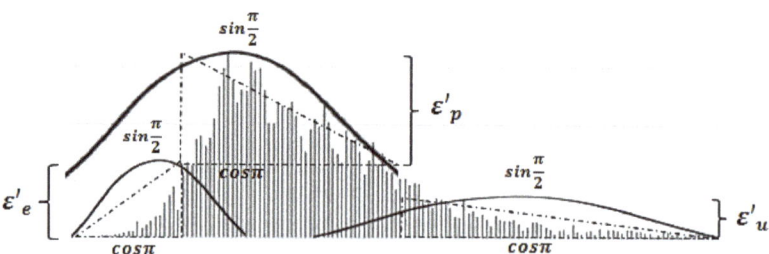

Figure 4. Considering the observation COVID-19 confounding scenario, it is presented the asymptotic strong seasonality force of HPALE (ε'_p) intervention and the narrow and unstable region (outbreak and control) of analysis for environmental and urban driving factors of seasonality ($\varepsilon'_e, \varepsilon'_u$).

Noting that the S and R compartments of the SIR model are needed for predictive analysis of infection dissemination patterns, these compartments might work properly under the third region of time series data: urban spaces ε'_u seasonality. To achieve results with a high uncertainty reduction, it is necessary to conceive S and R as in its most stable region of analysis, which should be influenced in a posterior scenario where ε'_p (HPALE) and ε'_e (environmental seasonality) already took effect. This is mandatory since, as far as policies are assumed in models or estimated with unreal quantitative parameters, uncertainty growth is promoted along with limitations to track real patterns within an urban space feature for S and R as a causation relation. For urban spaces seasonality forcing behavior, it is considered that inside and outside urban spaces promote limitations to HPALE due to the limiting action that it can face within these urban spaces (not all HPALE can reach some urban spaces features properly as it was designed to be). Environmental seasonality can also be present at this phase by influencing urban spaces limitations of taken HPALE actions. Therefore, ε'_e might find a growing point inside and outside urban spaces beyond ε'_p normalization (more explanation of this causation effect will be given in the Results section), which can be the cause of worldwide second waves or posterior waves.

Considering unexpected seasonal forcing ε'_p roughly defined as $\partial(t) = \partial_0 [1 \pm \varepsilon_0 \cos \pi < \varepsilon' < \sin \frac{\pi}{2}]$ [9] in a complex network model, where no periodic oscillation (sinusoidal) are to be found in a discrete form with $f(\varepsilon'_{e,p,u}) = \int_{-\infty}^{+\infty} Y(t), te^{-2\pi i w t} dw$, assume now a rupture of the $\sin(2\pi t)$, leaving the region the pre-assumed linearity $\theta(t) = \theta_0 [1 \pm \varepsilon \sin(2\pi t)]$ for S and R in the overall metrics of time series data T within one sample or among countries and understanding each iteration of the event as unconnected to the previous and future data if considering multiple time-series comparisons (among countries) or even in the same time series if considering long-term analysis. Since the I' is an asymptote to ε'_p, then ε'_u is limited by ε'_p on I', but not necessarily fully stable in terms of ε'_p present total control over environmental seasonality due to urban space features.

It is possible to verify that most of these SIR models are constructed based on ε'_p seasonality behaviors [45–48]. Following this phase, urban spaces and HPALE interventions might present a strong influence on the outcomes due to the unpredictability of S and R patterns to design appropriate contact rates, which still represents a limitation for the SIR model methods [27–34]. Nonetheless, it is still the most desirable region of analysis for data extraction.

3. Results

The overall scenario of spreading and dissemination patterns skewness concerning the environment, HPALE and urban spaces can be visualized in Figure 5, where seasonality forcing behavior assumes the following topological metric space. Considering all the possible seasonality types, $f(\varepsilon'_{e,p,u}) = \int_{-\infty}^{+\infty} Y(t), te^{-2\pi i \omega t} d\omega$, in continuous form of observation, with the need to discretize within causal roots of analysis due to heterogeneity and confounding scenario of analysis, HPALE seasonality can be understood as $f\varepsilon'_p = g \circ f(Y_t, t) = g(f(\varepsilon'_p))$, hence it can also be written as, $f\varepsilon'_p = h \circ (g \circ f(Y_t, t)) = h(g(f(\varepsilon'_p)))$ as a control phase of local epidemics. However, this phase might present high instability (spreading patterns fluctuations) at a worldwide level due to heterogeneity and confounding behavior of $f\varepsilon'_u$ and $f\varepsilon'_e$. Since SIR models require stable points for S and R, there is $f\varepsilon'_u = h \circ g(Y_t, t) = h(g(\varepsilon'_u))$, resulting in a stable asymptotic convergence only if $f\varepsilon'_p = h \circ (g \circ f(Y_t, t)) = h(g(f(\varepsilon'_p)))$. Since the outbreak might incur in unknown spreading and dissemination patterns for $f\varepsilon'_p$, $f\varepsilon'_e$ and $f\varepsilon'_u$, this region needs to be carefully considered. Therefore, environmental seasonality can be found as $f\varepsilon'_e = (h \circ g(Y_t, t)) \circ f = f(h(g(\varepsilon'_e)))$ or it is also possible to assume $f\varepsilon'_e = (\varepsilon \circ g(Y_t, t))$, being ε the undefined patterns of environmentally driven new infections for Earth seasonality or atmospheric factors, which was not fully resolvable in this research.

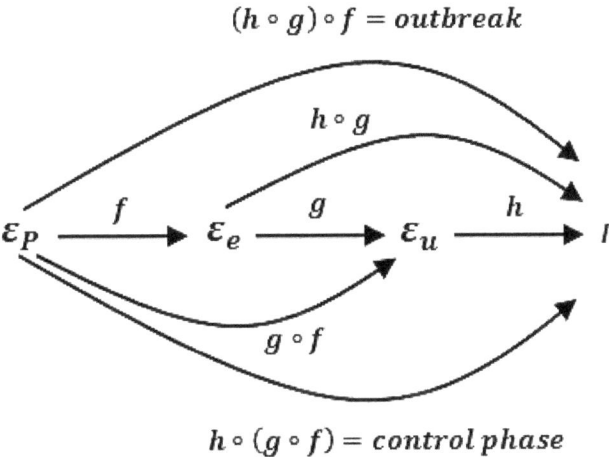

Figure 5. Schematically representation of the COVID-19 skewness properties: during epidemics evolution, HPALE influences the environment and urban spaces seasonality until a limit defined by its type and strategy of application; compartmental models during peak phase are influenced by HPALE, environment and urban spaces and present high uncertainty; at control phase, policies/HPALE finds its limitation by the environment and the type of urban spaces and finally, at outbreak, environmental factors present outcomes caused by the existing HPALE and urban spaces.

4. Discussion

Concerning urban spaces' spreading patterns, due to the vast diversity of public health infrastructure buildings design, outdoor and indoor building designs within natural physical features such as rivers, lakes, snow, culture, and urbanization developments, they exert influence on the region of environmental driven pattern and not only policies. Therefore, it is reasonable to understand that any assumption on S and R during the epidemic phase in its initial curvature is much more closed to uncertainty measures than ever due to several possible confluences. Countries may then diverge greatly in the urban space and environmental scenarios, and thus S and R compartments face calculation limitations during peak curvature, being uncertain how to predict virus spreading and dissemination patterns since policies/HPALE are not even fully developed or had adequate time to take effect while most of the models use policies as the basis of modeling the dissemination patterns. For this reason, the most reliable region of analysis for these compartments and where most of the models are currently situated/functioning remains at the control phase of epidemics. However, fluctuations may still occur worldwide due to the type of HPALE and urban space features. Therefore, urban spaces and environmental seasonality drivers are the main cause of aperiodic and unstable behavior for SARS-COV-2 spreading patterns worldwide. It is likely that environmental driven seasonality results found in many studies are, in truth, HPALE and urban spaces results, representing a need for further detailed research [48].

This was addressed in the research [49], where despite the vast review made, and the observation of confounding scenarios for each sample of analysis and type of climate conditions that influence COVID-19 spreading patterns, authors [49] have understood that there are homogeneity and heterogeneity in the statistical results and conclusions about the environmental influence on the virus dissemination patterns. This was addressed correctly in a systematic review [49] and further developed in this present study through a careful observation that environmental influence can be better understood in outbreaks and urban spaces by using graph analysis. Also, despite the analysis made in [49] considering only policies and climate conditions, further scenario need to be evaluated that is urban spaces, where human lifestyles are directly connected with a risk behaviour over contamination of infectious diseases, such as COVID-19, hence human behaviours also have great impact in the preventive measures efficacy.

Also, concerning evolutionary and game of life algorithms [50,51], predefined parameters and initial inputs are crucial for the machine learning analysis. However, beyond biological features as described in the last paragraph, unpredictable scale of infected individuals are found worldwide without vaccination or social isolation. The article aimed to analyze the problem without these predefined parameters being the basis and sensitivity of analysis. This can be mandatory since many countries are facing problems with vaccination speed and availability as well as social isolation as well as a severe lack of citizen compliance in many countries. Similarly, in Bateman SIZ analysis, this approach can be observed [52] regarding the uncertainty of models without using predefined parameters for sensitivity and robustness. These uncertain parameters lead the calculations to include new panoramic idea of how to combat COVID-19 without proper pre assumptions, thus giving for the real world skewness observed in predictive methods, a degree of uncertainty worldwide. This can be useful due to the lack of correlation between the sensitivity of models and real life complexity.

Concerning uncertainty and sensitivity, the article presents some references that address this point [8,30,33,45]. This research's main objective was to analyse the SIR model equation without pre-defined data input in terms of formulating a specific SIR model to perform predictive analysis with numerical results. For this reason, theoretical observations were made, considering references findings and the global sensitivity model used (policies and ALE, environment and urban spaces). Despite not considering numerical solutions of the problem, due to complexity issues for data collection in real life and chaotic behaviour of some events, the theoretical model proposed can be helpful to understand how pandemics should be investigated for future SIR model equations and also for the basic interpretation of epidemiological behaviour of SARS-COV-2. This is mandatory nowadays since many countries present unfitted vaccination prediction, unfitted social isolation prediction and unfitted SARS-COV-2 variants appearance. The validation of the data subject can be found in Section 2.2. Skewness validation and SIR model limitation. Since the model proposed in this article is not developed to numerical data or results, the theoretical basis of analysis was retrieved from references that already performed these numerical solutions of the problem. Therefore, compiling these findings, it was possible to observe how skewness properties of the issue express how the virus behaves worldwide without predefined spreading and dissemination patterns. This concept of an absence of predefined spreading and dissemination patterns was supported in the results section, aiming to describe how uncertainty and predictive constraints can be found based on the SIR model equation and its variants developed worldwide.

In the research results section, it is possible to observe that the most reliable region to investigate environmental seasonality remains at the outbreak and control phases. In contrast, best urban space seasonality observations remain at the control phase. This feature can be very useful for HPALE approaches since the actual fluctuations/instability in the region mentioned above are mainly caused by these two posterior forcing behaviors. Therefore, new strategies and measurements need to be adopted to keep the economy and prevention with similar power, which was already initially investigated by Sajadi et al. in June 2020 [46].

Note that there is a great difference between environment-driven seasonality caused by urban spaces influenced by HPALE limitations or otherwise caused by Earth and other natural (atmospheric) seasonality forcing behavior at outbreaks. This characteristic should be carefully considered when studying Earth seasonality among countries. The compartmental models are mostly in the control phase region and lose efficacy at outbreaks where no specific parameters are given, and environmental seasonality is not yet discovered in its true patterns. Another point regarding the control phase is that in which instabilities can occur, as far as urban spaces create a scenario where HPALE faces limitations, environmental seasonality finds a suitable place to grow its patterns [47]. Due to uncertainty growth over time and the lack of mean for defined intervals of t over T normal distribution shape for the whole data, Earth season ε gradually loses its effect with the possibility of random delays observed for each country of analysis (sample) being attributed by different patterns in which an outbreak occurs since existing HPALE are found within worldwide cultures, science, and education.

5. Conclusions

This research modeled SARS-COV-2 spreading and dissemination patterns sensitivity by defining and redesigning time series data extraction to SIR model equations. The approach opened a new scenario where seasonality forcing behavior was introduced to understand SARS-COV-2 skewness expressions due to heterogeneity and confounding epidemics scenarios where actual SIR models might find a high degree of uncertainty caused by oscillatory conditions found in the input of variables of the event.

The main research results are the elucidation of three birth and death forced seasonality phases that can explain how COVID-19 spreading and dissemination patterns skewness occurs worldwide. It can be understood in the following order: (1) the environmental variables (Earth seasons and atmospheric conditions); (2) health policies and adult learning education (HPALE) interventions; (3) urban spaces (local indoor and outdoor spaces for transit and social-cultural interactions, public or private, with natural physical features (river, lake, terrain).

These three forced seasonality phases were pointed to as the most effective explanation concerning uncertainty found in the predictive SIR model equations that might diverge in outcomes expected to express the disease's behaviour. Therefore, many distinct models were generated to cover COVID-19 confounded scenarios.

Regarding the forced seasonality model the following pattern was observed: HPALE can be the strongest stable point of seasonality during the epidemic peak phase and compartmental models are influenced mainly by HPALE, while environmental and urban spaces present a low or hidden influence on it. However, HPALE can still be limited at the control phase, depending on urban spaces and existing environmental conditions demanding SIR models to adapt to these new features. Finally, at outbreak and control phases, environmental factors present outcomes caused by the existing HPALE and urban spaces of a given sample, thus producing high uncertainty to predictive SIR model equations.

6. Limitations

ALE was considered in the view of effective practice mainly based on adequate policies adopted by countries. Nonetheless, it should be carefully addressed in the view of infodemics practices, in which ALE can assume one more seasonal force in epidemics, disrupting the peak and control phase and promoting new spreading and dissemination patterns during ε'_p seasonality. It can also enforce posterior waves and confirm spreading pattern fluctuations at outbreaks and urban spaces' stability and. therefore. demanding new modifications in SIR models.

Author Contributions: Conceptualization, C.R.T.; Methodology, C.R.T. and H.L.; Formal analysis, C.R.T.; Investigation, C.R.T.; Resources, H.L. and C.R.T.; Writing—original draft preparation, C.R.T.; Writing—review and editing, D.F., H.L. and C.R.T.; Supervision, H.L.; project administration, H.L. All authors have read and agreed to the published version of the manuscript.

Funding: Sponsored by social responsibility programme by Sharen to support COVID-19 open source publication.

Institutional Review Board Statement: Not applicable.

Informed Consent Statement: Not applicable.

Data Availability Statement: Some of the data used are available at Our World in Data and Outbreak website retrieved from: https://outbreak.info/data and https://ourworldindata.org, respectively.

Acknowledgments: The author feels very grateful for the researchers that made this article possible through conversations and revisions: Ralf Reintjs (Department of Health Sciences—Hochschule für Angewandte Wissenschaften Hamburg—Hamburgo), Ana-Maria CEAUP Universidade do Porto; UNDP) and Manuel Hernández Rosales (Universidad Nacional Autónoma de México).

Conflicts of Interest: The authors declare no conflict of interest.

References

1. Grassly, N.C.; Fraser, C. Seasonal infectious disease epidemiology. *Proc. R. Soc. B Biol. Sci. R. Soc.* **2006**, *273*, 2541–2550. [CrossRef] [PubMed]
2. Su, D.; Chen, Y.; He, K.; Zhang, T.; Tan, M.; Zhang, Y.; Zhang, X. Influence of Socio-Ecological Factors on COVID-19 Risk: A Cross-Sectional Study Based on 178 Countries/Regions Worldwide. *SSRN Electron. J.* **2020**. [CrossRef]
3. Telles, C.R.; Roy, A.; Ajmal, M.R.; Mustafa, S.K.; Ahmad, M.A.; de la Serna, J.M.; Frigo, E.P.; Rosales, M.H. Influence of countries adopted social distancing policy for COVID-19 reduction under the view of the airborne transmission framework (Preprint). *JMIR Public Heal Surveill.* **2020**, *11*. [CrossRef]
4. Block, P.; Hoffman, M.; Raabe, I.J.; Dowd, J.B.; Rahal, C.; Kashyap, R.; Mills, M.C. Social network-based distancing strategies to flatten the COVID-19 curve in a post-lockdown world. *Nat. Hum. Behav.* **2020**, *4*, 588–596. [CrossRef] [PubMed]
5. Ferguson, N.; Laydon, D.; Nedjati Gilani, G.; Imai, N.; Ainslie, K.; Baguelin, M.; Bhatia, S.; Boonyasiri, A.; Cucunuba Perez, Z.U.; Cuo-mo-Dannenburg, G.; et al. *Report 9: Impact of Non-Pharmaceutical Interventions (NPIs) to Reduce COVID19 Mortality and Healthcare Demand*; Imperial College London: London, UK, 2020. [CrossRef]
6. Chu, D.K.; Akl, E.A.; Duda, S.; Solo, K.; Yaacoub, S.; Schünemann, H.J.; El-Harakeh, A.; Bognanni, A.; Lotfi, T.; Loeb, M.; et al. Physical distancing, face masks, and eye protection to prevent person-to-person transmission of SARS-CoV-2 and COVID-19: A systematic review and meta-analysis. *Lancet* **2020**, *395*, 1973–1987. [CrossRef]
7. Lopes, H.; McKay, V. Adult learning and education as a tool to contain pandemics: The COVID-19 experience. *Int. Rev. Educ.* **2020**, *66*, 575–602. [CrossRef]
8. Alberti, T.; Faranda, D. On the uncertainty of real-time predictions of epidemic growths: A COVID-19 case study for China and Italy. *Commun. Nonlinear Sci. Numer. Simul.* **2020**, *90*, 105372. [CrossRef] [PubMed]
9. Roberts, M.; Andreasen, V.; Lloyd, A.; Pellis, L. Nine challenges for deterministic epidemic models. *Epidemics* **2015**, *10*, 49–53. [CrossRef] [PubMed]
10. Dong, E.; Du, H.; Gardner, L. An interactive web-based dashboard to track COVID-19 in real time. *Lancet Infect. Dis.* **2020**, *20*, 533–534. [CrossRef]
11. Altizer, S.; Dobson, A.; Hosseini, P.; Hudson, P.; Pascual, M.; Rohani, P. Seasonality and the dynamics of infectious diseases. *Ecol. Lett.* **2006**, *9*, 467–484. [CrossRef]
12. Bacaër, N.; Dads, E.H.A. On the biological interpretation of a definition for the parameter R_0 in periodic population models. *J. Math. Biol.* **2011**, *65*, 601–621. [CrossRef] [PubMed]
13. Siettos, C.I.; Russo, L. Mathematical modeling of infectious disease dynamics. *Virulence* **2013**, *4*, 295–306. [CrossRef] [PubMed]
14. Mari, L.; Casagrandi, R.; Bertuzzo, E.; Rinaldo, A.; Gatto, M. Floquet theory for seasonal environmental forcing of spatially explicit waterborne epidemics. *Theor. Ecol.* **2014**, *7*, 351–365. [CrossRef]
15. Zhang, Y.; You, C.; Cai, Z.; Sun, J.; Hu, W.; Zhou, X.H. Prediction of the COVID-19 outbreak based on a realistic stochastic model. *medRxiv* **2020**. [CrossRef]
16. Utsunomiya, Y.T.; Utsunomiya, A.T.H.; Torrecilha, R.B.P.; Paulan, S.D.C.; Milanesi, M.; Garcia, J.F. Growth Rate and Acceleration Analysis of the COVID-19 Pandemic Reveals the Effect of Public Health Measures in Real Time. *Front. Med.* **2020**, *7*, 247. [CrossRef] [PubMed]

17. Stübinger, J.; Schneider, L. Epidemiology of Coronavirus COVID-19: Forecasting the Future Incidence in Different Countries. *InHealthcare* **2020**, *8*, 99. [CrossRef]
18. Rock, K.; Brand, S.; Moir, J.; Keeling, M.J. Dynamics of infectious diseases. *Rep. Prog. Phys.* **2014**, *77*, 026602. [CrossRef]
19. Billings, L.; Schwartz, I.B. Exciting chaos with noise: Unexpected dynamics in epidemic outbreaks. *J. Math. Biol.* **2002**, *44*, 31–48. [CrossRef] [PubMed]
20. WHO. World Health Organization: Influenza Laboratory Surveillance Information by the Global Influenza Surveillance and Response System (GISRS). Available online: https://www.who.int/influenza/gisrs_laboratory/flunet/charts/en/ (accessed on 25 June 2020).
21. Li, Y.; Wang, X.; Nair, H. Global Seasonality of Human Seasonal Coronaviruses: A Clue for Postpandemic Circulating Season of Severe Acute Respiratory Syndrome Coronavirus 2? *J. Infect. Dis.* **2020**, *222*, 1090–1097. [CrossRef] [PubMed]
22. Smit, A.J.; Fitchett, J.M.; Engelbrecht, F.A.; Scholes, R.J.; Dzhivhuho, G.; Sweijd, N.A. Winter Is Coming: A Southern Hemisphere Perspective of the Environmental Drivers of SARS-CoV-2 and the Potential Seasonality of COVID-19. *Int. J. Environ. Res. Public Health* **2020**, *17*, 5634. [CrossRef]
23. Engelbrecht, F.A.; Scholes, R.J. Test for Covid-19 seasonality and the risk of second waves. *One Health* **2021**, *12*, 100202. [CrossRef]
24. Kanzawa, M.; Spindler, H.; Anglemyer, A.; Rutherford, G.W. Will Coronavirus Disease 2019 Become Seasonal? *J. Infect. Dis.* **2020**, *222*, 719–721. [CrossRef]
25. Grenfell, B.; Kleczkowski, A.; Gilligan, C.; Bolker, B. Spatial heterogeneity, nonlinear dynamics and chaos in infectious diseases. *Stat. Methods Med. Res.* **1995**, *4*, 160–183. [CrossRef]
26. Buonomo, B.; Chitnis, N.; D'Onofrio, A. Seasonality in epidemic models: A literature review. *Ric. Mat.* **2018**, *67*, 7–25. [CrossRef]
27. Telles, C.R. Reducing SARS-CoV-2 infectious spreading patterns by removing S and R compartments from SIR model equa-tion. *medRxiv* **2020**. [CrossRef]
28. Carlson, C.J.; Gomez, A.C.R.; Bansal, S.; Ryan, S.J. Misconceptions about weather and seasonality must not misguide COVID-19 response. *Nat. Commun.* **2020**, *11*, 1–4. [CrossRef] [PubMed]
29. Manzo, G. Complex social networks are missing in the dominant covid-19 epidemic models. *Sociologica* **2020**, *14*, 31–49. [CrossRef]
30. Merchant, H. CoViD-19 may not end as predicted by the SIR model. *BMJ* **2020**, *369*. Available online: https://www.bmj.com/content/369/bmj.m1567/rr (accessed on 30 April 2020).
31. Adam, D. The simulations driving the world's response to covid-19. How epidemiologists rushed to model the corona-virus pandemic. *Nature* **2020**, *580*, 316–318. [CrossRef]
32. Luo, J. *Predictive Monitoring of COVID-19*; SUTD Data-Driven Innovation Lab.: Singapore, 2020.
33. Best, R.; Boice, J. Where The Latest COVID-19 Models Think We're Headed—And Why They Disagree. Abc News: FiveThirtyEight. Available online: https://projects.fivethirtyeight.com/covid-forecasts/ (accessed on 11 June 2020).
34. Koerth, M.; Bronner, L.; Mithani, J. Why It's So Freaking Hard to Make a Good COVID-19 Model. Abc News: FiveThirtyEight. Available online: https://fivethirtyeight.com/features/why-its-so-freaking-hard-to-make-a-good-covid-19-model/ (accessed on 31 March 2020).
35. Liu, Y.; Ning, Z.; Chen, Y.; Guo, M.; Liu, Y.; Gali, N.K.; Sun, L.; Duan, Y.; Cai, J.; Westerdahl, D.; et al. Aerodynamic analysis of SARS-CoV-2 in two Wuhan hospitals. *Nat. Cell Biol.* **2020**, *582*, 557–560. [CrossRef] [PubMed]
36. Lin, K.; Marr, L.C. Humidity-Dependent Decay of Viruses, but Not Bacteria, in Aerosols and Droplets Follows Disinfection Kinetics. *Environ. Sci. Technol.* **2020**, *54*, 1024–1032. [CrossRef] [PubMed]
37. Morawska, L.; Milton, D.K. It Is Time to Address Airborne Transmission of Coronavirus Disease 2019 (COVID-19). *Clin. Infect. Dis.* **2020**. [CrossRef]
38. Roda, W.C.; Varughese, M.B.; Han, D.; Li, M.Y. Why is it difficult to accurately predict the COVID-19 epidemic? *Infect. Dis. Model.* **2020**, *5*, 271–281. [CrossRef]
39. Duarte, J.; Januário, C.; Martins, N.; Rogovchenko, S.; Rogovchenko, Y. Chaos analysis and explicit series solutions to the seasonally forced SIR epidemic model. *J. Math. Biol.* **2019**, *78*, 2235–2258. [CrossRef] [PubMed]
40. Dietz, K. The Incidence of Infectious Diseases under the Influence of Seasonal Fluctuations. In *Mathematical Models in Medicine*; Springer: Berlin, Germany, 1976; pp. 1–15. [CrossRef]
41. Telles, C.R. False asymptotic instability behavior at iterated functions with Lyapunov stability in nonlinear time series. In *Science and Information Conference*; Springer: Cham, Switzerland, 2020; pp. 673–693. [CrossRef]
42. Jiang, R.; Murthy, D.N. A study of Weibull shape parameter: Properties and significance. *Reliab. Eng. Syst. Saf.* **2011**, *96*, 1619–1626. [CrossRef]
43. Edelsbrunner, H.; Harer, J. Persistent homology-a survey. *Contemp. Math.* **2008**, *453*, 257–282. Available online: https://www.maths.ed.ac.uk/~{}v1ranick/papers/edelhare.pdf (accessed on 14 July 2020).
44. Cohen-Steiner, D.; Edelsbrunner, H.; Harer, J. Stability of persistence diagrams. *Discret. Comput. Geom.* **2007**, *37*, 103–120. Available online: http://math.uchicago.edu/~{}shmuel/AAT-readings/Data%20Analysis%20/Edelsbrunner,%20Harer,%20Stability.pdf (accessed on 25 August 2020). [CrossRef]
45. CDC. Centers for Disease Control and Prevention. CASES, DATA & SURVEILLANCE: Forecasts of Total Deaths July 2, 2020. Available online: https://www.cdc.gov/coronavirus/2019-ncov/covid-data/forecasting-us.html (accessed on 8 July 2020).

46. Sajadi, M.M.; Habibzadeh, P.; Vintzileos, A.; Shokouhi, S.; Miralles-Wilhelm, F.; Amoroso, A. Temperature, Humidity, and Latitude Analysis to Estimate Potential Spread and Seasonality of Coronavirus Disease 2019 (COVID-19). *JAMA Netw. Open* **2020**, *3*, e2011834. [CrossRef] [PubMed]
47. Lin, J.; Huang, W.; Wen, M.; Li, D.; Ma, S.; Hua, J.; Hu, H.; Yin, S.; Qian, Y.; Chen, P.; et al. Containing the spread of coronavirus disease 2019 (COVID-19): Meteorological factors and control strategies. *Sci. Total. Environ.* **2020**, *744*, 140935. [CrossRef] [PubMed]
48. Rucinski, S.L.; Binnicker, M.J.; Thomas, A.S.; Patel, R. Seasonality of Coronavirus 229E, HKU1, NL63, and OC43 from 2014 to 2020. In *Mayo Clinic Proceedings*; Elsevier BV: Amsterdam, The Netherlands, 2020; Volume 95, pp. 1701–1703.
49. Mecenas, P.; Bastos, R.T.D.R.M.; Vallinoto, A.C.R.; Normando, D. Effects of temperature and humidity on the spread of COVID-19: A systematic review. *PLoS ONE* **2020**, *15*, e0238339. [CrossRef]
50. Ghosh, S.; Bhattacharya, S. A data-driven understanding of COVID-19 dynamics using sequential genetic algo-rithm based probabilistic cellular automata. *Appl. Soft Comput.* **2020**, *96*, 106692. [CrossRef]
51. Machado, J.A.T. An Evolutionary Perspective of Virus Propagation. *Mathematics* **2020**, *8*, 779. [CrossRef]
52. Braun, P.; Haffner, S.; Woodcock, B.G. COVID-19 pandemic predictions using the modified Bateman SIZ model and observational data for Heidelberg, Germany: Effect of vaccination with a SARS-CoV-2 vaccine, coronavirus testing and application of the Corona-Warn-App. *Int. J. Clin. Pharmacol. Ther.* **2020**, *58*, 417–425. [CrossRef] [PubMed]

Article

The Double Phospho/Dephosphorylation Cycle as a Benchmark to Validate an Effective Taylor Series Method to Integrate Ordinary Differential Equations

Alessandro Borri [1,*], Francesco Carravetta [1] and Pasquale Palumbo [2]

[1] Institute for Systems Analysis and Computer Science "A. Ruberti", National Research Council of Italy (CNR-IASI), 00185 Rome, Italy; francesco.carravetta@iasi.cnr.it
[2] Department of Biotechnology and Biosciences, University of Milano-Bicocca, 20126 Milan, Italy; pasquale.palumbo@unimib.it
* Correspondence: alessandro.borri@iasi.cnr.it

Citation: Borri, A.; Carravetta, F.; Palumbo, P. The Double Phospho/Dephosphorylation Cycle as a Benchmark to Validate an Effective Taylor Series Method to Integrate Ordinary Differential Equations. *Symmetry* **2021**, *13*, 1684. https://doi.org/10.3390/sym13091684

Academic Editor: Lorentz Jäntschi

Received: 30 July 2021
Accepted: 8 September 2021
Published: 13 September 2021

Publisher's Note: MDPI stays neutral with regard to jurisdictional claims in published maps and institutional affiliations.

Copyright: © 2021 by the authors. Licensee MDPI, Basel, Switzerland. This article is an open access article distributed under the terms and conditions of the Creative Commons Attribution (CC BY) license (https://creativecommons.org/licenses/by/4.0/).

Abstract: The double phosphorylation/dephosphorylation cycle consists of a symmetric network of biochemical reactions of paramount importance in many intracellular mechanisms. From a network perspective, they consist of four enzymatic reactions interconnected in a specular way. The general approach to model enzymatic reactions in a deterministic fashion is by means of stiff Ordinary Differential Equations (ODEs) that are usually hard to integrate according to biologically meaningful parameter settings. Indeed, the quest for model simplification started more than one century ago with the seminal works by Michaelis and Menten, and their Quasi Steady-State Approximation methods are still matter of investigation nowadays. This work proposes an effective algorithm based on Taylor series methods that manages to overcome the problems arising in the integration of stiff ODEs, without settling for model approximations. The double phosphorylation/dephosphorylation cycle is exploited as a benchmark to validate the methodology from a numerical viewpoint.

Keywords: systems biology; enzymatic reactions; quadratization; ODE integration

1. Introduction

Protein phosphorylation is a ubiquitous regulatory mechanism for cells, generally working to activate or inactivate molecules [1]. From a biochemical viewpoint, to phosphorylate a molecule consists in the binding of a phosphoryl group PO_4^- [2]. The general model to deal with phosphorylation is to exploit the framework of enzymatic reactions, where the substrate M is supposed to be modified (phosphorylated, actually) into the product M_p by means of the preliminary formation of a complex C provided by the binding of an enzyme (called kinase, K) in charge to catalyze the phosphorylation, see the scheme in (1).

$$M + K \underset{k_{-1}}{\overset{k_1}{\rightleftarrows}} C_K \overset{k_2}{\longrightarrow} M_p + K \qquad (1)$$

Phosphorylations usually introduce conformational changes that activate/inactivate the enzymatic activity of a protein, or simply prime degradation processes, like the ones involved in the yeast cell cycle (see, e.g., in [3,4] dealing with the degradation of Sic1 and Whi5, respectively) or those involving tyrosine kinase pathways, regulating diverse cellular processes, and whose dysregulation is one of the leading causes of cancer progression [5]. In many important cases, multi-site phosphorylations are required to ensure the correct timing of activation [6,7]. Besides, according to specific conditions and biological frameworks, phosphoryl groups can be removed, making phosphorylation a reversible activation/inactivation mechanism. Moreover, in this case the dephosphorylation may be treated as a generic enzymatic reaction, with the enzymes that catalyze the reaction called phosphatases P:

$$M_p + P \underset{h_{-1}}{\overset{h_1}{\rightleftarrows}} C_P \overset{h_2}{\rightarrow} M + P \qquad (2)$$

Combinations of multiple phosphorylations/dephosphorylations have been selected by nature as devices, providing specific useful biological functions. Within this framework, the Double Phosphorylation/Dephosphorylation Cycle (DPDC) is a symmetric network motif consisting of a double reversible phosphorylation step required to activate a given substrate M:

$$M + K \underset{k_{-11}}{\overset{k_{11}}{\rightleftarrows}} C_1 \overset{k_{12}}{\rightarrow} M_p + K \qquad M_p + K \underset{k_{-21}}{\overset{k_{21}}{\rightleftarrows}} C_2 \overset{k_{22}}{\rightarrow} M_{pp} + K$$

$$M_{pp} + P \underset{k_{-31}}{\overset{k_{31}}{\rightleftarrows}} C_3 \overset{k_{32}}{\rightarrow} M_p + P \qquad M_p + P \underset{k_{-41}}{\overset{k_{41}}{\rightleftarrows}} C_4 \overset{k_{42}}{\rightarrow} M + P \qquad (3)$$

where the final product is the doubly phosphorylated M_{pp}. Ordinary Differential Equation (ODE) models of DPDC use to combine in a symmetric fashion the four enzymatic reactions [8], providing a bistability regime where the non-phosphorylated or the double-phosphorylated versions of the substrate is predominant [9]. A primary motivation in investigating the computation of the system solutions is that, in a recent paper [10], it has been proven that symmetry breaking in the dynamical solutions of such a network may lead to modify its emergent properties, including concentration robustness of different stationary solutions.

In this context, numerical integration of enzymatic reactions in ODE form has been a matter of investigation for more than a century [11,12], since the seminal works of Michaelis and Menten [13] providing an approximation (the celebrated Quasi Steady-State Approximation (QSSA) [14]) to cope with the double time scale arising whenever biologically meaningful parameters are assigned. Multi-timescale phenomena are very common in biology, see, e.g., the very recent cardiac cell model in [15].

Indeed, in enzymatic networks, the binding/unbinding reactions use to occur at a faster rate, thus leading to stiff ODEs, thus characterized by numerical instability when ordinary numerical schemes are employed for their integration. In particular, in the case of stiff equations, ad hoc integration methods, like the one illustrated in [16] for linear multistep methods, can be employed to approximate the solution efficiently. Like any approximations, there are limitations that may render unfeasible its concrete applicability. Indeed, in [17] we showed how the numerical integration of a basic enzymatic reaction model may create serious problems even to well established procedures like the ones implemented by Matlab in ode45 and ode15s functions. Besides, things become even more crucial in the DPDC, as it has been shown in [18] how the QSSA may miss the bistability property.

In order to deal with stiff ODEs, Taylor Series Methods (TSMs) can be used. These methods build up a polynomial approximation (up to some fixed order k) of the ODE solution around the initial point through Taylor series expansion, which amounts to the recursive calculation of the partial derivatives of the ODE function at the initial point, up to the order k. With respect to standard Runge–Kutta methods, TSMs do not exhibit worse performance in terms of numerical stability, and guarantee a better accuracy in the solution calculation for higher degrees of the approximating polynomial. We refer the interested readers to the works in [19–23] for an in-depth description of TSMs and their numerical properties.

The main issue with TSMs is that, as the approximation order k increases, the calculation of all the required derivatives becomes too cumbersome, and some preliminary transformations need to be applied to the original problem in order to simplify the derivatives calculation. To this end, in the present work, we employ some recent technical results published in [24,25], according to which ODE systems can be embedded into higher-order quadratic equations which, in spite of their dimensionality, allow for more efficient differentiation, which in turn can be exploited for numerical integration via TSM. These results have been already exploited in [17] for the class of simple enzymatic reactions (two differential equations), and are here extended to the more challenging DPDC case (seven differential equations). Simulations are promising as the numerical results show a higher qualitative accuracy of the method with respect to standard off-the-shelf solvers for an appropriate choice of the reaction parameters which make the equations stiff.

The paper is organized as follows. Section 2 reviews the methods involving quadratization and approximate integration of a class of differential equations. Section 3 adapts the framework to the context of Double Phosphorylation/Dephosphorylation Cycle. Section 4 provides some numerical simulations of the DPDC system. Finally, Section 5 offers concluding remarks and ideas for further developments.

2. Exact Quadratization and Approximate Integration of $\sigma\pi$ Differential Equations

This section recollects and adapts some results mainly developed in [24,25] for more general classes of dynamical systems than those developed in this work. Except where differently specified, we adopt the following vector and indices convention: *a vector v is always a column vector, and v' is its transpose*. With respect to indices, given a vector v, the scalar v_j denotes its j-th entry; instead, in case of double subscripts, like in $Z_{i,j}$, when dealing with a vector we mean a nested notation, where $Z_{i,j}$ is the j-th scalar/vector component of vector Z_i, and vector Z_i is the j-th vector component of vector Z; on the other hand, when dealing with a matrix, $Z_{i,j}$ refers to the usual scalar entry in row i and column j.

2.1. Exact Quadratization of $\sigma\pi$-ODEs into Driver-Type Differential Equations

We consider a first-order ODE system

$$\dot{x} = f(x), \qquad x \in \mathbb{R}^n, \tag{4}$$

where the function f is a *formal polynomial* of x, i.e., a polynomial writing where the exponents are allowed to be *any real number*. More formally, the components of f are in the form

$$f_i(x) = \sum_{l=1}^{\nu_i} \bar{v}_{i,l} X_{i,l}(x); \quad X_{i,l}(x) = \prod_{r=1}^{n} x_r^{p_{i,r}^l}, \tag{5}$$

where $p_{i,r}^l$ are real exponents, the ν_i quantities $X_{i,l}$ in (5) are named *monomials* and $\bar{v}_{i,l}$ are real coefficients. We refer to this kind of functions as $\sigma\pi$-*functions*, and to the associated system of differential equations as $\sigma\pi$-*ODE*.

For $\sigma\pi$-ODEs, the following theorem holds, by virtue of which the system (4) and (5) can be densely embedded in a higher-dimensional quadratic system.

Theorem 1 (*Exact Quadratization Theorem, adapted from the work in [24]*). *Any $\sigma\pi$-ODE in the form (4) and (5), with domain $V' \subset \mathbb{R}^n$, is quadratizable on the non empty, open and dense subset $U' = V' \setminus S$ (with S denoting the set of all coordinate hyperplanes in $\mathbb{R}^n$), and the quadratization is given by the following homogeneous Riccati equation in the indeterminates x_i and $Z_{i,l}$:*

$$\dot{x}_i = (\bar{v}_i' Z_i) x_i \tag{6}$$

$$\dot{Z}_{i,l} = \sum_{r=1}^{n} \pi_{i,r}^l (\bar{v}_r' Z_r) Z_{i,l} \tag{7}$$

where $\pi_{i,r}^l = p_{i,r}^l - \delta_{i,r}$, and $\delta_{i,r}$ being the Kronecker symbol: $\delta_{i,r} = 1$ (resp. $\delta_{i,r} = 0$) if $i = r$ (resp. $i \ne r$).

It clearly appears that the specific Riccati equation constituting the quadratization (6) and (7) includes the original state variables, so it is possible to define an augmented state such that the original ODE system (4) is now embedded in the following extended system evolving in $\mathbb{R}^m$, with $m \geq n$:

$$\dot{x}_i = \sum_{i=1}^{m} v_{i,j} x_i x_j = (v'_i x) x_i, \qquad (8)$$

where, with a little abuse, we keep the notation of x for a vector now living in $\mathbb{R}^m$, with the first n components provided by the n components of vector x in (4), and the other $m-n$ components provided by vector Z in (7). The coefficients $v_{i,j}$ are suitable linear functions of the coefficients $\bar{v}_{i,l}$ in (5). Equation (8) is called 'Driver-type' ODE form, while the matrix $V \in \mathbb{R}^{m \times m}$ collecting the entries $v_{i,j}$, $i,j = 1, \ldots, m$, is called 'frame'.

The interested reader is referred to the works in [24,25] for further notation (including multi-indices), technical details and full proofs.

2.2. Approximate Taylor Series Integration Method

With a slight abuse of notation, let $t \mapsto x(t)$ be the solution of (4) with initial condition $x(t_0)$, and consider the Taylor expansion of a generic scalar component $x_i(\cdot)$ with respect to the initial time instant t_0:

$$x_i(t) = \sum_{k=0}^{\infty} c_k(i) \frac{(t-t_0)^k}{k!}, \qquad c_k(i) = x_i^{(k)}(t_0). \qquad (9)$$

Numerical integration techniques based on the application of the truncated series in (9) to compute a solution of (4) are called Taylor Series Methods (TSMs). Unfortunately, such a series expansion cannot be straightforwardly applied to compute the solution for general systems as it requires the explicit computation of the derivatives of the solution at the initial point, which usually reveals to be too cumbersome. Below is reported a Theorem that allows to compute the coefficients of the Taylor expansion for a system in the 'Driver-type' ODE form (8).

Theorem 2 (from [25]). *Consider a 'Driver-type' ODE in the form (8). Then, the coefficients $c_k(i)$, $k > 0$, in the Taylor expansion (9) are given by*

$$c_k(i) = \sum_{i_1, \ldots, i_k \in S} v^{k+1}_{i, i_1, \ldots, i_k} \cdot x_i(t_0) x_{i_1}(t_0) \cdots x_{i_k}(t_0), \qquad (10)$$

where $i_s \in S = \{1, \ldots, n\}$, for $s = 0, 1, \ldots, k$ (we set $i_0 = i$), and the (constant) coefficients $v^{k+1}_{i,i_1,\ldots,i_k}$, are given by the following recursive equation

$$v^{k+1}_{i,i_1,\ldots,i_k} = v^k_{i,i_1,\ldots,i_{k-1}} \left(\sum_{j=0}^{k-1} v_{i_j, i_k} \right), \quad v^1_i = 1, \qquad (11)$$

where the coefficients $v_{i,j}$, $i, j = 1, \ldots, m$, are defined in (8).

Approximate numerical integration based on Theorem 2 can be readily performed by truncating the series (9) at a finite order $\bar{k}$, provided that the integration formula is reinitialized frequently enough to prevent numerical instability. This readily leads to the following iteration. Let $\hat{x}_i(j\Delta)$, $i = 1, \ldots, n$, for $j = 0, 1, \ldots$, be the approximate value of x_i

at time $j\Delta$ provided by the algorithm, where $t_0 = 0$ and a fixed sampling time $\Delta > 0$ are assumed for simplicity. Then, the approximate solution at all times $t \geq 0$ is given by

$$\begin{cases} \hat{x}_i(t) = \sum_{k=0}^{\bar{k}} c_{k,j}(i) \dfrac{(t-j\Delta)^k}{k!}, & t \in [j\Delta, (j+1)\Delta), \\ c_{k,j}(i) = \sum_{i_1,\ldots,i_k \in S} v_{i,i_1,\ldots,i_k}^{k+1} \cdot \hat{x}_i(j\Delta) \hat{x}_{i_1}(j\Delta) \cdots \hat{x}_{i_k}(j\Delta). \end{cases} \quad (12)$$

Note that, for $\bar{k} = 1$, the proposed integration scheme coincides with the forward Euler method.

3. The Double Phosphorylation–Dephosphorylation Cycle

According to the mass action law, the system of equations governing the dynamics of substrates and complexes in the DPDC scheme in (3) is

$$\begin{aligned}
\frac{dM}{dt} &= -k_{11}MK + k_{-11}C_1 + k_{42}C_4 \\
\frac{dM_p}{dt} &= -k_{21}M_pK + k_{-21}C_2 + k_{-41}C_4 - k_{41}M_pP + k_{32}C_3 + k_{12}C_1 \\
\frac{dM_{pp}}{dt} &= -k_{31}M_{pp}P + k_{-31}C_3 + k_{22}C_2 \\
\frac{dC_1}{dt} &= k_{11}MK - (k_{-11} + k_{12})C_1 \\
\frac{dC_2}{dt} &= k_{21}M_pK - (k_{-21} + k_{22})C_2 \\
\frac{dC_3}{dt} &= k_{31}M_{pp}P - (k_{-31} + k_{32})C_3 \\
\frac{dC_4}{dt} &= k_{41}M_pP - (k_{-41} + k_{42})C_4
\end{aligned} \quad (13)$$

where the following conservation laws hold:

$$M + M_p + M_{pp} + C_1 + C_2 + C_3 + C_4 = M_T, \quad (14)$$

$$K + C_1 + C_2 = K_T, \quad P + C_3 + C_4 = P_T. \quad (15)$$

Enzymes K and P can be replaced in (13) according to (15), so that the overall dynamics is not redundant and the system reduces to the following 7-dimensional ODE with the constraint (14):

$$\begin{aligned}
\frac{dM}{dt} &= -k_{11}M(K_T - C_1 - C_2) + k_{-11}C_1 + k_{42}C_4 \\
\frac{dM_p}{dt} &= -k_{21}M_p(K_T - C_1 - C_2) + k_{-21}C_2 + k_{-41}C_4 \\
&\quad - k_{41}M_p(P_T - C_3 - C_4) + k_{32}C_3 + k_{12}C_1 \\
\frac{dM_{pp}}{dt} &= -k_{31}M_{pp}(P_T - C_3 - C_4) + k_{-31}C_3 + k_{22}C_2 \\
\frac{dC_1}{dt} &= k_{11}M(K_T - C_1 - C_2) - (k_{-11} + k_{12})C_1 \\
\frac{dC_2}{dt} &= k_{21}M_p(K_T - C_1 - C_2) - (k_{-21} + k_{22})C_2 \\
\frac{dC_3}{dt} &= k_{31}M_{pp}(P_T - C_3 - C_4) - (k_{-31} + k_{32})C_3 \\
\frac{dC_4}{dt} &= k_{41}M_p(P_T - C_3 - C_4) - (k_{-41} + k_{42})C_4
\end{aligned} \quad (16)$$

Summing up all left hand sides of the system (16) yields zero, which, on the other hand, is entailed by (14), accounting that M_T (the total mass) is constant over time. The algebraic equation (14) defines a six-dimensional manifold in $\mathbb{R}^7$, invariant with respect to system (16), which means that, if one takes the initial value on this manifold, the evolution of system (16) remains on the same manifold at all times.

Remark 1. *Indeed, it can be readily proved the stronger result that the DPDC system is positive [26], as each non-positive term on the right-hand side of any equation in (16) multiplies the variable differentiated on the left-hand side of the same equation; in short, removal terms are linear in the variable of interest. This prevents the crossing of the coordinate hyperplane* **S** *already defined in Theorem 1, on which the aforementioned terms are zeroed; this will make the DPDC ODEs quadratizable (see the remainder of this section) on the same domain* $V' \subseteq \mathbb{R}^7_{\geq 0}$ *of the original variables, where the latter symbol denotes the non-negative orthant in* $\mathbb{R}^7$.

By setting
$$(x_1, x_2, x_3, x_4, x_5, x_6, x_7) = (M, M_p, M_{pp}, C_1, C_2, C_3, C_4),$$

it is readily seen that Equation (16) defines a $\sigma\pi$-ODE (see Section 2.1), with state dimension $n = 7$, where the exponents in (5) are integer. As a consequence, Theorem 1 can be applied so that the system is exactly quadratized, with the quadratization that can be expressed in the 'Driver-type' ODE form (8), with augmented state dimension $m = 24$, by extending the system with the following adjoint variables, whose dynamics is defined in (7):

$$x_8 = x_1^{-1}x_4; \quad x_9 = x_1^{-1}x_7; \quad x_{10} = x_2^{-1}x_5; \quad x_{11} = x_2^{-1}x_7; \quad x_{12} = x_2^{-1}x_6;$$
$$x_{13} = x_2^{-1}x_4; \quad x_{14} = x_3^{-1}x_6; \quad x_{15} = x_3^{-1}x_5, \quad x_{16} = x_4^{-1}x_1 \quad x_{17} = x_4^{-1}x_1x_5$$
$$x_{18} = x_5^{-1}x_2; \quad x_{19} = x_5^{-1}x_2x_4 \quad x_{20} = x_6^{-1}x_3; \quad x_{21} = x_6^{-1}x_3x_7$$
$$x_{22} = x_7^{-1}x_2; \quad x_{23} = x_7^{-1}x_2x_6 \quad x_{24} = 1. \tag{17}$$

Therefore, system (16) rewrites as follows:

$$\dot{x}_1 = (k_{11}x_4 + k_{11}x_5 + k_{-11}x_8 + k_{42}x_9 - k_{11}K_T x_{24})x_1$$
$$\dot{x}_2 = (k_{21}x_4 + k_{21}x_5 + k_{41}x_6 + k_{41}x_7 + k_{-21}x_{10} + k_{-41}x_{11} + k_{32}x_{12} + k_{12}x_{13}$$
$$\quad - (k_{21}K_T + k_{41}P_T)x_{24})x_2$$
$$\dot{x}_3 = (k_{31}x_6 + k_{31}x_7 + k_{-31}x_{14} + k_{22}x_{15} - k_{31}P_T x_{24})x_3$$
$$\dot{x}_4 = (-k_{11}x_1 + k_{11}K_T x_{16} - k_{11}x_{17} - (k_{-11} + k_{12})x_{24})x_4$$
$$\dot{x}_5 = (-k_{21}x_2 + k_{21}K_T x_{18} - k_{21}x_{19} - (k_{-21} + k_{22})x_{24})x_5$$
$$\dot{x}_6 = (-k_{31}x_3 + k_{31}P_T x_{20} - k_{31}x_{21} - (k_{-31} + k_{32})x_{24})x_6$$
$$\dot{x}_7 = (-k_{41}x_2 + k_{41}P_T x_{22} - k_{41}x_{23} - (k_{-41} + k_{42})x_{24})x_7$$

while we can use the chain rule to compute the dynamics of the adjoint variables, resulting, after some substitutions, into the following additional quadratic differential equations:

$$\dot{x}_8 = (-k_{11}x_1 - k_{11}x_4 - k_{11}x_5 - k_{-11}x_8 - k_{42}x_9 + k_{11}K_T x_{16} - k_{11}x_{17}$$
$$+ (k_{11}K_T - k_{-11} - k_{12})x_{24})x_8$$

$$\dot{x}_9 = (-k_{41}x_2 - k_{11}x_4 - k_{11}x_5 - k_{-11}x_8 - k_{42}x_9 + k_{41}P_T x_{22} - k_{41}x_{23}$$
$$+ (k_{11}K_T - k_{-41} - k_{42})x_{24})x_9$$

$$\dot{x}_{10} = (-k_{21}x_2 - k_{21}x_4 - k_{21}x_5 - k_{41}x_6 - k_{41}x_7 - k_{-21}x_{10} - k_{-41}x_{11} - k_{32}x_{12} - k_{12}x_{13}$$
$$+ k_{21}K_T x_{18} - k_{21}x_{19} + (k_{41}P_T + k_{21}K_T - k_{-21} - k_{22})x_{24})x_{10}$$

$$\dot{x}_{11} = (-k_{41}x_2 - k_{21}x_4 - k_{21}x_5 - k_{41}x_6 - k_{41}x_7 - k_{-21}x_{10} - k_{-41}x_{11} - k_{32}x_{12} - k_{12}x_{13}$$
$$+ k_{41}P_T x_{22} - k_{41}x_{23} + (k_{41}P_T + k_{21}K_T - k_{-41} - k_{42})x_{24})x_{11}$$

$$\dot{x}_{12} = (-k_{31}x_3 - k_{21}x_4 - k_{21}x_5 - k_{41}x_6 - k_{41}x_7 - k_{-21}x_{10} - k_{-41}x_{11} - k_{32}x_{12} - k_{12}x_{13}$$
$$+ k_{31}P_T x_{20} - k_{31}x_{21} + (k_{21}K_T + k_{41}P_T - k_{-31} - k_{32})x_{24})x_{12}$$

$$\dot{x}_{13} = (-k_{11}x_1 - k_{21}x_4 - k_{21}x_5 - k_{41}x_6 - k_{41}x_7 - k_{-21}x_{10} - k_{-41}x_{11} - k_{32}x_{12} - k_{12}x_{13}$$
$$+ k_{11}K_T x_{16} - k_{11}x_{17} + (k_{21}K_T + k_{41}P_T - k_{-11} - k_{12})x_{24})x_{13}$$

$$\dot{x}_{14} = (-k_{31}x_3 - k_{31}x_6 - k_{31}x_7 - k_{-31}x_{14} - k_{22}x_{15} + k_{31}P_T x_{20} - k_{31}x_{21}$$
$$+ (k_{31}P_T - k_{-31} - k_{32})x_{24})x_{14}$$

$$\dot{x}_{15} = (-k_{21}x_2 - k_{31}x_6 - k_{31}x_7 - k_{-31}x_{14} - k_{22}x_{15} + k_{21}K_T x_{18} - k_{21}x_{19}$$
$$+ (k_{31}P_T - k_{-21} - k_{22})x_{24})x_{15}$$

$$\dot{x}_{16} = (k_{11}x_1 + k_{11}x_4 + k_{11}x_5 + k_{-11}x_8 + k_{42}x_9 - k_{11}K_T x_{16} + k_{11}x_{17}$$
$$+ (k_{-11} + k_{12} - k_{11}K_T)x_{24})x_{16}$$

$$\dot{x}_{17} = (k_{11}x_1 - k_{21}x_2 + k_{11}x_4 + k_{11}x_5 + k_{-11}x_8 + k_{42}x_9 - k_{11}K_T x_{16} + k_{11}x_{17}$$
$$+ k_{21}K_T x_{18} - k_{21}x_{19} + (k_{-11} + k_{12} - k_{-21} - k_{22} - k_{11}K_T)x_{24})x_{17}$$

$$\dot{x}_{18} = (k_{21}x_2 + k_{21}x_4 + k_{21}x_5 + k_{41}x_6 + k_{41}x_7 + k_{-21}x_{10} + k_{-41}x_{11} + k_{32}x_{12} + k_{12}x_{13}$$
$$- k_{21}K_T x_{18} + k_{21}x_{19} + (k_{-21} + k_{22} - k_{21}K_T - k_{41}P_T)x_{24})x_{18}$$

$$\dot{x}_{19} = (-k_{11}x_1 + k_{21}x_2 + k_{21}x_4 + k_{21}x_5 + k_{41}x_6 + k_{41}x_7 + k_{-21}x_{10} + k_{-41}x_{11} + k_{32}x_{12}$$
$$+ k_{12}x_{13} + k_{11}K_T x_{16} - k_{11}x_{17} - k_{21}K_T x_{18} + k_{21}x_{19}$$
$$+ (k_{-21} + k_{22} - k_{-11} - k_{12} - k_{21}K_T - k_{41}P_T)x_{24})x_{19}$$

$$\dot{x}_{20} = (k_{31}x_3 + k_{31}x_6 + k_{31}x_7 + k_{-31}x_{14} + k_{22}x_{15} - k_{31}P_T x_{20} + k_{31}x_{21}$$
$$+ (k_{-31} + k_{32} - k_{31}P_T)x_{24})x_{20}$$

$$\dot{x}_{21} = (-k_{41}x_2 + k_{31}x_3 + k_{31}x_6 + k_{31}x_7 + k_{-31}x_{14} + k_{22}x_{15} - k_{31}P_T x_{20} + k_{31}x_{21}$$
$$+ k_{41}P_T x_{22} - k_{41}x_{23} + (k_{-31} + k_{32} - k_{-41} - k_{42} - k_{31}P_T)x_{24})x_{21}$$

$$\dot{x}_{22} = (k_{41}x_2 + k_{21}x_4 + k_{21}x_5 + k_{41}x_6 + k_{41}x_7 + k_{-21}x_{10} + k_{-41}x_{11} + k_{32}x_{12} + k_{12}x_{13}$$
$$- k_{41}P_T x_{22} + k_{41}x_{23} + (k_{-41} + k_{42} - k_{21}K_T - k_{41}P_T)x_{24})x_{22}$$

$$\dot{x}_{23} = (k_{41}x_2 - k_{31}x_3 + k_{21}x_4 + k_{21}x_5 + k_{41}x_6 + k_{41}x_7 + k_{-21}x_{10} + k_{-41}x_{11} + k_{32}x_{12}$$
$$+ k_{12}x_{13} + k_{31}P_T x_{20} - k_{31}x_{21} - k_{41}P_T x_{22} + k_{41}x_{23}$$
$$+ (k_{-41} + k_{42} - k_{-31} - k_{32} - k_{21}K_T - k_{41}P_T)x_{24})x_{23}$$

Finally, we obviously have
$$\dot{x}_{24} = 0$$
initialized to $x_{24}(0) = 1$, implying $x_{24}(t) = 1$ for all $t \geq 0$, which allows to turn linear into quadratic terms in the right-hand side of any $\sigma\pi$-ODEs.

4. Simulation Results

Numerical simulations of the system (16), quadratized in the form (8) as developed in the previous section, have been performed in the Matlab® suite. Inspired by the parameter choices in [14,17], we consider the following parameters:

$$k_{j1} = 4 \cdot 10^8 \text{M}^{-1}\text{s}^{-1}, \quad k_{-j1} = 25 \text{ s}^{-1}, \quad k_{j2} = 15 \text{ s}^{-1}, \quad j = 1,2,3,4, \quad (18)$$

with total amounts (14) and (15) equal to

$$M_T = \frac{k_{-11} + k_{12}}{k_{11}}, \quad K_T = P_T = 10^{-3} \cdot M_T. \quad (19)$$

We start from the initial conditions (at time $t_0 = 0$)

$$x_1(0) = 0.70 M_T, \quad x_4(0) = 0.25 M_T, \quad x_i(0) = 0.01 M_T \quad \text{for } i = 2,3,5,6,7, \quad (20)$$

where the initial states of the adjoint variables $x_j(0)$, for $j = 8, \ldots, 24$, are uniquely determined from (17) and (20). The sampling interval has been set to $\Delta = 0.015$ s and the overall simulation time is 1 s. For the given choice of parameters and initial conditions, simulations performed according to the standard ODE45 Matlab® solver, based on the Dormand–Prince Runge–Kutta method [27] with default settings, are aborted by Matlab for not being able to meet integration tolerances.

Figures 1–7 show the numerical solution obtained for variables $x_1, \ldots, x_7$ by means of the ODE15s Matlab® variable-order solver for stiff differential equations [28] compared with the method of quadratization and truncated TSM integration proposed in this paper. It is clearly observed that the substrate trajectories provided by ode15s oscillate, while our approach provides a smoother behavior. Regards to the complexes, ode15s trajectories become negative, which is qualitatively inconsistent by virtue of Remark 1, as we know that the system (16) is positive. The same occurs with C_1 for the TSM method with truncation order $\bar{k} = 1$ (Euler), see Figure 4, and with C_2 for the TSM method with $\bar{k} = 2$, see Figure 5. Instead, the TSM method applied to the quadratized system with truncation order $\bar{k} = 3$ exhibits non-negative solutions for all the variables.

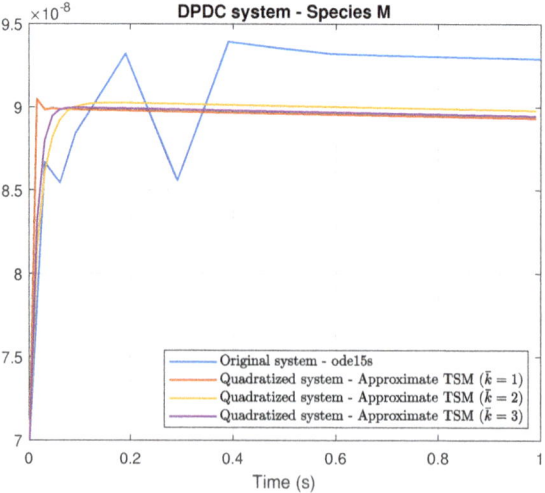

Figure 1. Trajectory of species M via quadratization of Equation (16) and approximate TSM method compared with the Matlab® ODE15s solution. The maximum truncation order has been set to $\bar{k} = 3$.

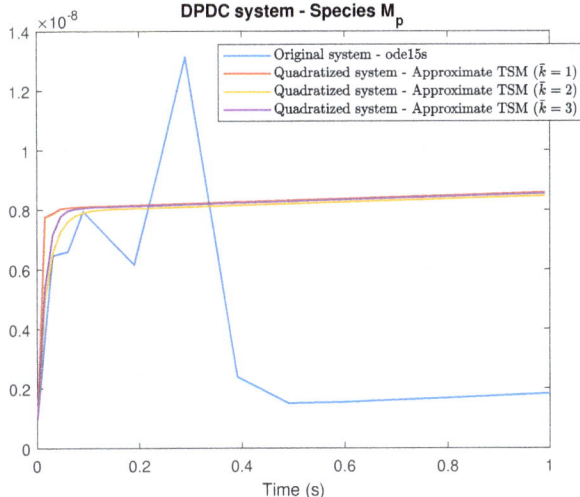

Figure 2. Trajectory of species M_p via quadratization of Equation (16) and approximate TSM method compared with the Matlab® ODE15s solution. The maximum truncation order has been set to $\bar{k} = 3$.

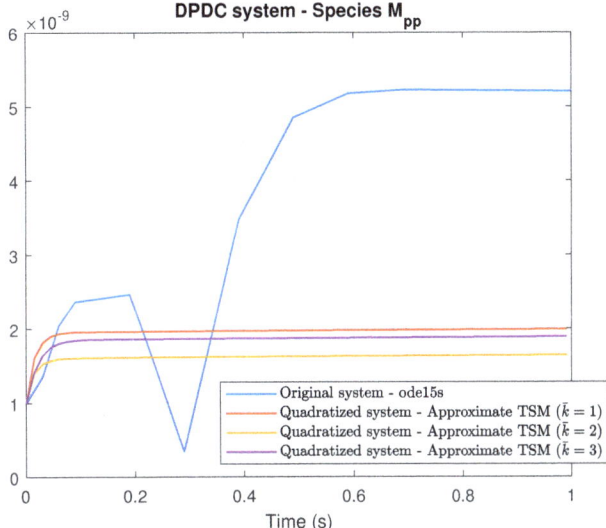

Figure 3. Trajectory of species M_{pp} via quadratization of Equation (16) and approximate TSM method compared with the Matlab® ODE15s solution. The maximum truncation order has been set to $\bar{k} = 3$.

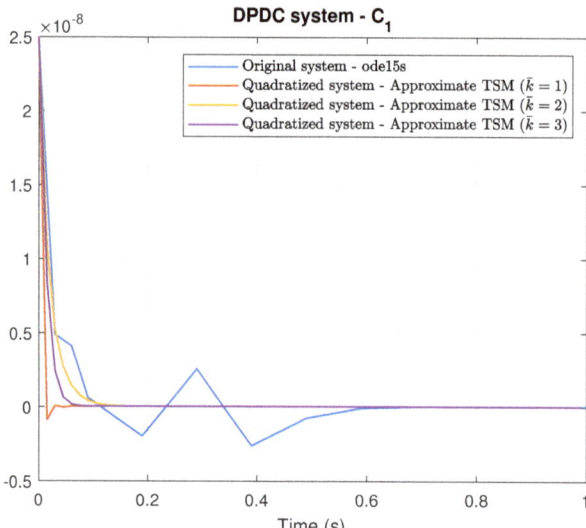

Figure 4. Trajectory of species C_1 via quadratization of Equation (16) and approximate TSM method compared with the Matlab® ODE15s solution. The maximum truncation order has been set to $\bar{k} = 3$.

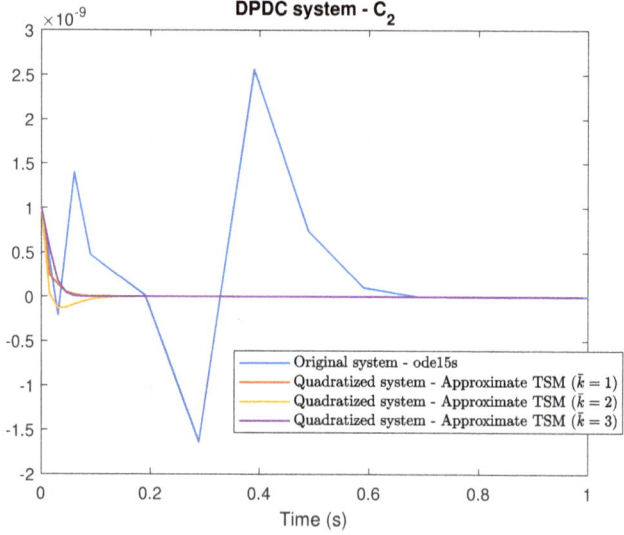

Figure 5. Trajectory of species C_2 via quadratization of Equation (16) and approximate TSM method compared with the Matlab® ODE15s solution. The maximum truncation order has been set to $\bar{k} = 3$.

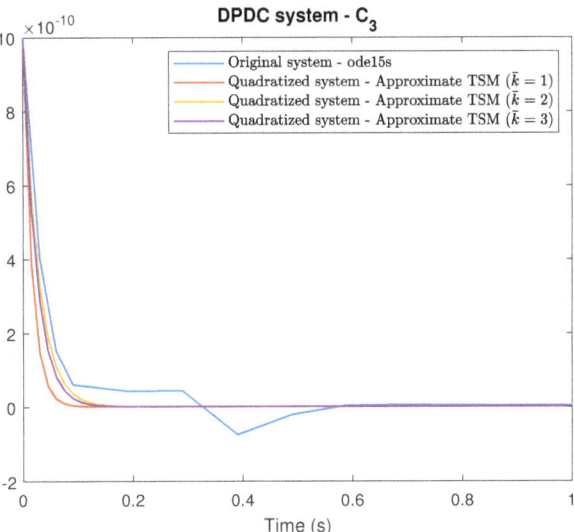

Figure 6. Trajectory of species C_3 via quadratization of Equation (16) and approximate TSM method compared with the Matlab® ODE15s solution. The maximum truncation order has been set to $\bar{k} = 3$.

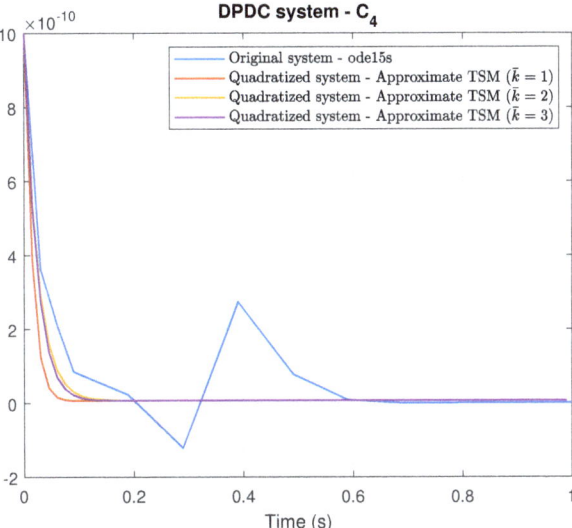

Figure 7. Trajectory of species C_4 via quadratization of Equation (16) and approximate TSM method compared with the Matlab® ODE15s solution. The maximum truncation order has been set to $\bar{k} = 3$.

Figure 8 shows the trajectories of complexes C_1 (top panel) and C_2 (bottom panel), obtained with sampling time $\Delta = 0.015$ s, compared with the same trajectories computed with a doubled sample interval $\Delta = 0.03$ s, and the same truncation order $\bar{k} = 3$ of the TSM method. It is apparent that the choice of a sufficiently small sampling interval, jointly with a sufficiently high truncation order, is crucial for the numerical stability of the algorithm. In particular, both C_1 and C_2 violate again the non-negativity constraint in the case $\Delta = 0.03$ s, as already observed for $\Delta = 0.015$ s and low truncation orders in Figures 4 and 5, with a notable oscillating behavior and an evident initial overshoot of species C_2. Note that the pattern of damped oscillations in Figures 4, 6, and 8 is not surprising in numerical simulation and identification in biochemical and biological contexts, for instance, a similar behavior may indeed result from the optimization of the power of the error in multiple linear regression under the assumption of generalized Gauss-Laplace distribution [29].

In summary, the method proposed in this paper seems to be able to return meaningful solutions in the numerical simulation of particular biological conditions when standard solvers may fail.

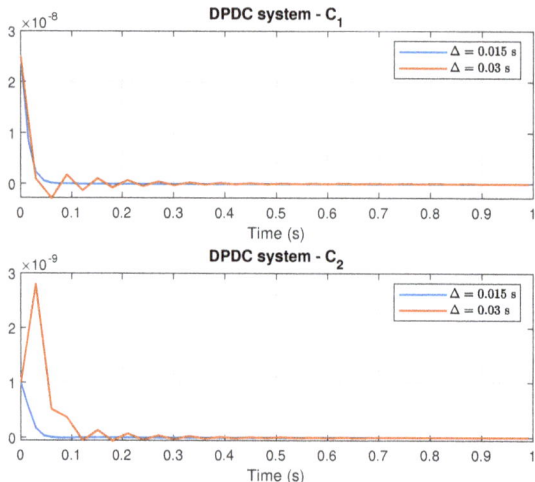

Figure 8. Trajectories of species C_1 (top panel) and C_2 (bottom panel) via quadratization of Equation (16) and approximate TSM method, with truncation order set to $\bar{k} = 3$, for two different values of the sampling interval Δ.

5. Discussion

In this work, we proposed a novel approach to the problem of integrating the solution of biological systems expressed by stiff differential equations (for example, those exhibiting an apparent double time-scale separation). To overcome typical numerical issues related to the numerical integration of this kind of system by means of existing solvers, we here rely on recent work exploiting the so-called *quadratization* of ODEs, which allows embedding the original dynamics in a higher-dimensional space where the system is quadratic and differentiation formulae of any order are computable by means of simple recursions. Such derivatives are exploited within a truncated Taylor Series expansion to build an approximate simple integration scheme, which is proved to work accurately in the in silico simulation of the Double Phoshphorylation/Dephoshphorylation Cycle (DPDC), which is an important regulatory mechanism present in cells. Ongoing and future work is focusing on the construction of a numerical scheme that might overcome the *curse of dimensionality* due to the computation of coefficients of the high-order terms in the Taylor series expansion for the augmented quadratized dynamics.

Author Contributions: Conceptualization, investigation, writing—review and editing, resources, A.B., F.C. and P.P.; writing—original draft preparation, formal analysis, A.B. and P.P.; methodology, F.C.; software, A.B.; supervision, P.P. All authors have read and agreed to the published version of the manuscript.

Funding: This research received no external funding.

Institutional Review Board Statement: Not applicable.

Informed Consent Statement: Not applicable.

Data Availability Statement: Not applicable.

Conflicts of Interest: The authors declare no conflict of interest.

References

1. Cooper, G. *The Cell, a Molecular Approach*; Sinauer Associates: Sunderland, MA, USA, 2000.
2. Chang, R. *Physical Chemistry for the Chemical and Biological Sciences*; University Science Books: New York, NY, USA, 2000.
3. Nash, P.; Tang, X.; Orlicky, S.; Chen, Q.; Gertler, F.B.; Mendenhall, M.D.; Sicheri, F.; Pawson, T.; Tyers, M. Multisite phosphorylation of a CDK inhibitor sets a threshold for the onset of DNA replication. *Nature* **2001**, *414*, 514–521. [CrossRef]
4. Palumbo, P.; Vanoni, M.; Cusimano, V.; Busti, S.; Marano, F.; Manes, C.; Alberghina, L. Whi5 phosphorylation embedded in the G1/S network dynamically controls critical cell size and cell fate. *Nat. Commun.* **2016**, *7*, 11372. [CrossRef]
5. Ionescu, A.E.; Mentel, M.; Munteanu, C.V.A.; Sima, L.E.; Martin, E.C.; Necula-Petrareanu, G.; Szedlacsek, S.E. Analysis of EYA3 Phosphorylation by Src Kinase Identifies Residues Involved in Cell Proliferation. *Int. J. Mol. Sci.* **2019**, *20*, 6307. [CrossRef]
6. Salazar, C; Höfer, T. Multisite protein phosphorylation—From molecular mechanisms to kinetic models. *FEBS J.* **2009**, *276*, 3177–3198. [CrossRef]
7. Salazar, C.; Brümmer, A.; Alberghina, L.; Höfer, T. Timing control in regulatory networks by multisite protein modifications. *Trends Cell Biol.* **2010**, *20*, 634–641. [CrossRef] [PubMed]
8. Ortega, F.; Garcés, J.L.; Mas, F.; Kholodenko, B.N.; Cascante, M. Bistability from double phosphorylation in signal transduction. *FEBS J.* **2006**, *273*, 3915–3926. [CrossRef]
9. Bersani, A.M.; Borri, A.; Carravetta, F.; Mavelli, G.; Palumbo, P. On a stochastic approach to model the double phosphorylation/dephosphorylation cycle. *Math. Mech. Complex Syst.* **2020**, *8*, 261–285. [CrossRef]
10. Ramesh, V.; Krishnan, J. Symmetry breaking meets multisite modification. *Elife* **2021**, *10*, e65358. [CrossRef] [PubMed]
11. Bersani, A.M.; Bersani, E.; Dell'Acqua, G.; Pedersen, M.G. New trends and perspectives in nonlinear intracellular dynamics: One century from Michaelis–Menten paper. *Contin. Mech. Termodyn.* **2015**, *27*, 659–684. [CrossRef]
12. Cornish-Bowden, A. One hundred years of Michaelis-Menten kinetics. *Perspect. Sci.* **2015**, *4*, 3–9. [CrossRef]
13. Michaelis, L.; Menten, M. Kinetics of invertase action. *Biochem. Z.* **1913**, *49*, 333–369.
14. Segel, L. On the validity of the steady state assumption of enzyme kinetics. *Bull. Math. Biol.* **1988**, *50*, 579–593. [CrossRef]
15. Barrio, R.; Martínez, M.A.; Pérez, L.; Pueyo, E. Bifurcations and Slow-Fast Analysis in a Cardiac Cell Model for Investigation of Early Afterdepolarizations. *Mathematics* **2020**, *8*, 880. [CrossRef]
16. Mohd Ijam, H.; Ibrahim, Z.B. Diagonally Implicit Block Backward Differentiation Formula with Optimal Stability Properties for Stiff Ordinary Differential Equations. *Symmetry* **2019**, *11*, 1342. [CrossRef]
17. Borri, A.; Carravetta, F.; Palumbo, P. Time series expansion to find solutions of nonlinear systems: An application to enzymatic reactions. In Proceedings of the 2020 European Control Conference (ECC), St. Petersburg, Russia, 12–15 May 2020; pp. 749–754.
18. Bersani, A.M.; Dell'Acqua, G.; Tomassetti, G. On stationary states in the double phosphorylation-dephosphorylation cycle. In Proceedings of the AIP Conference Proceedings, College Park, MD, USA, 28–31 July 2011; American Institute of Physics: College Park, MD, USA, 2011; Volume 1389.
19. Barton, D.; Willers, I.M.; Zahar, R.V.M. Taylor Series Methods for Ordinary Differential Equations—An Evaluation. In *Mathematical Software*; Rice, J.R., Ed.; Academic Press: New York, NY, USA, 1972; pp. 369–389.
20. Corliss, F.; Chang, Y.F. Solving ordinary differential equations using Taylor Series. *ACM Trans. Math. Softw.* **1994**, *8*, 209–233. [CrossRef]
21. Corliss, G.F.; Kirlinger, G. On implicit Taylor series method for stiff ODEs. In Proceedings of the SCAN 91: International Symposium on Computer Arithmetic and Scientific Computing, Oldenburg, Germany, 1–4 October 1991.
22. Barton, D. On Taylor series and stiff equations. *ACM Trans. Math. Softw.* **1980**, *6*, 280–294. [CrossRef]
23. Barrio, R. Sensitivity analysis of ODEs/DAEs using the Taylor series method. *SIAM J. Sci. Comput.* **2006**, *6*, 1929–1947. [CrossRef]
24. Carravetta, F. Global Exact Quadratization of Continuous-Time Nonlinear Control Systems. *SIAM J. Control Optim.* **2015**, *53*, 235–261. [CrossRef]
25. Carravetta, F. On the Solution Calculation of Nonlinear Ordinary Differential Equations via Exact Quadratization. *J. Differ. Equ.* **2020**, *269*, 11328–11365. [CrossRef]
26. Farina, L.; Rinaldi, S. *Positive Linear Systems: Theory and Applications*; John Wiley & Sons: Hoboken, NJ, USA, 2000.
27. Dormand, J.R.; Prince, P.J. A family of embedded Runge-Kutta formulae. *J. Comput. Appl. Math.* **1980**, *6*, 19–26. [CrossRef]
28. Shampine, L.F.; Reichelt, M.W. The MATLAB ODE Suite. *SIAM J. Sci. Comput.* **1997**, *18*, 1–22. [CrossRef]
29. Jäntschi, L.; Bálint, D.; Bolboacă, S.D. Multiple Linear Regressions by Maximizing the Likelihood under Assumption of Generalized Gauss-Laplace Distribution of the Error. *Comput. Math. Methods Med.* **2016**, *2016*, 8578156. [CrossRef] [PubMed]

Nonlinear Analysis of the C-Peptide Variable Related to Type 1-Diabetes Mellitus

Diana Gamboa [†], Carlos E. Vázquez-López [†], Rosana Gutierrez [†] and Paul J. Campos *

Posgrado en Ciencias de la Ingeniería, Tecnológico Nacional de México/I.T. Tijuana,
Blvd. Alberto Limón Padilla s/n, Mesa de Otay, Tijuana 22454, Mexico; diana.gamboa@tectijuana.edu.mx (D.G.);
carlos.vazquez@tectijuana.edu.mx (C.E.V.-L.); rosana.gutierrez@tectijuana.edu.mx (R.G.)
* Correspondence: paul.campos@tectijuana.edu.mx
† These authors contributed equally to this work.

Abstract: Type-1 diabetes mellitus is a chronic disease that is constantly monitored worldwide by researchers who are strongly determined to establish mathematical and experimental strategies that lead to a breakthrough toward an immunological treatment or a mathematical model that would update the *UVA/Padova* algorithm. In this work, we aim at a nonlinear mathematical analysis related to a fifth-order ordinary differential equations model that describes the asymmetric relation between C-peptides, pancreatic cells, and the immunological response. The latter is based on both the Localization of Compact Invariant Set (LCIS) appliance and Lyapunov's stability theory to discuss the viability of implementing a possible treatment that stabilizes a specific set of cell populations. Our main result is to establish conditions for the existence of a localizing compact invariant domain that contains all the dynamics of diabetes mellitus. These conditions become essential for the localizing domain and stabilize the cell populations within desired levels, i.e., a state where a patient with diabetes could consider a healthy stage. Moreover, these domains demonstrate the cell populations' asymmetric behavior since both the dynamics and the localizing domain of each cell population are defined into the positive orthant. Furthermore, closed-loop analysis is discussed by proposing two regulatory inputs opening the possibility of nonlinear control. Additionally, numerical simulations show that all trajectories converge inside the positive domain once given an initial condition. Finally, there is a discussion about the biological implications derived from the analytical results.

Keywords: type-1 diabetes mellitus; global analysis; β cells; regulatory system

1. Introduction

Diabetes is a severe long-term condition ranking as one of the first ten causes of death in adults; according to global estimations, around four million people worldwide died in 2017 from this disease. Since the year 2000, the International Diabetes Federation (IDF) has reported the regional, national, and global occurrence of diabetes, indicating that the worldwide population with diabetes may increase from 463 to 700 million in the next two decades [1]. Diabetes mellitus (DM) is a long-term condition resulting from the inability of the pancreas to produce enough insulin (type 1 diabetes, T1D) or from the incapability of the pancreas to process the insulin that the body produces (type 2 diabetes, T2D) [2]. Thus, an increase in blood glucose leads to a non-symmetric behavior in the body over time.

Some complications related with high glucose blood include hypertension, kidney failure, lower limb amputation, nerve damage, stroke, and blindness [3]. Studies investigating the trends in diabetes prevalence have been conducted since 2000 [4], including the diabetes prevalence forecast for 2030 [5], 2035 [6], 2040 [4], 2045 [7], and 2060 [8], based on the national and regional data, where the results were overwhelming. Recently, several mathematical models have been published describing the process of glucose-insulin into the regulatory system, and the so-called Bergman's Minimal Model is the most highlighted [9,10].

Recently, research applying mathematical algorithms to describe diabetes behavior and its outcomes is gaining attention [11,12]. Some of these algorithms are focused on both modeling insulin receptor or the body's insulin-glucose dynamics, diabetes cost-effectiveness, and glucose tolerance testing [13]. However, models used to describe the glucose's dynamic, insulin transport, and accuracy of glucose measurements, are challenging to assess in vivo.

Therefore, studying these non-symmetrical metabolic processes by mathematical approaches can help to understand these dynamics [14]. On the other hand, models based on Ordinary Differential Equations (ODEs) have been widely applied to describe real-life systems in physics, engineering, economics, and biomedicine. In particular, ODE models become a promising alternative to describe within-host dynamics, infectious or viral diseases, and even complex biomedical behaviors of the human body [15].

Currently, clinical studies and in silico data have demonstrated that C-peptide administration reduces renal disfunction, and combinations with insulin helps avoid microvascular issues. Hence, patients with C-peptide persistence are less prone to long-term complications than those without it [16]. The study of β cell population dynamics in long-time intervals becomes a key to understand the prevalence of C-peptide secretion in T1D [17].

Some studies demonstrate that C-peptide levels drop exponentially in the first seven years after diagnosis and could continue dropping throughout the years at a slower rate. Nonetheless, log-transformed C-peptide levels permit establishing differences, both pathophysiological and immunological, between glucose and pancreatic cells, giving essential knowledge to understand β cell survival. Therefore, broader attention should be paid to the progression of C-peptide loss in a longer duration of T1D, even with special focusing on the patient's age [18].

The Localization of Compact Invariant Set (LCIS) method is a reliable method commonly used in nonlinear ODE models with mathematical-biological implications, see [19,20]. This method helps to provide sufficient or necessary conditions that lead to a broad understanding of the long-term behavior of a dynamical model, even to establish requirements for possible treatments or reduce some undesired cell populations proliferation [19–21].

In the particular case of T1D, the LCIS method permits analysis of the β cell behavior in the presence of glucose [22] or with the immunological response [23]. The ODE's mathematical model was initially presented in [24] describing the dynamics between cytotoxic T cells, the β cell population, and the peptide level as a result of their interactions.

Our objective is to provide the conditions for a localizing domain, understand the global behavior of T1D's cell dynamics, and give viable cells stabilization conditions. Hence, our hypothesis aims at how maximum population cells behave in time, based on upper bounds computations.

The organized sections of this work are presented as follows. The first section describes a general scheme for the fifth-order nonlinear mathematical model where upper bounds for all variable states hold when the positive orthant domain is satisfied by the nonlinear model's positiveness. Some of the proposed localizing functions have no mathematical restriction on how they are defined or in the quantity limitations associated with a particular upper bound; however, the proposed function must not be the first integral, see [25,26]. Discussion resulting from applying local asymptotic stability by Lyapunov indirect method given the equilibrium point led to analyzing the stability criteria by closed-loop Lyapunov in which the input controls are analyzed. The second section shows some simulations that validate our previous mathematical results, and the last section presents the main conclusions of this research.

2. Preliminaries of Localization of Compact Invarian Sets Method

This section presents the necessary background to define the localizing domain that contains all the compact invariant sets of a nonlinear system represented by first-order ODEs. The general method of LCIS was proposed by Krishchenko and Starkov in [25,26] to determine the domain where all compact invariant sets of a differential equations system are located. This method is helpful to understand the long-time behavior of first-order ODE systems. This is considered an autonomous nonlinear system represented by:

$$\dot{x} = f(x), \tag{1}$$

where $x \in \mathbb{R}^n$, $f(x) = (f_1(x), \ldots, f_n(x))^T$ is a differentiable vector field. Let $h(x) \in C^\infty(\mathbb{R}^n)$ be a function such that h is not the first integral of the system (1). The function h is exploited in the solution of the localization problem of compact invariant sets and is called a localizing function. By $h|_U$ we denote the restriction of h on a set $U \subset \mathbb{R}^n$. $S(h)$ denotes the set $\{x \in \mathbb{R}^n \mid L_f h(x) = 0\}$, where $L_f h(x)$ is the Lie derivative in the vector field of $f(x)$. In order to determine the localizing set, it is necessary to define $h_{\inf}(U) := \inf\{h(x) \mid x \in U \cap S(h)\}$ and $h_{\sup}(U) := \sup\{h(x) \mid x \in U \cap S(h)\}$.

Therefore, for any $h(x) \in C^\infty(\mathbb{R}^n)$, all compact invariant sets of the system (1) located in U are contained in the set $K(U; h)$ defined as $\{x \in U \mid h_{\inf}(U) \leq h(x) \leq h_{\sup}(U)\}$, as well as, if $U \cap S(h) = \emptyset$, then there are no compact invariant sets located in U. Moreover, the Iterative Theorem can be applied to refine the localizing domain $K(h)$; this theorem is defined as follows [19–21,23]:

Theorem 1 (Iterative Theorem). *Let $h_m(x)$ be a sequence of C^∞ differentiable functions where $m = 0, 1, 2 \ldots$ Sets*

$$K_0 = K(h_0), \quad K_m = K_{m-1} \cap K_{m-1,m}, \quad m > 0,$$

with

$$K_{m-1,m} = \{x \mid h_{m,\inf} \leq h_m(x) \leq h_{m,\sup}\},$$
$$h_{m,\sup} = \sup_{S(h_m) \cap K_{m-1}} h_m(x),$$
$$h_{m,\inf} = \inf_{S(h_m) \cap K_{m-1}} h_m(x),$$

contain any compact invariant set of the system (1) *and*

$$K_0 \supseteq K_1 \supseteq \cdots \supseteq K_m \supseteq \ldots .$$

In summary, the general methodology to compute the LCIS of a nonlinear dynamical system described by first-order ODEs is as follows [27]:

1. A localizing function denoted as $h(x)$ must be proposed. $h(x)$ is a function that can represent a specific shape, such as a plane, hyperplane, cylinder, or sphere; in terms of the system's parameters and state variables.
2. Computing the Lie derivative of $h(x)$, defined as $L_f h$.
3. Calculate the infimum ($h_{\inf}$) and supremum ($h_{\sup}$) by computing $L_f h = 0$. From the latter, two cases can result:
   (a) $S(h)$ is compact, the Lagrange multiplier method or the polytope approximation may be applied;
   (b) the sign of $S(h)$ cannot be defined, a mapping must be performed to determine the sign of $h(x)|_{S(h)}$.
4. If it is not possible to define the sign of $S(h)$, the localization problem is not yet solved; therefore, a new localizing function must be proposed, and the process is restarted.
5. In the case of a satisfactory localizing domain, Theorem (1) could be applied to refine the localizing domain $K(h)$.

This methodology can be applied until a satisfactory solution is achieved.

3. Mathematical Model of Type-1 Diabetes Mellitus Related to C-Peptide

The mathematical model of Type-1 Diabetes Mellitus (T1DM) related to C-peptides was proposed by Mahay and Edelstein-Keshet, in 2007 [24], involving the immune response as the main factor that leads to a decrease in the β cell population in the body. It consists of five first-order ODEs describing the dynamical interaction between activated T cells

$(A(t))$, memory T cells $(M(t))$, effector T cells $(E(t))$, the C-peptide level $(p(t))$, and the β cell $(B(t))$ populations at time t. Therefore, the T1DM model related to the C-peptide is given as follows:

$$\frac{dA}{dt} = (\sigma + \alpha M)\frac{p^n}{k_1^n + p^n} - (\beta + \delta_A)A - \epsilon A^2, \tag{2}$$

$$\frac{dM}{dt} = \beta 2^{m_1} \frac{ak_2^m}{k_2^m + p^m} A - \frac{p^n}{k_1^n + p^n}\alpha M - \delta_M M, \tag{3}$$

$$\frac{dE}{dt} = \beta 2^{m_2}(1 - \frac{ak_2^m}{k_2^m + p^m})A - \delta_E E, \tag{4}$$

$$\frac{dp}{dt} = REB - \delta_p p, \tag{5}$$

$$\frac{dB}{dt} = -\kappa EB; \tag{6}$$

where Equations (2)–(4) correspond to the population level of activated, memory, and effector T cells; Equation (5) represents the peptide level and the remaining population of β cells by Equation (6). The parametrization and units of the model's equations are presented in Table 1.

Furthermore, to fulfill the positivity of the system (2)–(6), we evaluated each state variable at the border, i.e., $A = E = M = p = B = 0$. Evaluating Equation (6), we obtained that $\frac{dB}{dt} = 0$; Equation (5) gives that $\frac{dp}{dt} = REB$; Equation (4) gives that $\frac{dE}{dt} = \beta 2^{m_2}(1 - \frac{ak_2^m}{k_2^m + p^m})A$; whereas Equation (3) gives that $\frac{dM}{dt} = \beta 2^{m_1}\frac{ak_2^m}{k_2^m + p^m}$; finally, from Equation (2), we obtained that $\frac{dA}{dt} = (\sigma + \alpha M)\frac{p^n}{k_1^n + p^n}$; allowing us to conclude that, given nonnegative initial conditions, the system's dynamics are located in the non-negative orthant, i.e., they are located into the following domain:

$$\mathbf{R}_{+,0}^5 = \{A(t) \geq 0, M(t) \geq 0, E(t) \geq 0, p(t) \geq 0, B(t) \geq 0\}. \tag{7}$$

Table 1. Parameter description and units of T1DM related to C-peptides [24].

Parameter	Description	Value	Units
σ	Influence of naive T cells in the thymus	1–10	day^{-1}
α	Production rate of A per M	1–5	day^{-1}
β	Cell division rate	1–6	day^{-1}
δ_A	Mortality index, activated T cells	≈ 0.01	day^{-1}
δ_M	Mortality index, memory T cells	≈ 0.01	day^{-1}
δ_E	Mortality index, effector T cells	0.3	day^{-1}
δ_p	Peptide turnover rate	0–1	day^{-1}
ϵ	Competition parameter T cell	$1-5 \times 10^{-2}$	cells^{-1}day^{-1}
k_1	Peptide level for 1/2 of maximum activation	2	peptide units
k_2	Peptide level for 1/2 of the maximum memory cells	1	peptide units
m	Hill's coefficient, production of memory cells	2	—
n	Hill's coefficient for activation of T cells	3	—
2^{m_1}	Maximum number of memory cells produced by T cells proliferating	8	—
2^{m_2}	Number of effector cells produced by proliferating T cells	60	—
a	Maximum fraction of memory cells produced	<1	—
R	Peptide accumulation rate	10^{-5}	cells^{-1}day^{-1}
κ	Death of β cells by effector T cells	0.14×10^{-6}	cells^{-1}day^{-1}

4. Localization of Compact Invariant Sets-Peptide Variable Analysis

Localizing the compact invariant domain of a dynamical system depends on the system's complexity. Sometimes, it is possible to define the domain of attraction that contains all compact invariant sets by employing only one localizing function, resulting in symmetric shapes, such as ellipsoids, paraboloids, and cylinders [26]. These shapes are frequently obtained in three-dimensional systems.

However, biological systems are often modeled by more than three dimensions, making it impossible to define symmetric shapes by only one function and, at the same time, ensure all the dynamics of a system are bounded. Biological systems usually need more than one localizing function to describe the system's variables' maximum and minimum bounds [19]; therefore, the compact localizing domain is characterized by an asymmetric domain. Hence, the compact localizing domain and ultimate bounds for a T1DM related to C-peptide are achieved by exploring three localizing functions. First, we compute the maximum population of β cells with the following localizing function

$$h_1 = B - \ln B, \tag{8}$$

whose Lie derivative is given by $L_f h_1 = -\kappa EB - \left[\frac{-\kappa EB}{B}\right]$, defining the set $S(h_1) = \{L_f h_1 = 0\}$ as

$$S(h_1) = \{-\kappa EB + \kappa E = 0\}, \tag{9}$$

and, after solving for B, the set $S(h_1)$ is defined as

$$S(h_1) = \{B = 1\}; \tag{10}$$

further, expressing the constraint $h_1|_{S(h_1)} = B - \ln B$, and substituting $S(h_1)$, the maximum value of the function h_1 is as follows

$$K(h_1) = \left\{h_1 \leq h_1|_{S(h_1)} := 1\right\}. \tag{11}$$

Therefore, the location set of the β cell population is

$$K_B = \{B(t) \leq B_{max} := 1\}. \tag{12}$$

Now, to determine the upper bound for the C-peptide level, the following localizing function is proposed

$$h_2 = p - \ln p + B, \tag{13}$$

where its Lie derivative is defined by $L_f h_2 = REB - \delta_p p - \left[\frac{REB - \delta_p p}{p}\right] - \kappa EB$. The set is determined and analyzed by $S(h_2) = \{L_f h_2 = 0\}$, giving

$$S(h_2) = \left\{REB - \delta_p p - \frac{REB}{p} + \delta_p - \kappa EB = 0\right\}, \tag{14}$$

and it can be defined in terms of the interest variable of the localizing function as $S(h_2) = \left\{p = 1 - \frac{REB}{\delta_p p} - (\kappa - R)\frac{EB}{\delta_p}\right\}$, where, after some algebraic manipulation gives

$$S(h_2) - \{p - 1\}, \tag{15}$$

as long as the following condition can be satisfied

$$R \leq \kappa. \tag{16}$$

It is important that the constraint can be expressed by $h_2|_{S(h_2)} = p - \ln p + B$. Substituting (15) into $h_2|_{S(h_2)}$ and applying Theorem (1), the set $K(h_2)$ is defined as

$$K(h_2) \cap K(h_1) = \left\{ h_2 \leq h_2|_{S(h_2)} := 1 + B_{\max} \right\}; \tag{17}$$

allowing us to compute the set $K(h_2)$, which defines the maximum C-peptide level as

$$K_p = \{ p(t) \leq p_{\max} := 2 \}. \tag{18}$$

Finally, an upper bound for T cells is computed through the following localizing function

$$h_3 = A + M + E, \tag{19}$$

whose Lie derivative is given by

$$L_f h_3 = \{(\sigma + \alpha M - \alpha M) \frac{p^n}{k_1^n + p^n} + (\beta 2^{m_2} - \beta - \delta_A - \epsilon A) A \tag{20}$$

$$+ (2^{m_1} - 2^{m_2}) \frac{\beta a k_2^m}{k_2^m + p^m} A - \delta_M M - \delta_E E \}; \tag{21}$$

hence, after some algebraic rearrangement and mathematical analysis, the set $S(h_3) = \{L_f h_3 = 0\}$ is defined as

$$S(h_3) = \left\{ A = \frac{\sigma p^n}{\delta_A(k_1^n + p^n)} + \frac{(\beta 2^{m_2} - \beta)}{\delta_A} A - \frac{\epsilon}{\delta_A} A^2 - \frac{\delta_M}{\delta_A} M - \frac{\delta_E}{\delta_A} E \right\}, \tag{22}$$

as long as the next condition holds

$$2^{m_1} \leq 2^{m_2}. \tag{23}$$

Now, substituting the previous results and some algebraic manipulation, the constrain $h_3|_{S(h_3)} = A + M + E$ is defined by

$$h_3|_{S(h_3)} = \frac{\sigma}{\delta_A} + \frac{(\beta 2^{m_2} - \beta)^2}{4 \epsilon \delta_A},$$

as long as the following conditions must be satisfied at all time

$$\delta_A \leq \delta_M, \tag{24}$$
$$\delta_A \leq \delta_E; \tag{25}$$

then, it is possible to define the set $K(h_3)$ as

$$K(h_3) = \left\{ h_3 \leq h_3|_{S(h_3)} := \frac{\sigma}{\delta_A} + \frac{(\beta 2^{m_2} - \beta)^2}{4 \epsilon \delta_A} \right\}.$$

Summarizing the results shown through this section, the following statement is formulated regarding the ultimate bounds for the T1DM related to the C-peptide system.

Theorem 2. *If the conditions (16), (24), (25) are fulfilled, all the compact invariant sets of the T1DM related to C-peptide system (2)–(6) lie within the following domain location*

$$K_{se} = K_B \cap K_p \cap K_A \cap K_M \cap K_E, \tag{26}$$

where

$$K_B = \{B(t) \leq B_{max} := 1\}; \tag{27}$$

$$K_p = \{p(t) \leq p_{max} := 2\}; \tag{28}$$

$$K_A = \left\{A(t) \leq A_{max} := \frac{\sigma}{\delta_A} + \frac{(\beta 2^{m_2} - \beta)^2}{4\epsilon\delta_A}\right\}; \tag{29}$$

$$K_M = \left\{M(t) \leq M_{max} := \frac{\sigma}{\delta_A} + \frac{(\beta 2^{m_2} - \beta)^2}{4\epsilon\delta_A}\right\}; \tag{30}$$

$$K_E = \left\{E(t) \leq E_{max} := \frac{\sigma}{\delta_A} + \frac{(\beta 2^{m_2} - \beta)^2}{4\epsilon\delta_A}\right\}. \tag{31}$$

The skewness correlation between C-peptides and cells was also demonstrated in [24], as the time scale of the peptide dynamics is faster (hours) than the time scale of the cell dynamics (days), and thus an almost steady state is assumed in the peptide. The C-peptide clinical test, which is widely applied to measure pancreatic β cell function [28].

Considering the mathematical function $dp/dt = 0$, leads to the variable C-peptide as $p = (REB/\delta_p)$. In this case, the state variable is far from being defined as an invariant plane in the mathematical scope; further, C-peptide represents a function that relays in the β cell population with the immune response's presence through effector cell populations. A disadvantage of analyzing the C-peptide in terms of other variables implies that the maximum carrying capacity of β cells can be estimated in a general scheme. This research contributes by analyzing a whole model with the LCIS method to establish a scheme where the clinical test interpretation can lead to a mathematical preamble approach.

4.1. Local Stability

In this subsection is presented the mathematical results applying the Lyapunov indirect method and considering the equilibrium point $(A^*, M^*, E^*, p^*, B^*) = (0, 0, 0, 0, 0)$ in the positive orthant. To determine if the equilibrium is locally stable, the system of Equations (2)–(6) is linearized. First, the system's Jacobian matrix (J) is defined as follows

$$J = \begin{bmatrix} -(\beta + \delta_A) - 2\epsilon A & \alpha \frac{p^n}{k_1^n + p_n} & 0 & (\sigma + \alpha M)\phi_2 & 0 \\ \beta 2^{m_1}\phi_3 & -\frac{p^n}{k_1^n + p_n}\alpha - \delta_M & 0 & \phi_1 2^{m_1} - \phi_2 \alpha M & 0 \\ \beta 2^{m_2}(1 - \phi_3) & 0 & -\delta_E & -\phi_1 2^{m_2} & 0 \\ 0 & 0 & RB & -\delta_p & RE \\ 0 & 0 & -kB & 0 & -kE \end{bmatrix}, \tag{32}$$

where

$$\phi_1 = \beta \frac{amk_2^m p^{m-1}}{(k_2^m + p^m)^2} A, \tag{33}$$

$$\phi_2 = \frac{nk_1^n p^{n-1}}{(k_1^n + p_n)^2}, \tag{34}$$

$$\phi_3 = \frac{ak_2^m}{k_2^m + p^m}; \tag{35}$$

evaluating matrix J at the equilibrium point, we obtained the expression

$$J(A^*, M^*, E^*, p^*, B^*) = \begin{bmatrix} -(\beta + \delta_A) & 0 & 0 & 0 & 0 \\ \beta 2^{m_1} a & -\delta_M & 0 & 0 & 0 \\ \beta 2^{m_2}(1-a) & 0 & -\delta_E & 0 & 0 \\ 0 & 0 & RB & -\delta_p & 0 \\ 0 & 0 & -kB & 0 & 0 \end{bmatrix}; \tag{36}$$

thus, the eigenvalues of (36) are $\lambda_1 = -(\beta + \delta_A)$, $\lambda_2 = -\delta_M$, $\lambda_3 = -\delta_E$, $\lambda_4 = -\delta_p$, and $\lambda_5 = 0$.

Since $\lambda_5 = 0$, it is impossible to conclude local stability for the equilibrium by applying the Lyapunov indirect method theorem in Equation (36). In summary, the system of Equations (2)–(6) has only one equilibrium point; therefore, local asymptotic stability is not evident. Hence, the design criteria in which the authors initially based the system (2)–(6) in [24] opens the possibility of considering control inputs to define a complementary model.

However, implementing the LCIS method provided a positive domain where all nonlinear system's trajectories were held without a linear scheme or numerical approach; thus, establishing a solution to the system by defining the upper bounds given the conditions (16), (24), and (25). The domain defined by (26) contains the cell population; however, it is considered asymmetric regarding each cell dynamic.

Closed-Loop Analysis via Lyapunov Stability Criteria

In the particular case of biological models, proposing control inputs are complex to determine unless a real-world known variable can be measured or supplied in a laboratory, such as insulin. In this work, insulin is not directly involved; instead, we assumed that a more comprehensive understanding of blocking a direct targeting of the effector cells to the pancreatic cells would lead to unnecessary antigen scheme behavior.

Recent research suggests that a more in-depth development of the insulin proliferation due to the β cell behavior. In [29], the authors concluded that researchers worldwide must continue monitoring T1D incidence trends. In contrast, research associated with prevention areas, early detection, and improved TID treatment continues. Furthermore, in [30], the authors tackled the use of protein biomarkers associated with risk factors in developing cardiovascular diseases when diabetes family antecedents prevail and pass in offspring from the gestational diabetes stage. They concluded that a deeper understanding of a leading cause that diabetes develops could improve this research topic.

Therefore, considering the system dynamic and the obtained previous results, we decided to analyze the system in a closed-loop scheme, proposing control inputs that guarantee its overall stability. The model described by Equations (2)–(6) is expressed as follows:

$$\frac{dA}{dt} = (\sigma + \alpha M)\frac{p^n}{k_1^n + p^n} - (\beta + \delta_A)A - \epsilon A^2 + U_1, \tag{37}$$

$$\frac{dM}{dt} = \beta 2^{m_1}\frac{ak_2^m}{k_2^m + p^m}A - \frac{p^n}{k_1^n + p^n}\alpha M - \delta_M M, \tag{38}$$

$$\frac{dE}{dt} = \beta 2^{m_2}(1 - \frac{ak_2^m}{k_2^m + p^m})A - \delta_E E + U_2, \tag{39}$$

$$\frac{dp}{dt} = REB - \delta_p p, \tag{40}$$

$$\frac{dB}{dt} = -\kappa EB; \tag{41}$$

where U_1 and U_2 represent the control inputs that could regulate the T cell population increase rate. To determine the criteria for each input, we propose the following candidate Lyapunov function

$$V = q_1 A + q_2 M + q_3 E + q_4 p + q_5 B, \tag{42}$$

where its derivative is given by $\dot{V} = q_1\dot{A} + q_2\dot{M} + q_3\dot{E} + q_4\dot{p} + q_5\dot{B}$, with q_1, q_2, q_3, q_4, and q_5 as free parameters, after substituting Equations (37)–(41) into the derivative gives

$$\begin{aligned}\dot{V} &= q_1\left[\sigma\frac{p^n}{k_1^n + p_n} + \alpha M\frac{p^n}{k_1^n + p_n} - (\beta + \delta_A)A - \epsilon A^2 + U_1\right]\\ &+ q_2\left[\beta 2^{m_1}\frac{ak_2^m}{k_2^m + p^m}A - \frac{p^n}{k_1^n + p_n}\alpha M - \delta_M M\right]\\ &+ q_3\left[\beta 2^{m_2}A - \frac{ak_2^m}{k_2^m + p^m}\beta 2^{m_2}A - \delta_E E + U_2\right] + q_4[REB - \delta_p p] + q_5[-\kappa EB].\end{aligned} \quad (43)$$

Now, analyzing the Equation (43), we concluded that U_1 and U_2 are able to establish stability conditions; therefore, U_1 and U_2 are defined as

$$U_1 = -\sigma\frac{p^n}{k_1^n + p_n} - \alpha M\frac{p^n}{k_1^n + p_n}, \quad (44)$$

$$U_2 = -\beta 2^{m_2}A, \quad (45)$$

as long as the condition (46) holds

$$2^{m_1} < 2^{m_2}, \quad (46)$$

with

$$q_1 = q_2 = q_3 = q_4 = 1, \quad (47)$$

$$q_5 < \frac{R}{\kappa}, \quad (48)$$

and, in order to guarantee asymptotically stability by the Lyapunov direct method, also the following inequality must hold

$$\epsilon\left(A + \frac{(\beta + \delta_A)}{2\epsilon}\right) + \delta_M M + \delta_E E + \delta_p p > \frac{(\beta + \delta_A)^2}{4\epsilon}. \quad (49)$$

In summary, the condition for q_5, inequality (48), implies that, given the Equation (16), when $R = \kappa$, then $q_5 < 1$, in comparison with the positive free parameters (47) that are equal to one. Meanwhile, condition (46) holds as condition (23). This implies that set $K(h_3)$ in Equation (26) encompasses the system (37)–(41) only when $R = \kappa$; thus, Equation (49) is also contained in the positive domain of $K(h_3)$; leading us to a mathematical preamble that the system (2)–(6) is a baseline model that can guide a mathematical revaluation, i.e., a model where cell populations could be modified, in view of a possible treatment.

5. Numerical Simulations

This section presents numerical simulations obtained with the LCIS method. Figure 1, shows the behavior of the activated, effector, and memory T cells, as well as the behavior of the population level of β cells and C-peptides. The parameters considered were those corresponding to Table 1, and the initial conditions were $A(0) = 0.5$, $M(0) = 0$, $E(0) = 1$, $p(0) = 0$, and $B(0) = 1$. Figure 1 shows the number of circulating cells (scaled) against time (days); $A(t)$ is expressed as $\times 10^3$ cells. $M(t)(\times 10^4)$, $E(t)(\times 10^6)$, $p(t)$ tends to be a small population of cells, and $B(t)$ is a fraction of the remaining β cell mass. The β cell population decreased by 10% during the immune attack. Since the model does not address the replenishment of the β cells by reproduction or stem cell differentiation, the β cell mass remains constant after this isolated immune response, [31]. The proposed initial conditions leading to the immune response was resolved without chronic disease or cyclic waves.

In Figure 2, we present a first approach of the upper bound for the variable $A(t)$, only if the conditions (24) and (25) are fulfilled; whereas, the immunological response in the presence of β cell behavior is presented in Figure 3. Effector and memory cell dynamics are under the upper bound set $K(h_3)$, implying that C-peptide has a direct impact on them;

therefore, in mathematical sense, the model has a proximity approach to the biological scheme. Clinical procedures need to be considered to ensure a reliable approach between the mathematical and the physical dynamics.

Figure 3 and 4 show the maximum value of the set $K(h_3)$ for the two types of T cells. The condition of δ_A, in (25), implies that the death rate of the memory T cells must be lower than the death rate by effector cells. Figure 5 presents the dynamics under the upper bound K_p, given by the localizing function h_2 and satisfying the condition (16). The secretion of the peptide is directly associated with the activation of T cells. When the C-peptide reaches high levels, memory cell production stops, and, consequently, the C-peptide is gradually cleared. High T cell levels are associated with an immune response to attack the β cell population, while the C-peptide attempts to avoid their destruction.

Using the LCIS method, we determined the maximum β cell population; therefore, when the β cells are at the maximum, then the C-peptide level is at the minimum as long as the T cells remain inactivated, see Figure 1. However, the C-peptide secretion stops when the β cells are gone; otherwise, its secretion remains active and waiting for the following β cell-level change. An increased incidence of microvascular complications are correlated with low C-peptide levels. It would be interesting to determine whether C-peptide concentrations are associated with increased macrovascular morbidity and mortality. Moreover, the maximum population of β cells is given by the set K_B, see Figure 6.

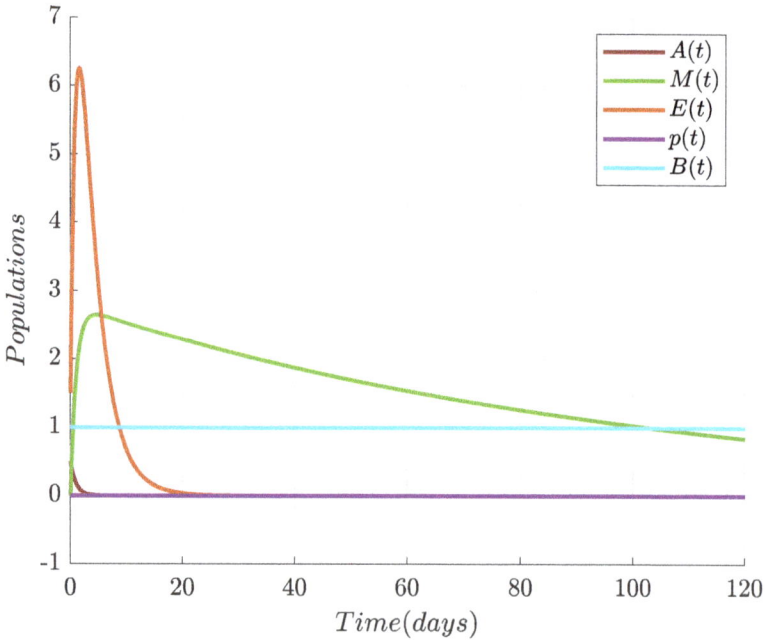

Figure 1. The dynamics of the circulating cell populations over time. $A(t)$ [$\times 10^3$ cells]. $M(t)$ [$\times 10^4$ cells], $E(t)$ [$\times 10^6$ cells], $p(t)$ [tends to be a small population of cells], and $B(t)$ [a fraction of the β cell mass remaining].

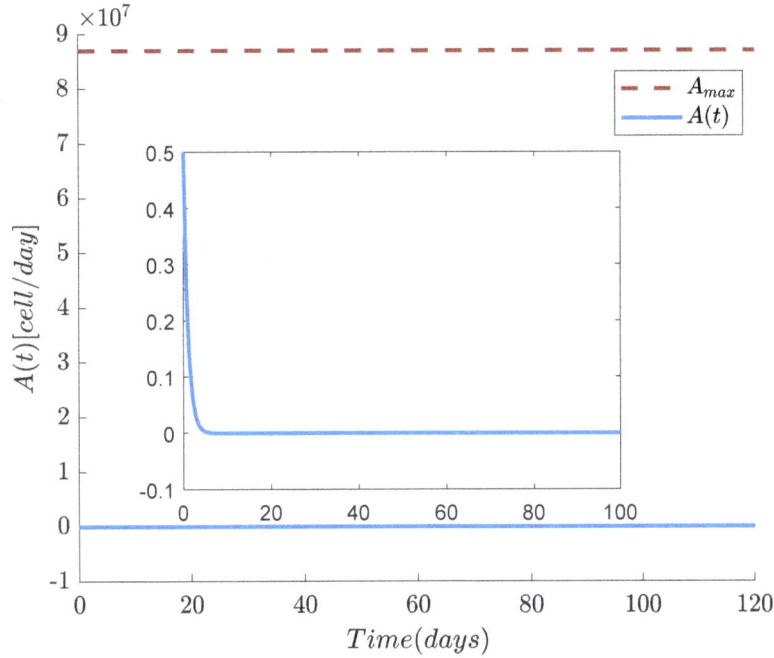

Figure 2. The presence of the upper bound for activated T cells by the set $K(h_3)$.

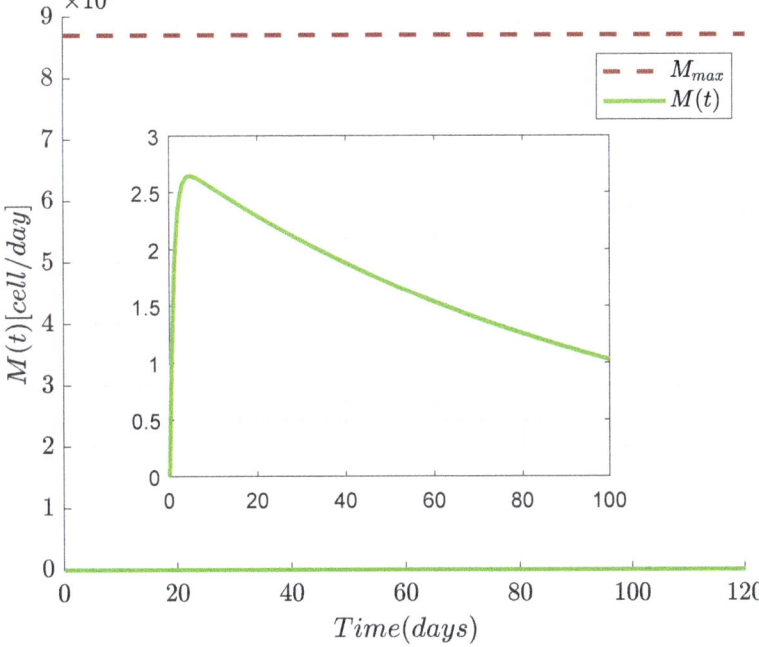

Figure 3. The immunological response in the presence of β cell behavior.

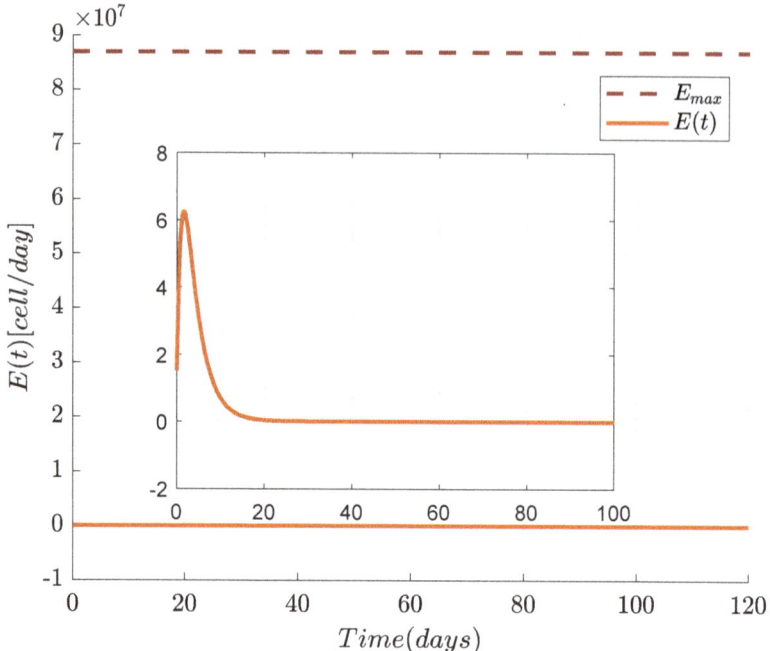

Figure 4. Effector cell dynamics under the upper bound set $K(h_3)$.

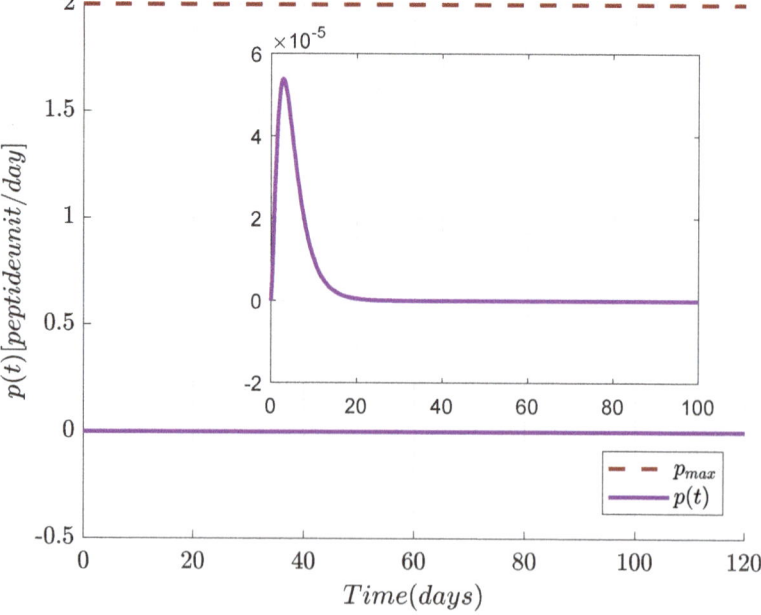

Figure 5. Upper bound for the C-peptide cell population by the set K_p.

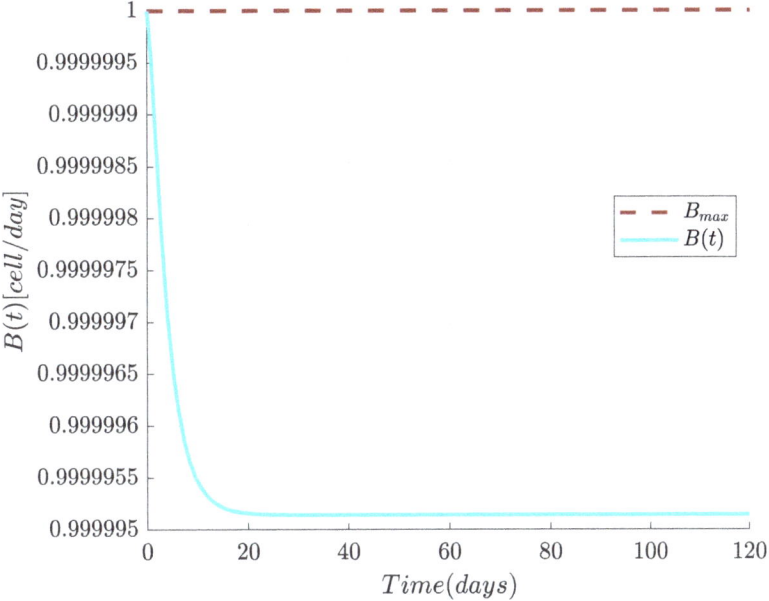

Figure 6. Upper bound for β cell population by the set K_B.

6. Conclusions

The localizing compact invariant set method provides the mathematical preamble to define the bounded positive invariant domain, i.e., the domain where all trajectories of the cell populations involved in T1DM are contained. It was also possible to mathematically describe the C-peptide level by proposing linear type localizing functions. The particularity in which the mathematical model is presented in [24], and discussed in this research implies that it represents a feasible scheme to analyze β cell targeting by the immune response. Thus, the estimated numerical values in Table 1 hold a reliable approach that can lead to a deeper pancreatic cell population understanding for experimental research in the future.

C-peptides are a useful indicator of β cell function, allowing discrimination between insulin-sufficient and insulin-deficient individuals with diabetes. Potential future uses of C-peptide are broad, including aiding appropriate diagnosis, guiding therapy choices, and predicting morbidity in diabetes; hence, the set of Equations (2)–(4) is one of the first nonlinear models involving a variable for C-peptide, and our results aim to contribute to future research involving a mathematical preamble.

The local stability of the systems through linearization was not concluded, since, in both cases, a matrix with a null eigenvalue was obtained, that is, one of the eigenvalues is equal to zero. Thus, this indicates the possibility of needing control inputs to ensure that the system regulates and breaks even.

The mathematical analysis of closed-loop systems suggests two control inputs directly related to the population of activated T cells and effector T cells. The control input U_1, see condition (44), implies the existence of a counterpart that prevents an increase in the population of activated T cells under the presence of β cells by suppressing the C-peptide level and the number of memory T cells produced by the body. On the other hand, the control input U_2, see (45), is associated with the effector T cell population's level, suggesting a population reduction effect of activated T cells to proliferate.

Therefore, a mathematical analysis considering control inputs based on a closed-loop system provides a theoretical basis to implement an immunotherapy treatment, if and only if, the conditions (46), (47), and (48) hold and, as a consequence, the condition (49) is also satisfied. In other words, these control inputs permit the conduction of all the cell populations to the desired state of equilibrium, i.e., being in symmetry with the desired level of each cell population.

This work did not discuss the idea of a nonlinear controller design at the moment; however, this is considered as future work given the conditions (44) and (45). We also intend to carry out the design of observers. We assumed, that the mathematical purpose of the observer is to identify or estimate those model's variables for feedback and to implement it as a possible or feasible treatment. Since the model deals with cell populations that do not have an easy way to measure themselves, considering their development outside the body is still a goal for the future.

Author Contributions: Conceptualization, D.G. and R.G.; Data curation, C.E.V.-L.; Formal analysis, D.G. and P.J.C.; Funding acquisition, C.E.V.-L.; Methodology, R.G.; Validation, P.J.C., C.E.V.-L. and R.G.; Writing—original draft, D.G.; Writing—review and editing, P.J.C. All authors have read and agreed to the published version of the manuscript.

Funding: This work was funded by Tecnológico Nacional de México (TecNM), Grant project ID: 10872.21-P. Title project: Análisis matemático de modelos no lineales relacionados a células pancreáticas y la respuesta inmunológica asociados a diabetes mellitus insulinodependiente.

Institutional Review Board Statement: Not applicable.

Informed Consent Statement: Not applicable.

Data Availability Statement: Not applicable.

Conflicts of Interest: All authors declare no conflict of interest in this paper.

References

1. Saeedi, P.; Petersohn, I.; Salpea, P.; Malanda, B.; Karuranga, S.; Unwin, N.; Colagiuri, S.; Guariguata, L.; Motala, A.A.; Ogurtsova, K.; et al. Global and regional diabetes prevalence estimates for 2019 and projections for 2030 and 2045: Results from the International Diabetes Federation Diabetes Atlas. *Diabetes Res. Clin. Pract.* **2019**, *157*, 107843. [CrossRef]
2. World Health Organization. *Global Action Plan on Physical Activity 2018–2030: More Active People for a Healthier World*; World Health Organization: Geneva, Switzerland, 2019.
3. Ampofo, A.G.; Boateng, E.B. Beyond 2020: Modelling obesity and diabetes prevalence. *Diabetes Res. Clin. Pract.* **2020**, *167*, 108362. [CrossRef]
4. Ogurtsova, K.; da Rocha Fernandes, J.; Huang, Y.; Linnenkamp, U.; Guariguata, L.; Cho, N.H.; Cavan, D.; Shaw, J.; Makaroff, L. IDF Diabetes Atlas: Global estimates for the prevalence of diabetes for 2015 and 2040. *Diabetes Res. Clin. Pract.* **2017**, *128*, 40–50. [CrossRef]
5. Whiting, D.R.; Guariguata, L.; Weil, C.; Shaw, J. IDF diabetes atlas: Global estimates of the prevalence of diabetes for 2011 and 2030. *Diabetes Res. Clin. Pract.* **2011**, *94*, 311–321. [CrossRef]
6. Guariguata, L.; Whiting, D.R.; Hambleton, I.; Beagley, J.; Linnenkamp, U.; Shaw, J.E. Global estimates of diabetes prevalence for 2013 and projections for 2035. *Diabetes Res. Clin. Pract.* **2014**, *103*, 137–149. [CrossRef]
7. Cho, N.; Shaw, J.; Karuranga, S.; Huang, Y.; da Rocha Fernandes, J.; Ohlrogge, A.; Malanda, B. IDF Diabetes Atlas: Global estimates of diabetes prevalence for 2017 and projections for 2045. *Diabetes Res. Clin. Pract.* **2018**, *138*, 271–281. [CrossRef]
8. Lin, J.; Thompson, T.J.; Cheng, Y.J.; Zhuo, X.; Zhang, P.; Gregg, E.; Rolka, D.B. Projection of the future diabetes burden in the United States through 2060. *Popul. Health Metrics* **2018**, *16*, 9. [CrossRef] [PubMed]
9. Bergman, R.N.; Cobelli, C. Minimal modeling, partition analysis, and the estimation of insulin sensitivity. *Fed. Proc.* **1980**, *39*, 110. [PubMed]
10. Bergman, R.N.; Ider, Y.Z.; Bowden, C.R.; Cobelli, C. Quantitative estimation of insulin sensitivity. *Am. J. Physiol. Endocrinol. Metab.* **1979**, *236*, E667. [CrossRef] [PubMed]
11. Fritzen, K.; Heinemann, L.; Schnell, O. Modeling of diabetes and its clinical impact. *J. Diabetes Sci. Technol.* **2018**, *12*, 976–984. [CrossRef]
12. Viceconti, M.; Cobelli, C.; Haddad, T.; Himes, A.; Kovatchev, B.; Palmer, M. In silico assessment of biomedical products: The conundrum of rare but not so rare events in two case studies. *Proc. Inst. Mech. Eng. Part H J. Eng. Med.* **2017**, *231*, 455–466. [CrossRef]
13. Aluru, S. *Handbook of Computational Molecular Biology*; CRC Press: Boca Raton, FL, USA, 2005.
14. Castillo-Chavez, C.; Blower, S.; Van den Driessche, P.; Kirschner, D.; Yakubu, A.A. *Mathematical Approaches for Emerging and Reemerging Infectious Diseases: An Introduction*; Springer Science & Business Media: Berlin/Heidelberg, Germany, 2002; Volume 1.
15. Miao, H.; Xia, X.; Perelson, A.S.; Wu, H. On identifiability of nonlinear ODE models and applications in viral dynamics. *SIAM Rev.* **2011**, *53*, 3–39. [CrossRef] [PubMed]
16. Wahren, J.; Ekberg, K.; Jörnvall, H. C-peptide is a bioactive peptide. *Diabetologia* **2007**, *50*, 503–509. [CrossRef]

17. Hao, W.; Gitelman, S.; DiMeglio, L.A.; Boulware, D.; Greenbaum, C.J. Fall in C-peptide during first 4 years from diagnosis of type 1 diabetes: Variable relation to age, HbA1c, and insulin dose. *Diabetes Care* **2016**, *39*, 1664–1670. [CrossRef] [PubMed]
18. Shields, B.M.; McDonald, T.J.; Oram, R.; Hill, A.; Hudson, M.; Leete, P.; Pearson, E.R.; Richardson, S.J.; Morgan, N.G.; Hattersley, A.T. C-peptide decline in type 1 diabetes has two phases: An initial exponential fall and a subsequent stable phase. *Diabetes Care* **2018**, *41*, 1486–1492. [CrossRef] [PubMed]
19. Valle, P.A.; Coria, L.N.; Salazar, Y. Tumor Clearance Analysis on a Cancer Chemo-Immunotherapy Mathematical Model. *Bull. Math. Biol.* **2019**, *81*, 4144–4173. [CrossRef]
20. Starkov, K.E. A Cancer Model for the Angiogenic Switch and Immunotherapy: Tumor Eradication in Analysis of Ultimate Dynamics. *Int. J. Bifurc. Chaos* **2020**, *30*, 2050150. [CrossRef]
21. Valle, P.A.; Coria, L.N.; Plata, C. Personalized Immunotherapy Treatment Strategies for a Dynamical System of Chronic Myelogenous Leukemia. *Cancers* **2021**, *13*, 2030. [CrossRef]
22. Gamboa, D.; Coria, L.N.; Cárdenas, J.R.; Ramírez, R.; Valle, P.A. Hardware Implementation of a Non-Linear Observer for a Diabetes Mellitus Type 1 Mathematical Model. *Comput. Sist.* **2019**, *23*, 4. [CrossRef]
23. Gamboa, D.; Vázquez, C.E.; Campos, P.J. Nonlinear Analysis for a Type-1 Diabetes Model with Focus on T-Cells and Pancreatic β-Cells Behavior. *Math. Comput. Appl.* **2020**, *25*, 23. [CrossRef]
24. Mahaffy, J.M.; Edelstein-Keshet, L. Modeling cyclic waves of circulating T cells in autoimmune diabetes. *SIAM J. Appl. Math.* **2007**, *67*, 915–937. [CrossRef]
25. Krishchenko, A.P.; Starkov, K.E. Localization of compact invariant sets of the Lorenz system. *Phys. Lett. A* **2006**, *353*, 383–388. [CrossRef]
26. Krishchenko, A.P. Localization of invariant compact sets of dynamical systems. *Differ. Equ.* **2005**, *41*, 1669–1676. [CrossRef]
27. Campos, P.J.; Coria, L.N.; Trujillo, L. Nonlinear speed sensorless control of a surface-mounted PMSM based on a Thau observer. *Electr. Eng.* **2018**, *100*, 177–193. [CrossRef]
28. Leighton, E.; Sainsbury, C.A.; Jones, G.C. A practical review of C-peptide testing in diabetes. *Diabetes Ther.* **2017**, *8*, 475–487. [CrossRef] [PubMed]
29. Lawrence, J.M.; Mayer-Davis, E.J. What do we know about the trends in incidence of childhood-onset type 1 diabetes? *Diabetologia* **2019**, *62*, 370–372. [CrossRef]
30. Lorenzo-Almoros, A.; Hang, T.; Peiro, C.; Soriano-Guillén, L.; Egido, J.; Tuñón, J.; Lorenzo, O. Predictive and diagnostic biomarkers for gestational diabetes and its associated metabolic and cardiovascular diseases. *Cardiovasc. Diabetol.* **2019**, *18*, 140. [CrossRef] [PubMed]
31. Thompson, P.J.; Shah, A.; Ntranos, V.; Van Gool, F.; Atkinson, M.; Bhushan, A. Targeted elimination of senescent beta cells prevents type 1 diabetes. *Cell Metab.* **2019**, *29*, 1045–1060. [CrossRef]

Article

Symmetric and Asymmetric Diffusions through Age-Varying Mixed-Species Stand Parameters

Petras Rupšys [1,2,*] **and Edmundas Petrauskas** [2]

[1] Faculty of Informatics, Vytautas Magnus University, Studentų Str. 11, LT-53361 Kaunas, Lithuania
[2] Agriculture Academy, Vytautas Magnus University, Studentų Str. 11, LT-53361 Kaunas, Lithuania; edmundas.petrauskas@vdu.lt
* Correspondence: petras.rupsys@vdu.lt

Abstract: (1) Background: This paper deals with unevenly aged, whole-stand models from mixed-effect parameters diffusion processes and Voronoi diagram points of view and concentrates on the mixed-species stands in Lithuania. We focus on the Voronoi diagram of potentially available areas to tree positions as the measure of the competition effect of individual trees and the tree diameter at breast height to relate their evolution through time. (2) Methods: We consider a bivariate hybrid mixed-effect parameters stochastic differential equation for the parameterization of the diameter and available polygon area at age to ensure a proper description of the link between them during the age (time) span of a forest stand. In this study, the Voronoi diagram was used as a mathematical tool for the quantitative characterization of inter-tree competition. (3) Results: The newly derived model considers bivariate correlated observations, tree diameter, and polygon area arising from a particular stand and enables defining equations for calculating diameter, polygon-area, and stand-density predictions and forecasts. (4) Conclusions: From a statistical point of view, the newly developed models produced acceptable statistical measures of predictions and forecasts. All the results were implemented in the Maple computer algebra system.

Keywords: Voronoi diagram; diffusion process; bivariate probability density function; diameter; polygon area; stand density

1. Introduction

Forest statisticians often need to address complex issues in important whole-stand, unevenly aged growth models with high levels of uncertainty that affect individual trees. Providing scientific evidence for effective decision processes in forest areas is a key issue, and stochastic calculus is an essential tool [1].

In the past few decades, mathematical models based on diffusion processes were fruitfully applied to describe stochasticity phenomena belonging to even extremely different disciplinary fields that range in scale from human population in biology [2] to cryptocurrency in finance [3] and from infectious disease in medicine [4] to networks in neuroscience [5]. Mixed-effect parameters diffusion processes provide a convenient tool to account for differences between several experiments or several subjects [6].

One of the important aims of modern forest regeneration is the investigation of the mapped tree community distribution in a stand area and its evolution through time. The distribution of individual trees depends both on the initial conditions present in a forest stand and the successive development of trees through changes in size components and mortality events. At present, results are large datasets of observations and statistical analysis acquired by using competition indices to both direct and indirect stand measurements [7]. To operate with these data, it is necessary to investigate information in a convenient form for the mathematical modeling of individual-based tree growth and yield. Independently of the type of an individual tree or whole-stand stochastic modelling (having a random variable), the consideration of a diffusion process has particular challenges. Diffusion processes allow for us to compute both the solution of the corresponding stochastic differential equation in a form of probability density function and their statistical moments, mainly mean, quantiles, and variance. The mechanism of the evolution of the competition among living trees in a forest stand can be successfully described by using a relatively young mathematical tool—continuous stochastic differential equations (SDEs). SDEs serve the purpose of analysis in a wide variety of generic growth models with different resolutions. The most advanced statistical models of this kind were formulated in terms of multivariate diffusion processes [8].

The process by which tree seedlings start to grow successfully in a new place is spatially multivariate, with numerous unknown variables. A potentially available area for an individual seedling embodies a variable representing the competitive strength of individual tree–tree interactions and varies through time. Several case studies were conducted to study the relationships between the potentially available area of a tree and its main biometrical attributes and competition indices [9]. The competition index is widely applied in plant ecology, but it has a smaller number of applications in individual-tree or whole-stand modeling. From a mathematical point of view, the Voronoi diagram [10] can be regarded as the best solution for neighboring effects on tree-size growth. To illustrate this study, we use the Voronoi diagram method, which is used by the individual-based tree-growth model. The Voronoi diagram formalizes a detailed structure of the position, size, and shape of a potentially available area of individual trees with respect to the number of trees per unit area and nearness of their contiguous neighbors. Moreover, Voronoi polygons reflect the local variation of the number of trees in a given location. A variable outlined by the value of the area of the Voronoi polygon is used as a descriptive parameter of spatial arrangement and as a predictor of stand density models.

Almost all the published research on natural mechanisms of maintaining tree-species diversity focuses on the principles of spatial measures and competition-index construction and their biological and mathematical reasoning [9]. Previous relationships on the key competition index include only local neighbors and are static. Unfortunately, it is insufficient, as each competition index systematically changes through time, which is of great importance and highly correlated with tree-size variables. Therefore, this paper focuses on the Voronoi polygon area of a tree and its dynamics. The dynamics of the polygon area is described by a diffusion process that accounts for the competition effect of contiguous neighbors and its correlation with tree-size or -stand variables.

This paper deals with whole-stand models from a diffusion process of view and concentrates on mixed-species stands in Lithuania. The innovation of this paper lies in the following: (1) the Voronoi diagram of potentially available areas to tree positions as the measure of the competition effect of individual trees, and its evolution through time is described using a Gompertz-type diffusion process; (2) the link of stand density with potentially available area and tree diameter is analyzed; (3) the mean and quantile attribute equations of the potentially available area, tree diameter, and stand density are described; and (4) the significance of differences in the distributions of different tree species is assessed. This paper carries out further research from the following directions: the first aspect analyzes the stochastic fixed-effect parameters process and then the stochastic mixed-effect parameters process; the third aspect illustrates the computational properties of the derived models.

The study was conducted in naturally and artificially regenerated areas by using data collected from over 58,000 trees positioned in a network of 50 permanent, rectangular sampling plots. As significant variables in the present study, we used such assessed attributes as species, the location of the individuals (Cartesian coordinates x, y), tree diameter at 1.3 m above ground level, and age. In order to determine the individual area of the i-th ($i = 1, \ldots, n$) tree, Voronoi polygon area P_i was calculated.

By utilizing the additive and multiplicative noise systems, we define the hybrid bivariate Vasicek–Gompertz-type SDE. The inclusion of random effects in the SDE produced a more accurate model to account for the error between model predictions and observed dataset. Model building in forestry was traditionally formalized by empirical models supporting the decisions of forest managers [11]. In addition, large published growth and yield systems were described by regression analysis, developed on a statistical basis that actually sought only to highlight the importance of a particular response variable in predicting the future, remaining static and deterministic. The stochastic differential equation approach opened the way to a stochastic dynamical formulation of the individual-tree or whole-stand growth process that appeared much later in statistical forestry [12–14].

2. Materials and Methods

2.1. Voronoi Diagram

Considering data in the form of a given set of n points $(x_i; y_i)$, $i = 1, \ldots, n$ within a planar region A, we can assign an area to $(x_i; y_i)$ consisting of that part of A that is closer to $(x_i; y_i)$ than to any other point $(x_j; y_j)$. A Voronoi diagram involves the partitioning of a planar region A into regions or polygons A_i on the basis of the distance to a specified discrete set of points [15]. The Voronoi diagram is a mathematical tool for the quantitative characterization of natural phenomena, such as inter-tree competition. In these polygons, trees with which the area neighbors are in direct competition for available light and nutrients are shown [16]. Each area A_i is a convex polygonal region. Voronoi polygons A_i vary with increasing time, and the number of trees decreases. Considering the dynamic of the Voronoi diagram allowed for both the quantification of its temporal dynamics and the characterization of the number of trees in a stand and its dynamics through time.

A generic definition of Voronoi diagrams was mathematically first introduced by Aurenhammer [17]. Voronoi cell A_i, associated with point $(x_i; y_i)$, is the set of all points in A, of which distance to point $(x_i; y_i)$ is not greater than their distance to other point $(x_j; y_j)$, where j is any index different from i. If we assume that $d((x; y), B) = \inf\{d((x; y), (a_1; a_2)) \mid (a_1; a_2) \in B\}$ denotes the distance between point $(x; y)$ and subset B, then:

$$A_i = \{(x; y) \in A \mid d((x; y), A_i) \leq d((x; y), A_j) \text{ for all } j \neq i\}. \tag{1}$$

The Voronoi diagram is simply the corpus of polygons A_i, $i = 1, \ldots, n$. In the past decade, mathematical algorithms and the rapid development of computational capacities provided a new chance to develop Voronoi diagram-based applications. In this study, we discuss mathematical models and their analyses based on areas of generated Voronoi polygons. To illustrate our work, we computed the Voronoi polygon of each individual tree in a plot, which was remeasured four times and is visualized in Figure 1, which shows that the areas of the Voronoi cells change through age (time).

2.2. Bivariate SDEs of Diameter and Polygon Area

In forestry studies, most tree attributes are considered to be functions of the tree diameter at breast height D [18]. For explaining the dynamics of tree-size variables, the incorporation of the distance of neighboring trees into a model improves predictions [19]. Moreover, appropriate evaluation of individual-tree size-variable is a fundamental requirement for the analysis of stand variables, such as the number of trees and volume per hectare. This study considers a stochastic approach for the parameterization of diameter D and polygon area P at age to ensure the proper descriptions of their link during the age (time) span of a forest stand. In this section, we state the stochastic mixed-effect bivariate (diameter D and polygon area P) model and derive the corresponding bivariate probability density function. We also introduce the procedure for random-effect calibration. The Vasicek–Gompertz-type bivariate hybrid stochastic mixed-effect parameters model was used to parameterize diameter and polygon area at age-discrete data. The univariate Gompertz-type model was applied to the analysis of stem volume and tree-stem taper from different tree species [20]. Below, stochastic vector $X^i(t) = \left(X_1^i(t), X_2^i(t)\right)^T = \left(D^i(t), P^i(t)\right)^T, i = 1, \ldots, M, t \in [t_0; T]$,

M is the number of individuals (plots), and T is a finite horizon, $T < \infty$. Hybrid bivariate Vasicek–Gompertz-type SDE is defined as:

$$dX^i(t) = A^i\left(X^i(t)\right)dt + D\left(X^i(t)\right)B^{\frac{1}{2}} \cdot dW^i(t) P\left(X^i(t_0) = x_0\right) = 1, \; i = 1, \ldots, M, \quad (2)$$

$$A^i(x) = \left(\beta_d\left(\alpha_d + \varphi_d^i - x_1\right), \left(\left(\alpha_p + \varphi_p^i\right) - \beta_p \ln(x_2)\right)x_2\right)^T B = \begin{pmatrix} \sigma_{dd} & \sigma_{dp} \\ \sigma_{dp} & \sigma_{pp} \end{pmatrix}, \quad (3)$$

$$\left(D(x)B^{\frac{1}{2}}\right)\left(D(x)B^{\frac{1}{2}}\right)^T = \begin{pmatrix} 1 & 0 \\ 0 & x_2 \end{pmatrix}\begin{pmatrix} \sigma_{dd} & \sigma_{dp} \\ \sigma_{dp} & \sigma_{pp} \end{pmatrix}\begin{pmatrix} 1 & 0 \\ 0 & x_2 \end{pmatrix}$$

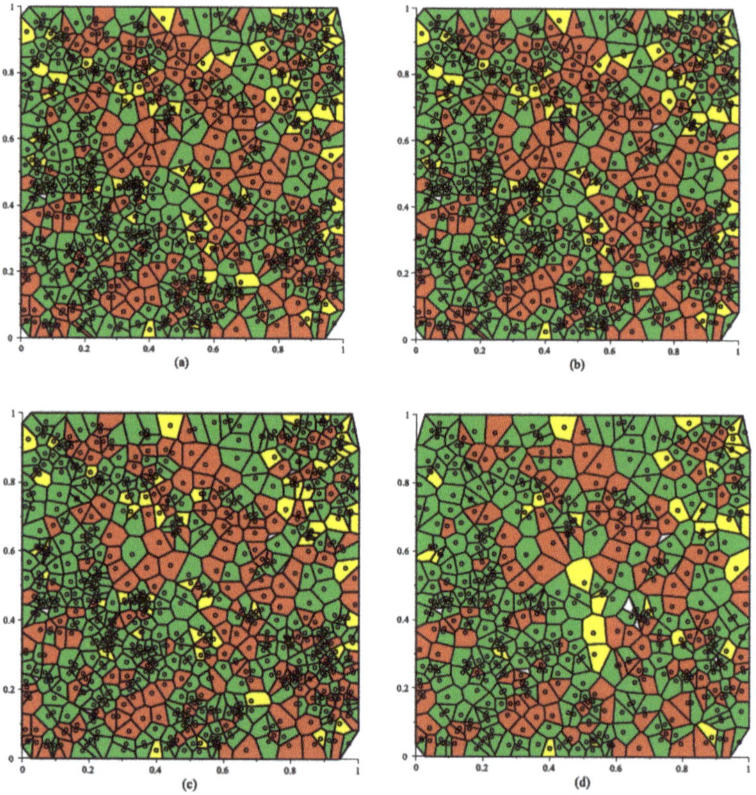

Figure 1. Voronoi diagram of plot remeasured on four succeeding occasions: (**a**) 1983rd-year cycle of measurement (mean age, 43.70 years); (**b**) 1988th-year cycle of measurement (mean age, 48.72 years); (**c**) 1996th-year cycle of measurement (mean age, 57.13 years); (**d**) 2019th-year cycle of measurement (mean age, 83.12 years); red, Scots pine trees; green, Norway spruce trees; yellow, birch trees; circles, tree position.

This study focusses on initial distribution, defined by deterministic initial value $\left(X_1^i(t_0), X_2^i(t_0)\right) = (x_{10}, x_{20}) = \left(x_{10}, \delta + \varphi_0^i\right)$, and δ is an unknown fixed-effect parameter to be estimated. SDE of form (2) consists of two parts. The deterministic part in the model is drift function $A^i(x)$. Random term $D(X^i(t))B^{\frac{1}{2}} \cdot dW^i(t)$, which corresponds to the uncertain part of the model, is referred to as the system noise. In Equation (2), $W^i(t) = \left(W_1^i(t), W_2^i(t)\right)^T$ represents the bivariate Brownian motion, of which the time derivative is white noise. Moreover, Brownian motion increments $dW^i(t)$, $i = 1, \ldots, M$, are considered to be independent across all plots. Random effects $\varphi_d^i \varphi_p^i$, and φ_0^i are

194

independent and normally distributed random variables with zero mean and constant variances, respectively, $\varphi_d^i \sim N(0; \sigma_d^2)$, $\varphi_p^i \sim N(0; \sigma_p^2)$, and $\varphi_0^i \sim N(0; \sigma_0^2)$. Fixed-effect parameters vector θ to be estimated is defined as:

$$\theta = (\alpha_d, \alpha_p, \beta_d, \beta_p, \sigma_{dd}, \sigma_{pp}, \rho_{dp}, \delta, \sigma_d, \sigma_p, \sigma_0) \sigma_{dp} = \sqrt{\sigma_{dd}\sigma_{pp}}\rho_{dp}. \qquad (4)$$

The solution of the Vasicek–Gompertz-type SDE (2) has bivariate normal-lognormal distribution $N_1 LN_1 (\mu^i(t|t_0, x_0); \Sigma(t|t_0))$ with mean vector $\mu^i(t|t_0, x_0)$ and variance–covariance matrix $\Sigma(t|t_0)$, defined as:

$$\mu^i(t|t_0, x_0) = \begin{pmatrix} \mu_d^i(t|t_0, x_{10}) \\ \mu_p^i(t|t_0, x_{20}) \end{pmatrix} = \begin{pmatrix} (\alpha_d + \varphi_d^i) + (x_{10} - (\alpha_d + \varphi_d^i))e^{-\beta_d(t-t_0)} \\ e^{-\beta_p(t-t_0)} \ln(\delta + \varphi_0^i) + \frac{1 - e^{-\beta_p(t-t_0)}}{\beta_p}\left(\alpha_p + \varphi_p^i - \frac{\sigma_{pp}}{2}\right) \end{pmatrix} \qquad (5)$$

$$\Sigma(t|t_0) = \begin{pmatrix} v_{dd}(t|t_0) & v_{dp}(t|t_0) \\ v_{dp}(t|t_0) & v_{pp}(t|t_0) \end{pmatrix} = \begin{pmatrix} \frac{1 - e^{-2\beta_d(t-t_0)}}{2\beta_d}\sigma_{dd} & \frac{1 - e^{-(\beta_d+\beta_p)(t-t_0)}}{\beta_d+\beta_p}\sqrt{\sigma_{dd}\sigma_{pp}}\rho_{dp} \\ \frac{1 - e^{-(\beta_d+\beta_p)(t-t_0)}}{\beta_d+\beta_p}\sqrt{\sigma_{dd}\sigma_{pp}}\rho_{dp} & \frac{1 - e^{-2\beta_p(t-t_0)}}{2\beta_p}\sigma_{pp} \end{pmatrix}. \qquad (6)$$

We can separately calculate the probability distribution of each random variable if we wish to restrict our attention to the value of just one, for example, diameter D or polygon area P. The marginal distribution of $X_1^i(t)|X_1^i(t_0) = x_{10}$ is normal $N_1(\mu_d^i(t|t_0, x_{10}); v_{dd}(t|t_0))$, and the marginal distribution of $X_2^i(t)|X_2^i(t_0) = x_{20}$ is lognormal $LN_1\left(\mu_p^i(t|t_0, x_{20}); v_{pp}(t|t_0)\right)$ with means $\mu_d^i(t|t_0, x_{10})$ and $\mu_p^i(t|t_0, x_{20})$ and variances $v_{dd}(t|t_0)$ and $v_{pp}(t|t_0)$, respectively.

For the diameter dynamic, the mean, median, mode, qth quantile $(0 < q < 1)$, and variance trends can be listed as:

$$m_d^i(t|t_0, x_{10}) = me_d^i(t|t_0, x_{10}) = mo_d^i(t|t_0, x_{10}) = \mu_d^i(t|t_0, x_{10}), \qquad (7)$$

$$mq_d^i(t, q|t_0, x_{10}) = \Phi_q^{-1}\left(\mu_d^i(t|t_0, x_{10}); v_{dd}(t|t_0)\right), \qquad (8)$$

$$w_d^i(t|t_0, x_{10}) = v_{dd}(t|t_0), \qquad (9)$$

where $\Phi_q^{-1}(\cdot; \cdot)$ is the inverse of the standard normal distribution function.

For the polygon area dynamic, the mean, median, mode, qth quantile $(0 < q < 1)$, and variance trends can be listed as:

$$m_p^i(t|t_0, x_{20}) = \exp\left(\mu_p^i(t|t_0, x_{20}) + \frac{1}{2}v_{pp}(t|t_0)\right), \qquad (10)$$

$$me_p^i(t|t_0, x_{20}) = \exp\left(\mu_p^i(t|t_0, x_{20})\right), \qquad (11)$$

$$mo_p^i(t|t_0, x_{20}) = \exp\left(\mu_p^i(t|t_0, x_{20}) - v_{pp}(t|t_0)\right), \qquad (12)$$

$$mq_p^i(t, q|t_0, x_{20}) = L\Phi_q^{-1}(\mu_p^i(t|t_0, x_{20}); v_{pp}(t|t_0)), \qquad (13)$$

$$w_p^i(t|t_0, x_{10}) = \exp\left(2\mu_p^i(t|t_0, x_{20}) + v_{pp}(t|t_0)\right) \cdot (\exp(v_{pp}(t|t_0)) - 1), \qquad (14)$$

where $L\Phi_q^{-1}(\cdot; \cdot)$ is the inverse of the standard normal distribution function.

Conditional distribution of $X_1^i(t)|X_1^i(t_0) = x_{10}$ at a given $(X_2^i(t) = x_2)$ is univariate normal $N_1\left(\eta_d^i(t, x_2|t_0, x_0); \lambda_d(t|t_0)\right)$, and conditional distribution of $X_2^i(t)|X_2^i(t_0) = x_{20}$ at a given $(X_1^i(t) = x_1)$ is univariate lognormal $LN_1\left(\eta_p^i(t, x_1|t_0, x_0); \lambda_p(t|t_0)\right)$, with means and variances given as:

$$\eta_d^i(t, x_2|t_0, x_0) = \mu_d^i(t|t_0, x_{10}) + \frac{v_{dp}(t|t_0)}{v_{pp}(t|t_0)}\left(\ln(x_2) - \mu_p^i(t|t_0, x_{20})\right) \qquad (15)$$

$$\lambda_d(t|t_0) = v_{dd}(t|t_0) - \frac{\left(v_{dp}(t|t_0)\right)^2}{v_{pp}(t|t_0)}, \qquad (16)$$

$$\eta_p^i(t, x_1|t_0, x_0) = \mu_p^i(t|t_0, x_{20}) + \frac{v_{dp}(t|t_0)}{v_{dd}(t|t_0)}\left(x_1 - \mu_d^i(t|t_0, x_{10})\right), \qquad (17)$$

$$\lambda_p(t|t_0) = v_{pp}(t|t_0) - \frac{\left(v_{dp}(t|t_0)\right)^2}{v_{dd}(t|t_0)}. \qquad (18)$$

For the diameter growth model, the conditional mean, median, mode, qth quantile ($0 < q < 1$), and variance trends can be listed as:

$$mc_d^i(t, x_2|t_0, x_0) = mec_d^i(t, x_2|t_0, x_0) = moc_d^i(t, x_2|t_0, x_0) = \eta_d^i(t, x_2|t_0, x_0), \qquad (19)$$

$$mqc_d^i(t, x_2, q|t_0, x_0) = \Phi_q^{-1}(\eta_d^i(t, x_2|t_0, x_0); \lambda_d(t|t_0)), \qquad (20)$$

$$wc_d^i(t|t_0) = \lambda_d(t|t_0). \qquad (21)$$

For the polygon area growth model, the conditional mean, median, mode, qth quantile ($0 < q < 1$), and variance trends can be listed as:

$$mc_p^i(t, x_1|t_0, x_0) = exp\left(\eta_p^i(t, x_1|t_0, x_0) + \frac{1}{2}\lambda_p(t|t_0)\right), \qquad (22)$$

$$mec_p^i(t, x_1|t_0, x_0) = exp\left(\eta_p^i(t, x_1|t_0, x_0)\right), \qquad (23)$$

$$moc_p^i(t, x_1|t_0, x_0) = exp\left(\eta_p^i(t, x_1|t_0, x_0) - \lambda_p(t|t_0)\right), \qquad (24)$$

$$mqc_p^i(t, x_1, q|t_0, x_0) = \Phi_q^{-1}(\eta_p^i(t, x_1|t_0, x_0); \lambda_p(t|t_0)), \qquad (25)$$

$$wc_p^i(t, x_1|t_0, x_0) = exp\left(2\eta_p^i(t, x_1|t_0, x_0) + \lambda_p(t|t_0)\right) \cdot (exp(\lambda_p(t|t_0)) - 1). \qquad (26)$$

2.3. Data

The field-study area is located in the municipality of Kazlų Rūda in Lithuania. A major part of the Kazlų Rūda municipality is located in the fertile Užnemunė lowland and is among the most wooded areas in Lithuania, with about 59.4% of the territory covered by large forests. The specific allocation comprises the area covered by stands of pine (*Pinus sylvestris*), 63.8%; spruce (*Picea abies*), 30.2%; silver birch (*Betula pendula* Roth and *Betula pubescens* Ehrh.), 5.8%; and others, 0.2%. All data were collected during fieldwork in 1983–2019 across the Kazlų Rūda forests (latitude, 54°44′54.222″ N; longitude, 23°29′27.7944″ E; altitude, 68 m). Mean temperatures vary from −16.4 °C in winter to 22 °C in summer. Precipitation is distributed throughout the year, although predominantly in summer; the average is approximately 680 mm a year. During the 1983–1987 period, 50 permanent experimental plots were established in the Kazlų Rūda forests in Lithuania. According to regeneration mode, the 50 field-sample plots vary between those naturally and artificially regenerated and spread in pure or mixed-species stands. Each sample plot consisted of about 0.16–0.72 ha and was remeasured several times, from 1 until 6 (see Figure 1, showing 4 cycles) at 2- to 36-year intervals. The attributes recorded for each tree in the considered plots were the tree species, age, location of the sample trees (planar coordinate position x and y), and diameter at breast height. The age of the i-th tree (i varied from all the trees until the 10th) in the first measurement was recorded by counting its growth rings on the increment core (for even-aged stands, from entries in documents), and the ages of the remaining trees were obtained from the arithmetic mean. The accuracy of planar coordinate position was 1 dcm, and diameter measurements were performed with approximately 1 mm accuracy. The 50 field-sample plot dataset was randomly divided into estimation and validation datasets.

The estimation dataset consisted of measurements from 40 plots, and the validation dataset compounded the remaining measurements from 10 plots. Table 1 shows the summary statistics of the field-sample data.

Table 1. Tree characteristics of sample plots (0.16–0.72 ha) selected for the study.

Species	Data	Number of Trees	Min	Max	Mean	St. Dev.	Number of Trees	Min	Max	Mean	St. Dev.
		Estimation					Validation				
Pine	t (year)	28,982	5.0	172.0	49.14	22.16	6997	7.0	197.0	67.90	19.06
	d (cm)	28,982	0.5	61.0	17.87	9.17	6997	3.0	59.2	24.35	9.02
	p (m^2)	28,982	0.09	120.21	9.24	7.56	6997	0.44	84.84	13.02	8.54
Spruce	t (year)	11,493	12.0	207.0	59.63	21.57	7001	7.0	191.0	67.94	21.01
	d (cm)	11,493	0.20	62.0	11.68	7.34	7001	3.0	61.8	13.24	8.51
	p (m^2)	11,493	0.11	160.24	9.17	8.32	7001	0.26	77.76	9.46	7.65
Birch	t (year)	2880	5.0	107.32	47.75	17.88	663	16.0	129.73	60.29	15.87
	d (cm)	2880	0.90	45.40	14.46	8.13	663	3.0	50.0	19.91	9.30
	p (m^2)	2880	0.33	173.82	8.70	7.01	663	0.89	51.93	9.88	8.05
All	t (year)	43,410	5.0	207.0	51.84	22.27	14,711	7.0	197.0	67.55	19.94
	d (cm)	43,410	0.20	62.0	16.0	9.07	14,711	3.0	61.80	18.87	10.35
	p (m^2)	43,410	0.09	173.82	9.18	7.73	14,711	0.26	84.84	11.16	8.29

3. Results

3.1. Parameter-Estimating Results

The key research problem in this study is the latest developments of accurate and computationally optimal parameter-estimation procedures based on the approximated maximum-likelihood technique, which cannot be implemented in the presence of a closed-form expression for the mixed-effect parameters SDE [21]. Our developed maximum-likelihood estimation technique relies on the fact that the conditional bivariate probability density function has an exact form. Therefore, the likelihood function maximization technique with respect to parameter vector θ for a given set of discretely observed diameter and polygon area data is defined by a two-step procedure.

To evaluate the proposed Vasicek–Gompertz-type mixed-effect parameters SDE (2), an approximated log-likelihood technique for estimating the parameters was set up on the basis of the discrete observations from estimation dataset $\left\{ (d_1^i, p_1^i), (d_2^i, p_2^i), \ldots, (d_{n_i}^i, p_{n_i}^i) \right\}$ on a fixed time interval $\left\{ t_1^i, t_2^i, \ldots, t_{n_i}^i \right\}$, $i = 1, \ldots, M$. The randomly selected 40 samples were used to fit the SDE model defined by Equation (2), and the results of the estimating parameters are summarized in Table 2. All parameters were statistically significant ($p < 0.05$).

Table 2. Vasicek–Gompertz-type system for diameter and polygon area: parameter estimates.

Species	α_d	β_d	α_p	β_p	σ_{dd}	σ_{pp}	ρ_{dp}	δ	σ_d	σ_p	σ_0
All	48.3358	0.0086	0.0875	0.0273	1.3363	0.0199	0.2405	1.7344	11.5987	0.0121	1.5185
Pine	59.8450	0.0081	0.0860	0.0251	0.8308	0.0174	0.2056	1.3111	11.3134	0.0098	0.9627
Spruce	77.4686	0.0030	0.0836	0.0280	0.6393	0.0250	0.2851	1.7769	26.8149	0.0120	1.3815
Birch	23.6670	0.0234	0.0802	0.0258	1.7425	0.0200	0.1823	2.0643	8.6172	0.0131	0.3988

3.2. Bivariate and Marginal Distributions

After the fixed-effect parameters were obtained in Section 3.1, which are listed in Table 2, they were used to evaluate the accuracy of the prediction and forecasting in subsequent sections by using data from the validation dataset. The bivariate mixed-effect parameters SDE model was developed by combining the two univariate models through a bivariate stochastic process. The model considered two correlated observations, tree diameter and polygon area, reflecting the high variation of stand density among *stands* of Lithuania. The main goal in an SDE modeling framework is to determine the probability density function of the solution, formulated as a diffusion process since it capacitates for calculating any univariate moment, which allows for calculating the mean, variance, and tolerance regions for bivariate cases. In our setting, the newly developed bivariate density and marginal and conditional densities were visually evaluated corresponding to the diameter and polygon area observed data from the validation dataset at a given average stand age. Therefore, the corresponding observed data from the validation dataset and its fitted distribution were graphically visualized. The Voronoi tessellations presented in Figure 1 show dynamic of polygon areas via stand age (time). These diagrams also demonstrate information about variations in the polygon area, which grows with age. Figures 2–5 illustrate the fitted marginal probability density functions and underlying frequency distributions (histograms) for new plots from the validation dataset with two cycles of remeasurements at an average stand age. All the fitted probability density functions take the values of the fixed-effect parameters from Table 2. Random effects φ_d, φ_p, and φ_0 for a new plot from the validation dataset were calibrated as:

$$\hat{\varphi} = \underset{(\varphi_d, \varphi_p, \varphi_0)}{argmax} \left(\sum_{j=1}^{m} \ln\left(f\left(x_{1j}, x_{2j}, t_j \middle| \hat{\theta}, \varphi_d, \varphi_p, \varphi_0 \right) \right) + \ln\left(\phi(\varphi_d | \hat{\sigma}_d) \right) + \ln\left(\phi\left(\varphi_p | \hat{\sigma}_p \right) \right) + \ln\left(\phi\left(\varphi_0 | \hat{\sigma}_0 \right) \right) \right) \quad (27)$$

where $\{(x_{11}, x_{21}), (x_{12}, x_{22}), \ldots, (x_{1m}, x_{2m})\}$ is the newly observed dataset, $t_0 = 4$, $(x_{10}, x_{20}) = (0.1, \hat{\delta} + \varphi_0)$, $f\left(x_1, x_2, t \middle| \hat{\theta}^1, \varphi_d, \varphi_p, \varphi_0 \right)$ is the bivariate normal-lognormal density function with the mean and variance defined by Equations (5) and (6), $\phi(\cdot | \sigma)$ is the univariate normal density function with zero mean and standard deviation σ, and the estimated values of fixed-effect parameters are denoted by "hat" (listed in Table 2).

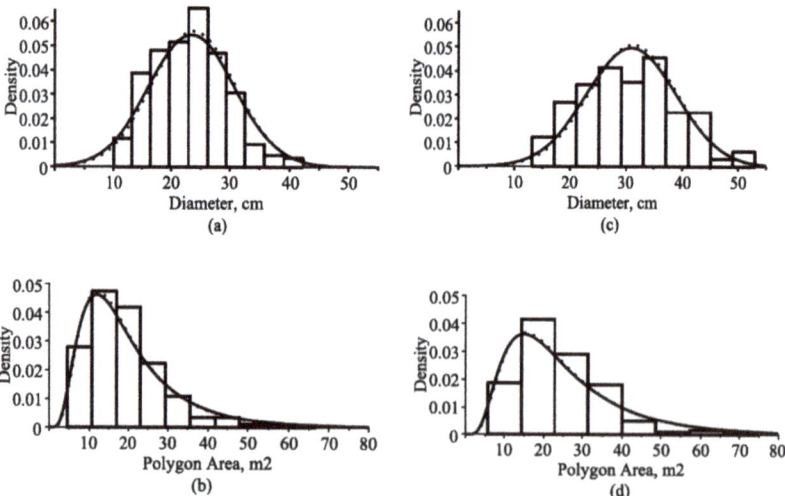

Figure 2. Estimated marginal and conditional probability density functions and frequency distribution for all tree species in a randomly selected stand from the validation dataset in two cycles of remeasurements: (a) diameter distributions (mean age, 71.9 years; and mean polygon area, 19.43 m²); (b) polygon area distributions (mean age, 71.9 years; and mean diameter, 23.12 cm); (c) diameter distributions (mean age, 106.4 years; and mean polygon area, 24.11 m²); (d) polygon area distributions (mean age, 106.4 years; and mean diameter, 31.06 cm); estimated marginal probability density functions, solid lines; conditional (diameter-dependent) probability density functions, dotted lines.

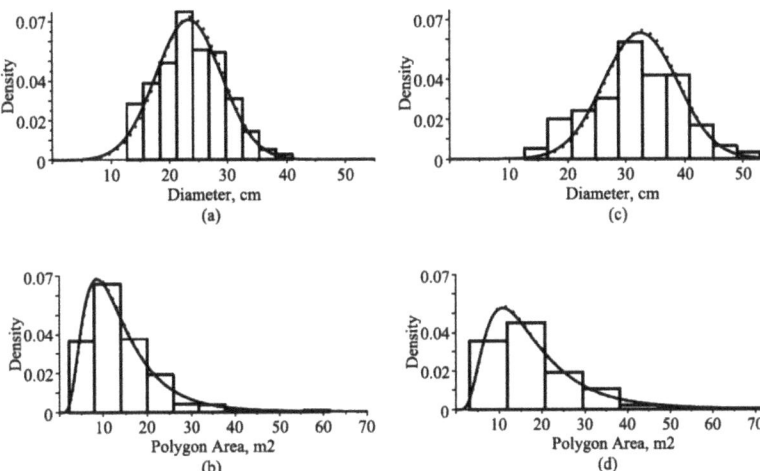

Figure 3. Estimated marginal and conditional probability density functions and frequency distribution for Scots pine tree species in a randomly selected stand from the validation dataset in two cycles of remeasurements: (**a**) diameter distributions (mean age, 63.7 years; and mean polygon area, 13.85 m^2); (**b**) polygon area distributions (mean age, 63.7 years; and mean diameter, 23.62 cm); (**c**) diameter distributions (mean age, 98.4 years; and mean polygon area, 17.52 m^2); (**d**) polygon area distributions (mean age, 98.4 years; and mean diameter, 32.33 cm); estimated marginal probability density functions, solid lines; conditional (diameter-dependent) probability density functions, dotted lines.

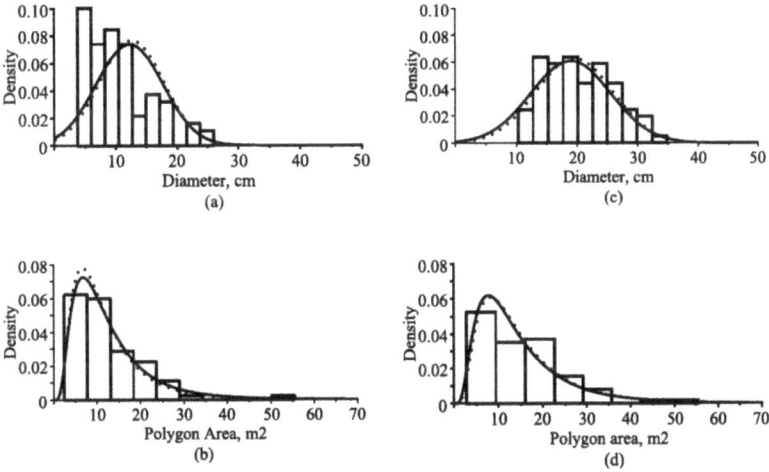

Figure 4. Estimated marginal and conditional probability density functions and frequency distribution for Norway spruce tree species in a randomly selected stand from the validation dataset in two cycles of remeasurements: (**a**) diameter distributions (mean age, 57.6 years; and mean polygon area, 12.26 m^2); (**b**) polygon area distributions (mean age, 57.6 years; and mean diameter, 10.64 cm); (**c**) diameter distributions (mean age, 91.3 years; and mean polygon area, 15.47 m^2); (**d**) polygon area distributions (mean age, 91.3 years; and mean diameter, 20.30 cm); estimated marginal probability density functions, solid lines; conditional (diameter-dependent) probability density functions, dotted lines.

Figures 2–5 show that univariate conditional probability density functions defined by inserting additional explanatory variable polygon areas or diameters undergo indistinguishable changes in comparison with corresponding univariate marginal densities. The similarity of the marginal and conditional distributions suggests that the additional explanatory variable (polygon area or diameter) has a relatively small effect on the values of the response variable (diameter or polygon area). Moreover, the figures superpose frequency distribution and estimated normal or lognormal probability distributions that correspond to the probability density function of the solutions of SDE (2). Frequency distributions are not exactly in agreement with the normal or lognormal distribution shapes due to the variation in tree age or probably did not arise from our presented form. The tree diameter histograms shown in Figures 2–5 confirm the assumption that the tree-diameter distribution in a particular forest stand has an approximately symmetrical shape. The lack of symmetry in Figure 4 for Norway spruce trees occurs probably due to the planned thinning in the stand, as lightening works are usually carried out in stands of this age. The symmetry and standard deviation of the diameter distribution increase with age. In contrast, the polygon area histograms reveal asymmetry of the distribution, and the long tail extends to the right. Histograms of the polygon area show a number of unusual observed values. This scenario may be the result of a directional felling or soil properties. Lastly, the newly derived bivariate probability density function was a good match for our validation data.

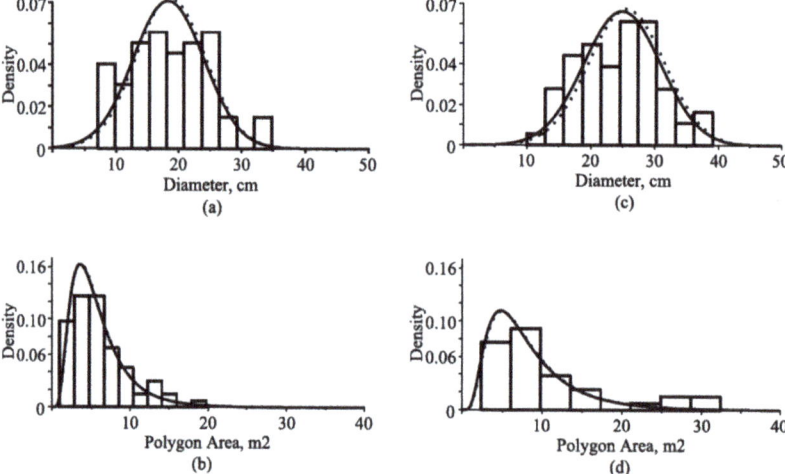

Figure 5. Estimated marginal and conditional probability density functions and frequency distribution for silver birch tree species in a randomly selected stand from the validation dataset in two cycles of remeasurements: (**a**) diameter distributions (mean age, 44.7 years; and mean polygon area, 6.11 m^2); (**b**) polygon area distributions (mean age, 44.7 years; and mean diameter, 18.60 cm); (**c**) diameter distributions (mean age, 81.0 years; and mean polygon area, 10.44 m^2); (**d**) polygon area distributions (mean age, 81.0 years; and mean diameter, 25.94 cm); estimated marginal probability density functions, solid lines; conditional (diameter-dependent) probability density functions, dotted lines.

For the observed diameter and polygon area data fitted with the bivariate Vasicek–Gompertz-type SDE (2), the tolerance region of mean vector $\mu^i(t|t_0, x_0)$, defined by Equation (5), takes the following well-known inequality [22]:

$$\left(\begin{pmatrix} x_1 \\ \ln(x_2) \end{pmatrix} - \mu^i(t|t_0, x_0)\right)^T [\Sigma(t|t_0)]^{-1} \left(\begin{pmatrix} x_1 \\ \ln(x_2) \end{pmatrix} - \mu^i(t|t_0, x_0)\right) \le \chi, \quad (28)$$

where χ is the tolerance coefficient [23]. For lognormally distributed polygon area data, we plot a tolerance region using a logarithmic axis. Figures 6–9 show the tolerance regions for $\beta = 0.95$ and confidence level $\gamma = 0.95$, which correspond to the randomly selected stand from the validation dataset with two cycles of remeasurements. The random effects were calibrated by Equation (27). For the tolerance region plots, the χ value was chosen from Table 1 in [23]: the setting $\beta = 0.95$ and $\gamma = 0.95$ produces a x of 10.02. The bivariate tolerance region for the Vasicek–Gompertz-type model (2) enables us to decide whether the newly developed distribution function corresponds well with the observed data of the diameter and polygon area. Figures 6–9 illustrate that the 95% tolerance regions had reasonable coverage rates for different tree-species scenarios. Information concerning tolerance regions is implicit in the hybrid bivariate distribution derived for the Vasicek–Gompertz-type SDE (2).

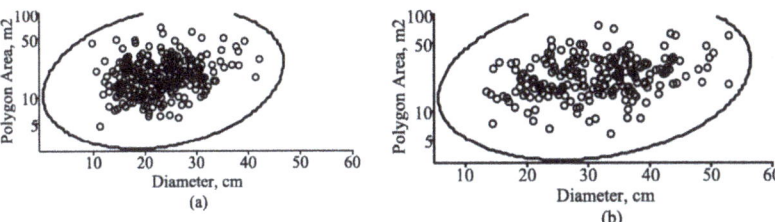

Figure 6. Tolerance region for mean vector with the observed sample from the validation dataset of all tree species in two measurement cycles: (**a**) tolerance region of diameter and polygon area for first cycle (mean age, 71.9 years; mean diameter, 23.12 cm; and mean polygon area, 19.43 m^2); (**b**) tolerance region of diameter and polygon area for fourth cycle (mean age, 106.4 years; mean diameter, 26.50 cm; and mean polygon area, 24.11 m^2); tolerance region, solid line; observed dataset, circles.

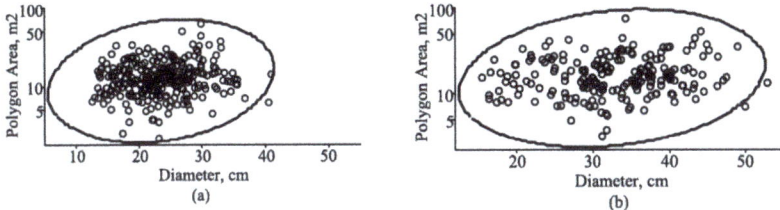

Figure 7. Tolerance region for mean vector with the observed sample from the validation dataset of Scots pine tree species in two measurement cycles: (**a**) tolerance region of diameter and polygon area for first cycle (mean age, 63.7 years; mean diameter, 23.62 cm; and mean polygon area, 13.85 m^2); (**b**) tolerance region of diameter and polygon area for fourth cycle (mean age, 98.4 years; mean diameter, 32.33 cm; and mean polygon area, 17.52 m^2); tolerance region, solid line; observed dataset, circles.

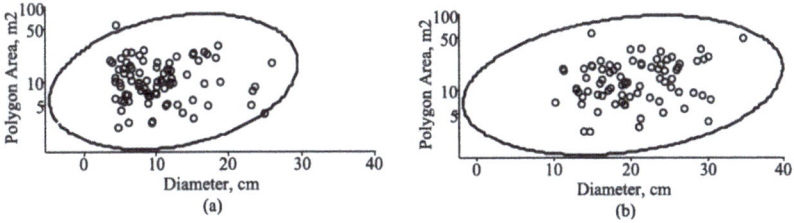

Figure 8. Tolerance region for mean vector with the observed sample from the validation dataset of Norway spruce tree species in two measurement cycles: (**a**) tolerance region of diameter and polygon area for first cycle (mean age, 57.6 years; mean diameter, 10.64 cm; and mean polygon area, 12.26 m^2); (**b**) tolerance region of diameter and polygon area for fourth cycle (mean age, 91.3 years; mean diameter, 20.30 cm; and mean polygon area, 15.47 m^2); tolerance region, solid line; observed dataset, circles.

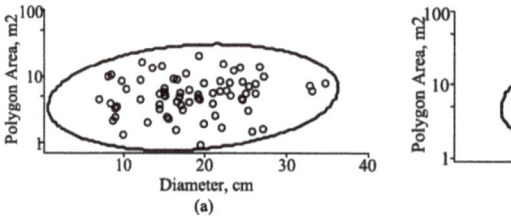 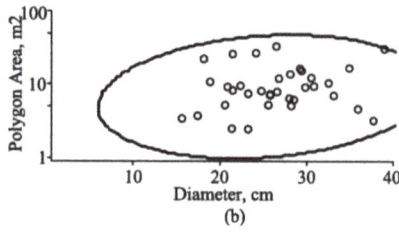

Figure 9. Tolerance region for mean vector with the observed sample from the validation dataset of silver birch tree species in two measurement cycles: (**a**) tolerance region of diameter and polygon area for first cycle (mean age, 44.7 years; mean diameter, 18.60 cm; and mean polygon area, 6.11 m^2); (**b**) tolerance region of diameter and polygon area for fourth cycle (mean age, 81.0 years; mean diameter, 25.94 cm; and mean polygon area, 10.44 m^2); tolerance region, solid line; observed dataset, circles.

4. Discussion

Figures 2–5 show that very high variation existed in the shape of the diameter and polygon area frequency distributions among plots of a given stand age. In our models, this variation was well accounted for by the used diffusion process defined by SDE (2). Since the observed sample plots represent forest stands in the region, the plot effects were generally included by using three random variables (effects). To properly test our mixed-effect model of diameter, polygon area, and number of trees per hectare, we used observed sample plots from the validation dataset to show its robustness in predicting (via current age) and forecasting (future age).

4.1. Modeling Tree-Diameter Dynamics: Predicting and Forecasting

Traditionally, individual-tree-diameter-growth regression models describe growth as a function of an age (tree or stand). Most individual-tree-diameter-growth models were framed using an algebraic difference approach [24] and its mathematical generalizations [25]. The SDE (2) developed in this study enables us to describe a wide range of tree- and stand-growth variables. To apply the mixed-effect SDE model defined by Equation (2), we had two adaptation strategies—prediction and forecasting. First, the underlying random effects of the model were precisely calibrated (using all remeasurement cycles from the validation dataset). Hence, random effects were calibrated by Equation (27) using data from the validation dataset in order to define the predictions (dynamic against the age) of the mean, variance, and quantiles of the diameter or polygon area in a particular stand. In this strategy, we could average the results of multiple realizations of tree diameters in different plots and obtain important characteristics (mean and variance) that could not be seen in one tree realization. Second, the underlying random effects of the model were not precisely calibrated (using only the first measurement cycle in a plot). Hence, random effects were calibrated by Equation (27) using measurements of diameter, polygon area, and age at the initial measurement cycle from the validation dataset in order to define the forecasts, at the 5-, 13-, and 35-year forecast periods, of the diameter or polygon area for each individual tree. Most remeasured plots from the validation dataset were unevenly aged and mixed-species. Figure and table illustrations are separately presented for all tree species, Scots pine tree species, Norway spruce tree species, and silver birch tree species. Figure 10 shows predictions of the mean diameter, 0.05 and 0.95 quantiles for all, Scots pine, Norway spruce, and silver birch tree species for two randomly selected stands from the validation dataset.

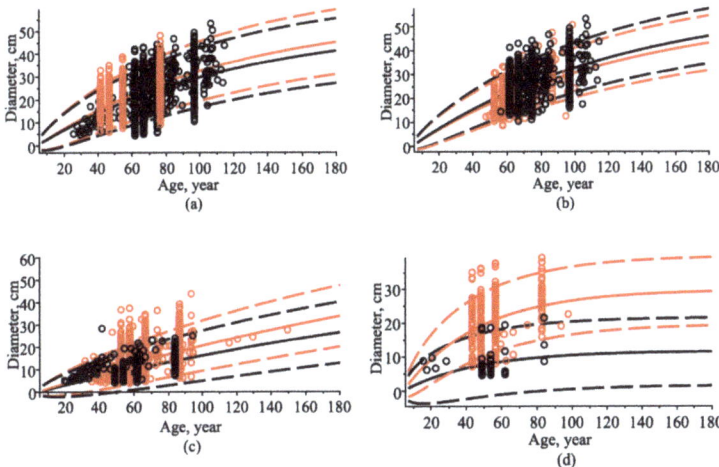

Figure 10. Dynamic of mean, 5%, and 95% percentiles of diameter with observed datasets for two randomly selected stands from the validation dataset: (**a**) all tree species; (**b**) Scots pine tree species; (**c**) Norway spruce tree species; (**d**) silver birch tree species; observed dataset of diameters, circles; mean trend, solid lines; percentiles, dashed lines; first stand, black; second stand, red.

The mean prediction error (percentage of prediction error, %) B, mean absolute prediction error (percentage of absolute prediction error, %) AB, root-mean-square error (percentage of root-mean-square error, %) RMSE, and coefficient of determination R^2 were used to evaluate the results of the mean diameter-marginal and conditional model fit defined by Equations (7) and (19), respectively. The calculated results of statistical measures using the validation dataset, the fixed-effect parameters from Table 2, and random effects calibrated by Equation (27) are presented in Table 3. The prediction performance of both models (marginal and conditional) showed that both models were highly capable of identifying the mean value of the diameter in a stand. Subsequently, only a small improvement in the statistical measures was found when we used the polygon area as an additional explanatory variable (conditional model (19)). Table 3 illustrates the accuracy of mean diameter predictions by using the observed validation dataset.

Table 3. Statistical measures for marginal and conditional models of mean (stand) diameter predictions.

Tree Species	Marginal Mean (Equation (7))				Conditional Mean (Equation (19))			
	B (%)	AB (%)	RMSE (%)	R^2	B (%)	AB (%)	RMSE (%)	R^2
All	0.019 (0.10)	0.798 (3.99)	1.133 (5.67)	0.949	−0.431 (−2.16)	0.782 (3.91)	0.989 (4.95)	0.961
Pine	−0.131 (−0.50)	0.841 (3.19)	1.141 (4.33)	0.973	−0.410 (−1.56)	0.846 (3.21)	1.158 (4.39)	0.972
Spruce	0.130 (0.90)	0.977 (6.80)	1.258 (8.76)	0.928	−0.345 (−2.40)	0.906 (6.30)	1.167 (8.12)	0.938
Birch	−1.038 (−5.94)	1.775 (10.15)	3.096 (17.71)	0.816	−1.354 (−7.74)	1.872 (10.71)	3.086 (17.65)	0.817

The marginal and conditional models defined by Equations (7) and (19) can also be used successfully as individual-tree-based models in forecasting tree growth regardless of species, age, and tree polygon area. In Equation (7), if initial point $(x_{10}, x_{20}) = (0.1, \hat{\delta} + \varphi_0^i)$ was changed by point $(x_{10}, x_{20}) = \left(d^i_{in,j}, p^i_{in,j} + 0.\right), i = 1, \ldots, K$ (K is the number of the observed sample plots from the validation dataset), we could calculate forecasts of individual-tree diameters and compare them with the observed dataset by determining the duration of the forecast period (5, 13, and 35 years), where $\left(d^i_{in,j}, p^i_{in,j}\right)$ is the diameter and polygon area of the *j*-th tree in the *i*-th plot at base age $t_{in,j}$, and random effects $\varphi^i_d \varphi^i_p$ and φ^i_0 are equated to 0. Table 4 shows the forecast statistical measures of a tree-individual scenario model calculated for the 5-, 13-, and 35-year forecast periods using the fixed-effect parameters estimates in Table 2.

Table 4. Statistical measures of diameter forecasts for 5-, 13-, and 35-year forecast periods.

Tree Species	5-Year Forecast Period				13-Year Forecast Period				35-Year Forecast Period			
	B (%)	AB (%)	RMSE (%)	R^2	B (%)	AB (%)	RMSE (%)	R^2	B (%)	AB (%)	RMSE (%)	R^2
All	−0.054 (−0.31)	0.949 (5.52)	1.440 (8.37)	0.977	−0.185 (−094)	2.140 (10.82)	2.911 (14.72)	0.914	−0.359 (−1.43)	4.606 (18.45)	5.654 (22.65)	0.739
Pine	−0.335 (−1.48)	0.982 (4.34)	1.447 (6.39)	0.968	−0.919 (−3.65)	2.178 (8.65)	2.816 (11.19)	0.886	−2.352 (−7.76)	4.469 (14.74)	5.674 (18.71)	0.615
Spruce	0.147 (1.24)	0.880 (7.42)	1.402 (11.82)	0.965	0.255 (1.83)	1.927 (13.85)	3.005 (21.60)	0.859	0.681 (3.62)	4.123 (21.89)	5.159 (27.39)	0.736
Birch	0.020 (0.10)	1.286 (6.85)	1.757 (9.38)	0.960	−0.321 (−1.50)	2.697 (12.59)	3.563 (16.64)	0.832	1.289 (4.92)	4.196 (16.03)	5.405 (20.65)	0.679

In general, the relative success of the 35-year forecast period in forecasting individual tree diameters showed that the values of statistical measures were considerably smaller than statistical measures were for the 5- and 13-year forecast periods. Therefore, the shorter (5 and 13 years) forecast periods provided us with reasonably accurate forecasts of tree diameters but performed quite poorly farther into the future. Compared to different tree species, Norway spruce species produced the lowest value of all statistical measures.

4.2. Modeling Tree Polygon Area: Predicting and Forecasting

The tree polygon areas show spatial tessellation based on closeness to trees in a particular stand. It was suggested by mathematician Voronoi [10] and named after him: Voronoi polygons (diagrams). A particular forest stand is driven with occasional events, and the spatial tree arrangement in it is featured with complexity and variability. Most studied Voronoi polygons are only static. A first approach for the dynamization of Voronoi diagrams could be an investigation by a procedure for inserting and deleting single trees (points), each in linear time. In modeling real dynamic scenes of a particular forest stand, parallel continuous changes of trees with a fast update of the Voronoi diagram are desirable. Four realizations at different times of a Voronoi polygon in a particular stand are presented in Figure 1. The main result of the present work consists in the dynamization of the underlying Voronoi polygon areas by the Gompertz-type diffusion process. Figure 11 shows predictions of the mean polygon area and 0.05 and 0.95 quantiles for two randomly selected stands from the validation dataset. Random effects were calibrated by Equation (27) using measurements of tree positions from the validation dataset, and the fixed-effect parameters are from Table 2.

The results of statistical measures of polygon area predictions, calculated using tree positions from the validation dataset, the fixed-effect parameters from Table 2, and random effects calibrated by Equation (27), are presented in Table 5, which clarifies the importance of the diameter employed in the modeling process. The prediction performance of both models defined by Equations (10) and (22) showed that both models were highly capable of identifying the mean value of the polygon area in a plot. On the other hand, only small improvement in the statistical measures was found (up to 3% in the coefficient of determination) when we used diameter as an additional explanatory variable in the conditional model defined by Equation (22).

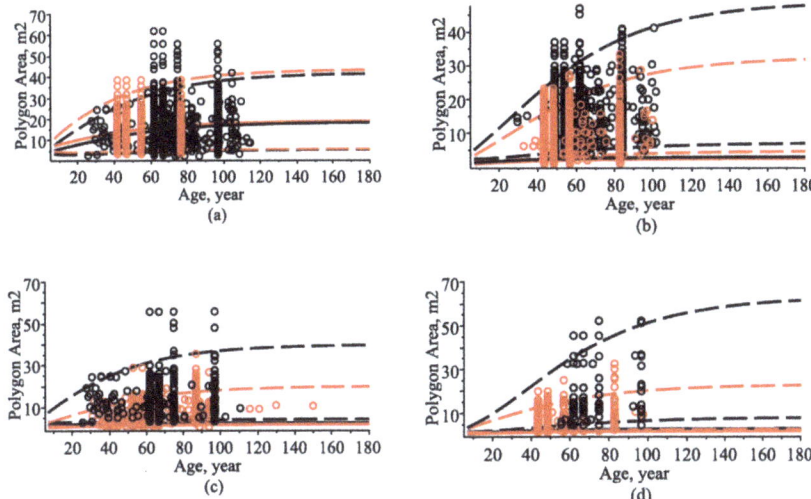

Figure 11. Dynamic of mean, 5%, and 95% percentiles of polygon area with observed datasets for two randomly selected stands from the validation dataset: (**a**) all tree species; (**b**) Scots pine tree species; (**c**) Norway spruce tree species; (**d**) silver birch tree species; observed dataset, circles; mean trend, solid lines; percentiles, dashed lines; first stand, black; second stand, red.

Table 5. Statistical measures for marginal and conditional models of mean polygon area predictions.

Tree Species	Marginal Mean (Equation (10))				Conditional Mean (Equation (22))			
	B (%)	AB (%)	RMSE (%)	R^2	B (%)	AB (%)	RMSE (%)	R^2
All	−0.305 (−2.46)	1.062 (8.58)	1.410 (11.26)	0.929	−0.184 (−1.49)	0.914 (7.39)	1.184 (9.57)	0.949
Pine	−0.392 (−3.17)	0.726 (5.87)	1.009 (8.16)	0.958	−0.276 (−2.23)	0.651 (5.27)	0.883 (7.14)	0.968
Spruce	−0.441 (−3.78)	1.155 (9.89)	1.597 (13.68)	0.913	−0.283 (−2.42)	1.062 (9.10)	1.454 (12.46)	0.928
Birch	0.202 (1.84)	1.628 (14.84)	2.318 (21.13)	0.790	0.442 (4.03)	1.571 (14.32)	2.145 (19.56)	0.820

Statistical measures of forecasts of trees' individual polygon areas using an observed validation dataset, the fixed-effect parameters from Table 2, and at random effects equal to zero, $\varphi_d^i = 0.$, $\varphi_p^i = 0.$, $\varphi_0^i = 0.$, $i = 1, \ldots, K$, are presented in Table 6 for the forecast periods of 5, 13, and 35 years. The conditional model defined by Equation (22) was evaluated using a data subset of diameters drawn from the validation dataset at the projected (forecast period) age and showed that the influence of diameters cannot greatly improve the forecast ability of a mixed-effect polygon area model. Statistical measures in Table 6 show that the accuracy of the model forecast decreases significantly with increasing the forecast period to 35 years.

Table 6. Statistical measures for the marginal model (Equation (10)) of polygon area forecasts for 5-, 13-, and 35-year forecast periods.

Tree Species	5-Year Forecast Period				13-Year Forecast Period				35-Year Forecast Period			
	B (%)	AB (%)	RMSE (%)	R^2	B (%)	AB (%)	RMSE (%)	R^2	B (%)	AB (%)	RMSE (%)	R^2
All	−0.601 (−6.01)	1.126 (11.26)	1.539 (15.38)	0.959	−0.555 (−4.69)	2.756 (23.31)	3.963 (33.51)	0.786	−1.581 (−11.09)	5.107 (35.83)	6.746 (47.33)	0.463
Pine	−0.762 (−6.34)	1.253 (10.43)	1.621 (13.49)	0.959	−1.194 (−8.72)	2.969 (21.70)	3.850 (28.13)	0.803	−3.655 (−23.78)	5.959 (38.66)	7.167 (46.50)	0.408
Spruce	−0.384 (−4.65)	0.983 (11.90)	1.466 (17.74)	0.953	0.221 (2.19)	2.601 (25.81)	4.238 (42.04)	0.725	0.664 (5.12)	4.575 (35.25)	6.798 (52.38)	0.405
Birch	−0.539 (−6.04)	1.004 (11.25)	1.198 (13.43)	0.971	−0.785 (−7.93)	2.504 (25.31)	3.373 (34.09)	0.827	0.201 (1.37)	5.788 (39.61)	7.458 (51.13)	0.491

4.3. Modeling Stand Density: Predicting and Forecasting

To manage the evolution of the number of trees per hectare from the early sapling stage to any stage in mixed-species, unevenly aged forests, reliable predictive and forecast models are needed. The complete size–density trajectory of a stand from an early development stage follows the form framed by the maximal size–density relationship [26]. Recently, diffusion processes were used to define maximal size–density equations [27]. Many various stand-density measures were developed as relationships of mean area available to trees in a particular stand [28,29]. The stand density expresses a stand occupancy in abstract form; consequently, in this study, the stand density per hectare dynamic is related to the dynamic of the polygon area, defined by Equations (10) and (22), in the following forms for all the tree species:

$$N^i(t|t_0, x_{20}) = \frac{10000}{m_2^i(t|t_0, x_{20})}, \qquad (29)$$

$$N^i(t|t_0, x_{20}, x_{11}) = \frac{10000}{\eta_2^i(t, x_{11}|t_0, x_0)}, \qquad (30)$$

and for constituent tree species:

$$N^i(t|t_0, x_{20}) = oc_{in} \frac{10000}{m_2^i(t|t_0, x_{20})}, \qquad (31)$$

$$N^i(t|t_0, x_{20}, x_{11}) = oc_{in} \frac{10000}{\eta_2^i(t, x_{11}|t_0, x_0)}, \qquad (32)$$

where oc_{in} is the occupation proportion of a specific tree species in a stand at an age of the first measurement ($0 < oc_{in} < 1$).

Sustainable forest management requires the comprehensive understanding of the long-term dynamics of stand density. The stand-density models defined by Equations (29)–(32) enable us to evaluate stand density in both prediction and forecasting scenarios. For calculating predictions of stand density, we used the fixed-effect parameters from Table 2 and the random effects calibrated by Equation (27), using a full validation dataset. Figure 12 shows the mean stand-density dynamics for all tree species and constituent tree species scenarios and compares with observed datasets for three randomly selected stands from the validation dataset. The accuracy measures of the mean stand-density predictions are presented in Table 7.

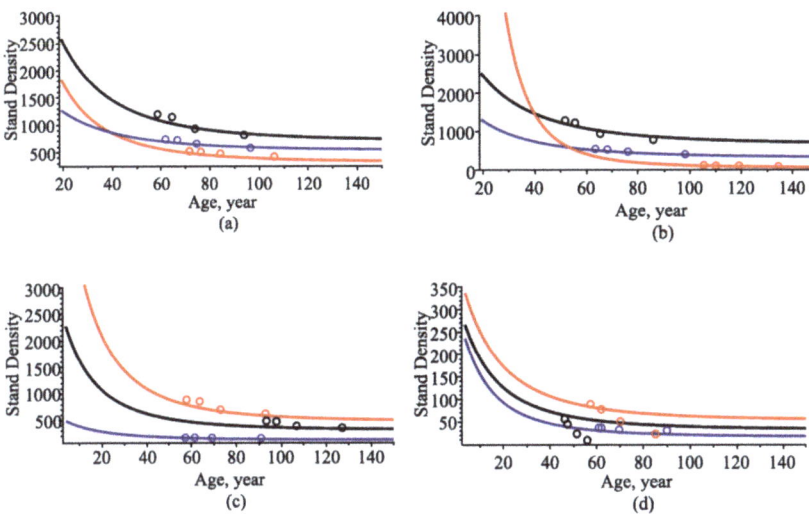

Figure 12. Dynamic of mean stand density with observed datasets for three randomly selected stands from the validation dataset: (**a**) all tree species; (**b**) Scots pine tree species; (**c**) Norway spruce tree species; (**d**) silver birch tree species; observed dataset, circles; mean trend, solid lines; first stand, black; second stand, red; third stand, blue.

Table 7. Statistical measures for marginal and conditional models of mean stand-density predictions.

Tree Species	Marginal Mean (Equation (29) or (31))				Conditional Mean (Equation (30) or (32))			
	B (%)	AB (%)	RMSE (%)	R^2	B (%)	AB (%)	RMSE (%)	R^2
All	0.686 (0.07)	102.23 (10.50)	166.149 (17.07)	0.873	−8.253 (−0.84)	90.608 (9.31)	147.297 (15.13)	0.901
Pine	19.339 (4.30)	37.682 (8.39)	49.302 (10.97)	0.966	16.429 (3.65)	34.762 (7.74)	44.767 (9.96)	0.972
Spruce	−3.720 (−0.62)	76.165 (12.74)	123.67 (20.67)	0.934	−14.901 (−2.49)	68.768 (11.50)	110.925 (18.56)	0.947
Birch	5.177 (7.89)	9.920 (15.12)	14.118 (21.52)	0.984	4.860 (7.41)	10.214 (15.57)	14.151 (21.57)	0.984

The Voronoi polygon of tree positions is a powerful tool for understanding the spatial competition properties on the basis of closeness to trees in a particular stand. Relatively few studies reported the construction of Voronoi polygons in forest-stand modeling [30] despite a wide array of potential applications. Dynamic Voronoi polygons have applications among stand-density models, as they can be used to accurately define the rate of natural mortality among trees within a forest. Results of diameter importance for stand-density modeling processes are shown in the conditional models defined by Equations (30) and (32), presented in Table 7, which shows that employing the diameter in the modeling process provided small improvement in statistical measures (up to 3% in the coefficient of determination).

In stand-density dynamic models, transition probability density functions only consider natural mortality that is influenced by competition, whereas general response functions account for the effects of the site index, basal area, and other factors [31]. The newly developed stand-density dynamic functions defined by Equations (29)–(32) were developed with the purpose of formalizing a whole-stand model for predicting and forecasting a given mixed-species forest stand. As such, the observed dataset (40 plots) from long-term remeasurements (from 1 until 6 cycles) of permanent plots was used to evaluate the fixed-effect parameters for both predicting and forecasting scenarios. Concerning the stand-density forecast scenario, the random effects for a new stand were calibrated by Equation (27) using the first measurement cycle observed sample from the validation dataset. Comparisons of stand-density forecasts (projections) among the forecast periods of 5, 13, and 35 years are presented in Table 8.

Table 8. Statistical measures of mean stand-density forecasts (Equations (29) and (31)) for 5-, 13-, and 35-year forecast periods.

Tree Species	5-Year Forecast Period				13-Year Forecast Period				35-Year Forecast Period			
	B (%)	AB (%)	RMSE (%)	R^2	B (%)	AB (%)	RMSE (%)	R^2	B (%)	AB (%)	RMSE (%)	R^2
All	−59.492 (−5.36)	60.113 (55.41)	72.799 (6.56)	0.981	−24.644 (−2.73)	94.991 (10.54)	118.212 (13.11)	0.897	62.025 (8.53)	103.635 (14.67)	125.749 (17.30)	0.605
Pine	−15.920 (−3.25)	40.292 (8.24)	53.640 (10.97)	0.966	31.761 (7.36)	46.707 (10.82)	56.766 (13.15)	0.938	74.438 (20.26)	87.838 (23.90)	105.201 (28.63)	0.751
Spruce	−24.434 (−5.50)	37.735 (8.50)	56.291 (12.68)	0.982	−58.010 (−15.04)	60.760 (15.73)	104.466 (27.08)	0.914	−19.460 (−6.57)	29.808 (23.90)	51.048 (17.26)	0.925
Birch	−68.224 (−9.68)	70.412 (9.99)	90.988 (12.91)	0.973	−82.303 (−15.26)	90.418 (16.76)	128.911 (23.90)	0.891	−36.060 (−8.68)	59.143 (14.25)	78.997 (19.03)	0.900

All the tested models for all the tree species provided good forecasts for data with high statistical measures. All the models for Scots pine, Norway spruce, silver birch, and all the tree species resulted in high coefficients of variation for the forecast periods of 5, 13, and 35 years in intervals of 96.6–98.2%, 89.1–93.8%, and 60.5–92.5%, respectively. Both scenario models for Scots pine trees were comparably better. Similar results were obtained in model ranking on the basis of B, B%, AB, AB%, RMSE, and RMSE%. Statistically, the marginal models defined by Equations (29) and (30) and the conditional models defined by Equations (30) and (32) provided similar forecasts for all forecast periods.

5. Conclusions

In this paper, we have studied the evolution of the mixed-species, unevenly aged forest stands by using a bivariate hybrid diffusion process and Voronoi diagram. The growth model considers two different system states (tree diameter and polygon area). In summary, derived individual-tree and whole-stand models describe how trees grow in diameter and how forest-stand structures are modified over time. On the other hand, one of the most fundamental features of our developed models is that they are strongly symmetrical, as they allow for forecasting trajectories in the future and the past. Numerical example by using experimental sample plots in Lithuania with measurements of tree position, age, and diameter at breast height showed high accuracy of the obtained results and the importance of the work. From a statistical point of view, the newly developed growth models produced acceptable predictions and forecasts. Our proposed bivariate hybrid diffusion process and Voronoi diagram approach also outperformed other existing techniques [32,33]. The newly developed hybrid bivariate distribution also provides a further in-depth understanding of the behavior of the stand basal area and volume.

Future work should try to extend our work to describe hybrid 3-, 4-, and 5-variate diffusion processes and copula approach for developing the link between state variables, as an example, diameter, height, crown width, crown base height, and available polygon area.

Author Contributions: Conceptualization, P.R.; methodology, E.P. and P.R.; software, P.R.; validation, E.P. and P.R.; formal analysis, E.P.; data curation, E.P.; writing—original draft preparation, P.R.; writing—review and editing, E.P. and P.R.; visualization, P.R.; supervision, E.P.; project administration, E.P. Both authors have read and agreed to the published version of the manuscript.

Funding: This research received no external funding.

Institutional Review Board Statement: Not applicable.

Informed Consent Statement: Not applicable.

Data Availability Statement: The data used in Section 2 is duly referenced.

Acknowledgments: We are greatly indebted to three anonymous reviewers for many helpful comments.

Conflicts of Interest: The authors declare no conflict of interest.

References

1. García, O. Estimating reducible stochastic differential equations by conversion to a least-squares problem. *Comput. Stat.* **2019**, *34*, 23–46. [CrossRef]
2. Nafidi, A.; Makroz, I.; Gutiérrez Sánchez, R. A Stochastic Lomax Diffusion Process: Statistical Inference and Application. *Mathematics* **2021**, *9*, 100. [CrossRef]
3. Dipple, S.; Choudhary, A.; Flamino, J.; Szymanski, B.K.; Korniss, G. Using Correlated Stochastic Differential Equations to Forecast Cryptocurrency Rates and Social Media Activities. *Appl. Netw. Sci.* **2020**, *5*, 17. [CrossRef]
4. Zhang, T.; Ding, T.; Gao, N.; Song, Y. Dynamical Behavior of a Stochastic SIRC Model for Influenza A. *Symmetry* **2020**, *12*, 745. [CrossRef]
5. Chow, C.C.; Buice, M.A. Path integral methods for stochastic differential equations. *J. Math. Neurosci.* **2015**, *5*, 8. [CrossRef] [PubMed]
6. Wiqvist, S.; Golightly, A.; McLean, A.T.; Picchini, U. Efficient inference for stochastic differential equation mixed-effects models using correlated particle pseudo-marginal algorithms. *Comput. Stat. Data Anal.* **2020**, *157*, 107151. [CrossRef]
7. Holmes, M.J.; Reed, D.D. Competition indices for mixed species northern hardwoods. *For. Sci.* **1991**, *37*, 1338–1349.
8. Rupšys, P.; Petrauskas, E. A New Paradigm in Modelling the Evolution of a Stand via the Distribution of Tree Sizes. *Sci. Rep.* **2017**, *7*, 15875. [CrossRef]
9. Pommerening, A.; Szmyt, J.; Zhang, G. A new nearest-neighbour index for monitoring spatial size diversity: The hyper-bolic tangent index. *Ecol. Model.* **2020**, *435*, 109232. [CrossRef]
10. Voronoi, G. Nouvelles applications des paramètres continues à la théorie des formes quad-ratiques. *J. Für Die Reine Und Angew. Math.* **1908**, *134*, 198–287. [CrossRef]
11. Weiskittel, A.R.; Hann, D.W.; Kershaw, J.A.; Vanclay, J.K. *Forest Growth and Yield Modeling*; Wiley: Hoboken, NJ, USA, 2011; p. 430.
12. Sloboda, B. Kolmogorow–Suzuki und die stochastische Differentialgleichung als Beschreibungsmittel der Bestandesevolution. *Mitt Forstl Bundes Vers. Wien* **1977**, *120*, 71–82.
13. Garcia, O. A stochastic differential equation model for the height growth of forest stands. *Biometrics* **1983**, *39*, 1059–1072. [CrossRef]
14. Rupšys, P.; Petrauskas, E. Quantifying Tree Diameter Distributions with One-Dimensional Diffusion Processes. *J. Biol. Syst.* **2010**, *18*, 205–221. [CrossRef]
15. Bormashenko, E.; Legchenkova, I.; Frenkel, M. Symmetry and Shannon Measure of Ordering: Paradoxes of Voronoi Tessellation. *Entropy* **2019**, *21*, 452. [CrossRef] [PubMed]
16. Diggle, P.J. *Statistical Analysis of Spatial Point Patterns*; Academic Press: New York, NY, USA, 1983; p. 148.
17. Aurenhammer, F. Voronoi diagrams—A survey of a fundamental geometric data structure. *ACM Comput. Surv.* **1991**, *23*, 345–405. [CrossRef]
18. Kuehne, C.; Weiskittel, A.; Simons-Legaard, E.; Legaard, K. Development and comparison of various stand- and tree-level modeling approaches to predict harvest occurrence and intensity across the mixed forests in Maine, northeastern US. *Scand. J. For. Res.* **2019**, *34*, 739–750. [CrossRef]
19. McTague, J.P.; Weiskittel, A.R. Individual-Tree Competition Indices and Improved Compatibility with Stand-Level Estimates of Stem Density and Long-Term Production. *Forests* **2016**, *7*, 238. [CrossRef]
20. Narmontas, M.; Rupšys, P.; Petrauskas, E. Models for Tree Taper Form: The Gompertz and Vasicek Diffusion Processes Framework. *Symmetry* **2020**, *12*, 80. [CrossRef]
21. Botha, I.; Kohn, R.; Drovandi, C. Particle Methods for Stochastic Differential Equation Mixed Effects Models. *Bayesian Anal.* **2021**, *16*, 575–609. [CrossRef]
22. Chew, V. Confidence, Prediction, and Tolerance Regions for the Multivariate Normal Distribution. *J. Am. Stat. Assoc.* **1966**, *61*, 605–617. [CrossRef]
23. Krishnamoorthy, K. Comparison of Approximation Methods for Computing Tolerance Factors for a Multivariate Normal Population. *Technometrics* **1999**, *41*, 234–249. [CrossRef]
24. Bailey, R.L.; Clutter, J.L. Base-Age Invariant Polymorphic Site Curves. *For. Sci.* **1974**, *20*, 155–159.
25. Cieszewski, C.J.; Bailey, R.L. Generalized Algebraic Difference Approach: Theory Based Derivation of Dynamic Site Equations with Polymorphism and Variable Asymptotes. *For. Sci.* **2000**, *46*, 116–126.
26. Zhang, X.; Cao, Q.V.; Lu, L.; Wang, H.; Duan, A.; Zhang, J. Use of modified Reineke's stand density index in predicting growth and survival of Chinese fir plantations. *For. Sci.* **2019**, *65*, 776–783. [CrossRef]
27. Rupšys, P. Modeling Dynamics of Structural Components of Forest Stands Based on Trivariate Stochastic Differential Equation. *Forests* **2019**, *10*, 506. [CrossRef]
28. West, P.W. Comparison of stand density measures in even-aged regrowth eucalypt forest of southern Tasmania. *Can. J. For. Res.* **1983**, *13*, 22–31. [CrossRef]

29. Zeide, B. Comparison of self-thinning models: An exercise in reasoning. *Trees* **2010**, *24*, 1117–1126. [CrossRef]
30. Li, X.; Chen, J.; Zhao, L.; Guo, S.; Sun, L.; Zhao, X. Adaptive Distance-Weighted Voronoi Tessellation for Remote Sensing Image Segmentation. *Remote Sens.* **2020**, *12*, 4115. [CrossRef]
31. Zhao, D.; Borders, B.; Wang, M.; Kane, M. Modeling mortality of second-rotation loblolly pine plantations in the piedmont/upper coastal plain and lower coastal plain of the southern United States. *For. Ecol. Manag.* **2007**, *252*, 132–143. [CrossRef]
32. Cao, Q.V. A unified system for tree- and stand-level predictions. *For. Ecol. Manag.* **2021**, *481*, 118713. [CrossRef]
33. Garcia, O. A parsimonious dynamic stand model for interior spruce in British Columbia. *For. Sci.* **2011**, *57*, 265–280.

MDPI
St. Alban-Anlage 66
4052 Basel
Switzerland
Tel. +41 61 683 77 34
Fax +41 61 302 89 18
www.mdpi.com

Symmetry Editorial Office
E-mail: symmetry@mdpi.com
www.mdpi.com/journal/symmetry

www.ingramcontent.com/pod-product-compliance
Lightning Source LLC
LaVergne TN
LVHW070400100526
838202LV00014B/1356